Mysterious Lands

Encounters with
Ancient
Egypt

Titles in the series

ENCOUNTERS WITH ANCIENT EGYPT

Mysterious Lands

Edited by

David O'Connor and Stephen Quirke

**Left
Coast
Press**
inc.

Walnut Creek, CA

LEFT COAST PRESS, INC.

1630 North Main Street, #400
Walnut Creek, CA 94596
http://www.LCoastPress.com

Copyright © 2011 by Left Coast Press, Inc.

Replaces edition of this book produced by Institute of Archaeology,
University College London under ISBN 1-84472-004-7 in 2003.
Originally published by UCL Press in 2003.

Library of Congress Cataloging-in-Publication Data available from the publisher.

ISBN 978-1-59874-207-7 paperback

Printed in the United States of America

The paper used in this publication meets the minimum requirements
of American National Standard for Information Sciences—Permanence of
Paper for Printed Library Materials, ANSI/NISO Z39.48–1992.

Cover illustration: Mounds of the Underworld from the "Book of the Dead"
(Early New Kingdom), Chapters 149 and 150 (© Musée du Louvre N3073;
Cenival 1992:12-14).

Series Editor's Foreword

This series of eight books derives from the proceedings of a conference entitled 'Encounters with Ancient Egypt', held at the Institute of Archaeology, University College London (UCL) in December 2000. Since then, many new chapters have been especially commissioned for publication, and those papers originally provided for the conference and now selected for publication have been extensively revised and rewritten.

There are many noteworthy features of the books. One is the overall attempt to move the study of Ancient Egypt into the mainstream of recent advances in archaeological and anthropological practice and interpretation. This is a natural outcome of London University's Institute of Archaeology, one of the largest archaeology departments in the world, being the academic host. Drawing on the Institute's and other related resources within UCL, the volumes in the series reflect an extraordinary degree of collaboration between the series editor, individual volume editors, contributors and colleagues. The wide range of approaches to the study of the past, pursued in such a vibrant scholarly environment as UCL's, has encouraged the scholars writing in these volumes to consider their disciplinary interests from new perspectives. All the chapters presented here have benefited from wide-ranging discussion between experts from diverse academic disciplines, including art history, papyrology, anthropology, archaeology and Egyptology, and subsequent revision.

Egyptology has been rightly criticized for often being insular; the methodologies and conclusions of the discipline have been seen by others as having developed with little awareness of archaeologies elsewhere. The place and role of Ancient Egypt within African history, for example, has rarely been considered jointly by Egyptologists and Africanists. This collaboration provides a stimulating review of key issues and may well influence future ways of studying Egypt. Until now, questions have rarely been asked about the way Egyptians thought of their own past or about non-Egyptian peoples and places. Nor has the discipline of Egyptology explored, in any depth, the nature of its evidence, or the way contemporary cultures regarded Ancient Egypt. The books in this series address such topics.

Another exceptional feature of this series is the way that the books have been designed to interrelate with, inform and illuminate one another. Thus, the evidence of changing appropriations of Ancient Egypt over time, from the classical period to the modern Afrocentrist movement, features in several volumes. One volume explores the actual sources of knowledge about Ancient Egypt before the advent of 'scientific' archaeology, while another explores knowledge of Ancient Egypt after Napoleon Bonaparte's expeditions and the unearthing of Tutankhamun's tomb. The question asked throughout these volumes, however, is how far fascination and knowledge about Ancient Egypt have been based on sources of evidence rather than extraneous political or commercial concerns and interests.

As a result of this series, the study of Ancient Egypt will be significantly enriched and deepened. The importance of the Egypt of several thousands of years ago reaches far beyond the existence of its architectural monuments and extends to its unique role in the history of all human knowledge. Furthermore, the civilization of Ancient Egypt speaks to us with particular force in our own present and has an abiding place in the modern psyche.

As the first paragraph of this Foreword explains, the final stage of this venture began with the receipt and editing of some extensively revised, and in many cases new, chapters – some 95 in all – to be published simultaneously in eight volumes. What it does not mention is the speed with which the venture has been completed: the current UCL Press was officially launched in April 2003. That this series of books has been published to such a high standard of design, professional accuracy and attractiveness only four months later is incredible.

This alone speaks eloquently for the excellence of the staff of UCL Press – from its senior management to its typesetters and designers. Ruth Phillips (Marketing Director) stands out for her youthful and innovative marketing ideas and implementation of them, but most significant of all, at least from the Institute's perspective, is the contribution of Ruth Massey (Editor), who oversaw and supervized all details of the layout and production of the books, and also brought her critical mind to bear on the writing styles, and even the meaning, of their contents.

Individual chapter authors and academic volume editors, both from within UCL and in other institutions, added this demanding project to otherwise full workloads. Although it is somewhat invidious to single out particular individuals, Professor David O'Connor stands out as co-editor of two volumes and contributor of chapters to three despite his being based overseas. He, together with Professor John Tait – also an editor and multiple chapter author in these books – was one of the first to recognize my vision of the original conference as having the potential to inspire a uniquely important publishing project.

Within UCL's Institute of Archaeology, a long list of dedicated staff, academic, administrative and clerical, took over tasks for the Director and Kelly Vincent, his assistant as they wrestled with the preparation of this series. All of these staff, as well as several members of the student body, really deserve individual mention by name, but space does not allow this. However, the books could not have appeared without the particular support of five individuals: Lisa Daniel, who tirelessly secured copyright for over 500 images; Jo Dullaghan, who turned her hand to anything at any time to help out, from re-typing manuscripts to chasing overdue authors; Andrew Gardner, who tracked down obscure and incomplete references, and who took on the complex job of securing and producing correctly scanned images; Stuart Laidlaw, who not only miraculously produced publishable images of a pair of outdoor cats now in Holland and Jamaica, but in a number of cases created light where submitted images revealed only darkness; and Kelly Vincent, who did all of the above twice over, and more – and who is the main reason that publisher and Institute staff remained on excellent terms throughout.

Finally, a personal note, if I may. Never, ever contemplate producing eight complex, highly illustrated books within a four month period. If you *really must*, then make sure you have the above team behind you. Essentially, ensure that you have a partner such as Jane Hubert, who may well consider you to be mad but never questions the essential worth of the undertaking.

Peter Ucko
Institute of Archaeology
University College London
27 July 2003

Contents

Note: No attempt has been made to impose a standard chronology on authors; all dates before 712 BC are approximate. However, names of places, and royal and private names have been standardized.

Contributors

James P. Allen is Curator of Egyptian Art at the Metropolitan Museum of Art. He has served as epigrapher for the University of Chicago's expedition in Luxor, Egypt, and as Director of the American Research Center in Egypt. He has held a research appointment at Yale University since 1986, and has taught there as well as at the University of Pennsylvania. His publications include *Genesis in Egypt: the philosophy of ancient Egyptian creation accounts* (1989); 'The Cosmology of the Pyramid Texts', in *Religion and Philosophy in Ancient Egyptian* (1989); *Middle Egyptian: an introduction to the language and culture of hieroglyphs* (2000); and *The Heqanakht Papyri* (2003). He is currently Vice-President of the International Association of Egyptologists. James received his doctorate from the University of Chicago.

Eric Cline is Assistant Professor of Ancient History and Archaeology in the Department of Classical and Semitic Languages and Literatures at The George Washington University in Washington, DC. He holds additional appointments in the History and Anthropology departments as well as on the Judaic Studies Programme. He is an experienced field archaeologist, with 17 seasons of excavation and survey in Israel, Egypt, Jordan, Cyprus, Greece, Crete, and the US. Eric is an award-winning author whose publications include *Sailing the Wine-Dark Sea: international trade and the Late Bronze Age Aegean* (1994); *Amenhotep III: perspectives on his reign* (1998, with David O'Connor); and *The Battles of Armageddon: Megiddo and the Jezreel Valley from the Bronze Age to the nuclear age* (2000). He received his PhD from the University of Pennsylvania.

Stephen P. Harvey is Assistant Professor of Egyptian Art and Archaeology in the Oriental Institute, and in the Department of Near Eastern Languages and Civilizations, University of Chicago. Since 1993, he has directed excavation of the monumental complex of King Ahmose at Abydos, southern Egypt, under the aegis of the University of Pennsylvania-Yale-Institute of Fine Arts Expedition to Abydos. His publications include *Gods of Ancient Memphis* (2001, with Melinda Hartwig), and other articles in the scholarly and popular press. In addition to extensive fieldwork at Abydos, Stephen has worked in Egypt at Giza and Memphis, as well as on archaeological projects in the United States, Syria and Turkey. He received his PhD from the University of Pennsylvania.

Robert Layton is Professor of Anthropology at Durham University, having spent seven years working as a research anthropologist in Australia, first for the Australian Institute of Aboriginal and Torres Strait Islander Studies in Canberra, then for the Northern Aboriginal Land Council in Darwin. His publications include *The Anthropology of Art* (2nd edition, 1991); *Uluru, An Aboriginal history of Ayers Rock* (1986); *An Introduction to Theory in Anthropology* (1997); and *The Archaeology and Anthropology of Landscape* (1999, co-edited with Peter Ucko). He received his PhD from the University of Sussex.

Antonio Loprieno is Professor of Egyptology at the University of Basel, Switzerland, after having served for 10 years as Professor of Egyptology and Chairman of the Department of Near Eastern Languages and Cultures at the University of California, Los Angeles. His research topics include comparative Afroasiatic and Egyptian linguistics as well as Egyptian history and literature. His publications include *Das*

Verbalsystem in Ägyptischen und im Semitischen (1996); *Topos und Mimesis* (1988); *Ancient Egyptian: a linguistic introduction* (1995); *La Pensée et l'écriture* (2001); and, as editor, *Ancient Egyptian Literature: history and forms* (1996). He received his PhD from the University of Turin, Italy, and his Habilitation from the University of Göttingen, Germany.

Dimitri Meeks is Director of Research with the French Centre National de la Recherche Scientifique. He has worked for the past 15 years at the University of Aix-en-Provence with a team of classical archaeologists. He is now resident Egyptologist at the Institut Français d'Archéologie Orientale, Cairo. He writes on the relations of Egypt with neighbouring countries, on the history of technology, and on ancient Egyptian lexicography, and he directs an international programme devoted to hieroglyphic palaeography. Dimitri's publications include the three volumes, *Année Lexicographique Egypte Ancienne* (1980, 1981, 1982), and *Daily Life of Egyptian Gods* (1996, with Christine Favard-Meeks). He received his PhD from the University of Paris-Sorbonne and his Habilitation from the University of Lyon.

David O'Connor is Lila Acheson Wallace Professor in Ancient Egyptian Art and Archaeology at the Institute of Fine Arts of New York University, Professor Emeritus of the University of Pennsylvania, and Curator Emeritus of the Egyptian Section of its Museum of Archaeology and Anthropology. He has excavated extensively in Nubia and at Malkata, Thebes, and at Abydos in southern Egypt since 1967. His publications include *Ancient Egypt: a social history* (1983); *Ancient Nubia: Egypt's rival in Africa* (1993); *Ancient Egyptian Kingship* (1995, with David Silverman); and *Amenhotep III: perspectives on his reign* (1998, with Eric Cline). He received his PhD from the University of Cambridge.

Stephen Quirke is Curator of the Petrie Museum of Egyptian Archaeology and Lecturer in Egyptology at the Institute of Archaeology, University College London, where he has worked since 1999. Previously he was a curator in the Department of Egyptian Antiquities at the British Museum. He has published extensively on Egyptian administration and religion, and his current research focuses on the collection of Middle Kingdom papyri from Lahun. Stephen's publications include *The Administration of Egypt in the Late Middle Kingdom* (1990); *Ancient Egyptian Religion* (1992); *Cultura y arte egipcios* (1998); *Hieroglyphs and the Afterlife* (1996, with Werner Forman); and *Middle Kingdom Stelae in the State Hermitage* (1999, with Andrey Bolshakov). He received his PhD from the University of Cambridge.

Peter Robinson is a member of the British Cartography Society and the Society for Landscape Studies. He has excavated in Britain, France and Greece and is a freelance Egyptology lecturer. With research interests in early maps and humanity's views and perceptions of the world, his publications include 'Mapping the Anglo-Saxon Landscape: a land-systems approach to the study of the bounds of the Estate of Plaish' (*Landscape History* 10, 15–24, 1988), and 'Crossing the Night: the depiction of mythological landscapes in the Am Duat' (*British Archaeological Reports*, forthcoming). He has a degree in Geography and received his M Phil from the University of Manchester.

Stephen Snape is Senior Lecturer at the School of Archaeology, Classics and Oriental Studies, University of Liverpool. He has directed archaeological fieldwork for the

Egypt Exploration Society and, for the University of Pennsylvania, has directed fieldwork in the Delta, northern Sinai, and at the temple sites of Abydos and Shanhur in Upper Egypt. Since 1994 he has been director of the Liverpool University excavations at the site of Zawiyet Umm el-Rakham, a Ramesside fortress in the western desert of Egypt. His publications include *Egyptian Temples* (1996). He received his doctorate from the University of Liverpool.

John Tait is Edwards Professor of Egyptology at the Institute of Archaeology, University College London. He has edited hieroglyphic, hieratic, demotic and Greek papyri, and studies Egyptian literary traditions. His publications include *Papyri from Tebtunis in Egyptian and in Greek* (1977) and *Saqqara Demotic Papyri* (1983, with H. S. Smith), and he has made several contributions to the work of the Project for the Publication of the Carlsberg Papyri (Copenhagen). He received his D Phil from the University of Oxford.

List of Figures

A note on transliteration from ancient Egyptian

The ancient Egyptian scripts convey 24 consonants, no vowels. Fourteen of these occur in modern English, written with one letter: b, d, f, g, h, k, m, n, p, r, s, t, w, y. Three more are also found in English, but usually written with two letters: to keep transliteration as direct as possible, these are transliterated by Egyptologists as follows:

š   'sh' as in 'sheep'

ṯ   'ch' as in 'chin'

ḏ   as in 'j' and 'dg' of 'judge'

The other seven Egyptian consonants do not occur in written English, and are transliterated by Egyptologists as follows:

ꜣ   the glottal stop (faintly heard if you start a sentence with a vowel in English)

i   a sound varying between glottal stop and y

ꜥ   the 'ayin' of Arabic, a deep guttural clenching of the throat

ḥ   a stronger 'h', found in modern Arabic

ḫ   found in Arabic, the 'ch' of Scottish 'loch'

ẖ   a sound varying between ḥ and š

q   a form of 'k' pronounced deeper in the throat, and found in Arabic

CHAPTER 1

INTRODUCTION: MAPPING THE UNKNOWN
IN ANCIENT EGYPT

David O'Connor and Stephen Quirke

'Mystery'

The 'mysteries' reviewed in this volume arise in the gap between what we think we know of the world from archaeology, geography and astronomy, and what we have found in Egyptian written and pictorial accounts of the world. The mismatch begins with the concept of mystery itself. An Egyptian word commonly translated into English as 'secret' or 'mystery' is *sštȝ*, related to the word *štȝ*, 'difficult'; the initial 's' is generally a prefix with causative meaning, indicating that the meaning of *sštȝ* should be 'caused to be difficult', 'obscured'. This is terrain unknown and, more importantly, rendered inaccessible because it involves what humans should not know. Excessive thirst for knowledge is an ancient Egyptian as well as a modern theme; the god Thoth governed knowledge, and especially communication by writing, and two ancient tales in particular indicate that he was not expected to share all his knowledge with human beings or even with the king. In the 'Tale of Setne Khamwase', known from Roman period manuscripts, the protagonist is a prince who almost destroys himself in his quest for a sacred book (Lichtheim 1980: 125–137); a second tale, 1,800 years earlier, seems to imply criticism of the king for desiring to know the location of chambers of Thoth (Lichtheim 1976: 219).

The lands inhabited by human beings were not part of this deliberately inaccessible terrain; a foreign land at the margin of ancient Egyptian knowledge might be 'land of god', and reaching it might require superhuman effort, but it does not seem that such efforts were considered impious excess. By contrast, otherworld and underworld lands outside living human experience required special access, just as special conditions applied to access by petitioners to the king, or even to his high officials, and as only specially designated individuals were permitted to enter inner parts of temples. From the mid-eighteenth Dynasty, the walls of the royal burial chamber were covered with the Amduat, a cycle of captioned images given the overall title 'writings of the hidden chamber which is in the underworld'. The opening phrases specify the content of this composition as knowledge (Forman and Quirke 1996: 117):

To know the powers of the underworld, to know their duties;
to know their transfigurations for Ra;

to know the secret powers, to know what is in their hours, and their gods;
to know his (the sun god's) summoning of them;
to know the doors and the road travelled by this great god (the sun god);
to know the course of the hours and their gods;
to know those who sing praises and those who are destroyed.

The European expansionist claim to possess time and space is alive here in the 15th century BC, but as knowledge appropriate to divine kingship. In the 'King as Priest of the Sun god', the detailed intimacy with the cosmos is a cardinal feature of the character and power of the king (Assmann 2001: 64–67). Exclusion formulae on the model 'let no-one see this' recur throughout New Kingdom funerary literature, emphasizing that not everyone should have this knowledge. In the trio sky-earth-underworld, the features and movements of sky and underworld carry too much power to be shared. In their domain the Egyptian writings readily assign the word *sšt3* 'secret' or 'mysterious', whereas the landscapes and the seasons of earth may merely be *št3* 'difficult'. Evidently our mysterious lands are not the same as those of the ancient Egyptians, and this difference reveals essential differences between our thirst for knowledge, our experience of the world, and the ancient Egyptian experience of being in, knowing, and not knowing the world. A self-critical historiography with archaeological method at its fore requires keen observation of the potential and the limitations of sources. Along with written and pictorial sources, this introduces the vast modern academic literatures of textual criticism and art history.

Lands and languages

The mapping of the world has been one of the primary expressions of European expansion since the high Middle Ages, when Genoa and Venice competed across the Mediterranean for knowledge of lucrative trade routes to the east, secrets as closely guarded as the highest technology of the 21st century. European 'science' has taken as if its birthright the exploration of all time and space; any obstacle to this quest, any mystery, is at once a defiant and enticing challenge to power, and a comforting reminder that human beings cannot always expect to have all the answers, that there are worlds that we cannot reach. In the archaeology of literate societies, any ancient name of a land beyond our (current) knowledge attracts at once scrutiny and, as can be seen in the scholarly arguments over unlocated lands, a passion that seems far from the claims of 'science' to objectivity. Those literate societies have left written evidence articulating in words their own perspectives on their world (see Allen, Chapter 2), and here modern preconceptions find good testing grounds.

In all human societies, landscapes involve acquired or cultural experience (Layton and Ucko 1999). Relation to the land is developed not only by the physical conditions and by individual psychologies, but especially by the methods developed in preceding generations for life, and more essentially for survival, in those landscapes. Language may illustrate something of the range of possible different personal and social relationships with the land. The syntax and vocabulary of landscape varies from one language to another; different languages offer different methods of appropriation, resistance or empathy – English, without syntactically gendered nouns, cannot deliver quite the same feeling of kinship as a language where the word for earth is syntactically masculine (as in ancient Egyptian), or feminine (as in modern French or modern German). This is just one part of the complex web of factors informing the way each human being experiences place. Local patterns of shelter and sustenance introduce the fundamental and historically specific conditions of any relation with landscape. Ways of inhabiting space, obtaining food, and communicating with one another and the world, are all so basic to life that it can too easily be forgotten how much historical conditioning goes into each, and how specific and, as is the fate of historically developed conditions, how unnecessary each modern way may be. In examining ancient space, the modern enquirer may have to travel farther than might be expected.

Lands in archaeology: the curse of writing

Egyptian writings provide plentiful references to foreign lands and peoples at all periods; and distinctively attired 'foreigners' are a recurrent feature in Egyptian art, both formal and informal. Surprisingly, however, some countries or peoples of considerable importance (to judge from what the Egyptians said about them) are documented only in Egyptian sources, and the same is true of many others mentioned, but not allotted particular significance, by the Egyptians. These circumstances are tantalizing to historians of Egypt, Africa and even the Near East and the Aegean, but also challenging and exciting. Archaeological fieldwork in relevant areas will surely locate some, maybe all, of the major 'missing' lands, and the cultures of their inhabitants, and any day hitherto undiscovered, or overlooked, texts and scenes from Egypt may also provide vital new data about some. A primary source of information is the archaeological record for foreigners settled and buried in Egypt itself. Such data have already been recovered about certain Nubian populations, specifically Medjayu – nomads from Nubia ('Pan-Grave' culture; Bietak 1966); C-Group people from northern Nubia (Friedman 2001); and even representatives of the Middle Bronze Age Kerma culture of central or Upper Nubia (Trigger 1976: 97). However, several other major groups of foreigners present in Egypt at various periods remain unidentified as yet in the Egyptian archaeological record.

During the Bronze Age in Egypt, ca. 3000–1000 BC, the lands and peoples who seem to have been most important to Egypt were, in a clockwise progression, located around the Aegean; in Anatolia and the Near East; to the south (Nubia, along the Nile) and south-east (between Nubia and the Red Sea, and perhaps across to Arabia); and finally to the west, primarily the better watered coastal regions such as Cyrenaica but also apparently regions further south, involving less hospitable regions of the Sahara (Figure 1:1). In the first millennium BC, Egyptian geographical knowledge expanded further as part of the Hellenistic, then Roman 'world systems', and one ground-breaking pharaoh – Necho II (ca. 610–595 BC) of the twenty-sixth Dynasty – purportedly sponsored the first known circumnavigation of Africa (Drioton and Vandier 1962: 584, 678). However, the main focus of this book is on the Bronze Age.

In terms of opportunity for identification on the ground, these lands are divided in two by the presence or absence of writing. As far as the Aegean, Anatolia and the Near East are concerned, many of the relevant regions are locatable because they are documented in other written sources as well as Egyptian ones, and their cultures have

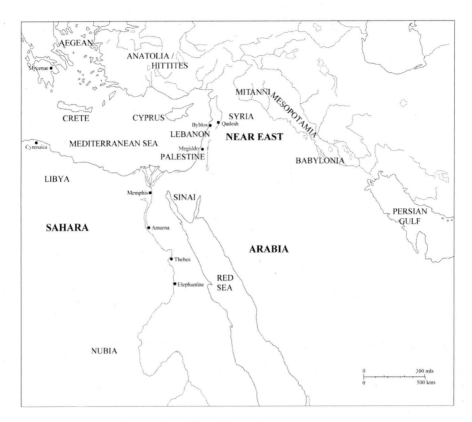

Figure 1:1   Map showing Egypt and its world.

been revealed by archaeologists. The Minoan and Mycenaean cultures of the Aegean were well known to Egyptians of the Late Bronze Age (ca. 1500–1000 BC) and, as regards the former, in at least indirect contact much earlier (Cline 1994; Kemp 1983: 147–149). Anatolia and the Tigris-Euphrates region appear to be *terra incognita* to Egypt prior to the Late Bronze Age, when they play a dominant role in the international relations for which correspondence survives in the form of the Amarna Letters of the 14th century BC and similar material (Cohen and Westbrook 2000; Moran 1992). Closer to Egypt, the lands of the Levant (today Syria, Lebanon, Israel-Palestine and Jordan) were in constant contact with Egypt throughout historic times and earlier (Matthews and Roemer 2003b; Redford 1992). Here, many of the states, places and peoples referred to in Egyptian writing and art can be located with a high degree of probability. Conversely, the available written sources in the Aegean and Near Eastern world refer to Egypt more or less in proportion to the Egyptian references to each land. The world of the written sources seems consistent in itself. The problems of identification multiply when the only relevant writing has come from one source, Egypt.

In the regions to the north-west, west, south and south-east of Egypt, no indigenous inscriptions were produced, or at least survive, until after the Bronze Age.

More seriously, most of these areas have been little explored archaeologically, if at all. Among countries or peoples featuring in Egyptian sources, perhaps the three most glaring examples of the 'missing' are Punt, apparently somewhere on the African or Arabian shores of the Red Sea (Meeks, Chapter 4; Harvey, Chapter 5), Irem, a substantial African land upstream of Wawat (northern Nubia) and Kush (central Nubia) (both Wawat and Kush are well known to ancient Egyptians and modern archaeologists alike; Adams 1977: chs. 6–9; O'Connor 1993: chs. 3–5), and finally Libya to the west, which presents a historically complex picture. Originally, the Egyptians referred to 'Libyans' as simply the Tjehenu and the Tjemehu, terms originally distinct but often used interchangeably. From about the 14th century BC, however, a medley of names of peoples appears relatively abruptly in the Egyptian records – the Ribu or Libu (ancestral to the Greek name Libya), Meshwesh and others (see Snape, Chapter 6).

Returning to the north, at the time that the Libyan 'tribes' begin to feature in Egyptian inscriptions, so do references to what modern historians call the Sea Peoples, identified by the Egyptians as inhabitants of foreign lands 'of the sea' or those who are 'in their islands' (Cline and O'Connor, Chapter 7). With names such as Shardana, Eqwosh, Teresh, Washosh and Lukki, these peoples joined Libyans in an invasion of Egypt in ca. 1209 BC. This onslaught was driven back, but 20 years later mainly new groups formed a migrating coalition that, some scholars believe, led to the collapse of the Late Bronze Age polities of Anatolia and the Levant, and a determined if unsuccessful attack upon Egypt itself. The homelands of these peoples remain mysterious; they may have extended as far west as Sicily and Sardinia, and may have been scattered through the Aegean and along the Mediterranean coast of Anatolia. Some have been identified as ancestral Greeks, the Danuna or the Danaians, a term later applied to Greeks in general (Redford 1992: 252) and the Eqwosh as the Achaeans of Mycenaean Greece (Gardiner 1961: 270–271). As a group, they seem to break abruptly onto the historical record, and equally abruptly drop out of it. Only one can be identified reasonably certainly with a later people, the Peleset being ancestral to the Philistines, a historically and archaeologically attested people of biblical fame (Machinist 2000). Otherwise, the available Near Eastern writings include only references to the Lukki, as seafarers and sometimes as enemies in the records from Hittite Anatolia and north-west Syria. This is fertile ground for speculation, but with mainly negative evidence in the archaeological record. As a result, there has arisen a rival school for interpretation of the 'Sea Peoples', according to which they are not a cause but a symptom of the collapse of the Hittite empire; according to this view, groups of island and coastal seafarers took advantage of the failure in security across Anatolia and the Levant, until the disappearance of the empire on which they had preyed (Kuhrt 1995). These elusive groups highlight the source of the mystery – a gap between the archaeological map and the written sources for it.

Topographical lists

References to foreign lands occur as early as the third millennium BC, and in the early second millennium BC detailed lists of names of foreign lands and rulers were written out on small clay figurines used in cursing rituals to protect the king and country

(Ritner 1993: 136–142). However, foreign place names are most impressively assembled together in 'topographical lists'. The earliest of these, the stela of general Mentuhotep from Buhen, dates to the early years of Sesostris I in the Middle Kingdom, ca. 1950 BC. There is then a gap in the record, until the inscription of the great majority of surviving examples in the New Kingdom and later periods.

In their longest versions, the lists are typically displayed upon temple pylons or external wall faces of temples, and consist of long series of place or people names, arranged in vertical columns or along horizontal registers. Each name is set in a cartouche-shaped oval which is a conventionalized representation of a fortified city wall, even if the people in question are non-urbanized nomads. Often, the top of the enclosure sprouts the upper part of a human figure, arms bound at the elbows behind its back, and representing the inhabitants of each place named. Topographical lists in these contexts are usually placed below, or adjacent to, emblematic representations of pharaoh preparing to smite a helpless group of pinioned foreign foes and hence are a statement about the 'world dominion' allotted each pharaoh by Egypt's deities and asserted by the military campaigning such emblematic scenes imply, with or without a basis in historical events (Figure 1:2). Shorter versions of such lists appear in a variety of other contexts: upon monumental stelae, royal throne daises or statue bases and even pharaoh's chariot (Figure 1:3).

These topographical lists sometimes comprise hundreds of people and places, as in the case of the several lists of King Tuthmosis III (ca. 1479–1425 BC) distributed

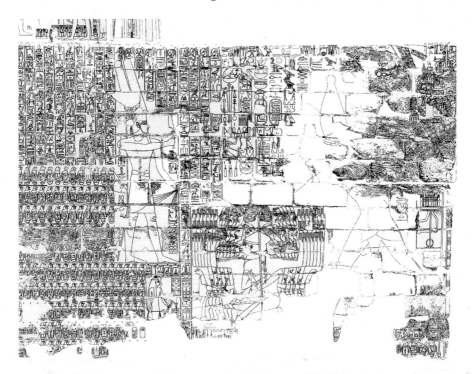

Figure 1:2   A twenty-second Dynasty example of a topographical list, commemorating Sheshonq I's campaign in Palestine (after Shaw 2000: 336; Cairo Museum, 120).

Figure 1:3   Depiction of foreigners on the chariot of Tutankhamun (Fox 1951: pl. 6).

around Karnak temple (O'Connor 1982: 928 n. 4). Typically, the sets of names are organized into geographically distinct groups, roughly 'northern', 'eastern', 'southern', and 'western' (for the Near Eastern category, see Edel 1966; Simons 1937; and for the Puntite and Nubian, O'Connor 1982: 928–933); the Nubian or southern group are often placed appropriately on the southern wing of a temple pylon, and the Near Eastern or north-eastern group upon the northern. The lists make no reference to scale: they incorporate a wide diversity of regions in terms of their specific areal and population sizes, without making any obvious distinctions between ones known, on other grounds, to be very disparate. Thus, imperial powers such as Khatte (the Hittite lands), Mitanni (on the upper Euphrates) and Babylon are found, without any special distinction, in lists incorporating more polities, and even places which were quite small but may have marked points along an itinerary (Redford 1992). Places named may lie within larger regional entities named before them in the relevant list. The spatial logic and distribution of each list cannot be assumed, and require decoding.

The geographical complexities within the lists are clear because many regions or places named in their Near Eastern segments have been precisely or approximately identified from cuneiform and biblical sources, and their spatial, distributional and other disparities made evident (Redford 1992). Despite the problems, the lists represent a very wide geographical knowledge about the world surrounding them on the Egyptians' part, even allowing for archaizing reuse of foreign toponyms which no longer existed in practice, and possibly even for fictitious names invented to fill up space and make complementary lists equivalent to each other in compositional terms. These problems probably comprise a minority, and the lists in general can be considered an accurate rendering of hundreds of foreign regions, places and peoples known to the Egyptians at that time.

Given the absence of corroboratory written source material, it is the southern (Puntite and Nubian) and western (Libyan) components of such lists that present the greatest problems in locating regions and peoples named. For example, the information provided about Nubian and Puntite regions by the lists of Tuthmosis III (O'Connor 1982: 928–933) is both intriguing and tantalizing. They display a certain underlying coherence and structure, but, as compared to the Near Eastern segments of the same lists, a vast majority of the names cannot be assigned even approximate, let alone precise, locations. The placement of certain key regions in the lists suggests that the lists comprise groups of toponyms within or close to Wawat (northern or Lower Nubia), Kush (central or Upper Nubia), Irem (southern Nubia), Punt (usually located between the Nile and the Red Sea, but see Meeks, Chapter 4), and the harsher, more arid lands occupied by the nomads known as the Medjayu (O'Connor 1993: ch. 3; Trigger 1976) and apparently lying north of Punt (Figure 1:4). An underlying structure is revealed if the Kush and Irem 'groups' are treated as a unit, followed by the Wawat group, a sequence moving along the Nile from south to north, similar to the way toponymical lists of places within Egypt were typically ordered (Gardiner 1947: 40). The compiler would then have moved east, listing first the Punt group, and then – moving from south to north again – the Medjayu group. Moreover, three of the groups are comparable in the number of toponyms assigned them: Kush plus Irem total 23, Wawat 24 and Punt 30, suggesting that toponyms of similar importance, or ones related in some way (e.g. key points along an itinerary), had been selected. Thirty-eight toponyms are found in the Medjayu group, but it is possible that this group actually incorporates another major region which we do not recognize (hence, two toponymical groups of roughly equal size might be involved), or that desert regions and loose tribal structures generate a larger number of relevant toponyms. In the total list of 116 toponyms, only a handful can be located on the ground, or equated with known material cultures (for an overly optimistic attempt, Zyhlarz 1958; for a more revealing compilation, Zibelius 1972).

Irem – a mysterious land in archaeology

The name of Irem is attested only, and then quite frequently, in the New Kingdom and later, in contexts making it clear that it is a Nubian region. It is often cited, in short lists, along with entities known to be substantial, such as Kush; Tuthmosis III noted that sons of the ruler of Irem were delivered to him as hostages, suggesting that his troops

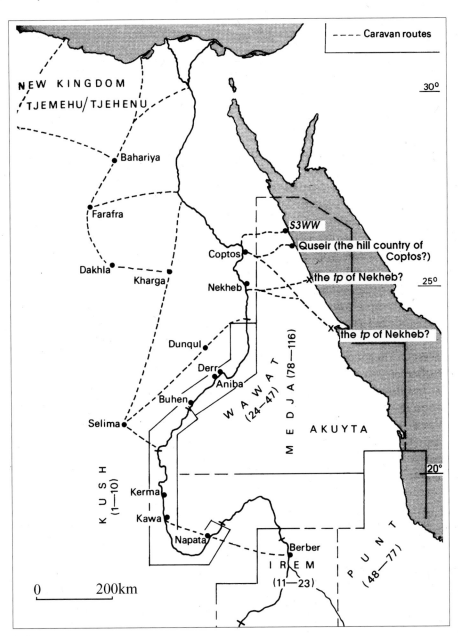

Figure 1:4   Map showing places mentioned close to northern Nubia (O'Connor 1982: 929, fig. 12.28).

may have campaigned there; and Seti I (ca. 1290–1279 BC) and Ramesses II (ca. 1279–1213 BC) certainly fought with Irem, while Amenophis III (ca. 1390–1353 BC) and Ramesses III (ca. 1187–1156 BC) may also have done so (O'Connor 1987). Moreover, Irem survived as a recognizable entity, its inhabitants being referred to as late as the reign of the Nubian king Irike-Amanote (ca. 431–405 BC; Welsby 1996: 208). However, in spite of the rather detailed description of the Seti I campaign, the location of Irem remains a matter of debate. Some scholars think it a comparatively small, if periodically rebellious, entity within Upper (central) Nubia, which was part of Egypt's Nubian empire during the New Kingdom. However, if Irem lay further south (as may be more likely) – perhaps along the Nile where it is joined by the Atbara – it might have been a relatively large polity, essentially independent of Egypt (O'Connor 1987). Hopefully, the discovery of *in situ* inscriptional evidence, or of a more geographically explicit inscription in Egypt, will resolve the issue.

A further interesting aspect of Irem is that it may be the later writing of the name of a Nubian region, attested much earlier: the land of Yam. Along with other Nubian regions the locations of which appear relatively certain (Wawat, Irtjet and Zetjau: O'Connor 1986), Yam is referred to in a number of Old Kingdom inscriptions, and later may be incorporated into other Nubian regional names of the Middle Kingdom (ca. 1975–1640 BC). Yam seems to have been relatively independent of Old Kingdom Egypt, but was clearly one of its important trading partners and an occasional ally in potential conflicts with other Nubian polities. Despite the importance of Yam, however, its actual location remains uncertain. The best evidence is provided by an early travel narrative, describing several trading expeditions made to Yam by Harkhuf, a high official based on Elephantine near Aswan during the sixth Dynasty (ca. 2325–2175 BC). On each occasion Harkhuf brought back for his overlord, the Egyptian king, a wide range of exotica (in one case, carried by 300 donkeys) such as incense, ebony, elephant tusks and, on one memorable occasion, "a dwarf of the god's dancers from the land of the horizon-dwellers" (Lichtheim 1976: 25–27), presumably meaning a place on the extreme periphery of the Egyptians' then geographical knowledge. The dwarf was therefore apparently not indigenous to Yam (which is never described in these terms), but had been acquired by the Yamites from a more remote region. Some scholars have identified him as a pygmy rather than a dwarf, in which case this might provide a fascinating glimpse of how wide, even if indirectly, Egypt's foreign contacts could be, for in recent times at least pygmies are a central or west, not east, African people.

Harkhuf's trips to Yam and back are stated to have taken seven to eight months, and donkey caravans were always used, not the river, at least insofar as the Nubian Nile Valley is concerned. On this basis, many scholars calculate that Yam lay somewhere in Upper (central) Nubia, and perhaps had the famous archaeological site of Kerma (Bonnet 1990; Kendall 1999) as its centre. However, this theory assumes that Harkhuf's donkey caravans began their trips at Memphis, far to the north, and returned thence. If Elephantine was their starting and return point, then Yam would have lain further south than Upper Nubia, in fact at about the confluence of the Nile and the Atbara, the same general location that can be suggested – on independent ground – for Irem in later times (O'Connor 1986). Again, only new archaeological discoveries, inscribed or otherwise, could resolve the issue.

Religious contents and contexts

The Egyptian data on these 'missing' foreign lands, as in those with locations which are fixed, are highly selective, and the factors making this so must be understood if the maximum possible information is to be gleaned from the available sources. These are primarily inscriptions and depictions which belong to religious or ceremonial contexts – temples, royal tombs, elite tomb-chapels and royal palaces. Inevitably, the presentation of the foreign in such contexts is heavily influenced by ideological and cosmological factors – foreign lands and peoples are presented as having a definite, subordinate and relatively powerless position in a hierarchical view of cosmos that assigns superiority to Egypt and its deities. Military records might have presented a different perspective, closer to the requirements of modern historians, but few such records survive (on military and other 'day-books', see Redford 1986: ch. 3).

From Egypt's theological and ideological perspectives, all lands and peoples have value, as products – like the Egyptians themselves – of the creator, so long as they function in accordance with the hierarchical position assigned them in cosmos, the created order often referred to as the personification, Maat (Assmann 1995). That hierarchy runs from the deities and their ruler, the lord of the cosmos – typically, the sun god Ra in a variety of manifestations (Quirke 2001) – down through Egyptians, then foreigners and finally the world of nature. Thus, foreigners, in terrestrial terms, lie on the frontier between human (the Egyptians) and non-human (nature, with its beasts, birds and reptiles). Like the world of nature, foreigners are expected to provide support and sustenance to Egypt and its deities, under whose control they, in theory, lie.

However, any land can be rebellious, i.e. can refuse to service the interests of the Egyptian king; it may resist, perhaps militarily, Egyptian influence, control or attack, and may even take the initiative, attacking Egyptian forces abroad, or attempting to invade Egypt itself. In all three circumstances 'rebels', from the cosmographic and ideological perspective, take on the character of Isfet, the limitless formlessness surrounding cosmos and generating hostile forces – demons and monsters – that ceaselessly attempt to abort the orderly, life-giving cycle of the sun god around cosmos and thus bring cosmos as a whole, and its carefully structured hierarchy, to an end (Hornung 1982a: 163–164; 1982b: chs. 5–7). In these circumstances, rebellious, defiant or invasive foreigners become equivalent to the wild beasts and birds of the natural world, and the demons and monsters that manifest aggressive chaotic force on the cosmic level.

The alien nature of the foreign, and the affinity to that which relates to chaos, is manifest in the generic terms the Egyptians applied to them. A foreign land was a *ḫȝst*, a word written with a depiction of a three-peaked, desert mountain ridge with a strip of green – the Nile Valley – at its foot (Gardiner 1957: 488, sign N 25). This indicates that foreigners lay beyond the ideal environmental and human order, i.e. the Egyptian Nile Valley and its inhabitants, and hence were on the frontier between order and chaos; and they lay behind the mountains defining the horizon, in a region wherein the sun god prepared himself for his renewal and re-ascent every day, but also had to be defended against the particularly intense attack of the demonic, with which foreigners were to be identified (O'Connor 2003: 174, Figure 9:12). Another term which included foreign lands was "the nine bows", written as a bow with nine strokes underneath (Gardiner 1957: 511, sign T 10), which, however, can also be read as the 'diffuse and multiple lands', highlighting chaotic aspects of foreigners that could be taken to distinguish them from the order represented by Egypt and its people. The term would imply that foreign lands are endlessly scattered, and foreign peoples uncountable, whereas, in contrast, Egypt is a finite geographical entity, with a specific population that can be counted (O'Connor 2003). These nine bows, however, contain some surprising features that may cause some rethinking of the assumptions brought to the discussion of contacts between Egypt and the world outside.

The nine bows

The phrase *pdt psdt* 'nine bows' appears in ancient Egyptian written sources on the theme of royal power from the third millennium BC. The bow presumably indicates the potential resistance that must be overcome, and the nine is perhaps an expression of totality (three being used to express the plural, three times three being a plural of plurals, a totality). From the New Kingdom, there is a standardized sequence of the bows specifying nine names of places or peoples (Osing and Rosati 1998: 48):

Egyptian	English translation
t3 šmˁ	Upper Egypt
t3 mhw	Lower Egypt
iwntyw sti	Iuntiu-people of Nubia
mntyw nw stt	Mentiu-people of Asia
thnw	Tjehenu-people
pdt šw	Bow-people of Shu/the feather
sht i3mw	Marshland of Iamu
š3t	Foreign land Shat
h3w nbw	Foreign land Hau-nebu

In the Ptolemaic Period, the same nine names were listed with explanatory notes on a wall in Edfu temple, and there are remnants of abbreviated versions on papyri of the Roman Period (Chassinat and Rochemonteix 1931: 196 ff):

added in manuscripts	added from Edfu temple
t3 swt (land of sut-plant)	*i3btyw* (easterners)
t3 mhty (north land)	*h3st h3rw* (foreign land of Syrians)
nhsyw (Nubians)	*styw nhsyw* (setiu-Nubians, nehesiu-Nubians)
h3rww (Syrians)	*p3 t3 n n3 išrw* (the land of the Assyrians)
pwdw (western nomads)	*p3 t3 n n3 pyt* (the land of the western nomads)
š3sw (bedouin)	*š3sw* (bedouin)
Wh3tyw (oasis dwellers)	*wh3tyw* (oasis dwellers)
not preserved	*p3 t3 n n3 hkr* (the land of the Hagrians)
not preserved	*n3 m3w n p3 ym hnˁ h3swt mhtt ˁš3 wrt* (the islands of the sea and very many northern foreign lands)

The lists run counter to Egyptological received opinion on the relation between Egypt and the outside world. First and foremost, the nine bows denote not 'foreign lands', but possible resistance to order, that is, to the king and his father the sun god. Egypt is not just a part of this world, but its starting point: the first two 'bows' are Upper and Lower Egypt, in that order. Along with the wetter climate of the Sahara in the fourth and third millennium BC, and the astonishingly dense network of desert roads either side of the Nile Valley, this inclusion cancels the simpler modern myths that posit ancient Egyptian isolation from its neighbours (and see Matthews and Roemer 2003a). Undoubtedly, then as now, there would not have been any adjacent population on a scale to match that supported by the fields along the Nile from north of Aswan. Egypt was probably always far more densely populated then even the settled lands of Nubia and the Levant, and the intermediate areas supporting nomadic rather than settled life would generally have provided an efficient buffer zone. Nevertheless, that is a condition of the longer term; in the shorter, more localized temporal and spatial horizons, the desert was a partner in life, and the inhabitants of the Nile Valley must have been in constant communication with their immediate neighbours.

Second, the worldview from Edfu temple appears to blur the dividing line between foreign and Egyptian, by aligning Lower Egypt (the Nile Delta and the area of Memphis) with Asia, under the explanatory note "foreign-land of Syrians". This is startling, even from the perspective of Edfu, a religious precinct at the very south of Upper Egypt. The hieroglyphic script includes determinatives, signs placed at the end of a word to denote the type of content, such as verbs of motion or verbs of action, and plants or animals or minerals. Determinatives remain among the most underexploited resources in the study of Ancient Egypt; the potential for using them to understand the Egyptian point of view is well illustrated in Loprieno (Chapter 3). The two commonest determinatives for place names are a circle denoting a town or settled area, for places in arable Egypt, and the triple mountain sign mentioned above, for places in the Egyptian deserts and beyond. These two signs divide the world in two, between the part where settled inhabitants spoke Egyptian, and the rest. The Edfu temple gloss for Lower Egypt seems to run counter to this basic division. Perhaps the note indicates direction, rather than content: Upper Egypt too is 'explained' with the word 'easterners', tying the inhabitants of the Nile Valley between Aswan and Memphis to the east, rather than removing Upper Egypt from the core of the Egyptian experience. In the word 'orientation', European languages also privilege the east and sunrise among the cardinal points. Yet the use of direction, of what is beyond, to explain the first two of the nine bows should be enough to demonstrate that they are all outside some other core. In the Ptolemaic and Roman Period lists cited above, the nine bows follow a series of seven "arrows of the goddess Bast" with their places of origin (Osing 1998: 253). These "arrows" designate physically destructive emanations of divine power; they first appear in the surviving record on an inscription of King Osorkon I of the twenty-second Dynasty at the temple of Bast in Bubastis. Together the bows and arrows represent the potential blows to the good order championed by the king on earth for the sun god: according to a composition revealed by Assmann (1970) as "the King as Priest of the Sun god", "the sun god placed the king on the earth of the living". The core of this operational system is a solar kingship. All hieroglyphic inscriptions and all the depictions in formal Egyptian art belong not to a human geography but to a superhuman or divine cosmography within which landscapes and peoples are treated uniformly as an accompaniment to the perpetual circuit of the sun, maintained by the king. Failure to recognise this, in literal readings of Egyptian written and pictorial sources, disables any useful reading of the past.

Kingship as the framing context

For Ancient Egypt, despite the survival of the monumental architecture that may be ranked its most overpowering achievement, paradoxically few direct explicit sources survive for the core of the civilization – kingship. Each chapter in this book reveals a dependency on sources and, in each 'mystery', a frustration at the missing core. The 'Book of the Two Ways', the 'Book of the Dead' (Chapters 8 and 9) and the Amduat may contain more or less direct echoes of a lost original, the cosmography developed for the Middle Kingdom kings; there are, though, no royal libraries, there is no single manuscript, from the twelfth Dynasty Residence Itjtawy, and the tombs of those kings are uninscribed. The evidence currently available does not reveal whether Middle Kingdom kings had guides to the underworld, or maps of any world. The pattern of communicating topography survives in a place removed from the Residence (el-Bersheh), or in periods removed from the Middle Kingdom. The surviving evidence is still abundant, but the absence of the core is a serious complication to modern knowledge about ancient knowledge, and may be fatal to modern knowledge if it is not recognized. The Egyptian view of the world as sky goddess arched over earth does not appear in the surviving record earlier than the reign of Seti I, in the early 13th century BC (Allen, Chapter 2); its contents agree with the general impression given by third millennium BC religious literature, but the articulation as an image is difficult to date, and difficult to assess in terms of its impact on the Egyptian perception of the world. Other elements in the temple of Seti I at Abydos find parallels in the Middle Kingdom, such as the appeal to the deity to come to his meal, on a ritual papyrus fragment from Lahun (Petrie Museum, UC 32091A, published on database at www.petrie.ucl.ac.uk). At present it is not possible to determine precisely when the image, and when its worldview, came into existence, and where, and for whom. As a result, knowledge of ancient Egyptian topography of the cosmos remains inexact, prone to generalization and inaccuracy. The damaged pictorial description of Punt in the Hatshepsut temple at Thebes dominates attempts to locate that land (Chapters 4 and 5); this is another source with highly uncertain historical context. Parallels are lacking, but it is difficult to assess whether it is original, or whether it might copy or develop earlier depictions in Theban or other temples of her predecessors in the eighteenth Dynasty. For one prominent inscription in her temple, on the selection of her four new names at accession, there is a poorly preserved parallel from a Fayum temple of the late twelfth Dynasty, four centuries earlier; the first topographical list in a scene of the king triumphant dates from the early twelfth Dynasty. Without clear historical location and diachronic development, the sources for ancient Egyptian geographical knowledge are left highly vulnerable to displacement and translation into foreign contexts: spatial diagrams, pictorial sub-plots and toponyms in art become fodder for the modern map maker, and are easily and conveniently built into the foundations of the next generation of archaeological and historical knowledge. The written and pictorial evidence can drown out the more direct archaeological evidence for human living in a landscape. The 'Book of the Fayum' shows how intensely and differently the ancient Egyptians encoded geographical space in two dimensions for a religious context (Tait, Chapter 10); it would be interesting to reconstruct from it a 'modern map', and compare that with the modern map of the Fayum. The Book of the Fayum can be appreciated best precisely by moving in the opposite direction, starting from the archaeological map on the ground, and comparing that with the data on the ancient two-dimensional rendering. The ancient experience of space can only be approached through the specific contexts of its material expression. This lesson has to be learned for the most elusive lands, those where the ancient description seems so close to modern patterns of describing that the ancient context can easily be forgotten. The inscriptions of Merenptah and Ramesses III celebrate defeat of foreign island peoples and western nomads (Chapters 5, 6 and 7); they are anchored in a world of kingship as expressed through the architecture and ritual of the ancient Egyptian temple, but have been set free from that religious environment to become histories of the end of the Bronze Age. The totality of archaeological sources across the eastern Mediterranean, including material culture in all its manifestations, inscribed or not, reveals a great range of factors and, at present, a material invisibility of island peoples outside their islands, with the one exception of the provincial Mycenaean material in coastal Canaanite towns. The power of the sea battle depictions and descriptions blinds the historian to its setting – spatially a temple wall, in genre a development of pictorial narrative cycles beyond the already epic scale and composition of the Battle of Kadesh in the celebration of kingship under Ramesses II a century earlier (Warburton 2003). From this perspective the so-called 'Sea Peoples' are another dazzling highlight in the artistic achievement of Ramesside Egypt. Certainly they offer an immense wealth of data on island peoples, whether or not we can identify those in their homelands or destinations. However, strictly speaking they constitute indirect rather than direct evidence. The historiography has to start from the material on the ground.

Differences of attitude in Egyptian sources: the case of the Libyans

Given the presence of kingship at the epicentre of most written and pictorial sources, it is not surprising to find foreigners assigned very specific and stereotypical roles in literature (including versions of royal victories inscribed on temple walls) and art. Typically, they are presented as gift-givers, representatives of each land or larger region presenting the produce of their land to pharaoh as if all were his subjects. The Egyptian gifts sent in return do not have a space in this formalized view, designed to perpetuate perfect order, but they surface in the 14th century BC correspondence between rulers: the Amarna Letters (Moran 1992). If hostile, foreigners are depicted as rendered helpless by pharaoh's divinely ordained power and reduced to a terrified mass being slaughtered by Egyptian troops (Heinz 2001; for typical literary equivalents, see Edgerton and Wilson 1936). The topographical lists, as noted above, also conform to this ideology. Despite the generic approach, Egyptian representations of the foreign can reflect their attitudes towards foreigners and the cosmological context they imagined for them in complex and nuanced ways; but, by the same token, these circumstances may impinge upon the reliability of textual and pictorial references insofar as the foreigners concerned are involved. A good case in point is provided by one of the 'missing' peoples, the Libyans.

As noted above, foreigners were depicted in art by representative type figures, each of distinctive appearance and accoutrements, and typically – when in groups – including Nubians, Levantines and Libyans, so as to express the universality of

Egypt's dominion (Figure 1:5). In literature and other texts, foreigners of different geographic origins are often treated in the same uniform, almost stereotypical way, for much the same reason. However, closer examination reveals that each foreign type

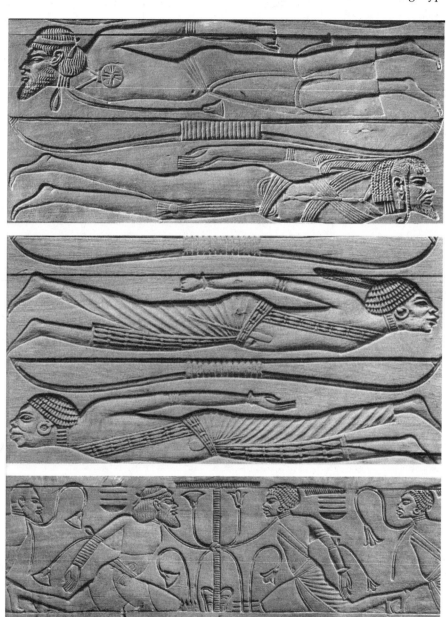

Figure 1:5   A typical collection of representative foreigners (from the "ceremonial" 'footstool' of Tutankhamun). Note from top to bottom: two bearded 'Libyans'; two 'clean-shaven' 'Nubians'; four kneeling 'Levantines' and 'Nubians' flanking the emblem of Egypt's own unity, tied round their necks with plant-stems (Desroches-Noblecourt 1989: 51, pl. xi).

is associated with a specific constellation of meanings, different from that of the others and derived from the Egyptian concept of cosmos, and its interaction with their historical experiences. All foreigners were alien, in that they lacked the normative human characteristics of orderly society – i.e. Egyptian ethnicity, language and culture – but some were more alien than others, according to a subtly structured hierarchy imposed by the Egyptians.

Using Libyans as the example, in terms of verbal metaphorical representation they are, especially in the New Kingdom, subject to a more pejorative treatment than other foreigners. For example, at the mortuary temple of Ramesses III at Medinet Habu, western Thebes, three actual historical events are described at considerable length – two attempted invasions of Egypt by Libyans, and one by the Sea Peoples, a powerful group of probably Aegean and West Anatolian origin (Cline and O'Connor, Chapter 7; Edgerton and Wilson 1936: 4–93). The status of both peoples is expressed metaphorically as well as by direct description, but the Sea Peoples are allotted much fewer metaphors than the Libyans, who are compared to trapped birds; threshed grain or harvested brush, reduced to ashes; demons destroyed by the god Seth, carried off by whirlwinds; ensnared wild cattle; and, most memorably, they are depicted as men turned into women who are giving birth, as a supreme example of the impotence, travail and helplessness their temerity has brought them to (Edgerton and Wilson 1936: 12 n. 116, 79 n. 23e, 81 n. 32d). All of the imagery cited was also applied to other kinds of foreigners, but an excessive amount of it was applied to the Libyans, unusually (although not uniquely) in an extreme form, such as in the references to childbirth.

Standardized Old Kingdom depictions of Libyans differ from those of the New Kingdom, but the two are clearly related. The dress, hairstyles and accoutrements assigned to Libyans are based on Libyan features also displayed in examples of Saharan rock painting of various dates (Hachid 2000: 54–55, 94–97, 106, fig. 120). However, it seems likely that the Egyptians reinterpreted the indigenous meanings of Libyan appearance in terms of their own prejudices and worldview. For example, Libyans were often depicted as nude, except for a so-called 'phallus sheath' (worn also by women! Hachid 2000: 94, figs. 87, 91, 97), whereas most foreigners were, like Egyptians, more modestly dressed. This may have conferred a certain animality upon Libyans, reinforced by their close association with animals as nomads, and the leather accoutrements worn by Old Kingdom Libyans or the leather cloaks worn by New Kingdom Libyans (necklets, chest bands, belt; Hachid 2000: 94, figs. 87, 88, 1st and 4th figs. from left, 91), which made them look like animals (Figure 1:6). Moreover, Libyans' gender was ambiguous from the Egyptian perspective; Old Kingdom Libyans had a slight beard, but wore their hair long and flowing, like Egyptian women (Hachid 2000: 94, fig. 87) or, if shorter – as in the New Kingdom – were elaborately dressed, again a characteristic of women rather than men to the Egyptians (Hachid 2000: fig. 91). These circumstances may explain why the insulting child-bearing metaphor was so frequently applied to Libyan enemies. Finally, the Libyans were, in some cases, uncircumcised, hence somewhat juvenile (and thus again akin to women), for to Egyptians and many foreign groups male circumcision marked the 'complete', fully socialized adult. To reinforce this point, New Kingdom Egyptians normally cut off the hand of slain enemies, in order to easily add up the total killed; but with slain Libyans they, presumably contemptuously, cut off the penises

Figure 1:6   Representations from the 'Book of Gates' of New Kingdom Egyptians, Asiatics and Nubians with the Libyan shown as nude under his robe (after Hachid 2000: 97, fig. 91).

(Edgerton and Wilson 1936: 14, 15, 67), a form of demoralization referring back to the feminine aspect of Libyans discussed above. These views of the Libyans persisted over a long period; in ca. 728 BC the Egyptianized and highly orthodox king of Nubia, Piye, defeated a coalition of Egyptian regional rulers who had resisted the expanding Nubian dominion over Egypt (Kitchen 1973: 363–366). Of the local kings who came to formally submit to him, three, of Libyan descent and still partly Libyan in attire, were barred from entering the royal palace because "their legs were the legs of women (i.e. smooth-skinned) and they were uncircumcised and ... eaters of fish, which is an abomination to the palace" (Lichtheim 1980: 80). The harsh judgment on Libyan ethnicity may be a back-handed compliment; in a sense, these were the most dangerous neighbours of Egypt, and came to be her rulers for much of the first millennium BC.

Mining the sources

The information on differential Egyptian attitudes demonstrates how much can be learned from these sources, provided the contexts are observed as carefully as the contents. Egyptian representations – textual and pictorial – of foreign lands and peoples must be analyzed carefully, with due regard to the influence upon them of Egyptian ideology, prejudice and historical experiences. Nevertheless, for 'missing' lands and peoples the Egyptian material remains an invaluable resource – our only glimpse, for the moment, into these otherwise lost worlds. Keeping the framing context of kingship and its ideology in mind, Egyptian literature and art do provide important information about foreigners, even when their homelands are as yet unlocatable. Just as Near Easterners and Aegean peoples are provided with distinctive appearances, hairstyles and costumes, so are Libyans, Puntites and Sea Peoples. More rarely, intriguing details of material culture are also indicated, but await archaeological confirmation. Did some Libyans really wield immense bronze swords 1.57 m (5'2") and 2.09 m (6'10") long (Edgerton and Wilson 1936: 66 with

n. 27e)? What do the strange helmets of some of the Sea Peoples consist of; feathers, a 'hoplite's plume', natural hair (Redford 1992: 251) or metalwork?

Moreover, important information is provided about the economies, technology and even military and political institutions of some of these as yet unlocated peoples. The pastoral nature of Libyan society is clearly indicated by their economic resource (animal herds), and, if it is not part of the Egyptian assumptions about pastoralists, the characteristic social structure of 'families' or 'clans' (Snape, Chapter 6). The ships of the migrant seafarers of the 12th century BC are to date only visible in an Egyptian depiction of their vessels of a type unique in Egyptian art. Sometimes political leadership is unequivocally described in Egyptian texts (as with Libyan invaders of Egypt under Merenptah and Ramesses III (Snape, Chapter 6, and in more detail, O'Connor 1990: 66–76); at other times leadership may be more obliquely referred to, and only in pictorial terms (Cline and O'Connor, Chapter 7).

The degree of detail is in itself a cautionary reminder of the relevance of context in each instance. The 'missing' homelands are not often described or pictured in any detail, and, when they are, the description may respond to literary requirements (Loprieno, Chapter 3). Thus, the southern Levant can be described both as, in part, a "good land", rich in fruit, grain and animals and with "more wine than water" (Lichtheim 1976: 226); but also, in part, as "short of water, bare of wood, its paths are many and painful because of mountains", its inhabitants nomadic, aggressive and treacherous, "Like a thief who darts about a group" (Lichtheim 1976: 104). Of course, environmentally different regions of the Levant may be involved, but the different descriptions involve selections to fit the mood and purposes of the different literary works involved.

Once, at least, one of the 'missing' lands stimulated production of a highly unusual rendering of a landscape, schematically organized into horizontal registers but incredibly rich in detail. This scene, in the mortuary temple of the female king Hatshepsut (ca. 1473–1458 BC) at Deir el-Bahri, Thebes, is usually taken to represent Punt, and has provided the crucial evidence for an African location for that land. However, it may include other southern territories as well, including the land of Irem, discussed above (Harvey, Chapter 5; see also O'Connor 1982: 934–939). The modern enquirer needs to return to the evidence itself and the circumstances of its discovery and original location. Too often the search starts from wherever the previous enquirer left off, when it should be the privilege and precondition of ancient history that its research begins directly from the primary source material.

Naming lands

In the enthusiasm for locating archaeological place, a simple distinction may be overlooked – the difference between name and place. The ancient Egyptian sources reveal the names that the Egyptians knew for lands and peoples around them; they do not record the sources for those names, although the other ancient literate societies make it possible to find corroboration, and there may be linguistic clues within the names that reveal a particular language, or language family. While the modern historian may fuse place and name in an archaeological hunt on the ground, the ancient Egyptian practice of naming implies belief in the identity of name and its object conferring power over the object from the knowledge of the name; the lists of foreign names were collected on cursing figures to be destroyed in rituals in order to disarm any possible threat to order, and the temple wall scenes with topographical lists served the same purpose. A name might be part of an equally powerful but less conflictual experience, as evoked in the literary celebrations of the home town (Loprieno, Chapter 3). These ancient experiences of place, more precisely of existence with intimate knowledge of a place, can scarcely be imagined by a modern city-dweller (Layton, Chapter 11). A different and more recent context offers some idea of the gulf between modern academic 'reportage' and the religious and literary contexts of ancient written sources:

> ... a modern road-map transmits knowledge of a kind that Celts would have found inconceivably abstract. Places would have been known to them as people were: by face, name and history. The last two would have been closely linked, for, as the Dindshenchas illustrates again and again, the name of every place was assumed to be an expression of its history.

> (Bowen 1975–1976: 115)

This comment on the *dinnsheanchas*, the medieval Irish literary corpus on place names, may also be applied to more recent experience:

> Placenames were a source of fascination to Thomas Murphy at all times. There were even some free-floating placenames that he didn't know where they really belonged any more. This was a major source of distress to him. One of them was a place called Slí Uisli, which seemingly was a gap in the cliffs over near where Cuan Iochtarach used to be, which he had heard of from his grandfather but had never been able to identify for himself.

> (Ni Dhomnaill 1996: 422)

This reflects the inclusiveness and intimacy of experience of the landscape, and the meaning of names in Ancient Egypt. This distant but instructive affinity extends in particular to the world beyond the human. The afterlife and desert creatures 'of the imagination' need more careful consideration than life sciences and earth sciences can usually accommodate:

> For the first and only time in his life he apprised me of his belief in merpeople. He was never to do so again, as later in his life he became rather coy and wary in speaking of mermaids or of fairy lore. The fact that I and my generation scoffed at him unmercifully from the heights of our newly acquired knowledge of biology and geology did not encourage him to pass on his knowledge to us. Twenty-five years down along the line, much humbler and more dog-eared, I feel in no position to laugh at him. Actually, I feel that his world view has much to offer us as a middle ground between the severities of scientific abstraction and the loneliness of the individual in contemplation of them.

> (Ni Dhomnaill 1996: 426)

There may be just such a high-handed tendency among Egyptologists and archaeologists not to take hybrid demons and otherworldly places so seriously, and to exclude the underworld from the series of lands to be studied. Such an omission would destroy the unity of the universe portrayed by the Egyptians. The full range of ancient Egyptian sources embrace a world comprising the earth of the living, the skies above, and the underworld beneath. The ancient historian tends to focus on compiling 'political history' or history event-by-event; 'short-wave' history. That may not be available for the Bronze Age, with its richer insights into cultural history and the operations of ancient kingship. It may also deflect attention from an experience of the world that was less exclusively focused on the physical, visible or tangible.

The destination of the modern quest for, and journey through, the mysterious lands of Ancient Egypt seems, then, as in most mental and physical journeys, to be the self, or more specifically a self-critical consciousness. Egyptology tends to be lambasted among the social sciences for its over-dependency on writing and art, its isolation from neighbouring disciplines and its disengagement from theoretical archaeology. This volume demonstrates the power of those written and artistic sources, and the need to incorporate them into the study of the past, on condition that their context remains visible and studied at least as much as, if not more than, their content.

CHAPTER 2

THE EGYPTIAN CONCEPT OF THE WORLD

James P. Allen

For the ancient Egyptians, as for most ancient cultures, their own land was the centre of the universe, and their experience of this land coloured their perceptions of the universe as a whole.

The Egyptian perception of Egypt itself was defined by the Nile. The river's flow from south to north determined the orientation of those who lived along its banks. South, where the river originated, was Up: the Egyptian word for "south", *rsw*, is related to the word meaning "awaken", and the root *ḫnt* means both "upstream" and "forward". Northern Egypt, where the river divided into several branches, forming the marshland of the Delta, was called *mḥw*, from the word meaning "immersed"; to go north was to go "downstream" (*ḫdi*). The Egyptians lived primarily in the arable land along both sides of the Nile and in the Delta, known as *kmt* "black (land)". The level nature of this primary zone of habitation is reflected in the Egyptian hieroglyph for "land" (*t₃*), which depicts a flat strip of earth. On either side of the "black land" lay the desert, which the Egyptians called "red (land)" (*dšrt*). Throughout the Nile Valley, the desert begins with a series of cliffs or hills, described by the Egyptian term *ḫ₃st*, written with a hieroglyph of three hills; the same word was regularly used to designate countries outside Egypt proper.

The Egyptian word for "land", *t₃*, also appears in texts with reference to the world as a whole, with the same duality as the English word "earth": for example, "the entire world (*t₃*), both sky and land (*t₃*)" (Coffin Texts Spell 335 (after de Buck 1951: 292)). The character of the hieroglyph with which this word is written suggests that the Egyptians thought of the earth as essentially a flat plate of land. The sky was visualized in similar fashion, as a flat surface with projections that touched the earth at its extremities; these projections were occasionally described and depicted in metaphorical terms as four sceptres or columns.

In Egyptian thought, the earth and sky were divinities, like all the forces and elements of nature. The earth was the god Geb and the sky his female consort, Nut; their sex reflects the grammatical gender of the two terms "earth" (masculine *t₃*) and "sky" (feminine *pt*). This worldview was occasionally depicted in the image of a recumbent god with a goddess arching over him, touching the surface on which he reclines with her feet and hands (metaphorical analogues of the four sceptres or columns of other depictions). The same images usually showed a second deity standing between Geb and Nut, his hands raised to support the goddess above him. This was the god Shu, the Egyptian personification of the air, wind and atmosphere. In one text, Shu describes himself as follows: "the air of life is my clothing ... the pressure of the wind is my skin ... the storm-cloud of the sky is my emanation, the storm of a dark day is my sweat. The length of the sky is my reach, and the breadth of the earth is my base" (Coffin Texts Spell 80; Allen 1988: 22).

The sky itself was the subject of detailed speculation. With nothing but the naked eye to rely on, Egyptian observers saw it as the surface of a vast body of water – like the Nile or the sea, blue during the day and black at night. Early texts refer to both its waters and its shores; the sky itself was sometimes called *ḳbḥw* "cool water" as well as a *bỉꜣ* "basin", and the name of its goddess, Nut, may mean 'the watery one'. The apparent motion of the sun and stars across it was understood, described and depicted as a voyage by boat.

Speculation about the nature of this celestial expanse centred on the sky at night, probably because it exhibits more diverse features than the unbroken stretch of the usual day sky in Egypt. The stars, like the sun, apparently move across the sky both during the night and in the course of the year, and for that reason they were viewed as voyagers over its surface rather than as fixed elements of its topography. The Egyptians identified stars both individually (notably, Sirius) and as members of constellations, including Orion and Ursa Major. They also recognized as distinct entities the five planets visible to the naked eye (Mercury, Venus, Mars, Jupiter and Saturn). The zodiac does not appear in Egyptian sources until the Roman Period (Neugebauer and Parker 1960: vii).

The major fixed feature of the night sky was known as the 'Winding Waterway', recently identified as the ecliptic (the 12 degree-wide arc that the sun, moon and visible planets follow in their course across the sky throughout the year). Running from east to west, the Winding Waterway divided the night sky in two, occasionally reflected in references to "the two skies". These two regions were home to the "Field of Rest" (also translated as "Field of Offerings"), in the north, and the "Field of Reeds", in the south. (The latter is the source of the Elysian Field of Classical myths, 'Elysian' deriving from the Greek pronunciation of the Egyptian word for reeds). Some stars were visible in these 'fields' for only part of the year, disappearing below the horizon for several months at a time. Others could be observed year round and were seen as permanent residents: the "Imperishables" in the north (the circumpolar stars) and the "Unwearying Ones" in the south.

Egyptian texts refer to the Field of Rest and Field of Reeds in terms indicating that both areas were understood as marshes, with regions of dry land as well as water. One early source describes the circumpolar stars as alighting on "the big island in the midst of the Field of Rest" (Pyramid Texts Spell 519; Faulkner 1969: 193). The extent to which the two fields were thought to occupy their respective halves of the sky is uncertain. They may have been seen as filling the entire sky north and south of the Winding Waterway to the horizon, or as narrower regions close to the horizon (the north celestial pole, "in the midst of the Field of Rest", lies about 30 degrees above the horizon when viewed from northern Egypt). In either case, these 'fields' undoubtedly reflected the Egyptians' experience of their own country, where the marshland of the Delta gives way to the open waters of the Mediterranean.

Whether open water or marshland, the sky was held above the earth only by the presence of the atmosphere, the god Shu. Together with the Duat, usually understood as a counterpart space below the earth, it formed the limit of what the Egyptians considered to be the entire world, often summarized as "sky, land, and Duat" (Allen 1988: 5–7). The world's boundaries are also reflected in the epithet "Lord to the Limits", given to the god Atum, source and sum of all matter in the world; as the atmosphere, the god Shu is called Atum's "utmost extent" (Coffin Texts Spell 75; Allen 1988: 15–18). In contrast, a hymn to the transcendental god Amun, who was thought to exist apart from nature, describes him as "farther than the sky ... deeper than the Duat" (P. Leiden I 350; Allen 1988: 53).

What lay beyond the sky and Duat was also the subject of Egyptian speculation, even though, like the Duat, it could only be intuited indirectly. Since the sky was seen as a watery expanse, the universe beyond was understandably thought to be water. The world as described above was therefore a kind of bubble within this infinite ocean: the name of the god Shu, its air, means both "empty" and "dry". The universal ocean itself was a god as well. In the earliest texts his name is Nu, the masculine counterpart of Nut, also meaning "the watery one" (Allen 1988: 4). Nu was seen not only as the ocean beyond the sky but also as the source of all the world's water.

Since he could not be observed directly, Nu's nature was defined by contrast with the known world. His essence as water contrasted with the world's dryness (particularly salient in Egypt). Where the world is lit by the sun, Nu lay perpetually in "uninterrupted darkness". The world is active; Nu was "inert" (this term was the source of his name in later texts, Nun). While the world is finite and defined, Nu was infinite and undefined ("lost", in Egyptian terms). And finally, Nu was "hidden", in contrast to the tangible world. Each of these qualities was recognized individually as a god: in early texts, Nu (water), Kuk (darkness), Huh (infinity), and Tenemu ("lostness") (Allen 1988: 20); in sources from the Ptolemaic Period, Nun (inertness), Kuk, Huh, and Amun ("hiddenness"). These gods were thought to have participated in the creation of the world, as a kind of dynamic potentiality that resulted in the reality of creation. Since the Egyptians envisioned creation in biological terms, each member of the quartet was also thought to have a female counterpart. Together the eight gods were known as the Ogdoad. Their cosmology was centred in the city of Hermopolis, which for that reason was called "Eight-town" (Bickel 1994: 28 for the question of the earliest date of this association).

The Egyptian view of the universe is represented most fully in the ceiling decoration of the cenotaph of Seti I at Abydos (Figure 2:1; Frankfort 1933: pl. 81). Carved ca. 1280 BC, it was reproduced 130 years later in the tomb of Ramesses IV in the Valley of the Kings, and its texts were copied, with commentary, more than a thousand years later in two papyri from the second century AD (Allen 1988: 1).

The ceiling depicts the sky goddess, Nut, supported by the god Shu standing on the earth, shown in this case as a flat surface labelled "sand". Nut's hands and feet extend slightly below the level of the earth, indicating that the Egyptians were aware of the earth's curvature beyond the visible horizon. Along her body are stars and a crescent moon, and a winged sundisk is represented at her mouth. These reflect one explanation of the daily solar cycle, in which Nut was thought to swallow the sun in the evening and give birth to it again at dawn. In this view, the interior of Nut's body

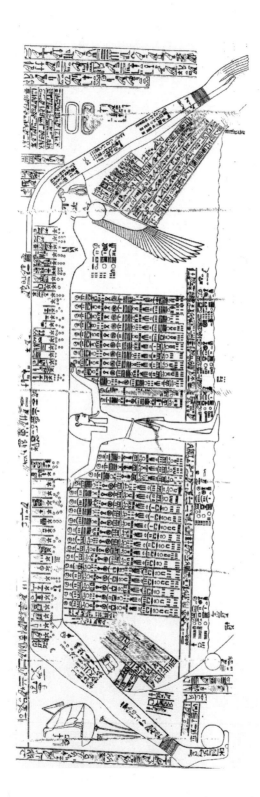

Figure 2:1   Depiction of the world on the ceiling of the cenotaph of Seti I at Abydos (Frankfort 1933: pl. 81).

was seen as the Duat, through which the sun was thought to travel during the night: text near the winged sundisk explains that "this god enters her mouth, inside the Duat" (for these and the other phrases inscribed around the image, see Allen 1988: 1–7). Though such a concept seems at odds with the alternative location of the Duat beneath the earth, Egyptian logic gave equal weight to both views.

Since the sun sets in the west, Nut faces this direction, as indicated by a label at her head: "Her head is the western Akhet, her mouth is the west"; in the same manner, her crotch is labelled "the eastern Akhet". The Akhet, often loosely translated "horizon", was a liminal zone between the Duat and the visible horizon. It represents the Egyptian explanation for the fact that light remains for some time after the sun has set and appears before the sun has risen.

A winged scarab at Nut's knee, reflecting the Egyptian hieroglyph for "come into being", represents the rising sun. The accompanying label reads: "This god comes forth at her rear; he is on course toward the world ($t3$), apparent and born; he produces himself afterwards; he parts the thighs of his mother, Nut; he distances himself toward the sky." The cycle of the stars is explained in a similar manner: "When this god enters her mouth, inside the Duat, it stays open after he sails inside her, so that these sailing stars may enter after him. They come forth after him and where they row is to their harbors."

The space above Nut represents the universal ocean. This is not depicted as such, but is described in several labels. The text above Nut's body reads: "What is above this sky exists in uninterrupted darkness, and its southern, northern, western, and eastern limits are unknown, these having been fixed in Nu, in inertness. There is no light of the Ram [a form of the sun god] there, he does not appear there – a region whose south, north, west, and east land is unknown by the gods or the akhs [spirits of the deceased], there being no brightness there. And as for every place devoid of sky or land, that is the entire Duat." This clearly identifies the outer space beyond the sky as a limitless expanse of water (Nu), inaccessible to the elements, forces and beings that inhabit the world. It also defines the Duat in negative terms as a place that is not sky or land. Since these last two elements are part of the world, the Duat was apparently also considered part of it as well. Its description as a place supports this interpretation, since the universal ocean itself was thought to contain no place as such ("lost"); in one text, the god Atum describes his existence before the creation of the world as "when I was alone with Nu, in inertness, and could not find a place in which to stand or sit" (Coffin Texts Spell 80; Allen 1988: 22).

The space above Nut's head and arms contains depictions of birds and is labelled: "The uninterrupted darkness, the cool water of gods, the place from which birds come. This extends from her north-western side up to her north-eastern side and is open to the Duat that is in her northern side, her rear being in the east and her head in the west. These birds exist with human heads and bird natures, each one speaking to the other with human speech. After they come to eat plants and get nourished in the black land, they alight under the brightness of the sky and have to change into their bird natures." As is still the case, Ancient Egypt saw the annual migration of flocks of birds from Europe into Egypt and the Sudan to its south. At the time this text was first carved, Europe was unknown to the ancient Egyptians: to them, the birds appeared to come from outer space. The birds' access to the "uninterrupted darkness" and their description as human is explained by the text's reference to a connection between the Duat and the universal ocean. Like the visible world, the Duat was thought to be inhabited by living beings; among these were the spirits of people who had drowned in the Nile, subsequently envisioned as floating in the waters of the Duat. The text apparently reflects the view that these spirits re-entered the world for a few months each year in the form of migratory birds.

Given the ancient Egyptians' view of the solar cycle as a circumnavigation of the world's limits, it was perhaps inevitable that they should also have come to see the world itself in circular terms. Indications of such a view can be found from as early as the Middle Kingdom, in characterizations of the world as "what the sundisk encircles", but unequivocal references to a circular world are not attested until late in ancient Egyptian history. The best illustration of this view exists on the lid of the sarcophagus of Wereshnefer, from Saqqarah, carved at the beginning of the Ptolemaic period and now displayed in the Metropolitan Museum of Art (Figure 2:2; Ransom 1914).

Encircling the scene is the body of Nut; stars and sundisks on her torso are meant to depict the nightly journey of these celestial bodies through the Duat, as in the image from the ceiling of Seti I's cenotaph. Winged sundisks at her mouth and crotch

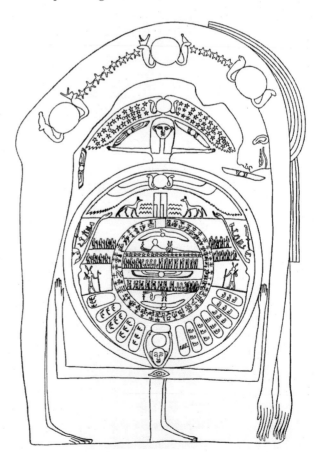

Figure 2:2   Depiction of the world on the lid of the sarcophagus of Wereshnefer (Metropolitan Museum of Art 14.7.1; Drawing MM 464 B).

represent the sun at sunset and sunrise. Below Nut's belly, the head and outstretched arms of the god Shu support both a large sundisk whose wings are sprinkled with stars and two smaller winged sundisks, together representing the night and day sky. Between Nut's hands and feet are a second pair of feet joined to two upraised arms. This image represents the earth god, Geb, and is meant to be understood both visually and as a hieroglyphic monogram of the god's name as it was pronounced in the Ptolemaic Period. Between Shu and Geb is a circle depicting the world, and Geb is shown standing in order to support it.

The circle itself is a complex amalgam of images. Though presented in two dimensions, it was intended to depict three – a true globe. The sundisk at the top of the outer circle and the images inside the inner ring belong in the same dimension as the depiction of Nut, Shu and Geb, while the rest of the circle is to be understood as rotated 90 degrees perpendicular to these. The winged sundisk represents the sun in the day sky. Despite their size, the images inside the inner ring should be seen as covering the full extent of the outer circle: they represent the visible world, at the top, and the Duat beneath it, at the bottom.

In line with the Egyptian perception of the world, Egypt itself lies at its centre. The images below the sundisk at the top of the larger circle represent the waters of the Nile (wavy lines) arising from caverns (the central rectangles) to Egypt's south. Stretched along the inside of the outer ring are the bodies of two goddesses, representing the west (right) and east (left). The boats at their arms are those of the sun god at sunset and sunrise, and the figures standing before them are the gods of the world's elements and forces. The ovals in the lower half of this circle are symbols of the lands surrounding Egypt. The inner ring is Egypt itself, represented by the standards of the 40 nomes (states) into which the country was divided at the time.

Conclusion

An eloquent summary of the ancient Egyptian view of the world, the scene on Wereshnefer's sarcophagus is also one of the earliest maps of the world as round. Though the Egyptians' perception of the world and the universe beyond did not correspond entirely to the reality we now know, it is nonetheless testimony to the persistence and ingenuity of their imagination.

Throughout ancient Egyptian history, that perception was remarkably uniform in its basic details. The extent to which it was shared in common by all Egyptians, however, is uncertain. The surviving texts and images that describe or reflect the Egyptian view of the world are almost exclusively limited to funerary literature and tombs, where they served as background to the mysteries of creation and daily rebirth. References are much less common in the more mundane writings of everyday life, such as the stories, instructions and autobiographies that constitute the bulk of ancient Egyptian literary texts, and they appear only rarely in hymns and prayers before the time of the New Kingdom.

In that respect we might be justified in concluding that the view of the world described above represented only the specialized knowledge of an educated few. Speculation, however, is a universal human trait. The farmers and artisans of Ancient

Egypt must surely have looked at the night sky with the same curiosity as their more learned contemporaries, and the limited evidence that does exist indicates that they saw it in the same way. Ordinary Egyptians may not have had the detailed understanding of the universe preserved in specialized religious texts and images, but even as early as the Old Kingdom some of them were named after gods such as Nu, the universal ocean (Ranke 1935: 206, no. 9), reflecting a fairly widespread knowledge of its basic elements. The fact that such knowledge appears never to have been codified in a specific myth also suggests that it reflects a common worldview rather than religious dogma promulgated by an educated elite.

As far as we can tell, the picture of the universe preserved in ancient Egyptian sources was one that was shared by all the inhabitants of Ancient Egypt and, at least in its major elements, remained essentially unchanged throughout Egyptian history.

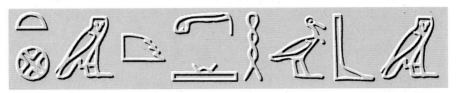

CHAPTER 3

TRAVEL AND FICTION IN EGYPTIAN LITERATURE

Antonio Loprieno

One of the most mysterious lands in ancient Egyptian writings is the "island of the spirit" at the heart of the 'Tale of the Shipwrecked Sailor', preserved in a single copy of ca. 1850 BC. An Egyptian is washed ashore after a storm at sea, and comes face to face with divinity in the form of a giant serpent of gold and lapis lazuli. When the Egyptian leaves, the island disappears. Deceptively simple in format and language, the tale is one of the most beautifully structured, as well as one of the earliest, examples of narrative fiction in the Egyptian language. This is just one in a series of accounts of the surrounding world that show physical travel to be central to the self-expression of Ancient Egypt. The relation between traveller and foreign lands in these tales changes over time, revealing deeper changes in Egyptian perception of the world outside and of Egypt itself. These literary spaces can only be explored if first we confront the problems surrounding our definition of literature in the Egyptian context.

Fiction and imagination

Ancient Egyptians did not convey to us a clear sense of which portion, if any, of their abundant written record they considered to be what we might term 'literary'. We can reasonably assume that a narrative about the adventures of a peasant on his way to the city (Gnirs 2000) is more likely to belong to a domain of 'literature' than a text containing the procedure to be followed in order not to become drunk while drinking beer (Borghouts 1970: 27). In content, though, the two texts exhibit a comparable amount of expressive sophistication, for example through a conspicuous use of wordplay (Loprieno 2001: 129–158). We only possess indirect ancient Egyptian hints at the features of literary discourse (Parkinson 2002: 29–32).

In their attempts to develop a cultural understanding of Egyptian literature, modern readers are torn between two options: form and content (Parkinson 2002: 17–21). The first option requires analysis of the formal aspects of Egyptian texts, trying to establish reasonable correspondences between the traits that we regard as crucial in defining our own literary discourse and similar traits in ancient Egyptian sources (Loprieno 1996a: 209–32). The 'Tale of Sinuhe' (Koch 1990; Lichtheim 1976: 222–235) has the introduction and narrative expression typical of the Egyptian autobiographical account, though it clearly departs from the conventions of the genre as we know it from funerary inscriptions: first, it is written on papyrus rather than on stone; and second, it provides a degree of detail and a sense of development absent from contemporary autobiographies on tomb walls. Today we might call it a 'fictional' autobiography, stressing by the use of this word its intended literary character. The inscriptions in the early Middle Kingdom tomb-chapel of Senet, wife of Intefiqer (Theban Tomb no. 60), include a hymn to the goddess Hathor, marked in two exceptional ways as a separate textual unit (Morenz 1996: 58–77). First, though within the funerary decorative programme, the text is written in vertical columns; this is unusual in this tomb-chapel, whereas columns are the regular format in contemporary hieratic papyri. Second, it is written in a more cursive hieroglyphic style than that generally found in tomb inscriptions; this feature again echoes the standard form of handwriting at the time, the hieratic script. To use the terminology of literary studies, these two features make the hymnic text 'self-referential' in the sense that it is clearly visualized as autonomous in its context on the wall, thus demanding that the viewer or reader recognize it as a separate textual reality.

Literary tradition usually establishes a more or less 'open canon' (Gorak 2001; Quirke 1996b: 379–380) that constitutes the object of cultural transmission. This transmission, or, to use the equivalent term in literary studies, 'reception', applies to a certain number of ancient Egyptian texts that were read and copied even many centuries after their putative date of composition (Fischer-Elfert 2003: 121; Morenz 2003: 102–104; Parkinson 2002: 53–55); they possessed, therefore, an educational function in the formation of the cultural identity of the Egyptian literate elite (Assmann 1996). The presence of the so-called colophon (such as the formula "here the text ends as was found in writing") is a sign of both self-referentiality and reception (Moers 2001: 82): by referring to itself and to its being the copy of an older writing, the text aspires to be viewed as the object of literary transmission (Loprieno 1996a: 226–231).

A second hermeneutic option consists in looking not at the formal features, but rather at the contents of Egyptian texts, possibly organized in genres (Parkinson 2002: 32–36). From this perspective, the domain of literature in Ancient Egypt includes those texts which explicitly express personal concerns: not the concerns of the gods, as is the case in theological texts such as solar hymns or cosmological treatises; not the concerns of the king, as they are presented in historical records such as annals or royal tales; not the concerns of the dead, as they are conveyed in funerary material such as religious spells or funerary stelae, but rather the concerns of the human individual in his or her personal dialogue with the big themes of life, whether the tone of the text be speculative or entertaining (Parkinson 2002: 130–146). In other words, the search for ancient Egyptian literature becomes a search for the 'human' aspects of a society that, through its written and pictorial records, usually appears to the modern observer to be preoccupied with gods, power and death.

The imaginary or 'fictive' dimension, the literary construction of a world with different conventions from the ones we are accustomed to, is probably one of the most visible signs of a textual concern for the life of the human individual, rather than for more abstract ideological expectations (Iser 1991: 19–24; Moers 2001: 22–27). While not every fiction is imaginary, all imaginary texts are necessarily fictional (Loprieno 1996a: 215): the concept of 'fictionality' refers to the setting of a text. When confronted with a fictional text, the reader implicitly agrees not to hold the author responsible for deviating from reality; the terms 'imaginary' or 'fictive', on the other hand, refer to the 'nature' of the world presented in the text: a fictive world is one in which, to take two Egyptian examples, a snake can talk or a prince can jump 70 cubits to reach a princess's window.

Ancient Egypt has bequeathed a variety of imaginary tales that depict wondrous beings or describe travels to marvellous lands. The number of these texts tends to increase during the history of Egyptian literature as it developed. Significantly, instructions and moral discourses, the more ideologically charged texts of the Middle (Parkinson 2002: 193–277) and New (Baines 1996: 157–174) Kingdoms, do not feature any journey into the unknown, but rather emphasize the advantages of a predictable scribal life. Even if a journey has to be made, the return from the journey seems to be taken for granted:

> I shall make you love the scribal activity more than your mother and let you clearly see its beauty. It is the greatest of all professions, there is none like it on earth. While still a child, the scribe is already hailed; he is sent on missions, and before he is back he already wears a gown.
>
> (after Helck 1970: IIIc–f)

The texts may criticize a son for having engaged in a trip abroad (Moers 2001: 232–245):

> You like to wander like a swallow and its fledglings: you returned to the Delta after a long tour, you intermingled with Asiatics after eating bread mixed with your own blood. You are out of your mind, you are nuts, you vagabond of the sea!
>
> (Guglielmi 1983: 148,4–6)

Or they may sing the praise of the Egyptian home-town (Guksch 1994):

> No work can succeed through my hand if my heart is forced to be away from its place.
>
> (Gardiner 1937: 39,11–12)

In the long history from the Old to the New Kingdom, Egyptian intellectuals seem to have become more sensitive to the charm of fantasy, but not more inclined to recognize the inherent value of the intellectual pursuit in travel, this most fictional of all fictional themes (Moers 1999: 43–61). Egyptian texts with imaginary contents were neither the most read in schools – many of them are only known through one manuscript – nor the favourite sources for quotations in later periods. Arguably, they may represent the works of elusive authors located at the margins of the prevailing channels of intellectual formation; and precisely because they are unorthodox, these texts are less likely to be a direct mirror of social expectations, but more likely to address the individual concerns of Egyptians.

Geography and Egyptian literature

One of the literary features that has been little investigated within the Egyptological tradition is the choice of hieroglyph as determinative at the end of place names, or what might be called the 'geographic sign'. These determinatives may help to reveal the Egyptian treatment and the organization of the narrated space. Where do the protagonists of a text live? Where do they go? What do they say about the place in which they happen to be? Of course, the subjective geography presented in Egyptian tales will not necessarily provide a faithful, objective image of contemporary geographic knowledge. Rather than a physical organization of space, the implicit geography contained in fictional texts should offer traces of underlying cultural hierarchies. Oppositions such as close versus far, domestic versus foreign, town versus country are all indicative of an intensely marked cultural universe.

Recent studies on the representation of travel and space in modern European fiction (Moretti 1997) have shown that there is a clear difference between the 'topography' of traditional folktales (such as those studied by Propp 1969) and the 'geography' of the novel from the 18th century onward. In the former we observe an opposition between two worlds, with clear borders and symmetrical movements, whereas the plots of Jane Austen or Walter Scott and the cities of Balzac or Dickens involve more diverse patterns that reflect the protagonists' social reality. In other words, in the development of a literature over time, the complexity of an organized geography tends to replace the magic topography of the traditional tale rooted in oral tradition. However, this literary history seems to be reversed in the case of Ancient Egypt. Instead of evolving from topography of the fable to geography of the novel, Egyptian texts seem to proceed from a focus on realistic trips during the Old and Middle Kingdoms to a topographical approach with fictive traits in later epochs.

Administrative journeys in Old Kingdom inscriptions

Scholarly work on the tomb as the cradle of Egyptian literary activity (Assmann 1983: 64–93) has shown that the autobiographies carved on the external walls of Old Kingdom tomb-chapels (Gnirs 1996: 191–241) already display the two main features of Egyptian literary discourse in later periods. The first is a concern for moral behaviour (the 'laudatory' biography), later to be expanded in 'wisdom literature'. The second is the narration of individual achievements (the 'event' biography), the motif elaborated in narrative literature.

Late Old Kingdom event biographies present the tomb owner's career achievements as the main justification for a funerary cult. One of the frequent themes is the expedition on behalf of the king, sometimes to a foreign country. This leads the protagonist to different territories which, if unknown, must be "opened" (wb3), i.e. explored, as in the case of Harkhuf:

> The Majesty of Merenra, my lord, sent me together with my father, the Sole Friend and lector-priest Iry, to Yam, in order to open a way to this foreign country. I did it in seven months, bringing back from there all sorts of beautiful and rare gifts.

> (Sethe 1933: 124,9–15)

In other instances, the land has to be "subdued" (ḫb3), as required by the hegemonic ideological model in which foreign countries represent a threat to the state's well-being, as in Pepinakht's account:

> The Majesty of my lord sent me to subdue Wawat and Irtjet. I behaved to my lord's satisfaction, killing many people there.

> (Sethe 1933: 133,9–12)

In such inscriptions, the geographic distribution is 'experience-driven': regions that belong to the Egyptian landscape are considered home territory, either agricultural entities, with the determinative (or lexical classifier – Goldwasser 1995) for cultivated land, or urbanized settlements, with the determinative for town (Figure 3:1). Yet, the opposition between home and abroad is present in a neutral, matter-of-fact way; one is not given a status higher than the other, and there is no visible effect on the

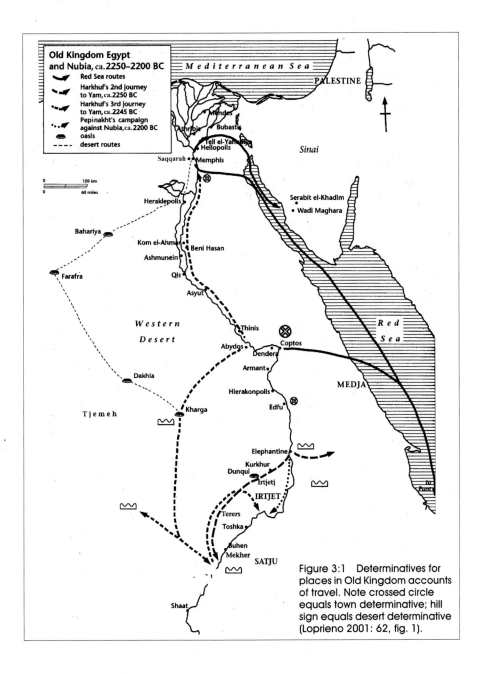

Figure 3:1   Determinatives for places in Old Kingdom accounts of travel. Note crossed circle equals town determinative; hill sign equals desert determinative (Loprieno 2001: 62, fig. 1).

personality of the official leading the expedition. Travelling is tantamount to fulfilling an administrative duty for which one receives praise, comparable to overcoming a tempest while sailing on the Nile. In the biography of Kaemtjenenet we read:

> I did not find anyone else who would travel because of the storm [...] on the river that day, when the tempest was most violent [...] as was my majesty's wish regarding this. You are his true helmsman [...] during a violent storm on the river.

> (after Sethe 1933: 182,15–183,5)

In these Old Kingdom inscriptions, travel means fulfilling a 'horizontal' mission to unknown places; none of the surviving narratives describes a fantastic journey as a rite of passage, as defined in Propp's (1969) structural analysis of traditional fables. Old Kingdom autobiographic narratives show no awareness of passing a border, or any emotional dimension to the hero's journey. Travel is presented as a matter of economic or political concern. Admittedly, the travelling official frequently holds the title of "head of the translators"; this is at least a recognition of linguistic diversity. However, any Egyptian practices and theories of translation go unrecorded.

Centripetal journeys in Middle Kingdom tales

In addition to the missions performed on the king's behalf, autobiographical texts of the Middle Kingdom emphasize the presence of officials at Abydos, the holy city of Osiris where Egyptian officials participated in the god's "mysteries" and often had a chapel built for themselves, to share in the eternal supply of festival offerings (Gnirs 1996: 225–228). From the early Middle Kingdom there is also a correspondence on papyrus between a landowner from Upper Egypt on a work-related journey in the north and his eldest son who was temporarily administering the family's affairs (James 1962). However, the horizontal geography seen in the inscriptions cited above appears radically challenged by literary compositions (Parkinson 2002: 293–321): teachings, discourses and tales which transcend the boundaries of the funerary context to acquire fictional traits. 'The Eloquent Peasant' (Gnirs 2000; Parkinson 1991a) is a complex literary composition that combines narrative and moral discourse. It is the story of a hunter-gatherer called Khuienanup, who undertakes a journey from his home in the oasis of Wadi Natrun to "Egypt" in order to sell his products. The destination is given more precisely as "southward to Herakleopolis", the capital of the country during the First Intermediate Period, the time when the story is set (though not necessarily when it was composed). This voyage leads the Middle Kingdom protagonist, conversely to his Old Kingdom predecessors, from the periphery of the Egyptian world – we know of the presence of a temple and fortress in the Wadi Natrun during the Middle Kingdom (Fakhry 1940: 845–848) – to its centre. Moreover, the list of products to be sold by Khuienanup in the central market (Junge 2000: 159–161) implies a wide range of places of origin. Some, such as natron or salt, would have been readily available in the Wadi Natrun; some are explicitly mentioned as coming from other regions of the Egyptian world, such as staves from Farafra Oasis (in Egyptian "cattle country"); still others, such as leopard skins or various types of herbs, are of more distant, entirely foreign provenance. These imports indicate the presence of intense commercial contact with central Africa, as well as illustrating the rhetorical potential inherent in lists of exotic landscapes and products (Figure 3:2).

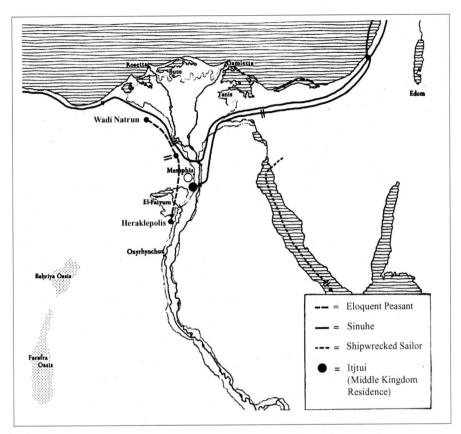

Figure 3:2   Journeys in Middle Kingdom literature (Loprieno 2001: 66, fig. 2).

During the descent by Khuienanup from the oasis to the city, near the fortress of Medenit, at the very transition between Upper and Lower Egypt, his passage is blocked by Nemtynakht, a servant of the High Steward Rensy. Nemtynakht beats up the traveller and seizes his goods. This is the turning point of the tale, which then becomes a moral discourse in the form of nine petitions delivered by the victim to the High Steward to remind him of his moral and administrative duty to re-establish justice in a case in which it had ostensibly been violated. It is important to recognize that the encounter of Khuienanup with his aggressor, set precisely at the juncture of the two traditional halves of the country, the Nile Valley and the Delta, is in every respect a liminal experience, a 'rite of passage' of the type absent from Old Kingdom accounts. It marks the literary change to a different stylistic genre, i.e. from 'narrative' to 'moral' discourse, and prepares for the transition to a higher degree of psychological awareness on the part of the protagonist: his travel has now turned into a moral journey. A description of exotic products has given way to an analysis of deep problems facing Egyptian society. This reveals the basic function of all journeys in Middle Kingdom literature: the hero's geographic movements are not simply 'horizontally' from a place 'here' to a place 'there', but from periphery to centre as a paradigm of an intellectual journey to a fuller understanding of humans in society.

A similar reading can also be applied to the most famous Middle Kingdom composition that centres on a hero's journey: the 'Tale of Sinuhe' (Koch 1990). During a military mission in Libya, Sinuhe, an official in the entourage of the king's family, hears that the reigning king Ammenemes I has died and fears – for whatever reason – that his successor Sesostris I may be less well-disposed towards him. Rather than return to the residence, where he expects dynastic troubles, he sets out southward (Figure 3:2 above). The text offers a very detailed description of his journey (Goedicke 1957: 77–85): Sinuhe crosses the Nile near the apex of the Delta, at a location very close to the place of the dramatic encounter between the Eloquent Peasant and Nemtynakht, and continues his journey along the border of the Delta, passing "the Walls of the Ruler, which were built to repel the Asiatic". He finally reaches Asia, the place beyond; at once, he is overtaken by thirst, which he associates with a "taste of death", but he gives himself courage and collects himself. He then hears the lowing sound of cattle and sees Asiatics: he is abroad.

During his flight to Asia, and more precisely at the "border of the cultivated land" and "on the verge of the road", Sinuhe encounters an unknown man whom he fears may stop him crossing the border. Here too, there are abundant indications that this journey involves more than just movement across geographical space: the emphasis on the transition from Egypt to Asia, accompanied as it is by a wealth of topographical and psychological details, makes it clear that the protagonist is entering a new phase in his life, an increased level of awareness. Accordingly, the land of Retjenu, where he is going to spend a sizeable portion of his adult life, is portrayed in Utopian terms, motivated by the hero's psychological state rather than by the objective observation of Palestinian landscapes:

> It was a good land, called Yaa. There were figs and grapes, and more wine than water.
> It had abundant honey and plenty of oil, and its trees carried all sorts of fruits. There
> was barley and emmer, and numberless kinds of cattle. He (i.e. Ammunenshi, the ruler
> of the land) made me chief of a tribe in the best portion of his land. Bread and drinks
> were made for me every day and wine as daily fare, cooked meat, roast fowl, and wild
> game. They would snare it for me and lay it before me, together with the catch of my
> hounds. Many sweets were made for me, and milk dishes of all kinds.
>
> (after Koch 1990: B 80–92)

Eventually, at the end of the tale, Sinuhe realizes that death is approaching and returns to Egypt at the king's explicit request. Once again, the protagonist moves from the periphery of the world back to its centre; once again, it marks a dramatic change in his life perspectives.

The third tale from the Middle Kingdom where a journey plays a prominent role is 'The Shipwrecked Sailor' (Blackman 1932: 41–48), which is at the same time the first Egyptian narrative to explore the realm of the imagination. The protagonist is a nameless "excellent follower" who accompanies an equally nameless "mayor" on a trip back from Nubia (Figure 3:2 above):

> Then the excellent follower said: 'Be courageous, mayor, we have reached home; the
> mallet is seized, the mooring-post staked, the prow-rope thrown on the ground. Praise
> is given and God is thanked, everybody is embracing his fellow. Our crew has returned
> safely, without losses to our troops. We left behind the end of Lower Nubia and passed
> the First Cataract. We have arrived in peace and reached our land. Hear me, mayor: I

do not exaggerate. Wash yourself, pour water on your hands, so that you may properly answer when questioned and speak to the king with presence of mind, replying without stammering. A man's word can save him, his speech can make one forgive him. But do as you like! It is tiresome to speak to you'.

(after Blackman 1932: 41,11–42,6)

The setting of the tale is once again a journey home, a return from the periphery of Nubia to the security of Egypt, which is identified here with the royal residence: Egyptian has the same word for 'home' and 'residence', one among many examples of wordplay in this first section of the text, a sign of its 'literary' character. The same applies to the anonymity of the two figures. If, in the case of the Palestinian ruler Ammunenshi in the 'Tale of Sinuhe', the possession of a name bestowed on him full human dignity, within the fictional world of the tale, then, in the tale of 'The Shipwrecked Sailor', the lack of name gives the mayor and follower paradigmatic status: they seem not to stand only for themselves, but to represent the individual in society.

The mayor is ostensibly under stress for having failed in a royal assignment. In order to show him that "a man's word can truly save him", the follower tells him a story that had happened to him during a mission to the mining region. A storm caused a shipwreck whose only survivor was the "excellent follower" himself. To this point the tale is rooted in reality as an Egyptian official might have experienced it; the passage recalls the use of a storm as a noteworthy event in the Old Kingdom autobiography of Kaemtjenenet. However, the shipwrecked sailor then found himself in a mysterious island, the "island of the Ka", which he describes in terms similar to those used by Sinuhe to describe his new Palestinian homeland (Gnirs 1998: 202):

I found there figs and grapes, and all kinds of fine vegetables, sycamore figs, ripe and unripe, and melons that looked as if they had been cultivated. There was also fish and fowl: there was nothing which was not in it. I ate to satiety and put something down, because I had too much in my arms. I cut a fire drill, made a fire and gave a burnt offering to the gods. Then I heard like a thunder and thought that it might be a wave of the sea, for the trees were splintering and the ground trembling. I uncovered my face and found that a snake was coming. He was thirty cubits long; his beard was over two cubits; his body overlaid with gold, his eyebrows of true lapis lazuli. He was bent upwards.

(after Blackman 1932: 43,1–9)

The landscape of this 'divine land' combines features of Syria with those of the mythical Punt, a Red Sea country with which Egypt entertained commercial contacts since the Old Kingdom (see Meeks Chapter 4, Harvey Chapter 5, both this volume). The supernatural snake presents himself as the victim of an equally tragic destiny: at first aggressive, he is swayed by the protagonist's humble speech and tells him that he is the sole survivor of a tribe of 75 snakes, annihilated by a falling star. Unlike himself, destined to remain alone and eventually to disappear into the water together with the island of the Ka, he predicts that the shipwrecked sailor will soon be picked up by an Egyptian ship. This indeed happens:

Then he gave me a load of myrrh, malabathrum, terebinth, balsam, camphor, perfume, eye-paint, giraffe tails, great lumps of incense, elephant tusks, greyhounds, monkeys, apes, and all kinds of precious things.

(after Blackman 1932: 46,16–47,4)

The innovative imaginary features of this Egyptian tale, which also displays unequivocal references to religious conceptions (Baines 1990: 62–65) or signals of fictionality such as the recourse to linguistic ambiguity (Loprieno 1991), may derive from the Semitic traditions on Yam and Astarte, which we know well from later Ugaritic mythology (Gnirs 1998) and from a New Kingdom tale probably composed in the time of Amenophis II (Collombert and Coulon 2000: 209–216).

These Middle Kingdom tales offer a completely different intellectual perspective on travelling and on the relationship between 'Egypt' and 'abroad' from that in the Old Kingdom career biographies. Its most visible feature is the opposition between a centre, often identified with the royal residence, and a periphery, which is the place where protagonists experience a form of psychological or intellectual transition. This type of cultural organization of space could be termed 'centripetal geography'. A basic characteristic of this geography is the 'rite of passage', an experience not expressed in official inscriptions. The literary representation of the contrast between 'Egypt' and 'abroad' is accompanied by the perception, on the part of the protagonist, of a border between two spheres: a border that needs to be overcome rather than simply passed, a border that is associated throughout world literatures with the experience of danger and of fear (Moers 2001: 191–245); in short, a liminal experience: in Sinuhe's words, "the taste of death".

We could generalize these observations and argue that Middle Kingdom literature conveys an orderly, hierarchical organization of space, founded on a clear border between 'here' and 'there'. This border is also ideologically underpinned; Ammunenshi, the Asiatic prince who welcomes Sinuhe to his tribe and to his own family, is the Egyptian king's ironical counterpart as vehicle of the author's views, and is told explicitly: "a Bowman (i.e. an Asiatic, a nomad) cannot befriend a Delta peasant (i.e. an Egyptian, a sedentary)." In this ideological model, Egyptians and Asiatics belong to two different worlds (O'Connor 2003), the cleavage between them being neutralizable only within the frame of 'fiction'. Between these two realities there are no intermediaries, which also explains why we do not encounter the contemporary 'translators' (Schenkel 1975: 1,116) in Middle Kingdom literature: Egypt as a whole, as a 'nation' (Moers 2000: 45–99) represents the theatre of literary fiction. An additional Middle Kingdom tale mentions a journey to the coastal town of Byblos, but only a small fragment is preserved (Simpson 1960; Parkinson 2002: 299–300). It is tempting to think that this lost tale again associated foreign travel with catastrophe in the life of a hero.

The development of such a concept of space can be observed in other Middle Egyptian texts and traced even more precisely from an historical point of view. In the wisdom text known as the 'Teaching of Khety' or, from its contents, as the 'Satire of Trades' (Helck 1970; Parkinson 2002: 273–277; 317–318), the fictional author journeys south to the residence, to place his son in the scribal school. This is the paradigm of an orderly journey, similar to the idealized excursion to the water-meadows praised in 'The Pleasures of Fishing and Fowling' (Caminos 1956: 1–7; Parkinson 2002: 226–234; 312):

On a happy day, we go down to the water-meadow, snare birds and catch many fish in the Two Waters. Let the fowl-catcher and the harpooner come to us, as we draw in the nets full of fowl, we moor our skiff at a thicket and put offerings on the fire for Sobek, Lord of the Lake.

(after Caminos 1956: A 2,1)

The journey abroad, on the contrary, characterizes the 'courier' as one of the wretched professions that the future scribe should avoid at all costs (another, by the way, being the fowl-catcher: not the idealized pastoral figure of the 'Pleasures', but a hard-working lowly man):

The courier goes to the desert, leaving his goods to his children: fearful of lions and Asiatics, only in Egypt can he pull himself together. When he reaches home at night, the march has worn him out; whether his house be of cloth or of brick, his return is without joy.

(after Helck 1970: XVI)

To complete the picture, the use of the determinatives 'town' versus 'desert' versus 'cultivated land' provides precious information on the cultural organization of geographic space (Figure 3:3). The Wadi Natrun, for example, the place of origin of the Eloquent Peasant himself, is determined by the 'mountain' sign in the oldest surviving manuscript, P. Berlin 3023 (Parkinson 1991: x). The centripetal journey leads the protagonist from a foreign periphery, through the transition of Nemtynakht's

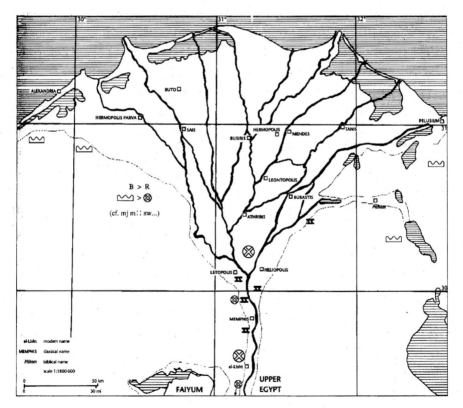

Figure 3:3   Determinatives for places in the journey of Khuienanup. Note crossed circle equals town determinative; hill sign equals desert determinative (Loprieno 2001: 71, fig. 3).

cultivated land, where he undergoes the liminal experience usually associated with the border, down to Egypt: "I make myself on my way to Egypt" are his parting words to his wife at the start of his adventure. By contrast, in a manuscript dated perhaps a hundred years later, P. Ramesseum A (Parkinson 1991a: xi–xiii), something strange happens: from being 'mountainous', i.e. foreign, the Wadi Natrun has now become 'urban', i.e. Egyptian. The hero's adventure causes his own place of origin to be fictionally promoted to the status of Egypt: the story now takes place wholly within Egypt. That this innovation is not the result of haphazard distribution, but rather the product of a specific cultural approach is shown by another difference between earlier and later manuscripts in the use of determinatives for place names (Parkinson 1991: xxv–xxviii). It is a difference that surfaces in the 'Tale of Sinuhe' as well: when Sinuhe discusses with the ruler Ammunenshi the psychological consequences of his flight, in the older version he says: "I do not know what brought me to this place: it was like a divine decision"; in the more recent manuscripts, he adds: "as if a Delta man saw himself in Elephantine, a Northerner in Nubia." Both the addition to the text of 'Sinuhe' and the change of lexical classifier for the Wadi Natrun in 'The Eloquent Peasant' can be dated to a period in which centralistic ideology organized space hierarchically, and neutralized domestic variety within a national perspective. If we read literary history against the background of political history, it is possible to interpret these two changes as the result of administrative centralization under Sesostris III, with the end of provincial autonomy and concentration of elites in the residence (Franke 1991), which provides the historical context for the graphic changes within the manuscript tradition. The older texts would then precede the administrative reform, whereas the younger manuscripts would follow it and document its effects in terms of the assimilation of a centralist ideology.

There is a striking parallelism with the history of European literatures in the 19th century. Recent work has shown that the emergence of the bourgeois novel is closely linked to the emergence of modern national ideology (Gumbrecht 1996: 6–10). It is possible to understand the organization of space in Middle Kingdom literature following the same lines and serving the same interests, i.e. those of an elite who displayed an emerging national identity. It is interesting to note that, both in Middle Kingdom Egypt and in bourgeois Europe, the hierarchization of space is paired with a questioning of social hierarchy: a humble oasis-man who wins his legal battle against the rich servant of a high official (the Eloquent Peasant), a fugitive whom the king himself asks to come back to Egypt (Sinuhe), an "excellent follower" who advises a mayor and enters dialogue with a divinity (the Shipwrecked Sailor).

The centrifugal geography of Ramesside literature

After the Middle Kingdom, with its centripetal representation of space accompanying the emergence of a form of national consciousness, dramatic changes took place. During the Second Intermediate Period, the northern portion of Egypt experienced the domination of the Hyksos, foreign rulers. The reorganization of a unified state in the seventeenth and eighteenth Dynasties was led by the Theban elite and charged with ideology: order had at last been restored and Egypt had been 'freed' from foreign domination. The consequence of this more international political perspective

(Assmann 1991: 288–302) was an increased dialogue with the outside world: in its 'globalized' culture, the Egyptian New Kingdom corresponds to the Late Bronze Age civilizations of Syria and Mesopotamia (see Matthews and Roemer 2003a: 9–10).

The first documents of a new attitude to the marvellous or the fantastic brought about by this confrontation with the foreign world come from the visual sphere. The outstanding examples are the scenes of the journey to Punt in the temple of Hatshepsut at Deir el-Bahri (see Meeks Chapter 4; Harvey Chapter 5, this volume), and the representation of exotic plants and animals in the Botanical Chamber of the Karnak temple, from the time of Tuthmosis III (Beaux 1990). A scene in a Theban tomb-chapel of the same period presents a distinctly un-Egyptian animal set in a fantastic landscape, evidence of an unusual encounter experienced by the tomb owner in Syria (Theban Tomb no. 85). It is easy to recognize here the signs of the more internationally inclined military culture of the Near East in the Late Bronze Age, in which royal display stresses heroic or sportive performances (Collombert and Coulon 2000: 217–222).

The seventeenth and eighteenth Dynasties frequently provide a retroactive context for literary compositions of the Ramesside era, the Golden Age of Late Egyptian literature. These tales (Quirke 1996a: 272–274, 1996b: 385–386) are all written in Late Egyptian and show a change in the treatment of fictional space, which is now often situated not in Egypt but abroad. The transformation is evident even when the centre of the action is within Egypt, as in the case of the 'Quarrel of Apophis and Seqnenra' (Gardiner 1932: 85–89; Goedicke 1986); its plot involves an improbable polemic between the Theban king Seqnenra of the seventeenth Dynasty and the contemporary Hyksos ruler Apophis over the noise allegedly made by the Theban hippopotamus that prevent the Hyksos in Avaris from sleeping. Unlike their Middle Kingdom predecessors, the fictional figures move in staccato leaps rather than in linear trajectories:

> After many days, king Apophis sent to the ruler of the Southern City the message that his scribes and his wise men had suggested him. The messenger of king Apophis reached the ruler of the Southern City. Then he was led to the presence of the ruler of the Southern City. Then the messenger of king Apophis was asked: 'Why have you been sent to the Southern City? Why have you travelled to me?' Then the messenger answered: 'King Apophis sends you the following message: "One should abandon the pond of hippopotami which is to the East of the City, for they prevent me from getting asleep by day and by night. Their voice is in the ears of the people of my city."'

(Gardiner 1932: 87,3–13)

The most significant text of Ramesside travel literature is certainly the 'Tale of the Doomed Prince' (Gardiner 1932: 1–9). Once upon a time, there was a king to whom, after insistent prayers, the gods decided to give a son whose fate was to die by a crocodile, or a snake, or a dog. The years of his youth pass, wholly pervaded by the fear that his fate might be fulfilled at any moment, even through his little pet dog. Finally, the prince decides to take his chances and face life:

> Now when many days had passed and the boy had become an adult, he sent to his father saying: 'Why do I have to sit around here? I am committed to my fate anyway. Let me go, therefore, so that I may live according to my heart, until the god decides to do what is in his heart.' And so a chariot was harnessed for him, equipped with all

kinds of weapons, and he was given a servant as follower. He was ferried over to the
eastern shore and told: 'Go wherever you wish.' He took with him his dog, went
northward to the desert, following his heart and living on the best of all desert animals.
He reached the ruler of Naharina. Now the ruler of Naharina had no children except
for one daughter, for whom a house had been built whose window was seventy cubits
away from the ground. The prince had sent a message to all the sons of all the rulers of
Syria, saying that whoever should reach his daughter's window would have her as
wife. When many days had passed and they were busy at their daily pursuit, the young
prince passed by them. They took him to their house, washed him and gave fodder to
his horse. They did everything for him: they anointed him, bandaged his feet, and gave
food to his follower. Then they asked him during a conversation: 'Where are you from,
good fellow?' He answered them: 'I am the son of an Egyptian officer. My mother died
and my father married another woman, a stepmother. She came to hate me, and so I
went away, fleeing away from her.' Then they embraced him and kissed him all over.

(after Gardiner 1932: 2,10–4,4)

"Naharina" is the land of Mitanni, the imperial power in northern Syria and
Mesopotamia during the first part of the Late Bronze Age (15th–14th centuries BC),
and the social context of the tale is the military culture of the maryannu (Helck 1987:
218–225), the Mitanni chariot drivers (Wilhelm 1995: 1,243–1,254). The tale is thought
to have been composed about two centuries later, and it was presumably set in the
earlier period because it perfectly suited the fantastic tenor of the events: an Egyptian
prince who rebels against his fate, conceals his own origin and travels into foreign
lands. The journey shares with Sinuhe's flight the geographic direction, but has
neither the richness of topographical details nor the cathartic psychological function.
It is a direct leap from Egypt to Asia, without intermediate stations, performed by a
timeless and nameless Egyptian prince, a figure of pure fantasy floating in a mythical
geographic universe. Eventually, the Egyptian prince will jump the impossible height
to the window, marry the Mitanni princess, and continue his lifelong challenge
against his pending fate. An interesting literary counterpart to the Doomed Prince
from 15th century Mitanni is provided by the literary biographical inscription of
Idrimi, king of Alalakh (Greenstein 1995: 2,423–2,428), who describes his own escape
from an "evil" at home, his long sojourn abroad and his eventual return to power.

Another journey to Asia, this time for military purposes, is the one undertaken by
Djehuty, a general who served under King Tuthmosis III, to conquer a foreign coastal
city, as related in the tale of the 'Capture of the City of Yoppa' (Gardiner 1932: 82–85;
Goedicke 1968). He adopts a similar stratagem to the one devised a few centuries later
by Odysseus, hiding his soldiers in baskets that are let into the city in order to free their
comrades and take prisoners:

One went out to say to the chariot driver of the ruler of Yoppa: 'Thus says your master:
Go and say to your lady (i.e. the ruler's wife): "Be happy! The god Sutekh has given us
Djehuty, his wife, and his children. Look, I myself have made them slaves." This you
should say to her concerning these two hundred baskets full of men, ropes and pegs.'
He went before them to inform the lady and said: 'We have captured Djehuty.' The
doors of the city were opened in front of the soldiers: they entered the city, freed their
comrades and seized the city, from old to young, and they immediately fastened them
with the ropes and the pegs. Thus pharaoh's mighty arm seized the city.

(after Gardiner 1932: 84,3–13)

The setting is again the milieu of the military elite of the early part of the Late Bronze Age; once again, the plot takes place outside the boundaries of Egypt. The extreme mobility of the protagonists of Late Egyptian stories can also be detected in tales with explicit mythological background such as the 'Contendings of Horus and Seth' (Broze 1996; Gardiner 1932: 37–60), a script-like, almost theatrical version (Verhoeven 1996) of the foundation myth of the Egyptian state. The most striking example is the 'Tale of the Two Brothers' (Gardiner 1932: 9–30), which describes the adventures of Bata: after being maligned by his brother's wife, he engages in a journey to a place called the "Valley of the Pine", perhaps a literary version of a Syrian landscape (Hollis 1990: 114–118), and various metamorphoses eventually lead to his rehabilitation and to the evil-doer's punishment:

> Then Bata said to his elder brother: 'Look, I am going to change myself into a great bull of beautiful colors of unknown kind, and you shall sit on my back. By the time the sun has risen, we shall be where my wife is, that I may avenge myself, and you shall take me to where the king is, for he will do for you every good thing. You shall be rewarded with silver and gold for taking me to pharaoh. For I shall be a great marvel, and they will rejoice over me in the whole land, and you shall depart to your village.' When it dawned and the next day came, Bata assumed the form that he had said to his elder brother. Then at dawn Anubis, the elder brother, sat on his back and reached the place where the king was.
>
> (after Gardiner 1932: 24,3–16)

These examples of Ramesside narrative literature revisit, in a fictive way, past historical periods or figures, offering many parallels with what is called the 'historical novel' of modern European literatures, such as Walter Scott's *Ivanhoe* or Alessandro Manzoni's *I Promessi Sposi*. In both genres, protagonists move away from the centre toward a periphery that neutralizes the relevance of the concept of 'border'. A fundamental element of this literature is a far less precise and organized geography than in 'Sinuhe' or 'The Eloquent Peasant': there are no detailed descriptions of the places through which the protagonists travel, but rather a fictive closeness between different narrative scenarios. To a certain extent, 'Egypt' and 'abroad' cease to be distinct entities: the former has lost hierarchical prominence over the latter. In this geography, narrative lines, whether temporal or spatial, are replaced by points. The border that the protagonist has to pass is no longer between Egypt and a foreign country, but rather between the 'real' and the 'imaginary' spheres. From the centripetal geography of the Middle Kingdom, we have now moved towards the centrifugal movements of the heroes of the Ramesside vernacular literature (Loprieno 1996a: 226–227).

The fragmentation of literary space

The most extreme version of such an attitude to topography comes after the end of the New Kingdom, during the transition from the Late Bronze to the Iron Age. In the 'Tale of Wenamun' (Gardiner 1932: 61–76), written at the very beginning of the Third Intermediate Period, the foreign land is not only the direct destination of the hero's journey, as was already the case in earlier Ramesside literature, but has in fact become itself the centre of the fictional space. Wenamun is an official of the Amun temple at Karnak, during the time that Smendes ruled the north and Herihor the south, in the peaceful political division that ended the New Kingdom (Egberts 1998). He undertakes a mission to the Phoenician coast in order to fetch wood for the sacred bark of Amun-Ra, king of the gods (Figure 3:4). What should be a routine administrative trip turns out to be an odyssey in which he becomes painfully aware of the irreparable loss of Egypt's prestige abroad:

> On the day of my arrival in Tanis, the place where Smendes and Tentamun were, I gave them the dispatches of Amun-Ra, king of the gods. They had them read out to them and said: 'Yes, I shall do as Amun-Ra, king of the gods, our lord has said.' I stayed in Tanis until the fourth month of the summer. Then Smendes and Tentamun sent me off with captain Mengebet and I went down on the great Syrian sea on the first day of the first month of the inundation. I arrived at Dor, a Sekel town, and its ruler Beder ordered that fifty loaves of bread, one jug of wine, and one ox haunch be brought to me. Then a man of my ship fled after having stolen one gold vessel worth 5 *deben*, four silver jars worth 20 *deben*, and a bag with 11 *deben* of silver, for a total of 5 *deben* of gold and 31 *deben* of silver. That morning, after rising, I went to the place where the ruler was and said to him: 'I have been robbed in your harbour. You are the ruler of this land, you are the one who controls it. Search for my money: it belongs to Amun-Ra, king of the gods, the lord of the lands; it belongs to Smendes; it belongs to Herihor, my lord, and to the other Egyptian potentates; it belongs to you; it belongs to Weret; it belongs to Mekmer; it belongs to Sekel-baal, the ruler of Byblos.' He said to me: 'Are you serious or are you joking? I can't understand what you demand of me! Had it been a thief who belonged to my land that had gone down to your ship and stolen your money, I would refund it to you from my treasury, until your thief, whoever he is, was found. But the thief who

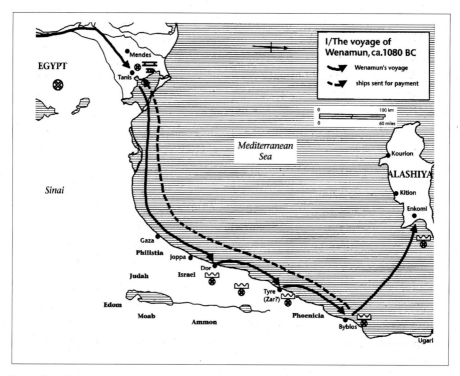

Figure 3:4   Determinatives for places in the journey of Wenamun. Note crossed circle equals town determinative; hill sign equals desert determinative (Loprieno 2001: 77, fig. 4).

robbed you is yours, he belongs to your ship! Spend a few days here with me; I will search for him.' I stayed nine days moored in his harbour. Then I went to him and said: 'Look, you haven't found my money. Let me depart with the ship captains, those who are experienced sea travellers.'

(after Gardiner 1932: 61,4–63,6)

Egypt seems lost in an administrative fragmentation, of the Theban High Priest Herihor versus the Lower Egyptian king Smendes, and the shared power of Smendes and Tentamun in the north. Its disunity jeopardizes its reception abroad, and the homeland has now turned into a narrative periphery (Eyre 1999). The selections of determinatives are again revealing (Figure 3:4). While Naharina in 'The Doomed Prince' or Yoppa in the tale of its taking were still determined by the sign of 'mountain', Dor and Byblos have been part-adopted, as it were, by the Egyptian author's fictional world: they are classified by a double determinative that characterizes them as 'Egyptian' and 'foreign' at the same time. They are places of what might be called a fictive Egyptization, places that are appropriated by the literary author because they represent the new centre of the literary space. This is also shown by a renewed attention to linguistic pluralism: in Alashiya, which corresponds to Cyprus, Wenamun asks prudently whether there is anyone around who understands Egyptian (Gardiner 1932: 75,5).

These features of the 'Tale of Wenamun', one of the literary peaks of late Ramesside Egypt (Baines 1999: 209–233), reveal a global renegotiation of the hierarchy of space that had emerged in the realistic 'national' journey of the Middle Kingdom and had already been challenged in the fantastic 'global' travel of Ramesside times. An organization of the fictional space very closely related to Wenamun's is displayed by this tale's *alter ego*, namely the 'Tale of Woe' of the high priest Wermai (Caminos 1977). Its content is a literary letter in which the protagonist describes to his friend, the royal scribe Wesermaatrenakht, how he became the victim of slander and was sent into exile in different regions of Egypt (Quack 2001). This text was discovered together with the sole copy of the 'Tale of Wenamun' and belongs to the same philological, linguistic and chronological horizon. In many respects, it represents the 'negative print' version of 'Wenamun', replacing the journey to the Syro-Palestinian coast with internal and foreign exile:

I was thrown out of office and became a wanderer on a hard path, while the land was in the flames of war in the South, in the North, in the West and in the East. I joined the crew of a stranger's ship, since mine was taken away under my eyes. I sailed through the land up and down and quickly passed over its depths, until I reached the North at Chemmis. I travelled through hills and marshes in the East of the land of the Pedjtyu-Shu and passed through their wells, then to the West of the land of the Tjemehu. I went to the land of the Tjehenu and wandered through this entire part of Egypt, until I came to Xois and proceeded to Tura. I reached the nome of Oxyrhynchus and entered the Great Oasis, after a speedy journey on both shores of Upper Egypt.

(after Caminos 1977: 2,10–3,4)

The richness of topographical details is so reminiscent of Sinuhe's journey to Asia that intertextual echoes seem plausible. The difference lies in the attitude to the geography. In Wermai's account, the extreme periphery of the Egyptian world has turned into the centre of the protagonist's experience, and thus of the literary space. The names of the

Libyan regions of the Tjehenu and Tjemehu, as well as the Asiatic localities Wermai passes through, end with the compound urban-mountain determinative and are, therefore, fictionally Egyptianized foreign regions (Figure 3:5). The Great Oasis, for its part, appears determined by the 'urban' sign, not the 'mountain' determinative typical since the Old Kingdom, and still found for oases in contemporary Onomastica (hierarchically organized lists of professions, localities, and other semantic realms of

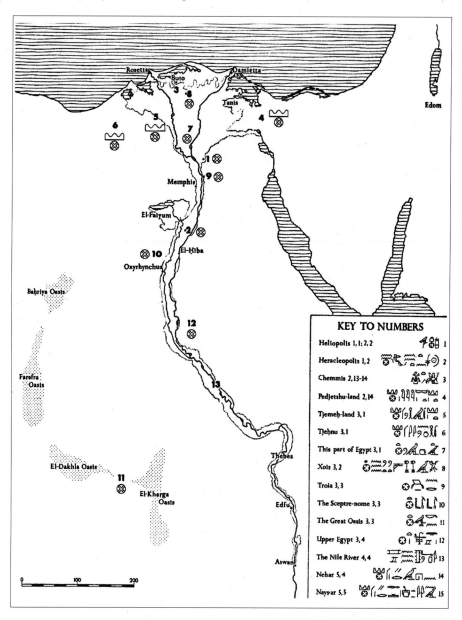

Figure 3:5   Determinatives for places in the journey of Wermai. Note crossed circle equals town determinative; hill sign equals desert determinative (Loprieno 2001: 80, fig. 5).

the Egyptian encyclopaedia – Gardiner 1947). While in the Middle Kingdom the journey of the protagonist was conceived according to 'national' contours, the wanderings of Wenamun and Wermai seem purely individual affairs. The author's subjective geography corresponds to the fragmentation of the contemporary political map of Egypt at the dawn of the Libyan domination.

From a geography of travel to a topography of wonder

The fragmentary geography that, at the end of the New Kingdom, replaces the centrifugal geography observed in Ramesside literature, was itself replaced by new representations of space in the Late Period texts, from the end of the twenty-fifth Dynasty, characterized by the triumph of geographic fantasy. After three centuries of literary silence, the seventh century BC sees the renewal of a fictional production in which the conventions of traditional geography appear neutralized. The new organization of space can be seen on a monument, perhaps dated to the period of the Persian domination in Egypt (525–404 BC), usually referred to as the 'Bentresh stela' from the name of the protagonist, or 'Bakhtan stela' from the name of the place in which the action takes place (Broze 1989). It may have been composed to emphasize putative historical connections between Egypt and Persia, and contains a pseudo-epigraphic narrative dated to the time of a king in whose name we can recognize a corrupted form of the great Ramesses II, and who had already then been dead for 700 years. The Egyptian king has a statue of the Theban god Khonsu sent to the land of Bakhtan to cure the princess Bentresh of a disease caused by a demon, and eventually it succeeds in healing the princess. Elsewhere in the surviving record, however, there is no country called Bakhtan, and the name seems to represent a literary fusion of Khatti in Anatolia and Baktriana in Iran. The journey of the god's statue would then be a voyage to a fictive location. At the beginning of the narrative, the Egyptian king is staying in Naharina, the land visited by the Doomed Prince, on geographically and politically identifiable soil: as usual, the country of Naharina is determined by the lexical classifier of 'mountain'. Equally expectedly, the Egyptian Thebes is determined by the urban sign. These are referential locations seemingly reinforced by a precise date: "The twenty-second day of the second month of the summer season of the fifteenth year" (Broze 1989: 3–4). But the core of the narration, the journey to Bakhtan, brings the divine statue to a space that is not only fictional, but also wholly imaginary. This move to a fictive scenario is also marked by a different choice of determinatives: not the foreign determinative, as in the case of the real-world Naharina, but rather the compound 'Egyptian-foreign' determinative (Figure 3:6).

This new imaginary geography of Late Period texts has its basis in the priestly elite. One composition, preserved in a single manuscript, P. Vandier (Posener 1985), relates the story of a King Sisobek who becomes ill with a mortal disease and of a magician Meryra who agrees to go to the Netherworld in the king's stead. In this tale "all of Egypt" is coextensive with "all the temples of Egypt" (Loprieno 1998: 20–22). The temple, which already in Ramesside times had developed into an autonomous socio-economic entity, has now become the intellectual referent, the ideal city, as indicated by the urban determinative. This implies that it is also the place where, typically, literature is written and read. In this religious setting, even "the West",

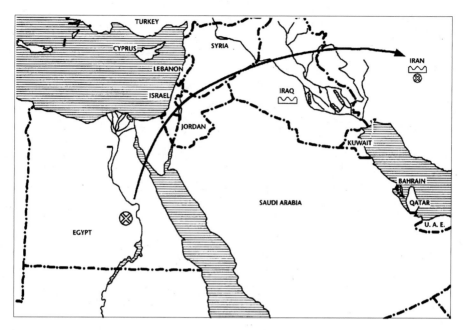

Figure 3:6   Determinatives for places in the Bentresh stela. Note crossed circle equals 'Egyptian' determinative; hill sign equals 'foreign' determinative (Loprieno 2001: 82, fig. 6).

meaning in Egypt the Underworld, is no longer a taboo, but has become a place that can be visited by a fictional protagonist, i.e. a place that can be fully integrated into literary geography.

This replacement of a geography of real places with a topography of fictive locations remains a feature of demotic literature: the location of the fight between Petekhons and the Amazons is a mythical Syria (Hoffmann 1995: 17–20), the heroes of the War for the Armour of Inaros travel in an instant from one place to the other (Hoffmann 1996: 45–48); the same happens to the rival Ethiopian and Egyptian magicians and kings in the 'Second Tale of Setne Khamwase', who during the night move from Egypt to Ethiopia and back (Griffith 1900). In a fragmentary papyrus from Copenhagen, Djoser and his vizier Imhotep begin a war against an Assyrian kingdom ruled by a woman (Hoffmann 1995: 25). The door to the Underworld had effectively been unlocked by Meryra, the hero of the tale in P. Vandier. Now it was wide open to literary heroes: in the second tale of Setne, the young Si-Osiri takes centre stage, leading his father through the kingdom of the dead, and the War for the Armour of Inaros begins when Osiris sends demons to the earth (Loprieno 1998: 12–23).

Conclusion

Throughout the historical evolution of Egyptian literary texts, different models for the representation of space can evidently be detected. In chronological sequence they indicate a gradual divorce between Egypt as a nation and Egyptian literature as cultural discourse. If Middle Kingdom literature was 'national' in the sense that the subjective geography of the protagonists – precisely like their intellectual and emotional concerns – tended to be modelled upon the official hierarchies of the Egyptian world, in the course of the following 15 centuries Egyptian literary discourse became more 'individual', in the sense of a more perfect authorial emancipation from political requirements. It also became more 'transnational', in the sense that themes and style moved closer to what was happening in the Levant in the case of the Late Bronze Age, and in the Hellenistic world in the case of demotic literature. The evolution towards the fictive journey begins with 'The Shipwrecked Sailor', with the common elements it displays with the Northwest Semitic cycle of Yam and Astarte (Collombert and Coulon 2000: 217–222; Gnirs 1998: 197–209), then continues with the narrative literature of the New Kingdom, some of whose motifs are also found in contemporary Mesopotamian literature (Greenstein 1995), and finally reaches its peak in the literary renaissance of the Late Period, when Egyptian literature shares with other literatures of the Mediterranean world a high number of rhetorical devices and conceptual features (Lichtheim 1983: 1–12).

To say that Late Egyptian literature is 'transnational' does not imply, of course, that the evolution is borrowed from foreign literary traditions. Rather, the term implies that national concerns do not of themselves play any major role in the creation of a literary space. That space, as in the case of the Hellenistic novel *Ephesiaka* (Papanikolaou 1973), is now characterized everywhere in the Mediterranean world by a break in the existing conventions of representation of time and by a recourse to fantastic or imaginary space. It took the rise of Enlightenment to replace the warm topography of the European fables with the cold geography of bourgeois novels; it took the contact with neighbouring literary traditions to change the realistic geography of Middle Kingdom journeys into the fictive topography of later Egyptian tales.

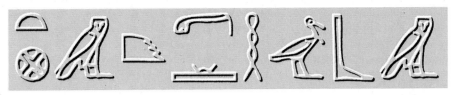

CHAPTER 4

LOCATING PUNT

Dimitri Meeks

Virtually no interest was expressed in the land of Punt during the early years of Egyptology. There were too few publications available at the time to enable researchers to appreciate how often this land, foreign to Egypt, was mentioned in texts, and to speculate as to its location. The position changed from the 1850s, after the new Antiquities Service of Egypt began the clearance of the great temples in Upper Egypt; Brugsch (1857: 48–49, 1858: 15–16, 1860: 63–64) suggested that Punt should be positioned in the Arabian Peninsula. It all looked straightforward enough. Punt was revealed to be the land of perfumes, which supplied aromatic, precious substances. According to the written sources it lay to the east of Egypt. This inevitably evoked the 'perfumes of Arabia' and all the mythology of aromatic materials, handed down by the Greeks. Brugsch's view was based in large measure on the inscriptions in the temples of the Hellenistic period, and was adopted without further discussion.

Two discoveries by Mariette transformed the situation: first, the recording of geographical lists of Tuthmosis III in the Amun temple at Karnak. These lists included Punt and its various toponyms in the series relating to the countries south of Egypt. Second, and most important, came the famous reliefs of the funerary temple of Queen Hatshepsut at Deir el-Bahri (mid-15th century BC). These give a detailed picture of the country, its inhabitants and its fauna and flora. Mariette (1875b: 60–66) ruled out the possibility that Punt was situated in Arabia and placed it in Africa on the Somali coast. Since then, a consensus has gradually taken shape: Punt could not be in Arabia, even if its exact location in Africa was still a matter for discussion. From that date onwards, texts subsequent to the New Kingdom have not really been taken into account, but it is precisely these texts which fit in least satisfactorily with an African location for Punt.

All recent studies concerning Punt start from the publication by Herzog (1968), who based his work on the fauna and flora in the scenes of the expedition to Punt in the funerary temple of Hatshepsut at Deir el-Bahri (Figure 4:1). He located Punt in the region of the Upper Nile between Atbara and the confluence of the White and Blue Niles, and concluded that the journey was undertaken partly overland, partly by river, but not by sea. This interpretation disregarded the setting of the scenes in question, by the shores of an expanse of water in which sea creatures are depicted, some of which are easily recognizable as Red Sea fauna (Danelius and Steinitz 1967: 15–24). In a lengthy review of Herzog, Kitchen (1971) not only corrected that particular mistake but took a new look at the whole question of Punt. Kitchen's article, along

Figure 4:1   Lower section of wall reliefs depicting Punt in the temple of Hatshepsut at Deir el-Bahri (after Kitchen 1983a: fig. 35.3).

with two other more recent ones (Kitchen 1993a, 1999), established the current accepted position on this subject (Degas 1995: 216; O'Connor 1983: 270). Still basing his conclusions on the Hatshepsut temple scenes, Kitchen (1993a: 604) assigned Punt to an area stretching from the Red Sea to the Nile, approximately between the latitudes of Port Sudan and Massawa. Earlier he had proposed that Punt might extend as far as Djibouti (1971: 185–188). He concluded that Punt must have been on the coast of the Red Sea on the basis of the depiction of marine creatures. He also stressed (1971: 188–193) that Punt could have been reached equally well by sea or by land, and this view has since been accepted as established fact (Leclant 1978: 69–73; Posener 1977: 341).

It is not so much the land itself which has fascinated researchers, as the representation of it in the reliefs in the temple of Hatshepsut. They occupy pride of place in all discussions, sometimes so much so that they overshadow other elements worthy of consideration. The reliefs have, in turn, influenced the way in which written sources have been analyzed. For example, the depiction of a giraffe has made it virtually impossible to consider the texts as relating to anywhere outside Africa. Nevertheless, Maspero had already commented that the presence of this giraffe was not conclusive evidence, even though he too eventually accepted the generally held opinion (Herzog 1968: 30 with n. 3).

The reliefs are the only pharaonic period example of an Egyptian pictorial representation of a country outside Egypt complete with its inhabitants and landscape. The unique nature of the reliefs contrasts with the relative abundance of written sources which mention Punt and which date from almost every period of ancient Egyptian history. Punt is the only land whose geographical reality is expressed so clearly, but – paradoxically – Egypt seems to be the only country to have known of Punt, and to refer to it. Punt virtually never seems to find itself in conflict with Egypt, or with any other country for that matter (though see below). Punt 'exists' as if in a void, previously Arabian, now African, but a void, nevertheless, the exact whereabouts of which remain more or less unknown. Punt exists in research, but its outline does not materialize on any map.

The giraffe and the rhinoceros

Despite the fragmentary condition of the scenes in the Hatshepsut reliefs (after the reconstruction in Smith 1962), it appears that the animals are more or less directly associated with a Puntite village. They mingle with domestic animals. A rhinoceros is shown in front of a herd of cattle: the giraffe (Figure 4:2) is in a register which includes a village hut. Both animals are shown as if in the village, although the poor preservation of the reliefs makes it impossible to determine whether they are captive or free.

Yet these 'African' (Gatier 1996) animals could have been transported by humans, even at considerable distances from their countries of origin. Both species were often used as diplomatic gifts in antiquity, appreciated for their rarity (Lion 1992). There are representations of giraffes from Egyptian tombs of the New Kingdom, and, in the sixth century BC a giraffe figures among gifts offered to the King of Kings in Persepolis (Gatier 1996: 929). Diodorus (II.51.1) describes the "cameleopards" of Arabia, and these may be giraffes, indicating that a number of giraffes could have crossed the country, which would have served as transit territory, and could then have been mistakenly identified as originally from there.

The Deir el-Bahri rhinoceros (Figure 4:3) only had one horn, rather short and curving backwards (Stork 1977: 221–222 with photograph and a facsimile by Keimer). This would normally have identified it as a representative of the Asiatic species living in the Indus Valley, since the various African species possess two horns. The

Figure 4:2   Detail of giraffe from upper register of wall reliefs depicting Punt in the temple of Hatshepsut at Deir el-Bahri (after Kitchen 1983a: fig. 35.4.e).

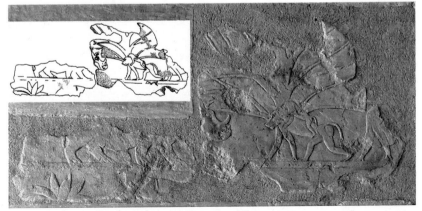

Figure 4:3   Photograph and drawing of rhinoceros from upper register of wall reliefs depicting Punt in the temple of Hatshepsut at Deir el-Bahri (© Dimitri Meeks).

rhinoceros, like the giraffe, can also be taken long distances for commercial or diplomatic reasons. King Shalmaneser III is said to have received a rhinoceros from a king of Egypt – probably Takelot II (Kitchen 1973: 327 with n. 462). For games in the circus, rhinoceros – both African and Asian – were brought to Rome (Colls *et al.* 1985: 108–110). In the 16th century a rhinoceros was still considered to be an appropriate diplomatic gift: Sultan Selim II received an Asian one in Istanbul (Störk 1992: 331–334).

The Nile Valley is not the only route which a rhinoceros might have followed. From the eighth century BC onwards the inhabitants of the southern part of the Arabian Peninsula had mastered ocean navigation and brought various spices back from India, and these may have been taken as far as the eastern Mediterranean and Mesopotamia (Salles 1989: 91–92). The question remains as to whether sea journeys of this kind were already being undertaken at the time of Hatshepsut; the proposition that the Punt rhinoceros could have been of Indian origin can certainly not be excluded.

Punt to the south of Egypt

Another argument has been used to prove that Punt was within Africa. The evidence consists of the various versions and copies of a list of toponyms first recorded from the reign of Tuthmosis III. This catalogue presents the foreign countries and cities known at the time and classified according to the four points of the compass, in theory all subject to pharaoh. In the series devoted to the lands of the south, Punt and the cities in it are mentioned alongside the lands of Kush, Irem, Wawat or Medja (Sethe 1906–1957: 796–798, no. 48 being Punt; version in later inscriptions, 1339; Kitchen 1983a: 67, 14 and 98), which we know to have been situated in Nubia. At first sight this makes Punt a country linked to the Nile and located somewhere to the south of Nubia. Yet the list also mentions the Tjehenu, the southern Libyans (Snape Chapter 6, this volume). The listing is therefore concerned with the south in a wider sense, and is not confined to the populations dwelling along the banks of the Nile upstream from Aswan. The lists of Tuthmosis III and similar sources are usually considered as a straightforward inventory of toponyms. However, to do so disregards their pictorial aspect: each place name is inscribed in an oval surmounted by a human head (Figure 4:4). The head served to classify the toponym according to ethnic categories, each traditionally defined by a face with characteristic features and attributes such as hair style, or the presence or absence of beards. That was how the ancient Egyptian artists distinguished between Asiatics, Libyans and Nubians. Modern publications of the list of Tuthmosis III only provide sketches, and to date there is no publication of a scientific standard. The heads on the place name ovals remain unpublished (Mariette 1875a: pls. 22–26; Sethe 1906–1957: 794–806). Old photographs of the list engraved on the western façade of the sixth pylon of the Karnak temple compensate to some extent for this omission (Mariette 1878, reprinted 1999: pl. 45). The heads of the Puntite toponyms (with Libyan or oriental features) differ markedly from those of the Kushite toponyms (African features) (O'Connor and Quirke Chapter 1: 16–18, this volume).

A copy of this list, probably inscribed during the reign of Amenophis II, divided these same southern lands into two quite distinct categories. The ovals in the first have heads which can be identified as belonging to Africans, while those in the second are

Figure 4:4   Place names written in ovals topped by different heads for different peoples, in the topographical lists of Tuthmosis III at Karnak (© Griffith Institute, Oxford).

identical to those on the ovals containing Near Eastern toponyms.[1] Punt and its toponyms belong to the second category. Fakhry (1937: 51) attributed this unusual detail to an error on the part of the sculptor, but the care in carving the heads has attracted comment from others (Epigraphic Survey 1986: 59). It seems more plausible that the complete set of lists would have grouped together all the toponyms from the south, regardless of whether they were located on one side of the Red Sea or the other, but distinguishing the African toponyms from the Arabian or Libyan ones by their different heads.

Punt to the north and east of Egypt

Other geographical lists, that of Amenophis III in Soleb (in Nubia) and its successors, locate Punt quite clearly to the north of Egypt among places known to have been in the Near East. Punt appears either between Pehal and Shosou, or in the sequence Mitanni, Shosou, Kadesh, Punt, Qatna, Tahse, Yenoam (Giveon 1971: 24 (Soleb), 85 (Karnak, reign of Ramesses II), 91 (Luxor, reign of Ramesses II); see below for Kom Ombo list, Roman period). Curiously these sequences have sometimes been taken, unquestioningly, to be the result of an error on the part of scribes and sculptors (Giveon 1971: 25 n. 2; Helck 1971: 263; but see Leclant 1964: 213–214).

Numerous texts, from at least the Middle Kingdom onwards, describe Punt as the land of the rising sun and locate it in the east, equating it with the eastern horizon

(Sethe 1906–1957: 1657, 2; cf. Kitchen 1975: 26, 13; de Buck 1947: 90d–f; Book of the Dead, 15c hymn to the rising sun; Chassinat and Rochemonteix 1918: 195, 2; and in general Kurth 1987: 173–174). As the source of the gum or resin ꜥnty, Punt is included among the "lands of the East" (Kitchen 1983a: 220, 4; Rochemonteix 1897: 110, 15, 151, 1), and as one especially closely linked to "eastern Shesmet" (Chassinat 1965; Chassinat and Rochemonteix 1918: 190, 12–13, 1929: 94, 13; Chassinat and Rochemonteix 1930: 379, 2, 1933: 141, 2; cf. Cauville 2000: 174, 1–2). Shesmet was reached by way of the Wadi Tumilat, east of the Nile Delta (Gardiner 1918: 218–223). The astronomical inscription in the Osireion of Seti I at Abydos (see Allen Chapter 2, this volume) also records that the sun is born in the south-east of Nut (the sky) beyond Punt (Neugebauer and Parker 1960: 44–45, pl. 44A; for the oblique south-easterly orientation, see Spalinger 1996: 229–230 n. 51).

Religious texts are not the only ones to cast Punt as an eastern country. A statue fragment, probably of the twenty-sixth Dynasty, refers to an expedition to Punt, "which is to the east of the provinces of the gods", that is to say to the east of Egypt (Hodjash and Berlev 1982: 212 no. 143; for the date, Betro 1996: 41–49). We also know that Punt was part of a vast territory, which the Egyptians called the "Land of God" (Kuentz 1920: 178–183; see also Saleh 1981: 107–117, locating the "Land of God" in southern Arabia). The Egyptians clearly understood this territory as a "land of the east" (Sethe 1906–1957: 615, 11–12). During the Ramesside Period, a military official in the Wadi Tumilat held the title "overseer of foreign lands of the Land of God" (Petrie 1906: pl. 31), which suggests that the wadi was one of the routes linking Egypt with the country in question. There are references to other points from which it was possible to set off to this land, such as Nebesheh in the eastern Delta (Chassinat 1934a: 128, 6).

Texts locating Punt beyond doubt to the south are in the minority, but they are the only ones cited in the current consensus on the location of the 'country'. All the other texts, despite their large number, have been ignored. Punt, we are told by the Egyptians, is situated – in relation to the Nile Valley – both to the north, in contact with the countries of the Near East of the Mediterranean area and also to the east or south-east, while its furthest borders are far away to the south. Only the Arabian Peninsula satisfies all these indications.

Puntites and Africans

The general appearance of Puntites in the temple of Hatshepsut and other sources is similar to those of the peoples of the Near East, and their skin is the same colour as that of the Egyptians (Saleh and Sourouzian 1987: 130a–c for colour reproduction). When Puntites and Africans are depicted on one and the same monument, care is taken to bring out the physical differences between them, as in the tomb of Amenmose at Thebes (Figures 4:5 and 4:6 (Puntites); Davies and Davies 1941: 131–136, pl. 24; Figures 4:7 and 4:8 (Africans); Davies and Davies 1941: pl. 25). Here the Puntites have none of the characteristic traits of the Africans; on the contrary they exhibit some features which are peculiar to them alone, and others which are also found elsewhere (Säve-Söderbergh 1946: 20–27). Proponents of the view that the Puntites were from Africa have recognized that the Puntites were not black Africans (Leclant 1978: 70; Saleh 1972: 258–261).

Figure 4:5 Egyptian depiction of Puntites, from the tomb-chapel of Amenmose at Thebes (after Davies and Davies 1941: pl. XXV).

Figure 4:6 Photograph of Puntites in the scene in Figure 4:5 (© Griffith Institute, Oxford).

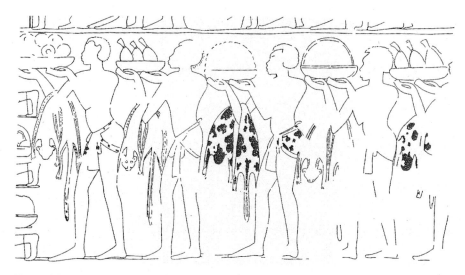

Figure 4:7   Egyptian depiction of 'black Africans' from the tomb-chapel of Amenmose at Thebes.

Figure 4:8   Photograph of 'black Africans' in the scene from Figure 4:7.

The Hatshepsut scenes include imperfectly preserved parts of three figures with black skins, contrasting with the rest of the population of the Puntite village (Naville 1898: pl. 71). The difference is most explicit in the depiction of a Puntite delegation in the tomb of Rekhmira (Figure 4:9). There the ethnic groups bringing their produce are divided between four parallel registers, each independent of the others. The Puntites are in the upper register; below them are Cretans and Mycenaeans, and below these are Nubians, while the fourth register presents Syrians. The four registers correspond to the four points of the compass – from top to bottom: east (Puntites), west (Cretans),

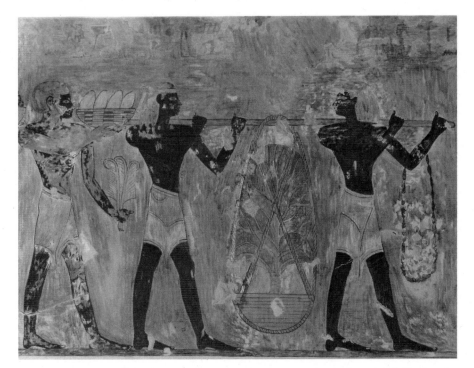

Figure 4:9 Egyptian depiction of Puntite delegation, from the tomb-chapel of Rekhmira at Thebes (after Davies 1935: pl. I).

south (Nubians) and north (Syrians). The Puntites and Nubians are clearly regarded as different ethnic groups, living in different places (Figure 4:10). The black-skinned men from Punt are shown mingling with a population, whose leaders ("the great man of Punt" or "the great men of Punt" referred to in texts) are always slender individuals with pale skin and thin, short beards. The presence of black Africans in a secondary position in relation to a population of 'notables' with paler skin may evoke the slave trade and slavery.

Meetings between Egyptians and Puntites

Two scenes, in two tombs of the eighteenth Dynasty, show Egyptians and Puntites meeting in a place that is not the land of Punt (Figure 4:11; Bradbury 1996: 40, 57; Kitchen 1993: 599–600). The fact that the Egyptians are armed and led by an officer on a horse-drawn chariot, and that the troop is using dogs, in one case, and donkeys as beasts of burden in the other (Figure 4:11), indicates that each scene shows special units involved in expeditions to the deserts bordering Egypt or to more distant lands. In both cases the Puntites bring produce which they lay down before the Egyptians. Nothing here recalls the landscape and environment shown in the Hatshepsut scenes. It is the Egyptians who welcome the Puntites. Moreover, one of the scenes shows Puntites on fragile craft (Figure 4:11) (Bradbury 1996: 40, 57; Kitchen 1993: 599, fig. 35.7; for the remnants of the accompanying inscriptions, see Sethe 1906–1957: 1,472–

Figure 4:10   Egyptian depiction of other ethnic groups from the tomb-chapel of Rekhmira at Thebes.

Figure 4:11   Egyptian depiction of Puntites meeting Egyptians outside the Nile Valley and Punt, from Theban tomb-chapel 143 (after Kitchen 1993a: fig. 35.7).

1,473). Their rigging is very simple: a triangular sail with a rope to manoeuvre it, and a single oar serving as a rudder. One of the registers depicts the arrival of the Puntites, and another their departure. In the accompanying text, the name of the place to which the Egyptians are returning has been largely destroyed, and attempts to reconstruct the name remain hypothetical. Enough survives, however, to show that it was neither Thebes nor Coptos.

The fragility, or at least apparent fragility, of the craft used by the Puntites raises a question. For Bradbury (1996: 39–46) these are rafts made of inflated goat-skins, on which there rests a deck made of planks. She considers that they would have made it possible to undertake a rapid journey from Punt via the Upper Nile to reach a trading point, which she would locate at Kurgus between the Fourth and Fifth Cataracts. Yet, the Egyptian caravans, which would have made their way to Punt or to meet the Puntites, have not left any trace of their route south of Wadi Hammamat. If the Nile Valley had constituted the normal access route for much of the way south towards that land, some indication of this would have been expected, since expeditions to the south left numerous rock inscriptions in Nubia. Moreover, Bradbury (1996: 43–44; cf. Casson 1989: 117–118) herself emphasizes that such rafts were regularly used on both sides of the Red Sea – African and Arabian. They were useful both for trading and for piracy, as witnessed by classical Greek and Latin authors from the third century BC onwards (Salles 1998: 97–98). The Puntite rafts could well have sailed at sea.

A text from Serabit el-Khadim in Sinai, dating from the time of Amenophis III, alludes to just one such meeting between Egyptians and Puntites, for which the latter had perhaps arrived on sailing craft:

> I travelled to the environs[2] of the Great Green in order to survey the precious products (*sr bi3yt*) from Punt and to accept delivery of aromatic gum resins, which the great ones had brought here in their ships (?) [the translation "ships (?)" follows Helck's interpretation of signs illegible on the original] as a supply from the lands which men do not know.
>
> (Gardiner *et al.* 1952: 165 no. 211, pl. 66; Helck 1954: 189–207)

The expression *sr bi3yt* is applied to state functionaries only in this example and, perhaps, in one other badly damaged Serabit inscription (Edel 1983/6: 183–185, fig. 7). In one particularly revealing context, the phrase refers to the king, in Thebes, enthroned on a stepped dais, welcoming an expedition which has returned from Nubia with various goods. It is said of him that he "surveys the precious produce (*sr bi3yt*) of his expedition" (Caminos 1968: 67, pl. 28; Edel 1983/6: 183 n. 36). In each case, attention is focused on the receipt of precious commodities and, in one way or another, going to meet those who are delivering them.

Min, patron deity of Coptos, caravan routes and distant expeditions, also receives this distinctive epithet (Yoyotte 1952: 125–137). An inscription in the temple at Dendera even states with regard to the king that the "*sr bi3yt* of Punt is like He-who-is-on-his-Platform" (Chassinat 1935a: 182, 9–10).

Min is usually represented on a stepped platform, yet clearly this has been assimilated here with the one used during the royal audience. In the city of Coptos, then, Min accepts from the height of his platform the precious substances which the caravans have brought in abundance. Together these epithets accord well with the scenes of the meeting with the Puntites, showing armed men on an expedition, with caravans made up of donkeys, a huntsman and his dog. In effect these scenes illustrate the activity designated by the phrase "*sr bi3yt* of Punt", and indicate that Egyptians would travel out of the Nile Valley in order to meet Puntites bringing produce. Given that the only secular examples of this expression are found in Serabit el-Khadim, it may be deduced that expeditions entrusted with "surveying the precious goods of Punt" passed that way.

Place-names of Punt and its neighbouring lands

Two inscriptions at Serabit el-Khadim in Sinai accord a particularly prominent place to a region known as Wetjenet (later as Wedenet/Wetenet) as an integral part of Punt. This toponym figures in the list of Puntite lands inscribed at Karnak (Edel 1976: 92, 100; Sethe 1906–1957: 799, no. 64). Ptolemaic and Roman period temple inscriptions also associate it with Punt and its aromatic substances (Chassinat and Rochemonteix 1932: 106, 7; 130, 16–17; 1933: 141, 7; Chassinat 1934b: 217, 11; Chassinat 1935b: 11, 14–15; 70, 4–5; 137, 5, 1965: 24, 3; Sauneron 1963: no. 20, 6). Usually this land is held to be near Suakin or Massawa (Edel 1976: 180 n. 34; Zyhlarz 1958: 23–24).[3] Yet the Egyptian sources make such a location highly unlikely. A hymn addressed by the "Easterners" to the rising sun, associates Wetjenet with the inhabitants of turquoise-producing regions, the *Mefkatyu, mfk3t* being the Egyptian word for turquoise (Assmann 1969: 127). The countries of Wetjenet are also known to have been inhabited by another tribe, the Qematyu (Favard-Meeks 1991: 34–35; Chassinat and Rochemonteix 1930: 185, 2–3). Mefkatyu are also associated with a country called Fek-heret (Gutbub 1995: 491 n. 372), a country also inhabited by the Qematyu (Chassinat and Rochemonteix 1931: 251, 17, 1932: 76, 13–14; Rochemonteix 1897: 132, 16). Wetjenet and Fek-heret must then be adjacent territories, and, moreover, in direct contact with the zones where turquoise was produced.

Whereas Wetjenet can only be situated vaguely to the south-east of Egypt, one inscription defines Fek-heret as "at the height of the land of Punt" (Chassinat and Rochemonteix 1931: 164, 7). Sauneron and Yoyotte (1952: 180 n. 2) have proposed that it might have been "a country called Fek distinguished from the Feka(t) (... or Mefka(t) ...) of Egypt and Sinai" by the adjective *ḥry/ḥrt* "upper". Fek-heret could then be translated as 'the upper Fek-land' (*fk* = land of turquoise?),[4] and thus adjoin Sinai, one way or another. This would support an Arabian location for Punt.

Another source worth examining is a geographical list carved at the beginning of the Roman period on the inner walls of the temple at Kom Ombo, in southern Upper Egypt (de Morgan 1895: 132 n. 174). In an initial sequence Fek-heret is mentioned as being between Kepen "Byblos" and Izy "Cyprus" (for Izy, see Osing 1980: 51; Quack 1996: 79–81). In a second series of names, Punt is listed between Upper Retjenou, corresponding to Palestine, and Pa-Bekhen, the mountainous northern part of Mesopotamia (Edel 1975: 51–54) on the one side, and Berber or Babylon (? – or a place name in southern Palestine: see Vandersleyen 1994: 39). Sasha or Susiana (?), and *prs* or Persia, on the other. Punt occupies a zone which would have to be that of the Arabian Peninsula. The list seems to place Fek-heret in Arabia Petraea. All this evidence combines to locate Punt and its constituent territories in the Arabian Peninsula. Moreover, an inscription in the 'court of the Cachette' at Karnak, dating from the reign of Ramesses III, treats the Puntites as part of the *ḥryw š* "the Dwellers-on-the-Sand", a term traditionally used to denote the Bedouin and oriental caravan-traders,[5] and places them on the east in a four part list corresponding to the four points of the compass: "the fear which you inspire reaches 'Those from the End of the World' (= west), breaks the heart of the Nubians (= south), devastates the lands of the Fenkhu (= north)[6] and penetrates Punt-of-the-Dwellers-of-the-Sands (= east)" (Kitchen 1983a: 240, 12–13). The geographical situation has remained essentially the same over a thousand years later.

Finally, the land of Qesenet, whose name means "the difficult (= inhospitable) country", also makes up part of the Puntite territories (Chassinat and Rochemonteix 1918: 200, 6; 201, 7; Rochemonteix 1897: 429, 9). Its inhabitants, the Qesentyu, are classified as Asiatics according to the dedicatory inscription in the temple treasury at Edfu (Chassinat and Rochemonteix 1918: 275, 4; Gutbub 1950: 34). All these texts agree in assigning Punt and its inhabitants to the Near East in more or less direct contact with the lands of the Mediterranean coast.

In a speech addressed to Queen Hatshepsut, the god Amun declares: "the Puntites, who did not know of the men (= of the existence of the Egyptians), the bearded men (*ḫbstyw*) of the Land of God, I have made them receptive to your plan" (Sethe 1906–1957: 345, 15). In Ptolemaic and Roman Period temple inscriptions, the *ḫbstyw* are Puntites, described as harvesting *ʿnty*, but also transporting it as far as Egypt. They are also the inhabitants of the land of Fek-heret, discussed above (Chassinat and Rochemonteix 1930: 133, 13–14). In a text for offering *ʿnty*, the king identifies himself as one of the "bearded men", when presenting the precious substance to the god, who is himself called "sovereign in Wetjenet" (Chassinat and Rochemonteix 1928: 144, 18–145, 1). The text specifies that he was "the excellent bearded man who takes the route via the *ḫ3rtt* in order to cense the divinity with his aroma". This indicates the route which the Puntites took to go to Egypt. *ḫ3rtt* is a common noun denoting a topographical feature rather than a country, and probably the same term as that in demotic texts, where it refers to a canal or channel intermittently filled with water like a wadi (Meeks 1972: 115–117; Pestman 1993: 395–397). Another text lists the minerals used to make the representation of Osiris at the time of the ceremonies at Khoiak, including a "turquoise of the *ḫ3rtt*". This must, then, be a place where turquoise was obtained, presumably Sinai. The "bearded men" of Punt were therefore able to take a land route passing across Sinai. This is one of the routes which Strabo (XVII.21) described: "entry into Egypt is difficult from the east as well, both coming from the regions near Phoenicia and Judaea, as well as departing from the Arabia of the Nabateans next to Egypt: for these are the regions crossed by the road which leads to Egypt" (Yoyotte *et al.* 1997: 117).

The gold of Punt

Gold and electrum are often prominent among those items brought back from Punt or delivered by Puntites. Yet the inscriptions never refer to them as "gold of Punt" or "electrum of Punt", but as the "gold" or "electrum from the land of Amu" (Posener 1977). The question then arises as to whether Amu is a region of Punt, or whether it is situated somewhere else, but within a Puntite sphere of influence. The land of Amu does not appear in the geographical lists of the New Kingdom. An eighteenth Dynasty rock inscription in the vicinity of the Third Cataract of the Nile records the presence of "the scribe (or draughtsman?) Userhat of Am (with foreign land determinative)" (Hintze and Reineke 1989: 184 n. 610; Vercoutter 1956: 70 n. 8); most researchers have considered this conclusive evidence for locating Amu in this region (Posener 1977: 340). However, as Kitchen (1993: 416, 1999: 174–177) has underlined, this region was entirely under Egyptian control at that period, and it is difficult to imagine Puntites extracting gold under the indifferent gaze of the Egyptians and then coming to exchange it with them for other commodities. As well as being a gold-mining area, therefore, Amu must have been situated outside the Egyptian sphere of influence and within the area under Puntite control. Kitchen (1999: 173–178) concluded that Amu must be located "in the easternmost Sudan, behind (W of) the coastal mountains, between latitudes of just N present-day Ras Shagara and just S of present-day Suakin". Amu would thus be situated almost exactly at the same level as Kurgus, with reference to the Nile, and it is Kurgus that Bradbury (1996) would identify as the trading point to which Puntites would have come to exchange goods with Egyptians. All this appears to form a coherent picture, particularly since Amu also supplied ebony and ivory to Egypt (Sethe 1906–1957: 524, 8). However, there remain areas of shade and contradiction.

The geographical situation of Amu seems fixed thanks to the list of the mining countries carved under Ramesses II at the Temple of Luxor. Here we find the following sequence: Nun (= the Primordial Ocean), the Throne of the Two Earths (= Gebel Barkal), Amu, Kush, Nubia (*ß sti*) (Kitchen 1979: 618, 2–10). This agrees perfectly with the proposed location. However, the sequence of Ramesses III at the Temple of Medinet Habu offers a different series of associations: the gold of Amu, the lapis lazuli of Tefrer, the turquoise of Ro-Shaut (*Medinet Habu* VI: pl. 452 = Kitchen 1983a: 328, 4). This is the sequence which becomes standard in Ptolemaic and Roman texts, which add to it the silver of Heh (Osing 1998: 107). Ro-Shaout has been linked with Sinai (Gardiner *et al.* 1952: 3). Tefrer, as the land of lapis lazuli, is probably located in Badakhshan (or other lands far from Africa – Hermann 1968: 21–59; Ohshiro 2000: 68). Almost all of Egypt's sources of silver were situated in the Near East (Harris 1961: 42), and there is silver in the Arabian Peninsula (Kisnawi *et al.* 1983: 78); it is therefore tempting to locate Heh in those areas as well. In any case, a Roman Period priestly manual specifically identifies the land of Heh as "the mountain of gold, Amu" (Osing 1998: 107, pl. 6A, fragment J21; Tait 1976: 49–54). The Ptolemaic and Roman Period lists of mineral-lands do indeed include Heh in sequences which are Near Eastern rather than African. The list in the temple of Edfu presents the following series of toponyms: "Land of God", Heh, Isternen, Tefrer, Ro-Shaut (Chassinat and Rochemonteix 1933: 71–72); the list from Philae places Heh immediately after Byblos and before Tefrer (Junker 1958: 85). Finally, Amu is directly linked with Isternen (Mammisi d'Edfou, 89, 7; Dendara V, 34, 5; Kom Ombo II, no. 864A), the location of which is not known, but which was inhabited by Asiatic nomads (the "Dwellers-on-the-Sands") and was in Asia (Setjet) (Chassinat and Rochemonteix 1918: 286, 12).

These inscriptions contradict the idea that Amu was in Africa. The graffito of "Userhat of Am" needs to be reconsidered in this light. The written form – Am – of the toponym differs from the written name of the land of Amu, which invariably include the final 'u', at least in the eighteenth Dynasty (Sethe 1906–1957: 329, 6; 384, 7; 436, 9; 524, 8; 630, 1). The two toponyms are probably different and denote countries which have nothing to do with each other.

In the Theban tomb-chapel of Qenamun, a depiction of Amenophis II's war chariot includes the caption "the one from the land of Amu", with the note that its wood had been "brought back from the Land of God, in the country of Naharina" (Davies 1930: pl. 22; Sethe 1906–1957: 1393, 9–10). This can be compared with an inscription from the reign of Seti I, in which the god Amun declares that he has "opened the roads of Punt" for the king (*Epigraphic Survey* 1986: pl. 17B, 14–15); the inscription belongs to the record of Asiatic campaigns, and therefore situates the "roads of Punt" in the east. Similarly, in an inscription of Ramesses III, the king records that he has raided Punt (Kitchen 1983a: 225, 1). All three New Kingdom sources indicate that Amu and Punt could have been involved, more or less directly, in Egyptian military campaigns in the Levant.

All this clearly makes Amu a territory situated within the Puntite zone, but one which would have been affected, however marginally, by the conflicts of the Near East in the New Kingdom. As a result it is hard to resist identifying it with the biblical land of Midian to the east of the Gulf of Aqaba, famous for its gold in antiquity (Bowersock 1996: 555 n. 14, 563; Kisnawi *et al.* 1983: 77–78). Indirect confirmation for this conclusion comes from a text linking the gold of Amu with the "Dwellers-on-the-Sands", the Bedouin of the Near East (Sethe 1906–1957: 436, 8–9).

The aromatic produce of Punt

Of all the products from Punt it was the aromatic gum resins which were the most highly prized. These are referred to by two different terms: *sntr* and *'nty*. From combined laboratory analyses and philological research it now seems clear that, by the New Kingdom at least, *sntr* designated the resin of the pistachio tree (Serpico and White 2000: 884–897). Since different varieties of this tree were very widespread in the Near East, this information cannot be used to locate Punt precisely, but it points more to Asia than to Africa.

The identity of the *'nty* tree is still a matter of controversy. Scholars hesitate between *olibanum*, deriving from various kinds of *Boswellia* in both Africa and the southern part of the Arabian Penuinsula (Amigues 1996; Hepper 1969), and myrrh produced from species of *Commiphora*, with the same distribution area (Germer 1979: 63–69). In an Edfu temple inscription that lists trees producing *'nty* there is a possible clue that the Egyptians preferred the resin of Arabian origin. It reflects interest first and foremost in trees from the lands of Punt and its dependent regions, and a note specifies that the varieties from the land of Kush are inappropriate for religious use (Chermette and Goyon 1996: 66). So this text differentiates between Punt and Kush, and, by implication, includes in the term Kush those African territories where *'nty* trees are found (Hepper 1969: pl. 15), Punt cannot, logically speaking, occupy the same territory in the mind of the author. It has to be situated elsewhere, in another region where resin exists, somewhere in the Arabian Peninsula.

There are two main varieties of *Boswellia*: *Boswellia papyrifera*, present among other places in the highlands dominating the Eritrean coastal plain, and the Somali *Boswellia frereana*, famed for the quality of its produce (Hepper 1969: 69 in favour; Kitchen 1993: 603–604 against). These regions could only have been reached by crossing the Bab el-Mandeb and travelling along the coast between the strait and Cape Guardafui. Apart from problems for Egyptian ships when trying to cross the strait, such a location does not fit the suggested land route all the way from Egypt, or the presence of mines recorded as being in the land of Punt. There then remains *Boswellia sacra*, which grows in the eastern Hadhramaut and in Dhofar, a zone straddling what are today south

Yemen and Oman. This was the most highly prized variety during the Ptolemaic and Roman Periods. Yet there must remain doubt as to whether ships from Hatshepsut could have ventured so far.[7]

Among the different varieties of *Commiphora* present within the Arabian Peninsula, *Commiphora myrrha*, which produces true myrrh and grows mainly in northern Yemen (Hepper 1969: 311), corresponds best to the trees in the Hatshepsut expedition (Baum 1994: 31, 1999: 430–443, noting the red colour of the ⟨nty tears in the Hatshepsut scenes, suggestive of *Commiphora*; Betro 1994: 44–48; Dixon 1969: 59–60). Additionally, chromatography and spectrography have been used to identify myrrh of Arabian origin in Egyptian samples dating from the twelfth Dynasty (Goyon *et al.* 1999: 116–117). More information on the analysis is needed, though, as it is doubtful whether chemical analysis can yet distinguish between species, in this case between an African and an Arabian variety of myrrh.

The various species of *Boswellia* and *Commiphora* grow equally well in both Arabia and Africa, and the Egyptians must have been well aware of those which grew in Africa. Indeed, the Edfu list clearly differentiates between ⟨nty from Kush and that of Punt, and in the Chronicle of Osorkon there is mention of ⟨nty from Nubia (To-Nehesy) (Caminos 1958: 126, 134 n. tt). However, Nubian ⟨nty is extremely rare in Egyptian written sources.

The roads of Punt

Texts of expeditions to Punt

Expeditions which left the Nile Valley in search of rare minerals or exotic produce marked their routes with a profusion of rock inscriptions and stelae. Routes through the Eastern or Western Deserts, those following the course of the river from Aswan deep into Nubia, and the routes through Sinai, are punctuated by written testimony in places where the caravans broke their journey or at their final destinations. Three regions preserve references to expeditions undertaken to the Land of Punt: Wadi Hammamat, Wadi Gasus and Mersa Gawasis, and Serabit el-Khadim in Sinai. No rock inscription mentioning Punt has been found south of Wadi Hammamat. This might indeed appear curious if this land lay near the upper Nile Valley. The inscriptions in the three sectors are all of equal importance, and yet they have been treated very differently by scholars, not because of their content, but because of their location with reference to an assumed African location for Punt. The Wadi Hammamat inscriptions have been closely studied (e.g. Bradbury 1988; Farout 1994; Vandersleyen 1989: 148–158), and there is therefore no need to examine them in detail here.

Two eighteenth Dynasty inscriptions from Serabit el-Khadim in Sinai record an expedition to Punt, with important details not found elsewhere (Gardiner *et al.* 1952: 165 n. 211, pl. 66, 173 n. 238, pl. 67; the first studied by Helck 1954: 189–207, the second by Edel 1983/6: 176–185, adding a third but highly fragmentary inscription). Several other inscriptions from Serabit mention crossing-points, implying that part of the journey there might be by sea (Gardiner *et al.* 1952: 11–13; Grandet 1994: 262–263). One inscription links the mission to Serabit and the expedition to Punt so closely that they seem to have taken place in the course of a single voyage – Gardiner *et al.* 1952: 13; Helck 1954: 207, section 6; cf. Sayed 1983: 31). In another case, the surviving inscription records a government official listing products which he had brought back from various countries of Punt (Edel 1983/6: 178). This would be difficult to explain if Punt is located in Africa. On the other hand, if Sinai had indeed been one of the access routes to Punt, nothing in these accounts would seem surprising.

The flight of Ptolemy X Alexander I to Punt

Once the construction of the temple at Edfu was complete, the priests decided to have inscribed on its walls an historical account of the events which marked the approximately one hundred years that the work had taken (Cauville and Devauchelle 1984: 31–55; Egberts 1987: 55–61). In connection with the dynastic feuds between Ptolemy IX Soter II and Ptolemy X Alexander I, they note laconically in relation to the latter: "he fled to Punt; his elder brother took possession of Egypt and was crowned king again" (Chassinat and Rochemonteix 1932: 9, 7–8). Other sources record that Ptolemy X fled to Cyprus, but Egyptologists have only mentioned the apparent contradiction without further comment (Ray 1986: 153). However ignorant one might assume Egyptian priests to be, they could scarcely have confused an island north of Egypt with the depths of Africa. Certainly, the events of 88 BC are rather involved, and numerous details remain obscure, particularly as regards the movements of the king (Samuel 1965; Van't Dack 1989: 136–150). Yet it seems certain that Ptolemy X, feeling threatened, left Alexandria in order to raise a mercenary force (in the provinces of Egypt according to some, in Syria according to others, e.g. Strabo Book XVII.8). Following defeat in a naval battle, Ptolemy X had to flee Egypt and ended up in Lycia. Some time later he tried to rally Cyprus but was killed fighting. He had therefore twice been in places quite near to Punt (if we accept the hypothesis that this country incorporated Arabia Petraea).

Ptolemais of the Hunts

In his research into the sea routes passing through the Red Sea, Ptolemy II gave orders for several expeditions to be undertaken, one of which founded Ptolemais Theron, "Ptolemais of the Hunts'" – the base from which elephant hunts would start. According to Desanges (1978: 272–274), this site must be in the vicinity of Aqiq on the Sudanese coast some 200 km south of Port Sudan. The African hypothesis would make that the coast of Punt. However, a hieroglyphic stela from Pithom gives a brief description of the founding of Ptolemais, and locates it in *phw nhsy*, "the rear land of Nubia" (Sethe 1904: 101, 8). At least this far south, priestly knowledge did not confuse lands of Africa (Nehesy) with Arabia (Punt). It seems reasonable to assume that if Ptolemais had been sited in an area recognized as part of Punt, the composers of the stela would have used the term 'Punt', not "the rear of Nubia" (much as we have seen that they distinguished Punt from Kush and Nehesy).

The Defenneh stela

A twenty-sixth Dynasty stela from Defenneh records how an expedition to Punt was saved from dying of thirst by unexpected rainfall in the mountains of this region (Griffith 1898; Kitchen 1993: 602–603; Posener 1960: 53–54, 1977: 342). According to the generally accepted reading of this text, it establishes a cause-and-effect link between the rain and the seasonal floods of the Nile. Not unnaturally this evidence has been fully utilized by those supporting an African location for Punt. The damaged inscription reads:

> (x + 1) ... His Majesty ... (x + 2) ... who is in Saïs ... (x + 3) ... was good; they said to His Majesty ... (x + 4) [entirely lost] (x + 5) ... on this mountain; the Majesty of ... said ... them (x + 6) ... the roads being impassable [because of the lack (127)] of water; for countless years people had not been crossing it (= the mountain) any more (x + 7) ...? ... in water (x + 8) ... the sky began to send down rain in the 4th month of Spring on Day 12 (x + 9) ... extremely (x + 10) ... in the manner of (x + 11) ... His Majesty. So the heart of His Majesty was glad of this more than of anything else ... the troop began to praise His Majesty (x + 12) [saying(?)]: "How great is thy power, O mighty King, ruler beloved of all the Gods! A marvel has come about during the time of Your Majesty (x + 13) [People had neither] seen or heard of this, that the sky should rain down on the mountain of Punt when there is little rain in the provinces of the South (of Egypt) (x + 14) [and] moreover the month during which it rained was not the season of rains in the cities of the North (of Egypt). (x + 15) [It is] your mother, Neith of Saïs, who had brought Hapy to you so that he might keep your troop alive". (x + 16) His Majesty had a great offering made to all the gods of this land, so that he might be granted life-longevity-power for ever. (x + 17) His Majesty [gave orders] for this stele made of pale schist (?) to be erected in the temple of Min, Lord of Coptos ... (?), ensuring that it should remain here for ever.

If the Egyptians of the twenty-sixth Dynasty had known of the link between tropical rains and annual Nile flood, it is unlikely that they would have treated the rainfall as a miracle out of season. The rains in question, just like the floods, which they caused, were annual and regular. The text states simply that Neith "had brought Hapy to you so that he might keep your troop alive" and not in order to inundate the valley of the Nile. Only the company of men sent by the king benefits from the intervention of Hapy. Now, we know that Hapy can denote the "celestial Nile-flood", that is to say rain, above all when one is far from Egypt. As early as the Amarna Period, the great hymn to Aten specifies that "all the distant lands, you enable them to live: you have placed Hapy in the sky, so that he should come down for them" (Sandman 1938: 95, lines 4–6; for the celestial Nile-flood, Drew Griffith 1997: 353–362; Sauneron 1952: 41–48). This is the Hapy secured by Neith in the Defenneh inscription for the company of men dying of thirst on the roads of Punt (Posener 1960: 54).

If we are considering tropical rains, which bring about the rise in the waters of the Nile, then the mountain of Punt, where the members of the expedition were, would correspond to the place where those rains fall annually. Wherever it is, this place must be desert most of the time, and must be not too far from the area in which *Boswellia* grows. However, when we superimpose a map showing the rainfall feeding the Nile (Stricker 1956: pl. 1) onto a map showing the distribution of *Boswellia* (Hepper 1969: 71, pl. 15), and then onto another map showing the distribution of products said to be "Puntite" in Africa (Fattovich 1991: 264), we obtain a territory more or less between the Eritrean coastal plain – from Aqiq to Adulis – and the region of Kassala. If we assume that the expedition would have been moving on foot, as was generally the case, in order to reach the rainfall zone, let alone *Boswellia*, it would have been necessary to go down the Nile as far as Atbara or even Meroe and then to commence a journey of at least 300 km to the east. For rainfall to appear exceptional, it would have been necessary to be significantly further north. However, if that were the case, the whole link with the rain giving rise to the floods would no longer exist. Yet the text clearly states that the Egyptians are on the mountain of Punt, a place known elsewhere to be a producer of ʿnty (Edel 1983/6: 177, fig. 6 for the mountain(s) of Punt). The data are incompatible with an African location for Punt.

The inscription dates the rainfall to the 4th month of Spring day 12. In the 'wandering' Egyptian calendar of 365 (rather than 365¼) days, during the twenty-sixth Dynasty the date must fall between mid-August and mid-September, or perhaps slightly later (Posener 1977: 342). This period corresponds exactly to the high-point of the floods (end of August in Aswan, mid-September at Saïs – Bonneau 1964: 23). Yet, the tropical rains of Ethiopia and Sudan fall in June–July (Bonneau 1964: 19; Stricker 1956: 5–6). There is, then, a gap of approximately one and a half months between the rains and the onset of the floods in Egypt. In Ethiopia the dry season lasts from September to March (Bonneau 1964: 18 n. 5). There are only two possibilities. Either the Egyptians in the text were in the zone at the moment when rains fell giving rise to the floods and they could not complain of drought or a shortage of water (the rains would have begun in April) – this means that the dates do not match; or they were there during the dry season, in which case there is no connection with the annual Nile flood in Egypt.

The question remains as to why a stela commemorating such an event should have been erected in Defenneh, in the eastern Nile Delta, where it has no obvious justification. However, if that town was on the expedition's route, at the point of departure or return, or both, then the reason for such a choice would be clear. In that case Punt could hardly be situated anywhere other than in the Arabian Peninsula, where rain is indeed very rare – so much so that it is known today as 'the mercy of God'.

All this points to the existence of a northern route leading to Punt. One of the favoured ways out of Egypt was through Wadi Tumilat, then crossing Sinai, passing among other places Serabit el-Khadim on the way to the Negev and Arabia Petraea. This route is well documented for the Hellenistic period and could have been used by Egyptians from at least the eighth century BC (Redford 1992: 348–351). Sinai features not merely as a destination for mining expeditions, but also as a place of preference for the exchange of goods, including the produce of Punt.

Ancient data and sailing towards Punt

The earliest mentions of the land of Punt can now be examined in the light of the above information.

The first historical mention of Punt is to be found in a fragment of the royal annals, known as the 'Palermo Stone', in the section covering the reign of Sahura, second king of the fifth Dynasty. In the course of one and the same year, near the end of that reign (ca. 2480 BC) the fragment records some wares brought from Punt, and others from the "Terrace of Turquoise" in Sinai (Sethe 1903: 246, 3–5). The second mention concerns a voyage in the reign of Isesi (ca. 2400 BC), but is recorded only indirectly. An official, Harkhuf, lived at the beginning of the reign of Pepi II (ca. 2240 BC) and brought back a dwarf from his travels; in the inscription on his tomb façade, he recalls that the latter "resembled the dwarf, whom the royal chancellor Wer-djeded-bau had brought back from Punt in the time of King Isesi" (Sethe 1903: 128, 17–129, 1). The presence of the dwarf is not sufficient in itself to explain why the journey of Wer-djeded-bau was still a living memory almost 150 years after it had taken place. Finds at Mersa Gawasis included a series of hieratic ostraca dating from the mid-twelfth Dynasty (ca. 1920–1840 BC), which may provide an answer to this problem. Two of them bear the single phrase "Wer-djeded-bau is strong" (Sayed 1983: 27). The name Wer-djeded-bau being otherwise only known for the chancellor of Isesi (Ranke 1935: 82 n. 6), both mentions may well refer to one and the same individual. In its structure the compound phrase Wer-djeded-bau + "is strong" recalls names given to Egyptian ships, such as "Aa-kheperu-Ra is enduring", "Aa-kheperu-Ra strengthens the Two Earths", "Isesi is powerful", "Men-kheperu-Ra lays waste the land of Khor" (Jones 1988: 231–233, nos. 5, 6, 16, 19). In each case the name is based on that of a king. The available publication of the ostraca does not reveal whether the expression "Wer-djeded-bau is strong" was followed by the determinative for ship, which would have removed all doubt. Meanwhile, a fragment of another inscription found at Mersa Gawasis, and again dating from the twelfth Dynasty, serves to reinforce the above analysis. On this it is possible to make out a list of three fragmentary names of ships, ending with the ship sign, and one of them is called "Sesostris is enduring in life". If the phrase "Wer-djeded-bau is strong" does indeed designate a ship, one reason as to why it incorporated the name of a traveller, who had lived almost six centuries earlier, could be that Wer-djeded-bau would have been the first (if not in reality at least in collective memory) successfully to have led a maritime expedition to Punt and back. In this case, the presence of a dwarf, in the Harkhuf expedition the sole attraction for the child king Pepi II, would have been merely a minor detail. Wer-djeded-bau would have brought back vital information for expeditions of this kind in the future, even though this is not actually mentioned in the texts.

Also in the time of Pepi II, but significantly later in his long reign, a certain Pepynakht was entrusted with a delicate mission:

> So, His Majesty, my master sent me to the land of the Asiatics, so that I might bring him back the Unique Companion, the Captain (?), the overseer of interpreters Anankhta, who was assembling (sp) a kbnt-ship there in order to travel to Punt, when the Asiatic-dwellers-on-the-Sands killed him together with the armed detachment which was accompanying him.
>
> (Sethe 1903: 134, 13–17)

The scene of the tragedy can scarcely be situated on the Mediterranean coast, as is sometimes believed, since it is unlikely that a ship would have been built on the Mediterranean coast when it was destined to be used on the Red Sea (Posener 1938: 264–265). The verb sp used here denotes the assembly rather than the complete construction process; once the ship was ready, it was meant to have sailed to Punt. A location at the end of the Gulf of Suez would seem to fit best with the text.

The problems raised by a maritime route to the land of Punt have for several years been at the centre of a debate as to whether the expression $w3d$ wr, the "Great Green", could mean the sea. However, the solution to this lexical problem is not the crucial factor in assessing the route taken by the Hatshepsut expedition to Punt. Even if, in the final analysis, $w3d$ wr could not denote the sea, her ships are depicted on water with sea creatures clearly identifiable as Red Sea fauna (Figure 4:1 above). As already seen, a ship journey to Punt could have begun in a region near Sinai, or it could have set out from Coptos. The fact that ships on their way back from Punt unloaded their cargoes on the coast near Mersa Gawasis or Quseir does not prove that there was no communication between Wadi Tumilat and the Gulf. Points of departure were dictated by the special circumstances of Red Sea navigation (see below). One stretch of water linked the Nile at the level of Heliopolis to the entrance at least of Wadi Tumilat, and was navigable in ancient times, as it was then a branch of the Nile. The date when it ceased to be a waterway and was replaced by a series of lakes is not known. These lakes are mentioned during the Ramesside Period (Winnicki 1991: 161 n. 40), suggesting that, by that date, direct journeys to the Gulf of Suez were no longer possible. The Hatshepsut temple record creates the impression that the ships left Thebes and reached Punt without any kind of transfer, and that the same applied on the return journey. Yet this could be a selective narrative. Current excavations in Wadi Tumilat show no trace of a canal predating the twenty-sixth Dynasty (Grandet 1994: 256–257; Kitchen 1998: 34–35; Redmount 1995: 127–135). It appears (Nibbi 1981: 88–94) that the fresh-water channel reaching the sea existed at the beginning of the dynastic era, and it is quite possible that it remained navigable during the Old Kingdom. It should also be noted that the Ramesside capital was located not far from the entrance to Wadi Tumilat and that all Late Period dynastic capitals lay in the Nile Delta (for the Middle Kingdom, see Bradbury 1988: 143). Whether full of water or not, Wadi Tumilat always constituted a favourite means of access to the Gulf of Suez and to Sinai.

Texts recording where ships for journeys to Punt were built or assembled during the pharaonic period do not give precise geographical landmarks. The unfortunate expedition of Anankhta during the reign of Pepi II was massacred by the Asiatic "Dwellers-on-the-Sands" while it was assembling a ship prior to setting off to Punt. This indicates that the scene of the action must have been both near Egypt and in a zone dominated to a greater or lesser extent by Asiatic nomads. In the reign of Mentuhotep III (ca. 2000 BC), the high official Henu led a large expedition leaving Coptos with a company of 3,000 men and an unspecified number of donkeys (Couyat and Montet 1912: 81–84, pl. 31). After crossing areas where the troops had to dig around 15 wells, he arrived near the "Great Green". There, to mark the success of that first stage, he made an offering of cattle and gazelles, presumably caught locally. He then built ships which departed for Punt. On their return, again near the "Great Green", Henu brought back their precious cargo to Coptos, passing through Wadi Hammamat. The outward route was not the same as the return journey, but it has not proved possible to identify the few places named in the account of the outward journey. Numerous hypotheses have been suggested for these two different routes (Bradbury 1988: 131–138; Kitchen 1993: 589–590; Schenkel 1965: 253–258). Some have proposed that Henu reached the sea near Berenice, but there is no evidence that that port was already in existence in the early Middle Kingdom. Others believe that he set off to Quseir or, following the discoveries at Mersa Gawasis, that he had been heading there. Henu left another inscription, this time in his tomb at Thebes, which clearly refers to the same journey (Hayes 1949: 43–49, pl. 4). It mentions an armed expedition, under his command, to the land of the "Dwellers-on-the-Sands".

The stela of the vizier Antefoqer and Ameny, found at Mersa Gawasis, from the reign of Sesostris I, appears to describe construction in two stages. The first, under the command of the vizier, took place in the naval shipyards of Coptos, while the second was supervised by Ameny on the shores of the "Great Green" (Farout 1994: 144; Sayed 1977: 170, pl. 16, 1983: 29; Vandersleyen 1996: 110–111). Since the inscription mentions not two expeditions, but only one, we must conclude that the construction of sea-going ships involved two different phases. The operation at Coptos was not exactly the same as that on the edge of the "Great Green". Evidently the ship planks and masts were prepared in Coptos, and then assembled during the second phase of the work (Kitchen 1993: 591). This procedure is well known from classical antiquity and later, and the few traces of it in Ancient Egypt should not be overlooked. Anankhta was assembling (*sp*) a ship, when he was killed with his companions by the "Dwellers-on-the-Sands". The term *sp* is very specific and normally applied to the assembly of papyrus rafts, the papyrus reeds being held together by ropes passed between them and pulled very tight (Newberry 1942: 64–66; Servin 1948: 82–88; for the Hellenistic and Roman periods, Vinson 1996: 197–204). Applied to a ship of wood, the term must denote an assemblage of component parts prepared in advance. Ancient depictions add support to the existence of this practice, and Lipke (1985: 34) concluded from study of the dismantled ship of Kheops that:

> It is not certain how (or if) the Ancient Egyptian got their vessels across the Eastern desert to the Red Sea, but had they wished to dismantle them for desert transportation it is hard to imagine a construction system more suited to reassembly with minimum of tools and time.

It seems likely that Ameny supervised the second stage of this kind of ship-building.

None of this provides direct information on the location of Punt, but it encourages consideration of whether there were several different places where the ships were assembled just before departure to Punt. We have seen that a link could be established between the "Great Green" and the region inhabited by the "Dwellers-on-the-Sands", both of them being situated somewhere in the Gulf of Suez. The details in P. Harris of an expedition sent by Ramesses III to Punt reinforce the impression that the northern end of this gulf, in all periods, provided a favourable point of departure for long distance expeditions (Grandet 1994: 255–260; Kees 1933: 122; Sayed 1983: 36–37). This seems in any case established for the Hellenistic, Roman and Islamic periods (Mayerson 1995: 17–18; Sidebotham 1986: 592–594). The choice of location stems from sailing conditions in the Red Sea, fully analyzed and expounded by various authors, often in great detail (e.g. Bradbury 1988: 127–130; Degas 1995: 219–221; Grandet 1994: 257–258; Kitchen 1971: 193–202; Salles 1998: 94 providing the main data for the following discussion; Sanlaville 1988: 20–21).

The ships of Hatshepsut, thanks to the positioning of the mast and sails, were able to use winds fairly close to the beam (Degas 1995: 217), but all vessels depended on the winds and prevailing currents which, in the Red Sea, are subject to remarkable seasonal variation (Bradbury 1988: 129; Degas 1995: 220). From June to September the winds and currents carry ships south, favouring the outward voyage for the Egyptians. The *Periplus of the Red Sea* recommends the month of September for departure to the south.[8] The winds and currents are reversed between October and May. The most favourable time of year for the return journey is January–February and in general the conditions are more complex for the return journey than for the outward one. Once they find themselves a little below the latitude of Berenice, ships coming up from the south encounter contrary currents and winds. By hugging the Arabian coast, a northbound ship can almost reach the mouth of the Gulf of Aqaba in this season. From there, however, the return to Egypt becomes more difficult. Northerly winds and currents in the Gulf of Suez make sailing further into the gulf extremely dangerous (Mayerson 1996: 119–120). A twisting current, however, together with the wind, drives the ships from the Arabian coast towards the African, enabling them to end up precisely in the area of Mersa Gawasis and Quseir.

These various constraints make it difficult to believe that a journey to Punt and back could be accomplished keeping solely to the African coast, even if that side is richer in food supplies and drinking water. Navigators needed to know both sides of the Red Sea coast. That being the case, from the aspect of sea voyages alone, there is no need to locate Punt in Africa; indeed the opposite is true. The sites of the harbours and ports can be explained by natural conditions but also by the chosen destinations.[9] If Punt occupied the whole western side of the Arabian Peninsula, there would have been a variety of possible routes.

The site of Mersa Gawasis was very important in the Middle Kingdom (Frost 1996: 869–902; Sayed 1977: 140–178, 1978: 69–71, 1980: 154–157, 1983: 23–27). Several stelae have been found there, an inscribed monument constructed from re-used anchors, and hieratic ostraca – all dating to the first half of the twelfth Dynasty. Several of these documents contain references to the land of Punt. From the quantity and coherence of these written sources, it seems impossible to maintain, as some scholars do, that they amount to a collection of enigmatic objects brought to Mersa Gawasis from elsewhere and abandoned there for no discernible reason (Vandersleyen 1996: 110–114). All these objects are clearly associated with this specific site as a point on one of the routes to or from Punt. The inscriptions inform us first of all that the voyages of which they tell were connected with "the mine of Punt" (*bi3 n pwnt*) rather than Punt in general (Sayed 1977: 176–177; for *bi3*, Gardiner *et al.* 1952: 1–2). The location of this mine is unknown; it could have been at any point on the Red Sea coast. The arid, isolated nature of the area makes it difficult to imagine a large company of men staying there long enough to assemble ships and having access to adequate supplies of drinking water and provisions. It would also have been unlikely that the thousands of men recorded as taking part in such expeditions would all have been able to go to Punt. Only a small group would have stayed on at Mersa Gawasis in tents, awaiting the return of the expedition. This, at least, can be deduced from the finds made on site. Thus, the fragments of planks with mortise slots, pegs and pieces of rope indicate that ships really had been assembled or dismantled here (Sayed 1980: 156–157, 1983: 36–37). Even anchors, some unfinished, have been found, along with fragments of copper alloy chisels; these suggest that there might have been an improvised workshop, although the blocks of stone had been brought in from elsewhere (Frost 1996: 882–884). A series of stone piles or 'cairns' could have helped to guide the returning ships, on lookout for the harbour entrance (Frost 1996: 876–877).

The choice of Mersa Gawasis, as with Quseir or even Berenice later on, seems justified, then, by the specific conditions of Red Sea navigation. Whatever the period and point of departure, the aim was, of course, to facilitate the outward journey there – by shortening it, for example – but, above all, to enable the returning ships to reach Egypt again without inordinate danger, when it came to unloading their cargoes. The inscriptions at the site show that they were composed on the return journey. The points situated furthest to the north, like Mersa Gawasis, also permitted a different sea journey: a ship departing from the Gulf of Suez and hoping to reach the Gulf of Aqaba would be well advised not to choose the most direct route, round Ras Muhammad. The inexperienced Aelius Gallus attempted that manoeuvre, and as a result lost some of his ships and suffered serious damage to the rest of his fleet (Mayerson 1995: 21–23). Ships emerging from the Gulf of Suez are naturally carried towards the Arabian coast. This is one of the reasons why the Egyptians must have known that coast. The landing point could vary, according to the navigational conditions, between Aynunah in the north and the area around al-Jar in the south. Significantly, this is the stretch of coast where Leukê Kome is assumed to have been founded (Sidebotham 1986: 596–598). From there, ships could sail on southwards, or, alternatively, sail back up the coast towards the north in small stages, mostly using oar-power so as to reach the Gulf of Aqaba. This would have been one of the routes available to the Egyptians for reaching the mines at Timna, and the name Geziret Faraoun, "the Island of the pharaohs", doubtless reflects memory of their transit (Flinder 1977: 127–139; Hafiz et al. 1994: 81–93, 1998: 39–119). Whatever solution was chosen, ships would land at points where the expeditionaries could exchange merchandise with the caravan traders of the Arabian Peninsula, either on the Red Sea coast or in the Gulf. On their return from the Gulf of Aqaba winds and currents would again carry the ships towards the Egyptian coast in the general area of Mersa Gawasis. Perhaps the "mine of Punt" was precisely the goal of such a journey.

Archaeological evidence, like the written sources cited above, fits neatly with the description in P. Harris of the expedition sent by Ramesses III to Punt:

> I built great ships ... which were equipped with countless crewmen. Laden with products beyond number from Egypt ... (and then) sent to the great Sea of Muqed, they reached the mountains of Punt without any misfortune befalling them ... The ships were then laden with produce from the Double Land of God ... with quantities of *anty* from Punt ... They came back safe and sound to the mountain of Coptos; they moored peacefully, laden with the produce they had brought back. These were then loaded on to donkeys and men as a caravan, and transferred to river boats at the landing-stage in Coptos. After they had been sent north (= towards the royal residence) and welcomed ashore in festivity and then brought before (me) as presents ... I offered them to the ennead (company of gods) of the lords of this land.

> (Grandet 1994: 338–339)

The king does not say exactly where the ships were built, but he does tell us that they sailed on the "Great Sea of Muqed" in order to reach Punt. Muqed is usually understood as two words, *mw ḳd*, meaning 'the reverse water (the water which flows backwards)'. For those who do not accept the possibility of a sea journey, the name implies the bend in the Nile between the Third and Fifth Cataracts, where part of the river flows from north to south and part in the opposite direction. For others, the expression alludes to the south-flowing currents in the Red Sea, which are the reverse of the currents of the Nile (Kitchen 1993a: 608 n. 19). Yet two essential details seem to have been overlooked. First, Muqed is the name of a region: the expression is determined by the sign for the desert, which usually accompanies the name of lands outside Egypt (noted by Grandet 1994: 257). Second, Muqed appears in several series of toponyms devoted to Syria-Palestine, at Aksha, Amara and Soleb, and comes at the beginning or end of the series. These lists were closely linked with the name of Punt (Kitchen 1979: 211 n. 1 and 28, 216 n. 28). A papyrus from the reign of Ramesses IX confirms that this land was bordered by the sea, and states that it was inhabited by Shosu bedouin (Giveon 1969–1970: 51–53; Helck 1967: 148 (46), 150 (72)). Together the data lead us to Sinai, with Muqed as one or all of its coastal zones.

Coptos lies at the point where the Nile flows closest to the Red Sea, and it is on the way to the place where ships were virtually obliged by natural forces to land on their return journey, as in the case of Aelius Gallus (Sidebotham 1986: 590). Coptos could also have served as a point of departure for land journeys to Sinai northwards along the coast and then, after reaching the peninsula, back again by the same route. It would thus be possible to associate Sinai and the land of Punt in a single undertaking, whether by sea or by land. The documentation seems to indicate that the route to the aromatic materials did not change from the pharaonic to the Hellenistic and Roman Periods.[10] The sheer age of Coptos and its wealth in the fourth millennium might already then have been linked with the distant contacts for which its location made it so suitable. There are indications that Upper Egypt and Lower Nubia on the one hand and Susa and Sumer on the other may have been in at least indirect contact during those very early periods (Smith 1992: 235–246; Warburton and Matthews 2003).

Conclusions

Apart from the few notable exceptions reviewed above, the name of Punt disappears from non-religious texts after the New Kingdom. If Punt was a territory in Africa, this might be explained first by the break in relations with countries south of Aswan, then by limited re-conquest during the twenty-sixth Dynasty, and finally by the emergence of a power block in Sudan forming a barrier between Egypt and Punt. However, when contacts had been re-established at least by sea during the Hellenistic era, two points would remain unexplained: the reference to the "Nubian borders" (*phw nhsy*) in connection with Ptolemais of the Hunts, and the flight of Ptolemy X to, or through, Punt.

If Punt occupied the western part of the Arabian Peninsula bordering on the Red Sea from Arabia Petraea to the Yemen (Figure 4:12), a more coherent explanation is possible. From the eighth century BC, Egypt's relations with the Arabian Peninsula and its inhabitants underwent significant change. A land, previously inaccessible even at its closest point, and of which outsiders had known mainly just the fringes, becomes an area occupied by small kingdoms of caravan traders, in frequent contact with the Near East, controlling the commercial routes for aromatic resins in an organized way, and specifically identified with these trade routes (Robins 1997: 48–52).

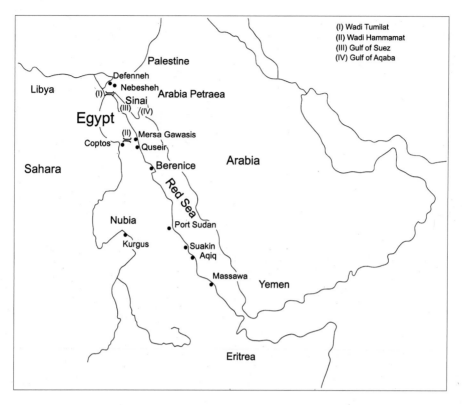

Figure 4:12   Map relating to the proposed location of Punt.

While Punt still figures relatively frequently in religious inscriptions, the more vernacular vocabulary of place names tends to reflect more accurately this new geopolitical reality. The expression "Land of Arby" denotes the north-east and the south of Sinai, at least from the time of the demotic onomasticon onwards, dated to the fourth–second centuries BC (Yoyotte and Chuvin 1986: 51 n. 49; Zauzich 1987: 88). This might seem strange at first glance, but 'Arby' is, without doubt, used here with its primary meaning of 'shepherds' or 'nomads', as it first appears in a Minian text of the sixth century BC (Robin 1991: 72–73). On the other hand, the term Heger, "Hagrians", is preferred for Arabia proper, or at least for its inhabitants; this is the place name on the Red Sea canal stelae of the Persian king Darius and on his statue at Susa, in a sequence "Ashur, Arabia (hgr), Egypt (kmt), Libya (t3 tmḥw), Nubia (t3 nḥsy), Oman (Mag), India" (Posener 1936: 186–197; Yoyotte 1972: 256). These Heger appear by the name of Hagraioi in Diodorus (XVI.4.2). The term is already known in the twenty-sixth Dynasty, and becomes common after the last indigenous dynasties. A demotic papyrus dating from the reign of Ptolemy XII supplies some names of these Hagrians, also identified as Nabateans, Sabians or Minians (Lüddeckens 1988: 56, h). Finally, a demotic papyrus of the Persian Period mentions "Min Lord of Heger" (Posener 1969: 148), which is none other than a 'modernization' of the older epithet "Min Lord of Punt", well known from written sources.

However imprecise the space designated as Punt in the Old Kingdom and later may have been, in general it corresponded to a reality, which continued to grow richer over the centuries. It is significant that, during the Old Kingdom, Punt only appears in autobiographical or historical texts. It does not figure in religious texts until the Middle Kingdom, at the very time when expeditions there begin to grow in scale. The restriction of the name Punt in the Late Period to religious texts does not imply that the land was some intangible feature that had finally disappeared. Rather, these texts retain the vocabulary of earlier periods, as is to be expected from their role as guardians of sacred heritage.

Elsewhere, I have examined further questions such as Egyptian deities linked with Punt, the various elements of fauna and flora, the varied products of that land, the transplanting of ꜥnty trees, huts built on piles, dwarfs and pygmies, the "Nubian (nḥsy) of Punt", the Medjay, and the Egyptian antiquities found in the Arabian Peninsula (Meeks 2002). All lead to the same conclusion. The hypothesis of an African location for the land of Punt is based on extremely fragile grounds. It is contradicted by numerous texts and has only become an established fact in Egyptology because no one has taken into account the full range of evidence on the subject regardless of place of origin or date. When all the evidence is assembled, the incoherent and implausible character of such an African hypothesis becomes self-evident. The only way to reconcile all the data is to locate Punt in the Arabian Peninsula. The territory of Punt began quite close to that of Egypt, once Sinai had been crossed, in Arabia Petraea or the Negev. It incorporated, probably in a rather imprecise manner, the whole coastal zone of the Red Sea down as far as present-day Yemen and the actual heart of Punt probably corresponded more or less to Yemeni Tihama.

Notes

1   From blocks reused in the Roman fortress around Luxor temple (Fakhry 1937: 51–56); this copy of the list is usually ascribed to the reign of Amenophis II (see Fakhry 1937: 40–41; Sethe 1906–1957: 1,338–1,340; Porter and Moss II, 338, lower).

2   The expression *her gswy wꜣd wr* is also found in the Hatshepsut expedition inscriptions (Sethe 1906–1957: 325, 13 and 326, 6). My translation is based on a Middle Kingdom invocation of the eye of Ra: "your black area is in your centre, your white area on your edges (*r gswy*)" (Roccati 1970: 28(22) and pl. recto 21–22).

3   The supposed reference to Wetjenet on the stela of the Napatan king Nastesen is a misreading for the name of King Kambadusen (Hintze 1959: 17–20; Zyhlarz 1958: 23–24).

4   For *Feka(t)* as an abbreviated form of *Mefka(t)*, see Gardiner *et al.* 1952: 1 n. a, 11 n. b. Note too that a people called Fekatyu (for Mefkatyu?) bring the produce of Punt (Rochemonteix 1897: 498, 11 with nn. i–j).

5   These are the Asiatic nomads in Sethe 1903: 34, 16, and later also some of the inhabitants of Naharina: Sethe 1906–1957: 1,233, 2, cf. Giveon 1971: 172 n. 18.

6   The Fenekhu inhabit a region of uncertain definition, but covering the Mediterranean coast from the south of Palestine (Green 1983: 40–43; Leclant 1984: 455–460; Vandersleyen 1971: 102–119). Note that the Qematyu of Punt can be closely linked to the Fenekhu in Ptolemaic temple inscriptions: Rochemonteix 1897: 30, 16; 132, 8–9.

7   The *Periplus of the Red Sea* indicates that in ancient times (before the monsoonal winds were used for navigation to India, from the end of the second century BC) ships coming from Egypt did not venture beyond Aden (Casson 1989: 65 (§ 26: 8, 27–30); Salles (1988: 75–102) demonstrates that the southern face of the peninsula, from Red Sea to Persian Gulf, was unknown until the time of Alexander at the earliest.

8   Which would be the time of the ꜥnty harvest (Amigues 1996: 675; Bradbury 1988: 130 n. 17; Casson 1989: 55 § 6: 3, 6–7; 65 § 24: 8, 11–12).

9   By harbour I refer to simple way-stations for maritime travel; Red Sea travel did without any port buildings for most of antiquity, the sailors making use of the natural shelter offered by coastal bays, in Arabic *mersa* (Degas 1995: 222–227; Frost 1996: 870–871; Kitchen 1971: 193).

10   An inscription in the tomb-chapel of Petosiris, dating to the early Ptolemaic period, explicitly refers to use of the aromatic produce of Punt in his perfume-producing workshop. The list of produce of Punt can also be compared with the produce listed on the Pithom stela and in the *Periplus of the Red Sea* (Paice 1993).

CHAPTER 5

INTERPRETING PUNT: GEOGRAPHIC, CULTURAL AND ARTISTIC LANDSCAPES

Stephen P. Harvey

The realms of the gods have been described in the writings, and the highlands of Punt can be explored ...

(Book of the Dead, Chapter XV,
P. Ani, trans. Foster 1995: 91)

Prior to the geographer Claudius Ptolemy's attempt in the second century AD to chart the known world (Butzer 1977; Thomson 1965), ancient Egyptian representations of the world appear to have been limited mostly to symbolic images of the cosmos intended for sacred purposes (Lesko 1991; O'Connor 1997). Rather than illustrating earthly itineraries, such images had as their goal the description of the sun's daily path through the day and night skies, or the roads and gates of the underworld, all for the benefit of the deceased (Allen Chapter 2, this volume; Hornung 1999; Robinson Chapter 8, this volume). With the exception of one particularly detailed geological map of a gold-mining region preserved on papyrus (Scamuzzi 1965: pl. LXXXVIII), no maps in the modern sense survive from Ancient Egypt prior to Late Antiquity, although it seems likely that maps of foreign locales must have existed for military and trading purposes. In their absence, scholars for the past two centuries have attempted to recreate maps of the Egyptian world using an extensive range of ancient information, including lists of foreign place names, scenes of far-off triumphs, and the archaeological testimony of trade products and imported raw materials.

The Egyptian artists' ability to document natural and human variety in the service of religious art is perhaps best exemplified in the representations of Queen Hatshepsut's expedition to the land of Punt carved on the walls of her mortuary temple, located in the area of western Thebes known as Deir el-Bahri (Naville 1898: pls. 49, 69–86; Smith 1962: 61). The southern wall of the Middle Colonnade of Hatshepsut's terraced temple is covered with six narrow registers, each no higher than 50 cm, densely populated with scenes of a landscape located at the edges of the Egyptians' known world (Figure 4:1 above; 5:1). Perhaps best known for its depictions of the ruler of Punt, Parahu, and his enormous wife named Iti, the registers detail an exhilarating environment of stilted thatch-roofed houses, a forest of precious trees, and animals foreign to the Egypt of Hatshepsut's time, such as a giraffe (Figure 4:2 above) and a rhinoceros (Figure 4:3 above). The adjacent western wall depicts the voyage by ship to Punt, and the return to Egypt of those ships laden with the precious

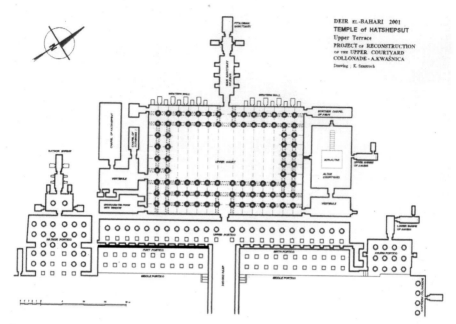

Figure 5:1   Hatshepsut's Temple at Deir el-Bahri (after Szafrański). Note that the Punt scenes occupy the wall behind the lower terrace, south side.

cargo of live trees, ebony logs, gold, incense, electrum, ivory, ebony, baboons, panthers, and ostrich eggs. Above this, the presentation of these goods to Hatshepsut by chiefs of Punt and the neighbouring territories of Irem and Nemayu is shown. The purpose and the aim of the entire Punt episode, the presentation of incense by Hatshepsut to Amun, forms both the coda and starting point for the scenes of the expedition, and serves as visual witness that Hatshepsut has fulfilled one of her sacred obligations to her divine father.

According to the texts accompanying Hatshepsut's offerings to Amun, her expedition to procure incense and other goods from Punt came about in response to an oracle of the state god Amun, who commanded her to search out the roads to Punt (Breasted 1906: 116). The goal of the Punt expedition was not just to procure large amounts of incense, but to capture live, transplantable trees to create a regenerating, incense-producing garden for Amun on the soil of Thebes (Dixon 1969), literally a Punt in Egypt. In a broader sense, the expedition formed part of her obligation to "satisfy the gods", a major duty of the Egyptian ruler along with the presentation of funerary offerings to the dead and the judgment of humankind, according to traditions that predate the New Kingdom (Loprieno 1996b: 282–283). At the successful conclusion of the expedition, Hatshepsut is recognized by her subjects as divine through her sweet, incense-like aroma and the golden colour of her skin, features which signal her transformation into a deity (Hornung 1982a: 64).

Unlike the English noun 'incense', which derives from a Latin root meaning "to burn", the major generic term for incense in ancient Egyptian, *sntr*, is formed from a causative verb meaning literally "to make divine" (formed from the root *ntr*, meaning "god"). Incense was not a mere luxury to the Egyptians, but an absolute requirement for proper religious worship. Just as burnt food offerings might nourish divine beings through their scent or essence, so too was the burning of aromatic resins thought to satisfy and bring pleasure to the gods. The mention of incense in Egyptian texts evokes two aspects of divinity: the vital pleasure that the gods take in smelling the scent of aromatic gums and resins, as well as the power of incense to transform human-made places and things into ones worthy of divine inhabitation. Both *sntr*, which is probably to be associated either with frankincense or with resin from *Pistacia* trees, and *ʿnty*, which may be myrrh, a resin from *Commiphora* trees, were products sought in Punt by Egyptian royal expeditions (Serpico 1997: 438–442). Incense was vital in Egyptian ritual for the purification and consecration of statues and temples, both of which might serve as temporary houses for divine power. This consecrating power of incense even extended to the human body, which after death might be anointed with myrrh and sticky resins during the mummification process in the effort to transform transitory human flesh into an appropriate and lasting home for the eternal spirit (Serpico 1997: 464–468). The offering of aromatic substances is deeply ingrained in religious practices from ancient times to the modern day, and royal gifts of aromatics find a distant reflection in Christian theology in the gifts of myrrh and frankincense brought to the infant Christ by the three *magi*, wise men from the East. Myrrh also played an important role in ancient Egyptian perfumes, and its rich scent was closely linked both to Punt and to divinity. The allure of Punt for the ancients was thus inextricably tied to scent and sensation.

In contrast to lands surrounding Egypt such as Retjenu (Syria-Palestine), Tjehenu (Libya), or Kush (Nubia), each of which was at some point dominated by Egypt, or in turn exercised control over it, the Egyptian relationship with Punt was never more than a distant one. Despite thousands of years of indirect and occasionally direct Egyptian trade with Punt, there is no evidence that Punt was ever dominated militarily by Egypt. Nor is the famous Punt scene in Hatshepsut's temple cast in the visual rhetoric of conquest; it instead reflects official exchange between emissaries of the Egyptian court and the local rulers of Punt.

Although the eighteenth Dynasty provides the most extensive evidence for travel to Punt, texts show that the securing of a steady supply of incense was a concern for Egyptian rulers since the Old Kingdom, beginning with the reign of King Sahura of the fifth Dynasty. Punt and its wonders figure significantly in a number of royal and non-royal sources, all of which seem to reflect expeditions carried out under the pharaoh's initiative. Royal command, rather than a divine oracle, led Old Kingdom high officials to travel to Punt and the land of Yam in search of, among other treasures, pygmies or dwarfs to perform sacred dances for Kings Djedkare Isesi and Pepi II. A more sober account, also from the reign of Pepi II, relates an expedition sent out to retrieve the corpse of an official who was murdered by Bedouin while preparing a ship for travel to Punt, although the text does not state precisely where these preparations had been taking place. More in line with the goals of Hatshepsut's Punt travel is the evidence for an expedition in search of "fresh myrrh" commissioned by eleventh Dynasty ruler Sankhkara Mentuhotep, recorded in a graffito left by the expedition's leader, Henu, in the Wadi Hammamat, a major ancient route to the Red Sea (for the above texts, see Kitchen 1993b and Bradbury 1988).

For any detailed visual evidence of Punt and its inhabitants, we must rely almost entirely on royal and private art of the eighteenth Dynasty. Fortunately, the Punt scenes from Hatshepsut's temple at Deir el-Bahri are not the only known representations of Puntites and the products of their land. A particularly fascinating scene in a Theban tomb dating to the period of Kings Tuthmosis III/Amenophis II shows the Punt trade in reverse: Puntites arrive in rafts under sail to deliver incense and other typical products of their land to Egypt (Theban Tomb 143, illustrated and discussed in Bradbury 1996; Figure 4:5 above). Scenes in other Theban officials' tombs of the eighteenth Dynasty showing myrrh and other products of Punt brought in tribute are likely derivative of the Punt scenes in Hatshepsut's mortuary temple; these include Theban Tomb 39 of Puyemra (Davies 1922: pls. 30–34), Theban Tomb 89 of Chief Treasurer Amenmose (Davies and Davies 1941: pl. 25), and Theban Tomb 100 of Rekhmira (Davies 1943: 17–20, pls. 16–23). A fragmentary scene from the tomb of Hepuseneb (Theban Tomb 67, Davies 1961) has been taken to represent the cutting down of incense-producing trees in Punt, but may more likely represent the felling of ebony trees, as in the Hatshepsut scenes. With the exception of fairly uninformative scenes of what seem to be Puntites presenting myrrh, as in the tomb of the official Meryra at Tell el-Amarna during the reign of King Akhenaten of the late eighteenth Dynasty (Davies 1905: pl. 41), all later mentions of Punt are purely textual. Aromatic plants were apparently brought from Punt and transplanted in Egypt during the reigns of Ramesses II and Ramesses III, most likely employing the same routes that Hatshepsut's officials had reopened centuries before.

Punt as a geographic landscape

After more than 150 years of intense academic interest in the Punt scenes at Deir el-Bahri, and in the face of much textual and pictorial evidence, the geographical location of Punt and the routes that the Egyptians used to reach that land continue to be the object of surprisingly lively ongoing debate (see Meeks Chapter 4, this volume). Major contributions to these debates have been made by Herzog (1968) and Kitchen, whose attempts to localize Punt over the past three decades have been extensively cited (Kitchen 1971, 1993, 1999). The overwhelming ancient association of Punt with the incense-producing trees that were its main product has meant that all attempts to identify the location of Punt have logically sought a region famed for the production of aromatics. Since incense trees, principally *Boswellia* sp. (frankincense) and *Commiphora* sp. (myrrh), flourish on both the eastern and western coasts of the Red Sea, cases have been made since the second half of the 19th century either for Punt's location in western Arabia, or in the eastern coastal region of Africa, in modern eastern Sudan, Ethiopia, or Somalia (for extensive discussion, see Meeks Chapter 4, this volume). Attempts to fix Punt more precisely on the map have depended mainly upon satisfying all of the environmental factors reflected in ancient lists of Puntite products, as well as features depicted in the visual narrative of Hatshepsut's expedition. Particular attention has been paid to the identification of plant and animal species represented in the Punt scenes, in an attempt to narrow down the broad range of possible locales.

As straightforward as it might seem, this process of associating ancient words and artistic images with features of culture, environment and topography is plagued with interpretive problems at many levels. Aside from elementary questions relating to the nature of representation in Egyptian art, a basic issue surrounds distinguishing items (aside from myrrh) which are truly Puntite products from those which are not. For example, while gold is a major part of the goods offered to the Egyptian emissaries by the ruler of Punt, it may be erroneous to expect gold mines within Punt itself. The Deir el-Bahri texts make clear that at least some of this gold derives from a place called Amu, and thus may reflect interregional trade beyond the borders of Punt itself (Meeks Chapter 4, this volume; Posener 1977).

Although the representation of a giraffe, that quintessentially African animal, in the Deir el-Bahri landscape might well be expected to establish once and for all the Africa location of Punt, the objection has been raised that animals could be removed from their natural habitats in antiquity (Meeks Chapter 4, this volume). The relationship between the scenes clearly situated in Punt on the lower registers and the topmost two registers containing the giraffe and rhinoceros depictions is also problematic, not the least because of the poor preservation of the upper wall (see the reconstruction in Smith 1962). While the entire six registers of the southern wall of the Punt colonnade at Deir el-Bahri have been viewed by most scholars as a visual catalogue of the natural and cultural traits of Punt, some doubts have been aired regarding this traditional view.

O'Connor (1982: 935–938, 1987) has pointed out that the upper two registers, those apparently depicting rhinoceros, giraffe, panthers and cheetahs, may in fact depict the landscape of Irem or the more obscure Nemayu (possibly the same as the Amu mentioned above), toponyms that are probably to be associated with the Berber-Shendi reach of the Upper Nile. This idea is supported by a similar division in a scene on the adjacent wall, where darker-skinned rulers of Irem and Nemayu are shown in a register above the rulers of Punt, all of whom offer the distinctive tribute of their lands to Queen Hatshepsut. If correct, this means that any attempt to take into consideration the natural environment of these animals may in the end have no bearing on the location of Punt (for a dissenting view, see Kitchen 1999: 177 n. 26). It would still be logical to assume that Punt is adjacent to the locales that produced these items, and recent attempts to accommodate them all on a map of the Horn of Africa reflect this possibility (notably in Kitchen 1999). Aside from place names that seem to reflect regions adjacent to Punt, textual sources also give the names of territories within Punt. These include Wetjenat, a source of ebony and resin/gum (O'Connor 1982: 931), and Wekemet, a source of resin that is listed in texts from the Sinai, and on topographic lists of Tuthmosis III (Kitchen 1993a: 600).

The routes from Egypt to Punt that Hatshepsut claims to have reopened are almost as much a subject of debate as the location of Punt itself. A considerable amount of Middle Kingdom textual evidence indicates that the trip to Punt began at ancient Coptos (modern Qift) on the Nile, and proceeded along one of the traditional roads leading through the Eastern Desert to the Red Sea. The discovery of twelfth Dynasty shrines built in part of recycled stone ships' anchors at the ancient port of Sawaw (modern Mersa Gawasis) on the Red Sea coast would seem to provide solid evidence for the route taken by at least some expeditions heading to Punt (Bradbury

1988; Sayed 1977, 1978). Fish and other aquatic life (such as spiny lobsters and squid) shown in watery strips beneath the arriving and departing Egyptian fleet have been identified as consisting of several types native to the Red Sea (Danelius and Steinitz 1967).

Despite this evidence, Vandersleyen (1996, 1999) has objected that the ancient Egyptian term "Great Green", consistently employed in descriptions of the Egyptian route to Punt, never refers to the sea, but instead relates exclusively to the Nile River. Objections have also been raised to the sea-going capabilities of Egyptian ships in the Pharaonic era (e.g. Herzog 1968, but see Kitchen 1993a). However, the metaphoric phrase "Great Green", which almost certainly *can* encompass both the Red Sea and at times the Nile itself, is in the case of Punt travel most certainly to be linked with the Red Sea. Although it is conceivable that some travel to and from Punt made use of a Nilotic route (cf. Kitchen 1993a: 587–589), it is hard to reconcile this suggestion with the Deir el-Bahri reliefs, especially given the presence of Red Sea marine life in the scenes themselves. In any case, attempts to determine the location of Punt based primarily on philological evidence are problematic, leading one scholar to position Punt in the environmentally inappropriate surroundings of Sinai (Nibbi 1981).

Punt as a cultural landscape

Beyond the requirements of the natural environment, the Hatshepsut reliefs have been closely read for clues regarding the cultural traits of the Puntites. Thatched houses on stilts, the exotic appearance of the wife of the ruler of Punt, and elements of Puntite adornment and appearance have all featured in a kind of comparative ethnography, primarily making use of known features of present-day African tribal groups living well to the south of Egypt proper (Herzog 1968). Despite the importance of these attempts, no linkages have been convincingly established between these artistically stylized features of the Punt scene and any surviving cultures nearly 3,500 years after the fact, although in general stilt houses seem to be a feature of many regions of east Africa. A basic problem is the 'reliability' from a modern perspective of ancient Egyptian images, intended not as reportage but as temple decoration, not as historical record or publication, but as an illustration of the distances to which a pious pharaoh will go to satisfy religious obligations.

While Punt was certainly of sufficient interest to the Egyptians to inspire a detailed visual and textual account of its wonders, the Punt scenes are part of a continuum in Egyptian representations of non-Egyptian people and their surroundings, a consistent theme in Egyptian culture during all periods. Yet, Egyptologists have found in this image of an Egyptian encounter with a less 'civilized' people a reflection of their own assumptions about sub-Saharan Africa, tending to link New Kingdom Egypt either explicitly or implicitly to European exploration and conquest, and Punt to a more 'primitive' African other (e.g. Erman 1894: 511–512). Alternatively, the Puntites have at times been grouped together with the Egyptians as members of a lighter-skinned 'Semitic' race, in contrast to a darker 'Hamitic' (i.e. African) one (e.g. Davies 1943: 19). In the wake of the *Black Athena* debates of the past two decades (Bernal 1987, 1991, 2001, 2003; Lefkowitz and Rogers 1996), scholarly and public awareness of the relevance of Egypt's location on the African continent has gradually grown, better enabling us to view the Punt episode in the context of foreign affairs among two essentially African cultures.

An intriguing aspect of the Punt scenes as an ethnographic document is the extreme obesity of the wife of Punt's ruler, a feature that has been linked by several scholars to African notions of wealth, beauty and royalty that are documented ethnographically in a number of sub-Saharan cultures (Herzog 1968: 58–61), and equated by other scholars with monstrosity (e.g. Fischer 1987: 24). In ancient records, obese women are prominently featured in depictions of queens and queen mothers in the Meroitic culture, centred in the region of the Fifth Cataract of the Nile in modern Sudan (Scholz 1984). In contrast to scholarly accounts which stress the monstrous or primitive appearance of Punt, its stilt houses, or the fat wife of its ruler, nothing in the Egyptian texts expresses anything but admiration for the wonders of this land. The decision of the artists of the Punt reliefs to step outside of Egyptian artistic conventions and depict extreme obesity is in keeping with the approach to other forms of physical difference such as dwarfism (cf. Dasen 1993). Thus, the wife of the ruler of Punt and her donkey mount need not be seen as any more remarkable than the high-status Egyptian dwarf Seneb's curious appearance in sculpture and relief deriving from his tomb of Old Kingdom date (Dasen 1993: 126–131, fig. 9.19, frontispiece).

One of the major attractions of the Deir el-Bahri scenes to modern viewers is its representation of an apparently sub-Saharan African cultural and natural landscape dating from a period prior to indigenous written documentation. Several recent reviews have sought to identify Punt with non-literate archaeologically documented cultures of the second millennium BC and later in east Africa (Fattovich 1991, 1993; Phillips 1997). Only the discovery of direct traces of New Kingdom Egyptian presence would positively identify Punt once and for all; it has been suggested that a shrine or temple erected by Hatshepsut might one day be located (O'Connor 1982: 918; Posener 1973). As Fattovich (1991: 260) has remarked, however, "The cultural frame of Eastern Sudan and Western Eritrea in 2500–1000 BC is still fragmentary". Definition of archaeological cultures for this period is only partial, and a single basic, definable culture, the Atbai Ceramic Tradition, may be identified across a broad zone from the Red Sea to the White Nile (Fattovich 1991: 260–261). At the present state of research, it is nearly impossible to connect archaeological cultures in the Upper Nile or northern Ethiopia and the Horn of Africa with Punt, especially due to the almost total lack of second millennium Egyptian trade goods in excavated contexts. Much as the reconciliation of biblical accounts with actual remains provided an impetus for archaeology in Egypt and much of the Near East during the late 19th century (Jeffreys 2003b: 5; Wilson 1964: 112), the archaeological quest for Punt may well lead during the coming decades to the intensification of archaeological reconnaissance in the entire region, including the investigation of how and whether the Arabian coast enters into the equation during the Late Bronze Age/New Kingdom.

Punt as a literary landscape

The mystery of Punt to the ancient Egyptians derived both from its association with aromatic substances vital to divine worship and their alluring scent, and from its distant location at the border between the human world and the world of the gods.

Such was the distance of Punt from the main sphere of Egyptian interaction and domination that the Egyptians associated it with the "God's Land", a liminal space beyond the controlled order of the Nile Valley (Osing 1977). The goddess Hathor, to whom Hatshepsut constructed a shrine at Deir el-Bahri adjacent to the Punt colonnade, is connected with distant lands and frequently termed the "Lady of Punt" (Inconnu-Bocquillon 2001: 197–198). Thus, the Punt expedition evokes an aspect of divinity: the theme of departure to the God's Land and return to Egypt, accompanied by the divine scents and qualities of distant places.

Although Punt was recognized by the Egyptians as an actual land at the fringes of their world, and one that could be visited and explored, from early times Punt also maintained a separate but related existence as a literary landscape synonymous with wonder. Egyptian love songs evoked the name of far-off Punt in connection with the heady scents of myrrh and frankincense: "When I hold my love close, and her arms steal around me, I'm like a man translated to Punt, or like someone out in the reedflats, when the world suddenly bursts into flower" (Foster 1974: 25). The transformative power of Punt's main product is similarly evoked in this Ramesside hymn dedicated to the god Amun:

> ... The people of Punt come to you, and the god's land blossoms for love of you; ... to make your temple fragrant with aromas of festival, and incense trees, and abundance of myrrh which wafts to you sweet odors to mingle with your breathing ...

(Foster 1974: 68)

Punt plays a significant role in the Middle Kingdom tale conventionally called the 'Tale of the Shipwrecked Sailor', in which an Egyptian castaway on a distant island is saved by an awesome, god-like serpent who refers to himself as the "ruler of Punt" (trans. and commentary in Parkinson 1997: 89–101; Loprieno Chapter 3, this volume). Although the island is never named in the story, it is referred to as "island of *ka*", a term meaning life-force or sustenance, reinforcing the sense that the products derived there are ones basic for both physical and spiritual survival. Indeed, the long list of products given by the serpent-ruler to the shipwrecked man to take home with him to Egypt is almost identical to the item to those listed in Hatshepsut's Punt scenes. The serpent's insistence on knowing who brought the sailor to this isolated region unknown to mankind is mirrored at Deir el-Bahri in the questions posed by the Puntites upon the arrival of the Egyptian expedition in their land: "How come you have arrived here, in this land unknown to (other) people?" (trans. Kitchen 1993a: 594). Here we encounter the discourse of royal narratives, which frequently posit non-royal astonishment, objections or surprise in order to offset the decisive actions of the pharaoh (cf. Loprieno 1996b: 280).

The narrative cycle depicted on the northern portion of the Middle Colonnade at Deir el-Bahri, showing the divine birth of Hatshepsut from the union of Amun and Hatshepsut's mother, Queen Ahmose, forms a pendant to the Punt expedition (trans. Breasted 1906: 75–86; Brunner 1964; scenes in Naville 1898: pls. 47–55). Although the two cycles at first seem to be unrelated, their point of connection centres around Hatshepsut's obligations to her divine father, Amun, and both scenes are suffused with the notion of the god's taking pleasure, whether sexual, reproductive or recreational. Punt is even evoked in the text of Hatshepsut's divine birth scenes in phrases that reflect secular and sacred love songs: "When he came before her, she rejoiced at the sight of his beauty, his love passed into her limbs, which the fragrance of the god flooded; all his odors were from Punt" (Breasted 1906: 80). The scent of the god, who here assumes the form of Hatshepsut's earthly father Tuthmosis I in order to impregnate Queen Ahmose, forms a textual link to the nearby Punt scenes. Like the Punt narrative, the divine birth cycle outlines a process by which far-off divine essence and vitality are brought home to Thebes and germinated, this time in the womb of Hatshepsut's human mother.

Punt as an artistic landscape

Despite abundant evidence in Egyptian hieroglyphic texts for travel to Punt, and other representations of expeditions to Punt and emissaries from that land, the study of ancient Punt mainly rests on the interpretation of a single artistic cycle: that of Hatshepsut's temple. Thus, the questions that arise from analysis of the Punt reliefs need to be examined as much from an art historical as from a geographical, ethnographic or biological perspective. While most studies have taken into account some of the basic problematic issues surrounding Egyptian artistic representation, including the access of Hatshepsut's artists to their source material, less attention has been paid to the scenes in their cultural and architectural context.

In the attempt to understand Egypt's foreign relations, by far the greatest source of information comes from the monumental record of temple and tomb walls, upon which pharaohs and elite members of the court sought to document civil and military expeditions. While the primary interest in carrying out the actual campaigns was no doubt economic and military, their documentation in temple and tomb art served a primarily religious goal. Scenes of foreigners bearing tribute to the pharaoh's court, or mass slaughters of enemy soldiers, served to symbolically reinforce the subjugation of foreign peoples, places and products to the centralized Egyptian empire and its state gods (e.g. Gaballa 1976: 100). This kind of statement can be made in either a concise fashion by means of personified lands bearing offerings, or more expansively through narrative scenes and associated texts, as at Deir el-Bahri. The complexity of the scenes of Hatshepsut's Punt contrast sharply with simple personifications of the land of Punt carrying aromatic resin, known from the Old Kingdom, as well as from the eighteenth Dynasty at Luxor Temple in eastern Thebes (Kitchen 1993a: 587, 601). Even in the complexity of the Deir el-Bahri scenes, however, the point is not the means (whether war, trade, tribute or diplomatic exchange) by which the outside world is drawn into Egypt, but the result of that process, the presentation of goods from all regions to the ruler, and thence to the gods.

The creation of a highly specific environment complete with flora, fauna, minerals and human life reinforces the documentary sense that the expedition leaders reached not a mythical land but an actual, livable place. Groenewegen-Frankfort (1970: 120) considered the Punt scenes to be one of several "minor heresies indulged in by adventurous artists ...", forming an exception from the rule of the "strong, deep-rooted anti-narrative bias in Egyptian relief and painting ...". While the literary structure of royal narratives is reflected in the Punt scenes, with their sequence of divine commission, royal command, effective outcome and presentation to the god, these events are not couched in military terms.

Time is also evoked in a complex way: the whole wall may be taken in all at once, or in its narrative sequence either from bottom to top, or top to bottom. Seen as a whole, the southern wall of the Punt scene forms a dense, unified landscape, unusual for Egyptian temple art. As a series of states, rather than unfolding actions, the scenes in the narrative may be conceptually reshuffled by the viewer, while still retaining its essential meaning and character. The narrative reflects deep traditions in Egyptian language and literature, in that actions are represented as already accomplished, perhaps reflecting the usual way that the ancient Egyptian language expresses a completed motion in terms of a state: e.g. "I am come" instead of "I have come", "I am arrived" versus "I have arrived", a feature that Egyptian shares with other languages, such as French and German (Allen 2000: 205–206).

More surprising than the narrative structure of the reliefs, however, is the fact that they do not place the visual emphasis on the image of the ruler at all. The Punt landscape is not dominated by a royal figure, lending to the southernmost wall of the Middle Colonnade the appearance of multi-register miniature scenes of expeditions and tribute in private tombs of the New Kingdom. This interest in the exotic reminds us of the nearly contemporary images of Syrian flora and fauna depicted by Tuthmosis III in a suite of chambers in Karnak temple, eastern Thebes. According to recent architectural studies, this chamber would have been all but inaccessible to any but divine viewers; these too were considered products of "God's Land" (Beaux 1990: 42). The ease with which modern tourists and visitors may walk up to and examine decorated temple walls stands in sharp contrast with the greatly restricted access of these same temple walls to ancient Egyptian viewers, who were prevented from entering all but the outer, relatively public courtyards of temples except during rotations into priestly service or great public festivals.

The feature of a high degree of visual specificity, as well as the effect of a pastoral landscape, are reflected in Egyptian royal and private art in other genres and during other periods. In their tendency toward specificity and narrativity, the Old Kingdom 'seasons' reliefs in the sun temple of Niuserra at Abu Ghurob form an important precursor to the Punt cycle, with their representations of specific aspects of the life cycle and agricultural year including migration, mating, birth, seeding, sowing, and reaping (Edel and Wenig 1974).

Similarly, the Punt scenes recall market and barter scenes in private Old Kingdom tombs, which also feature absorbing detail and sub-themes, such as the policeman with his attacking monkey chasing a youthful thief fleeing a market stall in the tomb of Niankkhnum and Khnumhotep at Saqqarah (Moussa and Altenmüller 1977: 82, fig. 10). Such details in private art served to relieve the repetitive nature of the basic transactions that are at the heart of the scene, and their introduction into royal monumental art is one of the many innovations of eighteenth Dynasty temple decoration. The artist or artists of Hatshepsut's Punt landscape seem to have been given licence within the limitations of space and within the decorum of the scene's basic intentions. Examples include a rhinoceros facing-off with a baboon mother and her young, in addition to the narrative sub-theme of the family of the ruler of Punt. Perhaps this freedom developed out of painting on mud plaster in palaces or tomb-chapels during the Second Intermediate Period, examples of which we have only scant traces.

Within the architectural setting of the innovative terraced form of Hatshepsut's temple, the Punt scenes also play a role in a broader, more esoteric narrative. Royal and divine ships form a common thread, rising from the lowest terrace to the third, uppermost terrace. Massive ships lift a pair of granite obelisks hewn from the quarries at Aswan on the lowest terrace, representing another sacred obligation to Amun, this time based on the southern border of Egypt. Travel by ship to Punt in the Middle Colonnade provides a visual link between the lower cycle and that of the Upper Colonnade, where ships appear in the form of sacred barques bearing divine images. Reliefs in the Upper Colonnade are concerned with the themes of sustenance and sacrifice, as well as solar veneration. The Punt cycle thus serves as a middle ground between Egypt and the divine world, mirroring its broader significance in religious topography. Egyptian funerary temples, or "mansions of millions of years" (Haeny 1997: 86), serve less as arenas for public display of achievements than as an environment that is sufficient for self-perpetuating eternal worship. Just as food production scenes in the Upper Colonnade relate to the production and provision of basic foodstuffs and cosmetics for the deceased ruler, so the scenes of the trip to Punt answer a perceived need for life-force. It is possible that the exotic plant and human life of Punt, the procuring of necessary gifts to the gods, and the divine births all combine to form a precursor to visual representations of solar hymns, more directly reflected in palace and temple paintings at the city of Amarna (O'Connor 1989).

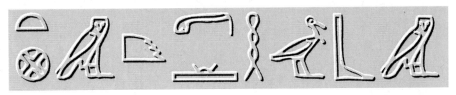

CHAPTER 6

THE EMERGENCE OF LIBYA ON
THE HORIZON OF EGYPT

Steven Snape

Introduction and definitions

In their discussions of foreign contacts, Egyptologists have tended to dwell on Nubia and Syria, but the Ancient Egyptians themselves acknowledged a third pre-eminent neighbour in their relations with the outside world: Libya. In the late second millennium BC, the inhabitants of the lands west of Egypt brought about the greatest upheaval with the longest-lasting effects in Egyptian history. They attacked and eventually overpowered Ramesside Egypt; most of the 'Egyptian' kings of the first millennium BC were of western origin, as reflected by their un-Egyptian names – Sheshonq, Osorkon, Psamtek, and Nekau. Yet, before the Ramesside Period, the Western Desert seems to have been populated only sparsely, and archaeologists have had difficulty in filling the gap between prehistory and that dramatic historical record.

In the mid-eighteenth Dynasty, the time of Egypt's greatest power, few if any officials involved in the operation of that empire seem to have been concerned with the Libyans. At that period a complex network of international relationships had developed in the Near East and eastern Mediterranean, based on competition for security, territory and economic resources, and negotiated through warfare, diplomacy and trade. Libya seems to have been very much out of the picture. This is the impression given by the evidence for foreign contacts from Egypt itself (see Matthews and Roemer 2003b; Tait 2003: 3–4), which refers to Libya and Libyans in a rather cursory or formulaic way. Surviving royal inscriptions of this period, most within temples, describe in some detail campaigns waged in the Levant and Nubia, but Libyans appear only in the role of 'traditional' enemies deemed to be under the generalized control of the Egyptian king. On wall scenes in private tomb-chapels at Thebes, a variety of foreigners are shown bringing goods to Egypt, and these are mainly Nubians, Syrians and even Aegeans; Libyans rarely appear. Within the Amarna Letters, from the international correspondence of King Amenophis III and Akhenaten, Libya appears neither as a vassal nor as a state governed by a 'brother' king.

From the beginning of the dynastic period, over a millennium and a half earlier, there are Egyptian references to the presence of a distinctive group of people living to the west, along what was by far its longest land border. However, they never receive the same attention in early Egyptian records as other peoples and lands. Nubia was clearly Egypt's most strategically important neighbour for most of its history. Egypt and Nubia are united by the Nile river much more decisively than they are divided by the outcrops of rock impeding river travel, as at the Upper Egypt/Lower Nubia boundary at the First Cataract, or at the Second Cataract, which formed the border during the Middle Kingdom. Egyptian policy towards Nubia from the Archaic Period to the end of the New Kingdom was one of depopulation, destabilization and colonial integration, all with a double purpose. The first was the prevention of a competitor Nilotic state developing immediately to the south of Egypt – a fear realized in political integration of Lower Nubia in the First Intermediate Period, Kerma in the Second Intermediate Period and the Kushite Kingdom in the late Third Intermediate Period. The second factor was control over valuable economic assets which included access to sub-Saharan Africa and its goods, and Nubian products, especially gold. Egypt's policy to the east was motivated by similar concerns. The acquisition of a Levantine empire early in the New Kingdom created an effective buffer against potentially hostile rival empire-builders, particularly Mitanni and the Hittite Kingdom. In the Second Intermediate Period, north-eastern Egypt had been taken over by an Asiatic population led by the Hyksos, "rulers of foreign lands". However, contacts with the east also offered opportunities, with long-standing economic relationships based around the acquisition of raw materials from unique sources (e.g. high-quality Lebanese timber via Byblos attested from the Old Kingdom to the end of the New Kingdom) or from economically more productive regions (copper from Cyprus rather than Sinai), and of technically sophisticated finished goods (e.g. glass from the Levant). The importation of skilled economic migrants from the east was also a relevant factor.

Libya seems to have offered none of these advantages. On the economic map it was, in many respects, a dead end. There was no need, at least until the nineteenth Dynasty, to acquire and hold a Libyan buffer zone against a competing empire to the west. The largely barren Western Desert, with particularly intractable areas like the Qattara Depression, provided a barrier rather than a corridor, and seems to have been occupied by low numbers of nomadic pastoralists. These seem to have offered no significant threat to the Egyptian state beyond occasional border raids, and there are no known urban centres or concentrations of raw materials that might have attracted Egyptian economic interest. Only towards the end of the eighteenth Dynasty does the Egyptian textual and pictorial record introduce a range of Libyan imports, albeit still on a modest scale; raw materials (cattle products), exotica (ostrich eggs and feathers) and skilled migrants (the increased presence of Libyans as mercenaries in the Egyptian military). The records do not specify the contents of the reciprocal economic exchange between Egypt and Libya, but traded items might have included technologically advanced finished products, perhaps especially metal tools and weapons.

It should be noted that the use of the term 'Libyan' in this chapter is necessarily wide and vague. It is not limited to occupants of an area now known as the modern state of Libya, nor is it restricted to a particular self- or externally-identified group. Following the example of the ancient Greek authors, and in accordance with what we know of Egyptian terminology, the word 'Libyan' denotes all non-Egyptians who lived in the region to the west of the Nile Valley and Delta. The northern boundary of the region in which these people lived can be delimited precisely in the north (the

Mediterranean coast) and the east (the fertile land watered by the Nile in the Valley and Delta), but its western and southern boundaries are less easy to define. It is likely, but by no means certain, that the Libyans discussed within this chapter – that is to say those with whom the Egyptians had some sort of contact during the dynastic period – operated within an area which included Cyrenaica to the west and stretched as far south as Lower Nubia. Some of the attempts to identify more exact locations for specifically named Libyan groups are discussed below (and see Figure 6:1).

Archaeological evidence from Libya

Archaeological activity within the area defined above has been limited. Part of the problem is the sheer size of the area involved, the difficulty of the terrain and, perhaps most significant of all, the limited amount of surviving evidence for nomadic pastoralists of the Bronze Age. In general, archaeologists have had more success in identifying earlier Holocene activity in what is now Egypt's Western Desert but which

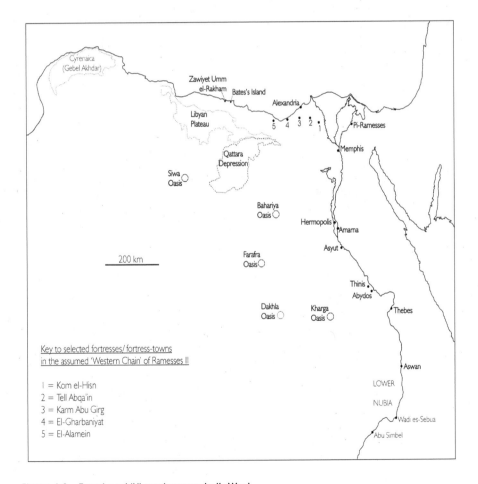

Figure 6:1   Egypt and 'Libyan' groups to its West.

was, up to the end of the Old Kingdom, habitable savannah land. With the exception of the oases and the Mediterranean coast, anything like large-scale settlement would have been impossible in almost all of ancient Libya (as defined above). Even on the Mediterranean coast, the most likely area of occupation, few Bronze Age Libyan sites have been clearly identified. White (1994) discusses the presence of Bronze Age Libyans at Mersa Matruh from the excavations of Bates (1927), to the survey of the region undertaken by Carter (1963) and the potential for future fieldwork on the Libyan coast. More recent survey work around Zawiyet Umm el-Rakham by Hounsell (2001) and Hulin (1999) has also been successful in identifying remnants of Libyan occupation on desert plateau sites. However, this recent work has shown how difficult it may always prove to identify a specifically Bronze Age Libyan cultural horizon within the archaeological record; the surviving material cultural evidence consists of simple ceramics and lithics, and crude dry-stone architecture, together known as the Capsian Tradition (Barker *et al.* 1996; Hounsell 2001). This 'cultural horizon' seems to be present in the region from the Neolithic until at least the 19th century AD, and is present over an area which exists far to the west of the zone of Libyan occupation noted above. The distribution suggests a mosaic of Libyan groups, each with a broad zone of economic activity that perhaps comprised coastal settlement and seasonally exploited interior, as in early modern Cyrenaica (Johnson 1973: 30–33). Their lands would have stretched from the Nile Delta to the Maghreb in the far west. Within this huge area the archaeological detection of these groups is extremely problematic, and only well established at a small number of sites (e.g. Haua Fteah – McBurney 1967). Even well-organized survey projects find the location of this Capsian material difficult (e.g. the Unesco Valleys Survey in Tripolitania – see Barker *et al.* 1996).

The oases of the Western Desert represent a special case. The presence of various Libyan groups within the oases is occasionally mentioned in Egyptian sources, and the oases provide a series of watering/trading points for anyone in the desert. Together they act as an alternative to the Nile river as a line of communication between Libya and Nubia; this was exploited in the late nineteenth Dynasty when the peoples of those two lands co-ordinated their efforts against the Egyptian king Merenptah. However, the oases have been remarkable for the lack of specifically identifiable Libyan material there (Hounsell 2001: appendix 1).

The most important region still to be examined in detail is Cyrenaica. It has been suggested (O'Connor 1990: 38 with bibliography) that the much greater carrying capacity of the Gebel Akhdar when compared to the Marmarican coast, and certainly to the desert interior, makes this the likeliest area for any substantial settlements of Bronze Age Libyan groups. However, the required intensive regional survey concentrating on the detection of Bronze Age Libyan sites has not yet been carried out (Barker *et al.* 1996: 1). Instead, some Late Bronze Age Aegean sherds associated with what is assumed to be a local Libyan ceramic product have been recovered from pre-Greek levels at a small number of classical sites, including Cyrene (Barker *et al.* 1996: 103–104).

For these largely logistical reasons, the archaeological study of pre-Greek 'Libya' has not developed. Instead, the textual and pictorial record of dynastic Egypt has been the major source for attempts to assess aspects of Libyan culture and activity, and

Egyptologists have been prominent in trying to identify and understand the people generally referred to as 'Libyans'.

Libyans in Egyptian sources

The Egyptian record, in both texts and pictorial depictions, is rich in attestations of Libyans. They are referred to by a series of specific names, which may refer to particular tribal groups (see below), and are iconographically distinct in their appearance. The most important attempts to collect this data on Libyans in Egyptian sources are those of Hölscher (1937), Osing (1980) and O'Connor (1990). The latter work is especially important in that it also reviews scholarly discussion on a number of questions crucial to the debate concerning Libyan identity and activity, including the issue of whether it is possible to define to any degree the 'homeland' of the various Libyan groups, and whether Egyptian sources allow the reconstruction of social structure and economic activity among the Libyans. O'Connor concentrates on the material from the Late New Kingdom, when new Libyan groups appear in Egyptian sources.

It should be noted that although references to Libyans within the dynastic Egyptian record are fairly common, detailed textual material is rare. The principal detailed Egyptian texts are those which describe the Libyan campaigns of Merenptah and Ramesses III of the nineteenth and twentieth Dynasties. Earlier detailed material is rare, the most significant exception being the autobiography of Harkhuf (Loprieno Chapter 3, this volume; and see below). Other attestations are ambiguous, such as the introductory section to the 'Tale of Sinuhe' where King Sesostris I returns from a campaign against the Libyans; as this is a work of fiction, it is not clear what historical reality this might reflect (Loprieno Chapter 3, this volume). The Egyptian sources have most often been used to construct a historical geography of the various Libyan groups named within the Egyptian sources. This has led to the construction of 'ethnogeographic' maps, such as that of Bates (1914), which attempt to find a homeland for these different groups in various parts of the Western Desert/Marmarica/Cyrenaica. However, the paucity of the available evidence cannot really justify such detailed reconstructions.

Egyptian references to Libyans concern not geographical locations but groups of people who are regarded as having some form of common, self-recognized identity. This in itself may be a strong indicator that the Egyptians themselves were aware that the Libyans were primarily defined not by where they happened to be living, but by their clan/tribe/family identity. Such a view is supported by other evidence, in both the Egyptian record and the limited archaeological evidence from Libya, which suggests a semi-nomadic pastoral basis for at least the longest-known Libyan groups, the Tjemehu and Tjehenu. These two names of Libyan peoples are the earliest to appear in the Egyptian record; a hieroglyph for 'Tjehenu' is probably to be identified amid trees and associated with herds of animals on the so-called 'Libyan Palette' of the late fourth millennium BC (Quibell 1900). From this early appearance it has been assumed that they lived immediately adjacent to the Nile Valley. Bates placed the Tjemehu immediately to the west of the Nile Valley and at least as far south as the First Cataract (Bates 1914: 41–72). The southern range is supported by the important autobiography of the late Old Kingdom official Harkhuf, inscribed on his tomb at Aswan (Lichtheim 1973: 23–27), which describes his activities as an Egyptian envoy in Lower Nubia, including his involvement in a dispute between the Nubians of Lower Nubia and the Tjemehu. It seems unlikely that groups in Nubia would find reason for conflict with a Tjemehu-land if the latter was primarily on the Mediterranean coast. However, it is possible that a primarily northern Tjemehu were extending their activities southwards along the oasis route and therefore challenging Nubian territorial ambitions. In the reign of Ramesses II, the desert to the west of Lower Nubia was certainly regarded as Tjemehu land; the Viceroy of Nubia, Setau, conscripted local Tjemehu Libyans to work at Wadi es-Sebua in year 44 of that reign (Kitchen 1980: 92–94).

Egyptian texts may sometimes seem vague and contradictory concerning the locations of Tjemehu-land and Tjehenu-land. In the 'Tale of Sinuhe', King Sesostris I campaigns in Tjemehu-land and brings back Tjehenu prisoners. Possibly Tjemehu was used as a general term for Libyans, while Tjehenu had a more precise meaning (O'Connor 1990: 30). The confusion perhaps arises from a modern desire for precision in geography; ancient Egyptian readers may have understood that the Tjemehu were not people who lived in Tjemehu-land , but rather that Tjemehu-land would be wherever the nomadic Tjemehu groups happened to be active, for example for seasonal grazing.

Egyptian contacts with 'new' Libyan groups

Low-intensity contact between Egyptians and Tjemehu/Tjehenu typifies Egypto-Libyan relations from the beginning of the dynastic period to the late eighteenth Dynasty. A second phase may be said to have begun at the end of that period, and is characterized by the attempts of Libyan groups to migrate in large numbers into Egypt itself. This is best attested by the records of the great Libyan war in year 5 of Merenptah, most famously on the so-called 'Israel Stela' and on a companion text at Karnak, and by the textual and pictorial accounts of two major Libyan wars in years 5 and 11 of Ramesses III. In both these reigns 'new' Libyan groups, especially the Meshwesh and Libu, take the lead, although accompanied by other 'older' Libyan groups and smaller new ones of whom little is heard before or after. It is likely that the Meshwesh and Libu were groups which possessed more substantial settlements than the Tjemehu/Tjehenu, probably, at least in part, within Cyrenaica (O'Connor 1990), although this location for the Meshwesh/Libu is far from universally accepted (Spalinger 1979).

Unambiguous evidence for increased contact with the Meshwesh and Libu can be detected from the late eighteenth and early nineteenth Dynasties. The first occurrence of the word Meshwesh is in the reign of Amenophis III, where it is recorded as a source of cattle/cattle-products provided to the royal palace at Malkata (Hayes 1951). Although the name Libu only appears from the reign of Ramesses II, the specific iconographic appearance of Libyans bearing ostrich eggs and enlisted in the paramilitary forces of Akhenaten at Amarna may suggest their identification as Libu (O'Connor 1982: 900). The two new groups, Meshwesh and Libu, apparently offered some greater level of economic opportunity than the 'traditional' Libyan groups, but they also brought a level of threat which became manifest at the end of the eighteenth Dynasty. A fragmentary illustrated papyrus from Amarna seems to depict conflict between Egyptians and Libyans in the reign of Akhenaten or shortly after (Parkinson and Schofield 1993; Schofield and Parkinson 1994). O'Connor (1982: 919) has argued that the Karnak reliefs depicting Seti I's Libyan war should, if the Egyptian records are iconographically consistent, be regarded as being against the Meshwesh. Evidently the Meshwesh/Libu threat began to dominate Egypt's security concerns in the nineteenth and, especially, twentieth Dynasties.

Egyptian accounts of the Merenptah and Ramesses III Libyan wars mention a range of different named Libyan groups. The extent to which these lists are complete or whether on occasion they represent a conflation of different events into a single war has been the subject of much discussion (O'Connor 1990: 38–41). Whatever the sequence of events, they amount to full-scale invasion, the stimuli for which remain unclear. It is unlikely that external pressure from Sea Peoples' invasions of Libya would displace Meshwesh and Libu; the presence of Sea Peoples in the Libyan 'coalition' against Merenptah might be seen as a successful attempt by Libyan rulers to employ Sea Peoples mercenaries, as Ramesses II had already done. The Merenptah war text refers to Libyans "hungry and land-hungry" (Kitchen 1990: 20); this may reflect some climatic crisis in Cyrenaica, or may simply, as Richardson (1999) believes, be a manifestation of local competition over resources between Libyan groups in Marmarica/Cyrenaica spilling over into Egypt itself. Whatever the case, the migratory hordes of Libyans were certainly substantial in number. Although it is difficult to assess the veracity of stated numbers of dead enemies, prisoners and captured herds, estimates derived from a combination of sources suggest a total migrant population in the Merenptah wars of 30,000+ and for the Ramesses III year 11 war of possibly 19,000 Meshwesh (O'Connor 1990: 40–45). It remains unknown what the residual population of Cyrenaica (assuming that to be the most likely Meshwesh/ Libu homeland) would have been at the time of the migrations.

Egyptian royal inscriptions emphasize the defeat of major migratory invasions, but the infiltration of both Delta and Valley continued for the rest of the New Kingdom. By the Third Intermediate Period new political units called "great chiefdoms of the Ma/Meshwesh)" had emerged in the western Delta. The Libyan settlement of the Nile Delta constitutes a third and decisive phase in Egypto-Libyan relations, when Libyan generals became the kings of Egypt. The build-up of pressure can be detected in Egyptian writings. P. Harris records that Ramesses III was forced to build fortifications around a number of major temples in Middle and Upper Egypt to protect them against "Asiatics and Tjehenu", including Asyut, Hermopolis, Thinis, and Abydos. These sites were all on the west bank of the Nile and were therefore particularly vulnerable to sudden raids from the desert.

The third phase of Egypto-Libyan interaction, in the Third Intermediate Period, followed not only infiltration, but also a deliberate settlement of Libyan prisoners of war in the eastern Delta, in cities that were to become emergent political power bases at the end of the New Kingdom, notably Bubastis, home to the twenty-second Dynasty and Tanis, capital of Egypt from the twenty-first to twenty-third Dynasties. The Egyptian policy of settlement must have encouraged the integration of Libyan groups into the power structure of the Delta; the percentage of Libyans or Egyptians of Libyan descent in the population as a whole remains unknown. Libyan leaders chose to retain at least some of their distinct cultural identity, including the title "great chief of the Ma/Meshwesh", and Libyan personal names. The various Egyptian opinions of the new rulers are not made explicit in the surviving sources, and Third Intermediate Period Libyans in Egypt do not have a different appearance; without the titles and names, they would be indistinguishable from Egyptians. Nevertheless, the accession of Libyans to the throne, and the emergence of Libyan "chiefdoms" on delta soil, amount to a political and historical transformation of the order of the Norman Conquest of Saxon England. It is scarcely possible to understand the next thousand years of Egyptian history without some analysis of the origins of Libyan power and the Egyptian reaction to them.

The most substantial piece of evidence for the initial Egyptian response to a perceived threat from new Libyan groups before the war of Merenptah, and for the interaction of Egyptians and Libyans within Libya itself, comes from the Ramesside site of Zawiyet Umm el-Rakham. Under Ramesses II the most spectacular developments in foreign policy terms were certainly in the east: the Kadesh campaign and its aftermath, the foundation of Pi-Ramesses as a capital/military base in the eastern Delta, and the settlement of the Hittite peace treaty (Warburton 2003). In Nubia, the reign was marked by a building programme to rival that in Egypt itself. The site of Zawiyet Umm el-Rakham shows that the west too received its share of Ramesside attention.

Western defences under Ramesses II

The most obvious manifestation of Egyptian concern over a possible Libyan threat before the reign of Merenptah was a programme of fortification in the west undertaken by Ramesses II. The building of large, new exterior walls at western Delta sites such as Tell Abqa'in (Thomas 2000b) was one response to an apparently unprecedented Libyan threat. More radically, a series of military installations were constructed westwards along the Mediterranean coast, representing the farthest extension of Egyptian control along this coast in the dynastic period. The exact nature and extent of this project is uncertain. Whether traces of structures dating to the reign of Ramesses II on Mediterranean sites such as el-Gharbaniyat and el-Alamein can be taken as indications of the presence of full-scale fortresses there is arguable, and a whole range of possible locations for links in a 'chain' of forts running westwards have been suggested (Habachi 1980). However, there was a clear resolve to insert a substantial Egyptian presence deep within the land of the Libyans; the scale of the fort at Zawiyet Umm el-Rakham, located 300 km west of the Delta, makes that assertion evident enough. This substantial Egyptian site on Libyan territory was largely self-sufficient, and it is not necessary to envisage a well-used supply route from Egypt to the fort. Nevertheless, some system of fortified stopping points, perhaps a day's march apart, would presumably have been constructed to facilitate the movement of troops, specialist supplies and, importantly, intelligence reports from Zawiyet Umm el-Rakham to central military command in Egypt. It is also likely that a regular series of coastal installations existed, not only for military reasons (see below).

The specifics of the Egyptian/Libyan relationship during the reign of Ramesses II, at both a macro and more local level, is best seen from the material so far excavated at Zawiyet Umm el-Rakham. The site was discovered by chance in 1948, briefly investigated by Rowe (1948, 1954) and then, in the mid-1950s, partly excavated by Habachi (1980), who revealed its nature as a military installation, with outer defences and stelae naming military officers stationed at the site. His excavation of the temple suggested a substantial and long-term occupation (see Figure 6:2). Excavations since 1994 have confirmed that the fortress-town was surprisingly massive given its location. The core fortress-town has a square (140 x 140 m) mud-brick enclosure wall averaging 5 m thick and probably around 10 m tall and containing 1.6 million bricks,

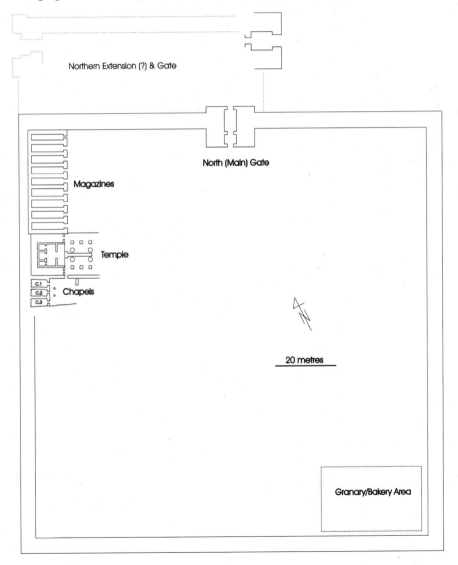

Figure 6:2   Zawiyet Umm el-Rakham (after Habachi 1980: fig. 2).

each of such size (42 x 21 x 16 cm) and weight that a man could comfortably carry only two at a time. The only entrance of any size was a massively towered gateway in the centre of the northern wall. From this gateway area came a series of inscriptions.

The gateway itself had a central stone corridor and lintels for a doorway at each end. Although badly damaged and surviving less than 1.5 m above ancient ground level, the outer (northern) faces of this gate contained inscriptions which seem to indicate at least part of the reason for the existence of this fortress-town. A fragmentary text referring to "fortresses on the hill-country of the Tjemehu" (Snape 1998) supports the argument for a chain of fortresses of which Zawiyet Umm el-Rakham is just one, and it is also the only example of an Egyptian reference to a Libyan region found in the Libyan region itself, rather than simply a text from Egypt describing one of these Libyan regions/peoples as 'somewhere else'. It remains unclear whether the reference to Tjemehu-land is specific or generalized. A series of stone doorjambs and lintels were inscribed with the cartouches of Ramesses II and an accompanying epithet of the king. From the area of the main gate have come a series of displaced doorjambs – presumably part of a now-lost internal arrangement of corridors and rooms within the gate area – which have their counterparts in similar jambs and lintels from the frontage of the magazines. The short texts refer to Ramesses II crushing foreign enemies, and only the Libyan groups Tjemehu, Tjehenu and Libu are mentioned. No Sea Peoples are mentioned, which strongly suggests that Zawiyet Umm el-Rakham and any other forts in a western chain were constructed against a Libyan threat, not a Sea Peoples threat.

The question remains as to how the fortress functioned as an effective military installation for the defence of Egypt against Libyan incursions. It might have been the outermost element in an early warning system to warn against Libyan incursions. Good quality intelligence would have been crucial to the Egyptian military. The specific value of such intelligence is underlined by the threat posed by the intended co-ordinated attack on Egypt by Libyans and Nubians that was forestalled by the prompt action of Egyptian military intelligence in Merenptah's Libyan war. In the aftermath of the defeat of the Libyans, the king received a report from the commander of the "fortress of the west" to say that the enemy chief Meryey had passed by the fort on his way home (Kitchen 1982b: 7). However, the fortress seems disproportionately large to be a mere observation post, even taking into account the military need to maintain such a post in potentially hostile territory. Its ground area exceeds those of New Kingdom forts on the eastern Delta frontier and the great Middle Kingdom fortresses in Nubia. Both the Merenptah and Ramesses III war texts/reliefs make it clear that the attempted penetration of Egypt by the Libyans in the Late New Kingdom concerned a mass migration by whole communities bringing their animals and possessions, not a military strike by an army made up of warriors. Zawiyet Umm el-Rakham, at the edge of the plateau and less than a kilometre from the coast, would be an obvious place in which to site a fortress whose function is to monitor, and perhaps to hinder, such migrations.

The main gate text at Zawiyet Umm el-Rakham mentions the "fortresses on the hill-country of the Tjemehu" and continues with a reference to the "wells/springs which are within them" (Snape 1998). Such wells would have been vital not only for the garrisons, but also for any migratory groups; the construction of the fort around a well would have transferred ownership of the water source from the Libyans to the Egyptians, with economic and military advantage. The extent to which the Libyans would have been able to undertake siege warfare against fortresses like Zawiyet Umm el-Rakham is debatable. It has been argued that the Libyans, though numerous and likely to be able to overwhelm the Egyptian garrisons in a pitched battle, would have been technically unsophisticated when faced with siege warfare. However, it can be argued that Libyans who served in the Egyptian army and then returned to Cyrenaica would have taken with them the detailed knowledge required to reduce even a major Egyptian fortress (O'Connor 1990: 88–89). The fragmentary text of the Karnak version of Merenptah's Libyan war suggests that not only were Libyans capable of capturing Egyptian fortresses/fortified towns, but they may actually have done so (Kitchen 1982: 4). The Merenptah text referring to retreating Libyans bypassing the "fortress of the west" (= Zawiyet Umm el-Rakham?) (Kitchen 1982b: 7) after their defeat suggests that at least some were simply ignored due to the difficulty in their investiture.

A base figure for the garrison size may be suggested by an unpublished stela recovered by Habachi depicting two officers, each a "Standard Bearer", a title used in the New Kingdom for the commander of a "company". The company was the largest unit of the Ramesside army of a relatively standard number of men, perhaps 200 (Faulkner 1953: 45) or 250 (Schulman 1964: 26–32). Since two Standard Bearers are shown together on this stela, it is reasonable to assume that they served as officers at Zawiyet Umm el-Rakham at the same time, with an establishment of some 400–500 men.

The forts on the road called the "Ways of Horus" east of the Nile Delta, a well-used trade route, derived some resources from local suppliers (e.g. ceramics – see Oren 1987), while other important commodities came from either the west (Egyptian Delta) or east (Canaan via Gaza). By contrast, Zawiyet Umm el-Rakham appears to have been at the western end of a tenuous supply chain which was not going anywhere beyond. If an enormous fortress utilizing the most up-to-date military architecture would have been, if adequately manned, more than capable of defending itself against an otherwise numerically overwhelming force of Libyans, access to the agricultural hinterland would, inevitably, have been dependent on local goodwill. The raiding and burning of fields of grain would have been a much more effective weapon available to the local Libyan population than attacking the walls of the fortress themselves, if it can be assumed that the departure of the Egyptian garrison was a desired result.

A distinction should probably be made here between local Libyan groups, Tjehenu or Tjemehu, and incoming/invading Libyan groups among whom the Libu and Meshwesh take a lead. The departure of the Egyptian garrison might not have been desired by the local Libyans, if they had developed a mutually beneficial relationship. In the south-east corner of the fortress was a major provisioning area, the main activities within which seem to have been the preparation of, presumably, official daily 'rations' of bread and beer for the garrison. All stages in the acquisition and production of the basic staples are represented archaeologically, from bread ovens and beer jars, wells dug down to drinkable groundwater, numerous saddle-querns, substantial circular granaries, and flint denticulates, some of which show distinctive sickle-sheen. This indicates that, rather than being supplied from Egypt, the basic food staples were produced by the garrison using local resources. Substantial amounts of agricultural land outside the fortress walls must have been cultivated for grain, harvested and stored in order to feed the garrison throughout the year.

A remarkable discovery was the so-called 'spinning bowls', whose sole function seems to have been the spinning of flax, a fibre that needs to be kept wet while being spun. Importation of raw flax to Marmarica to be turned locally into linen seems improbable. As with the grain, it seems more likely that the Egyptian garrison were also cultivating flax to supply themselves with linen cloth. Such fields of flax within Tjemehu-land might go some way towards explaining the otherwise puzzling reference to linen-wearing Libyans (O'Connor 1990: 63). There is nothing among the domestic material found at Zawiyet Umm el-Rakham that could not have been produced locally. Initial study of animal bones recovered from the site indicates the presence primarily of sheep and goat, while most of the pottery seems to be of a locally produced utilitarian fabric. The presence of significant quantities of ostrich eggshell introduces a more exotic item, obtained locally either by the Egyptian garrison itself or through exchange with local Libyan groups. There is no evidence for any active local Libyan opposition to the presence of the Egyptian garrison. The extent of such symbiosis will, it is hoped, be further elucidated by future work at the site. It is tempting to speculate that the fortresses in Marmarica were created as a response to the threat from 'new' Libyan groups (Meshwesh and Libu) encroaching from further west, while the Egyptian garrisons could rely at least in part on the co-operation of the long established Tjehenu/Tjemehu Libyans.

Excavations in the magazines north of the temple, in the re-excavated chapels south of the temple, and in the food-processing area have yielded a series of imported ceramics, including Levantine transport pottery and coarse-ware 'stirrup jars', the standard features of Late Bronze Age sea trade in the eastern Mediterranean (Snape 2000). These vessels indicate that Zawiyet Umm el-Rakham was another point on the maritime trade circuit that included the Aegean, the Levant and Cyprus. The Ramesside fortress would then have come into existence not only to defend against the Libyans, but also to facilitate foreign trade. On present evidence, such Egyptian coastal installations did not yet exist in the eighteenth Dynasty. Perhaps only the combination of the rising Libyan threat and the maritime trade made the construction of the 'Western Chain' worthwhile. The mid-14th century BC (late eighteenth Dynasty) could have seen the first increase in Meshwesh/Libu activity in the Marmarican region, precipitating the first clashes with the sea traders; this is apparently illustrated by the Amarna papyrus mentioned above, where men with Egyptian and Mycenaean military gear appear in conflict with men in Libyan costume (Parkinson and Schofield 1993; Schofield and Parkinson 1994).

All inscribed material found at Zawiyet Umm el-Rakham dates to the reign of Ramesses II, although it might have continued in use later. In the absence of any evidence from the reigns of Merenptah and Ramesses III, it may be concluded that Zawiyet Umm el-Rakham was abandoned soon after Merenptah's Libyan war, if not before. There is no sign of a destructive sacking of the fortress, but a short-lived squatter occupation seems to have followed, probably immediately, the main

Egyptian occupation of the site. Within a century Libyan leaders and their forces held the balance of power in Egypt itself.

Conclusions

The archaeological revelation of a great western fortress transforms the historical image of the emergence of Libya; it permits a full appreciation of, first, the scale of Ramesside involvement in the region and, second, the relative brevity of that episode. The history of late second millennium Libya and Egypt can now be read in sharper outline, even if the details remain obscure.

In the third and early second millennia, the two lands remained largely separate, with a sedentary Egyptian population and nomadic Libyan peoples called, if Egyptian sources are reliable, Tjemehu and Tjehenu. Something happens after 1400 BC to overturn the stability of life in the western deserts. A major catalyst for change may have been the establishment of the eastern Mediterranean trade circuit in the Late Bronze Age; by the 14th century BC, there were traders and perhaps even metalworking on Bates' Island (White 1990). A trading colony or colonies, permanent or seasonal, might be expected to have altered the balance of local socio-economic and political structures; traders as new economic agents could have stimulated the formation of 'classes' with privileged access to resources within existing ethnic groups, and the presence of traders could have been the magnet to attract groups previously absent from the region. Economic competition was a prime cause of conflict as depicted in the Amarna papyrus (mid-14th century BC), where two partners in eastern Mediterranean trade (Egyptians and Mycenaeans) seem to be ranged against Libyans. At the same time as this military development, new names appear in the Egyptian sources: Meshwesh and Libu. The 13th century Egyptian response is tangible in the construction of the great fortress at Zawiyet Umm el-Rakham. For a century Egyptian inscriptions record the successes of the nineteenth and twentieth Dynasties in repelling attempted migrations of Libyans into Egypt, but, in the twenty-first Dynasty (ca. 1070–945 BC), the Libyans emerge as masters of an Egypt that they have now transformed.

Broad parallels can be drawn between this outline and other histories of developments of peoples. Within ancient Egyptian foreign relations, a similar pattern can be charted in Lower Nubia during the third and early second millennia BC (see above). A mid-third millennium BC Egyptian trading presence, with a colony at Buhen, was extinguished in the late third millennium BC by a unified Nubian state, that had come into existence in part out of that trade. Then, during the early second millennium BC, Nubia was occupied by Egyptian forces, with a series of fortresses to the Second Cataract. These were abandoned by the end of the 17th century BC, when a more formidable Nubian state based at Kerma became more powerful than Egypt. In the eighth century BC, a later Nubian empire, that of Napata, succeeded in conquering Egypt, where its kings ruled for almost 50 years as the twenty-fifth Dynasty. A record of the triumph of the Napatan king Piye is preserved on the monumental stela which he had set up at Gebel Barkal. No such Libyan triumph survives in writing, but the scale and longevity of the Libyan ascendancy far exceed the more visible Nubian success. Only archaeological exploration on Libyan land can reconstruct the symbiosis of Egypt and her western neighbours that led to the violence of colonization from both sides.

Acknowledgments

I wish to mark my gratitude to Daniel Hounsell, Susanna Thomas and Fiona Simpson, all of whom have worked on material from Zawiyet Umm el-Rakham and with whom I have had many stimulating discussions on aspects of the site and its role in Egypto-Libyan relations in the Late Bronze Age.

CHAPTER 7

THE MYSTERY OF THE 'SEA PEOPLES'

Eric H. Cline and David O'Connor

Introduction

For some historians, the story of the Sea Peoples is a dramatic one. In this version of their story, the Sea Peoples came sweeping across the Mediterranean ca. 1200 BC, wreaking havoc and creating chaos, leaving smoking ruins and destroyed cities in their wake. To them is attributed the collapse of the Hittite empire, the downfall of Cyprus, the destruction of Syro-Palestinian and Canaanite petty kingdoms, and perhaps even the demise of the Mycenaeans and the Minoans (Figure 7:1). In this version, in effect, the Sea Peoples are held responsible for the very collapse of Bronze Age civilization in the Aegean and eastern Mediterranean and for bringing on a centuries-long Dark Ages that followed.

This dramatic historical account, based almost entirely on a handful of Egyptian inscriptions, provides an explanation for major change in the archaeological record, where Bronze Age is followed by Early Iron Age, amid a series of massive shifts in centres of political power and major upheavals in a series of key Late Bronze Age centres of population. Yet, in the archaeological record, in the ceramic traditions and architecture of the various civilizations around the eastern Mediterranean, the Sea Peoples remain curiously difficult to identify. As a result, the Sea Peoples continue to perplex and mystify historians and archaeologists of the ancient Mediterranean. Inscriptions celebrating Egyptian kingship in the 13th and especially 12th centuries BC present them as a major and aggressive force in the eastern Mediterranean, upon which they had an impact that to some scholars seems catastrophic. Yet even in this apparently detailed written record, the Sea Peoples, on present evidence, seem to come suddenly from nowhere, cause widespread disruption, take on some of the greatest powers of the region, and equally abruptly disappear from history, save for one or two historic peoples of later times (e.g. Redford 1992: 289–294).

Texts produced for Merenptah and Ramesses III, and large-scale scenes carved on the latter's mortuary temple at Medinet Habu in West Thebes, are the principal sources of information about the Sea Peoples (for these and other texts, see Appendix, pp. 135–138). At the heart of the Sea Peoples mystery is a short text inscribed on the walls of the mortuary temple of pharaoh Ramesses III (ca. 1187–1156 BC). It is laconic but explicit, and awe-inspiring in its implications:

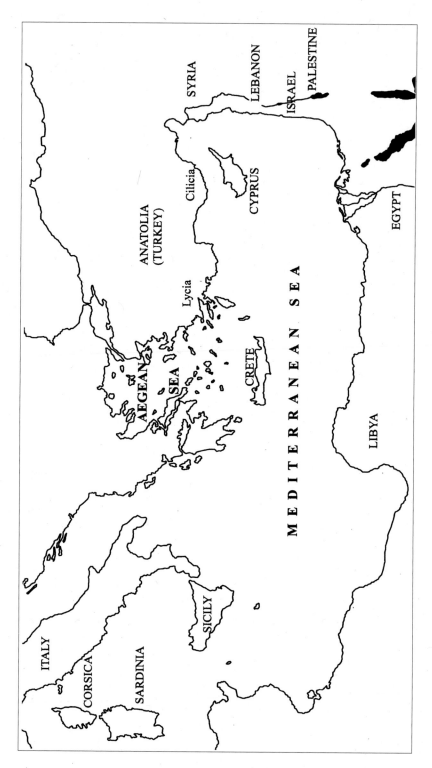

Figure 7:1   Map of the eastern Mediterranean.

The foreign countries made a *conspiracy* in their islands. All at once the lands were removed and scattered in the fray. No land could stand before their arms, from Hatti, Qode, Carchemish, Arzawa, and Alashiya on, being cut off *at [one time]*. A camp [was set up] in one place in Amor. They desolated its people, and its land was like that which has never come into being. They were coming forward toward Egypt, while the flame was prepared before them. Their confederation was the Philistines, Tjekeru, Shekelesh, Denye(n), and Weshesh, lands united. They laid their hands upon the lands as far as the circuit of the earth, their hearts confident and trusting: 'Our plans will succeed!'

(Wilson 1969: 262)

In hieroglyphs, this passage occupies less than three vertical columns of text, but it has generated an enormous amount of scholarly literature and public speculation since it was first published in 1844 (e.g. Oren 2000). The Sea Peoples, as modern historians call them, are the "foreign countries ... in their islands" referred to above, and have long provoked scholarly debate because the most fundamental questions about them still have no definitive answers.

The Egyptian sources provide the names of at least nine Sea Peoples. With these names the problems of the historian begin, for the Egyptian scripts record only consonants, whereas the contemporary cuneiform scripts of Mesopotamia record syllables; from the start, it is difficult to be sure that a name in one script corresponds to a name in another. An additional problem is the lack of a sign regularly denoting the sound 'l' in the hieroglyphic script; various solutions were possible, such as 'n'+'r', or a single 'r', but there are often uncertainties in reading, particularly for foreign names. New Kingdom writing introduces a selection of signs in combinations that appear to echo the syllabic structure of cuneiform, but there remains extensive debate over the vocalization of each name. Here we follow Redford (1992: 251, 248 n. 34, 251, 252, 476, 483, 485, 488); an exception is Lukki, for which see Gardiner (1947: 314, 316). The nine names attested are, in the text of Ramesses III (above), the Peleset, Tjekru, Shekelesh, Danuna or Da'anu, and Washosh, and, in other sources, the Eqwosh, Lukki, Shardana and Teresh. Given the problems in reconstructing the vowels between the consonants in the Egyptian writings, it is not surprising that these names usually have not been identified yet with specific regions, whether those from which the Sea Peoples originated, or those in which they resettled themselves after the events described during the reign of Ramesses III. The Sea Peoples are bound to remain elusive, as long as they exist only as names rendered in Egyptian scripts. Identifications with names in other scripts and languages may help, though they grow more speculative the greater the gap in time; without corroboration in the material unearthed in secure archaeological contexts, it is difficult to know whether a name is even intended to denote a separable 'people' rather than a less distinct part of a larger movement (Kuhrt 1995). The questions remain: who is giving which names, and on what grounds, to whom in this Egyptian reflection of history? Equally mysterious are the cultures and organizations of the Sea Peoples, and the degree of their diversity when at least nine different 'ethnic' names were involved. Although the Sea Peoples are depicted in Egyptian art, and perhaps appear in sources from various parts of the Levant and the Aegean, and although Egyptian texts provide some glimpses of the Sea Peoples' political and military structure, and of their material culture, all in all the data remain meagre.

Perhaps most important of all – because it implies so much about the capabilities and nature of the Sea Peoples – is that, according to the most dramatic reading of the Egyptian writings, they created an aggressive coalition so powerful and effective that it brought about the collapse of some of the most powerful contemporary kingdoms in the Levant and they even aimed to invade Egypt itself.

The extant list of states unable to resist the Sea Peoples appears to include the names of cities and empires regardless of scale, and securely located place names as well as more problematic ones (Figure 7:1 above). Some authors, such as Redford (1992: 251, 473, 480, 484), have ventured the identification of geographical and 'ethnic' locations: Khatte was the imperial state of the Hittites, which had dominated much of Anatolia and Syria but was perhaps weakening at this time. Arzawa and Qode would be large polities on the south Anatolian coast, with Qode extending further. Carchemish lay in modern Syria, while Alashiya probably represented all or much of the large island of Cyprus. Finally, the region in which the Sea Peoples set up their camp and which was devastated as a result was Amor, generally identified as the better attested Amurru (Redford 1992: 474), an extensive coastal region straddling modern Syria and Lebanon. Moreover, not only did the Sea Peoples advance on Egypt, by land and sea, but, in the reign of Ramesses III, the Egyptians had to fight two great battles to halt the onslaught. According to the inscriptions and depictions in the temple to his cult at Medinet Habu, one took place, on land, in Djahy (roughly, modern Israel and Palestine); the other in what the Egyptians call 'the mouths of the river', by which term some area along Egypt's Mediterranean coast is apparently meant.

Recent scholars have drawn very different opinions from the same basic data. Redford (2000: 13) and many others concluded that both battles actually took place, and Redford even hypothesizes where: the land and sea battles may have taken place within sight of each other just beyond the mouth of the Pelusiac branch (Redford 2000: 13) of the Nile. Drews (2000) accepts the sea or river mouth battle, but doubts that the land battle occurred. Cifola (1988) suggests that there were no large-scale battles, but instead many lesser conflicts between Egypt and the Sea Peoples extending over a long period of time, conflicts which the Egyptian sources misleadingly telescope together. And, in any event – whatever the specific details of the Sea Peoples' invasion of the eastern Mediterranean might have been – it still remains to be shown that, as Redford (1992: 243–244) argues, "the movement of the Sea Peoples ... changed the face of the ancient world more than any other single event before the time of Alexander the Great".

Various Sea Peoples interacted with Egypt and other lands 26 years before Ramesses III clashed with the Sea Peoples in his eighth regnal year (ca. 1180 BC). Monumental inscriptions from the reign of King Merenptah record that in his fifth regnal year (ca. 1209 BC) Egypt's western Delta was invaded by a Libu (Libyan) army, which had originated in, probably, the then Libyan homeland of Cyrenaica (O'Connor 1990: 37–38; Snape Chapter 6, this volume). The Libyan forces were accompanied by contingents of Sea Peoples, namely the Eqwosh, Teresh, Lukki, Shardana and Shekelesh, as allies or mercenaries; the combined attack by Libyans and Sea Peoples was defeated (Breasted [1906] 2001: 238–264; Iskander 2002). This prelude to the struggles under Ramesses III broadens the timeframe and number of 'peoples' involved, but leaves the principal questions unsolved: namely who the Sea Peoples were, where they had come from, and where they finally settled.

Unified society or ad-hoc alliance?

The primary Egyptian sources on the Sea Peoples date to the reigns of Merenptah and Ramesses III, and include a wall inscription, a stela and two inscribed columns, all celebrating King Merenptah's victory over the Libyans and the Sea Peoples. The wall inscription occurs at Karnak temple (Breasted [1906] 2001, 3: 241–252); the stela is from Kom el Ahmar or ancient Athribis (Breasted [1906] 2001, 3: 253–256); one column is in Cairo Museum (Breasted [1906] 2001, 3: 252–253; Edel 1961: 101–103); and the other is at Heliopolis (Bakry 1973). The Ramesses III sources comprise a series of large scenes along the external north face of his mortuary temple at Medinet Habu (western Thebes) and with a long text accompanying a scene on the west wall of that temple's first court (*Medinet Habu* I 1930: pls. 29–44, 46). In addition, Ramesses' defeat of the Sea Peoples is briefly described in P. Harris, a document actually prepared during his successor's reign (Breasted [1906] 2001, 4: 201). Other textual references to the Sea Peoples are provided in the Appendix.

Together, the texts of Merenptah and Ramesses III provide all known names for specific Sea Peoples, but the overlap between the two seems limited. The inscriptions from the reign of Merenptah refer to the Eqwosh, Teresh, Lukki, Shardana and Shekelesh; Ramesses III's list comprises Shekelesh, Peleset, Tjekru, Danuna and Washosh (cf. Breasted [1906] 2001, 3: 239–256 with Edgerton and Wilson 1936: 30, 35, 45, 47–48, 53, 130–131). P. Harris provides an almost identical list to that of Medinet Habu (Breasted [1906] 2001, 4: 201) but substitutes Shardana for Shekelesh, and, being less close in time to the actual events, may offer a less accurate record. In addition, Sandars (1985: 112) notes that although the Teresh are not listed at Medinet Habu by Ramesses III as part of the Sea Peoples whom he defeated, a captive chief of the Teresh is shown among his prisoners in the pictorial reliefs there, and that a later stela of Ramesses III mentions the Teresh in the same breath as the Peleset.

In Merenptah's texts, the Shardana, Shekelesh and Eqwosh are described as "foreign lands of the sea" (Breasted [1906] 2001, 3: 249, 255). The Teresh and Lukki are listed alongside the others, and all five are described collectively as northerners who came from every land (Breasted [1906] 2001, 3: 241); since the relevant texts are very fragmentary, the Teresh and Lukki too may have been identified as "of the sea". The texts of Ramesses III specifically identify all five peoples named as foreign countries (who) made a conspiracy in their isles (Edgerton and Wilson 1936: 53) and elsewhere refer to them generally as the northern countries who were in their isles (Edgerton and Wilson 1936: 41) and as the countries who came from their land in the isles in the midst of the sea (Edgerton and Wilson 1936: 42). The translation of the relevant word (*iw*) as isle or island is accepted by most Egyptologists (Faulkner 1999, 12; Gardiner 1947: 281; Lesko and Lesko 1982: 21). P. Harris also refers to the Danuna "in their isles", and the Shardana (= Shekelesh?) and Washosh "of the sea" (Breasted [1906] 2001, 4: 201).

The Lukki

The Lukki (Egyptian *Lk*) are well known from numerous additional inscriptions, Hittite as well as Egyptian; possibly because they were notorious pirates. Most scholars see the Lukki as originating in Anatolia. Although there is some discussion as to where exactly in Anatolia they came from, most agree that it was probably south-western Anatolia, in the area later known as Lycia and Caria. They are believed to have raided Cyprus upon occasion, as recorded in the Amarna Letters of the mid-14th century BC, and to have fought on the side of the Hittites against the Egyptians at the Battle of Kadesh ca. 1286 BC (Warburton 2003).

Very unfortunately, evidence for the Lukki in Anatolia is purely textual; no cultural remains have yet been definitely identified as being able to identify such a 'Lukki group' (Bryce 1979, 1986: 1–41, 1992: 55–57; Sandars 1985: 37, 107).

The Shardana

The Shardana (Egyptian *šrdn*) appear already in the Amarna Letters of the mid-14th century BC, where they are found serving as part of an Egyptian garrison at Byblos (Moran 1992: 201–202). They were mercenaries and, as such, fought both for and against Egypt in various conflicts during the latter part of the Late Bronze Age. Sandars (1985: 50, 106) notes in particular a fragmentary inscription of Ramesses II from Tanis which reads: "Shardana, rebellious of heart ... [and their] battleships in the midst of the sea" and which claims that Ramesses "destroyed [the] warriors of the Great Green [i.e. the Mediterranean], and lower Egypt spends the night sleeping peacefully" (Gardiner 1947, 1: 195). None of the texts give a homeland for the Shardana. In the Egyptian pictorial reliefs, they are shown wearing horned helmets and frequently carrying round shields, but these facts are of little help in ascertaining their origin (Sandars 1985: 106–107). From the similarity between the words 'Shardana' and 'Sardinia', scholars frequently suggest that the Shardana came from there. On the other hand, it is equally possible that this group eventually settled in Sardinia after their defeat at the hands of the Egyptians and only then gave their name to this island, as Maspéro and others have suggested (see detailed discussion of the various hypotheses in Drews 1992: 21–22, 1993: 53–61). For the time being such equations between similar-sounding names must be treated with the greatest caution in the absence of any corroboratory evidence.

In P. Harris, the deceased Ramesses III declares that the Shardana (and the Washosh) were brought as captives to Egypt, that he "settled them in strongholds bound in my name", and that he "taxed them all, in clothing and grain from the store-houses and granaries each year" (or that he 'supplied them with clothing and grain', following the interpretation by Grandet 1994, 2: 243 n. 920) (after Breasted [1906] 2001, 4: 201; Sandars 1985: 133). This would seem to indicate that the Shardana had been settled somewhere close enough to be taxed or supplied every year, and so an area no further away than Canaan. This location may be further substantiated by the Onomasticon of Amenemope, a composition dating to ca. 1100 BC, which lists the Shardana among the Sea Peoples who were settled on the coast there (Gardiner 1947, 1: 194–199; Knapp 1992: 124; Sandars 1985: 133). If this is the case, then perhaps the Shardana came originally from Sardinia and were eventually settled in coastal Canaan. However, the Shardana are listed – in P. Wilbour – as living in Middle Egypt during the time of Ramesses V, which would suggest that at least some of them were settled in Egypt (Leahy 2001: 259). It is also significant that the Shardana are the only foreign people mentioned among the subjects of the deceased king Ramesses III, in his address to his subjects in P. Harris, where they are listed among the military contingents (column 75, line 1; Grandet 1994, 1: 335).

Scholars often call attention to the ruins found on the island of Sardinia – in particular the Bronze Age circular stone structures known as *nuraghi* whose function is still debated – and hypothesize about their relationship to the Shardana (e.g. Knapp 1992: 119–122, 124–125; Vagnetti 2000). Most recently, Zertal (2001) claims that Iron Age El-Ahwat in Israel has stone architectural features which appear similar to those found on Sardinia. He hypothesizes that El-Ahwat may have been one of the villages/ towns/cities established by the Shardana when they were settled in Canaan by the Egyptians. So far, however, there is no identifiable Shardana pottery found at this or any other site in the region, and the interpretation of the architecture at El-Ahwat remains open to question.

The Teresh

The Teresh (Egyptian *Trš*) do not feature in Egyptian texts before the time of Merenptah, when they appear in both his Great Karnak Inscription and on the Athribis (Kom el Ahmar) stela. It has been suggested that the Taruisha mentioned in Hittite texts and probably located in north-western Anatolia (i.e. Troy) are to be linked with the Teresh, but this is highly speculative. Other suggestions link the Teresh with the Greek Tyrsenoi and the Tyrrhenians of central western Anatolia mentioned much later by Herodotus. Herodotus claimed that the Tyrrhenians migrated from central western Anatolia to central Italy, where they found later fame as the Etruscans (Drews 1992; Sandars 1985: 111–112). On the Teresh, it has recently been proposed (Drews 2000: 177) that they are to be identified with Tyrsenia, said to be the original Greek name for Italy. This still leaves unanswered the question of whether the Teresh would have come from Italy or would have gone there after being defeated by the Egyptians. It remains difficult to assess such connections, given the gap of centuries between alleged event and written source. The link seems possible, if still speculative, only in conjunction with the other alleged western Mediterranean associations of Sea Peoples (see above, on the Shardana, and below on the Shekelesh).

Amidst all these hypotheses, the reality remains that there is no archaeological evidence to support any of the above identifications, and there are, as yet, no archaeological remains which can be shown to be distinctively Tereshian.

The Shekelesh

The Shekelesh (Egyptian *šklš*) may be the "Sikilayu who live in ships" mentioned in a letter sent by the Hittite king to the last king of Ugarit. In Egyptian texts, the Shekelesh first appear in Merenptah's Sea Peoples inscriptions (Drews 2000: 178–180; Sandars 1985: 112). Based on the similarity between the words 'Shekelesh' and 'Sicily' – but without any supportive archaeological evidence – scholars have frequently suggested that the Shekelesh came from the island of Sicily. However, linguistically speaking, it is equally possible that this group settled in Sicily only after their defeat at the hands of the Egyptians and only then gave their name to this island. As Sandars (1985: 112–113) notes, the colonizing Greeks of the eighth century BC found people known as the Sikels already living on this island whom they believed had migrated to the island from southern Italy after the Trojan War. Instead of migrating to the island from southern Italy, however, they may have come all the way across from the final battlegrounds in the Egyptian Delta.

It is still quite conceivable that there was in fact no connection at all between the Shekelesh and Sicily. Very unfortunately, as a result of the paucity of reliable archaeological evidence, the significance for so-called Sikil remains – including pottery and incised cow scapulas possibly used for divination and/or musical instruments (Stern 1994, 1998, 2000) – at a number of sites located south of Mount Carmel in modern Israel, remains unclear, with detailed parallels not specified.

Other sites on the Carmel coast which have yielded possible Sikil remains include Tel Zeror and Ein Hagit, as well as the famous engravings of ships found on the rocks of the Carmel ridge, which could be representations of the ships of the Sea Peoples (Raban and Stieglitz 1991: 37–38, 41–42).

The Eqwosh/Akawasha

The Eqwosh (Egyptian *Ikwš*; also called the Akawasha) are a little-known group who are mentioned only in Merenptah's Sea Peoples inscriptions. It has often been claimed that the Eqwosh might be the Egyptian attempt to reproduce the word *Achaioi* – that is to say, the Achaeans, i.e. Homer's Mycenaeans, coming from mainland Greece, Crete, and the Cycladic islands of the Bronze Age Aegean (see Drews 2000: 181–182). A possible linguistic link with the Ahhiyawa mentioned in Hittite texts has also been suggested, but the identification of Ahhiyawa with the Achaeans/Mycenaeans is itself a hotly contested matter (Niemeier 1998).

As for most of the other Sea Peoples, there are no distinctive archaeological remains attributable specifically to the Eqwosh or Akawasha.

The Tjekru

The Tjekru (Egyptian *Tkr*) are elusive in Egyptian and other texts prior to the time of Ramesses III, but are found later in the story of Wenamun, details of which may date to ca. 1100 BC (Loprieno Chapter 3, this volume; Pritchard 1969: 25–29). As Sandars (1985: 158, 170) has noted, the Tjekru have long been suggested to have connections with the Teucri of the Troad, and with the Greek Teucer, the legendary founder of Salamis in Cyprus after the Trojan War, but this does not help in determining their origins, for the chronology of these connections is unclear, if the connections really did indeed exist at all.

The Onomasticon of Amenemope, perhaps composed ca. 1100 BC, provides a nugget of information by listing the Tjekru in between the Shardana and the Philistines. If the details found in the story of Wenamun and the Onomasticon of Amenemope are correct, then perhaps the Tjekru eventually settled (or were forcibly settled) on the coast of Canaan near the Sharon Plain following their defeat by Ramesses III. Indeed, one potentially revealing line in the story of Wenamun describes his travails in a harbour town in Syria-Palestine, beginning: "I reached Dor, a town of the Tjekru ..." (Dothan 1982: 4–5; Gardiner 1947: 199–200; Niemeier 1998: 47; Pritchard

1969: 26). Dor is precisely the coastal town where Stern excavated remains that he interpreted as material culture of the 'Sea Peoples' (see above, under Shekelesh). Stern refers to the Sea Peoples at Dor as Sikils rather than Tjekru, suggesting that the final letter should be vocalized as an 'l' rather than as an 'r' – i.e. that the name should be seen as *Tjekel* rather than *Tjekru* – this providing a linguistic connection to Sicily and the Sikels. *Tjekel* would then be an alternate name for the Shekelesh. Indeed, it has been suggested that the Shekelesh of Merenptah's inscriptions and the *Tjekel* of Ramesses III's inscriptions form one and the same group, just as Merenptah's Eqwosh and Ramesses III's Danuna may be two names for the same group (Drews 2000: 78–180, citing earlier bibliography including Edel 1984). If this is correct, then Sicily may have been the original source of, and coastal Canaan a final destination for, the Tjekru/Tjekel/Shekelesh/Sikels. However, the names Tjeker and Shekelesh appear side by side, for example in the Ramesses III inscription quoted above, and this may be thought to negate attempts to equate the two. Nevertheless, the identification of Dor as a Tjeker town in the 'Tale of Wenamun' – i.e. after the end of the New Kingdom/Bronze Age – provides one answer to the question of where at least some of the Sea Peoples settled (and compare the case of the Peleset, below).

The Danuna

It has long been suggested that the Danuna (Egyptian *Dnjn*) are to be equated with the land of Danuna. If so, then they – or rather their land – are mentioned in Hittite letters and in the Amarna Letters as being located in south-eastern Turkey in the Adana region of Cilicia, to the north of the city of Ugarit (Moran 1992: 238–239). It has also been frequently suggested that the Danuna should be equated with Homer's Danaans or Danaoi, his alternate name for the Achaeans. Currently, nothing is agreed, although those who equate the Danuna with the Danaans/Danaoi suggest that they would have come from the Aegean region, while those who equate them with the land of Danuna suggest that they would have either come from, or settled in, the coastal region of south-eastern Turkey or northern Syria.

Most recently, Drews has noted the similarity between the *Dnjn* of the Sea Peoples inscriptions and the *ti-nꜣ-ii* (vocalized as *Tanaja*) of the earlier eighteenth Dynasty inscriptions, primarily of Tuthmosis III and Amenophis III. Tanaja has been identified as the expression in Egyptian texts for the Mycenaeans of Bronze Age mainland Greece. He suggests that Danuna and Tanaja are two words for the same place and people and that the Danuna should be equated with Homer's Danaans/Danaoi rather than with the Hittite land of Danuna. He also observes that the Danuna (= Tanaja/Danaoi?) of Ramesses III's Sea Peoples inscriptions have apparently taken the place of the earlier Eqwosh (= Achaoi/Achaeans?) of Merenptah's Sea Peoples inscriptions (Drews 2000: 181–182). It is possible that the Danuna had an Aegean origin, with a final settlement in the coastal region of south-eastern Turkey (i.e. the area of Adana in Cilicia).

Another suggestion relates the Danuna to the biblical tribe of Dan, which would suggest that Sea Peoples also ultimately re-settled or were settled by the Egyptians in Canaan. If so, some of the archaeological remains uncovered by the excavations at the site of Tell Dan in northern Israel may be pertinent (Machinist 2000: 67; Raban and Stieglitz 1991: 41; Sandars 1985: 162–164; Yadin 1968: 9–23).

The Peleset

The Peleset (Egyptian *Prst/Plst*) are almost universally identified with the Philistines of the Bible (Drews 1998: 50–61; Machinist 2000; Sandars 1985: 164–166). The Peleset first appear in Egyptian texts under Ramesses III. There is no indication as to their origin, although they were 'islanders' (see above). Suggestions have ranged from Crete to Arzawa in Anatolia to Canaan, but there is as yet no clear evidence to resolve the question (Drews 1993: 54–72, 1998: 53–57; Niemeier 1998: 47).

However, if the Peleset really are synonymous with the Philistines, then we know where they ended up – for the Bible talks at great length about the Philistine cities in Canaan. We know this from other sources as well; for instance, the Onomasticon of Amenemope, perhaps composed ca. 1100 BC, lists the Peleset among the defeated Sea Peoples who re-settled or were settled by the Egyptians on the coast of Canaan (Drews 1998: 50; Gardiner 1947: 200–205; Knapp 1992: 124). In addition, the archaeological remains of the Philistines are numerous, primarily pottery, but also including full-blown architecture and other material goods from sites such as Tell Qasile, Tell Miqne/Ekron, Ashdod, and Ashkelon in Israel. Perhaps most significant in this context is the identification of so-called Mycenaean Late Helladic IIIC: 1b Aegean-inspired pottery which seems to be locally made in Syro-Palestine – and the question arises as to whether Philistine pottery can be described as a degenerate form of Mycenaean pottery and used to support a hypothesis that at least some of the Philistines originated in the Aegean (Brug 1985; Dothan 1982, 1995, 1998, 2000; Dothan and Dothan 1992; Finkelstein 2000; Killebrew 2000; Kling 2000; Mazar 2000; Oren 2000). As Killebrew (1998: 166) notes:

> Thus, in my opinion, the appearance of large quantities of Aegean-inspired locally-produced Mycenaean IIIC: 1b and its related wares at a number of sites in Syria-Palestine is a classic case study in material culture of the incursion of new peoples settling at several centers on the southern coastal plain of Canaan at the close of the Bronze Age. Though the material culture has its tradition in the Aegean, these peoples, termed Philistines in the biblical account, probably originated on Cyprus, Rhodes, and/or in southern Anatolia.

The Washosh

In contrast to the Peleset/Philistines, "of the shadowy Washosh", Sandars (1985: 158) once said, "virtually nothing is known, unless they had any connection with the 'Wilusa' (Wilusiya) of Hittite writings, that may have lain in south-western Anatolia, or with 'Ilios' (Troy) in the north-west". We may know nothing about the origins of the Washosh, but we can make an educated guess as to where some ended up. In P. Harris, Ramesses III says that the Washosh (and the Shardana) were "brought as captives to Egypt", that he "settled them in strongholds bound in my name", and that he "taxed them all, in clothing and grain from the store-houses and granaries each year" (Breasted [1906] 2001, 4: 201; for a recent alternative interpretation as 'supplied' rather than 'taxed', see above under Shardana). This would seem to indicate that at least some of the Washosh had been settled in Egypt itself. However, there is as yet no identifiable archaeological material which can be associated with them.

The Sea Peoples in general

According to the Egyptian sources, the Shekelesh, Peleset, Tjekru, Danuna and Washosh were all islanders, each living on land entirely surrounded by water, and the Shardana and Eqwosh occupied territories which, at the least, had a coast fronting the sea. The status of the Teresh and Lukki, in these regards, remains uncertain, although it is generally accepted that the Lukki are to be associated with the south-western coast of Anatolia, as the area is later known as Lycia. Moreover, again according to the Egyptian texts, the specific Sea Peoples were all northerners relative to Egypt, while those named in Ramesses III's texts apparently originated west of central Anatolia and Cilicia, to judge from the geographical sequence of the kingdoms which they attacked.

From this we must infer that the five Sea Peoples who collaborated in the Libyan attack on Merenptah's Egypt must have sailed to Libya to do so, because the invasion originated in the Libyan homeland – in all probability Cyrenaica (O'Connor 1990: 37–38). The Sea Peoples in question could not have traversed the Egyptian Delta and the land route (controlled by Egyptian fortresses) to Cyrenaica. As for the rather different set of Sea Peoples involved in the invasion of Egypt in the time of Ramesses III, the Egyptian texts state they came by sea (Edgerton and Wilson 1936: 30, 55) but also, more surprisingly, by land (Edgerton and Wilson 1936: 30, 55). Moreover, the contingent moving by land was apparently a very big one, for Ramesses seems to have organized a large military force to deal with it (Edgerton and Wilson 1936: 35–39) and earlier the Sea Peoples had set up a substantial camp, "in one place" (Edgerton and Wilson 1936: 53), from which base they supposedly devastated the entire and extensive land of Amor or Amurru.

The Sea Peoples' advance by land may have been due to two factors, insofar as the Egyptian evidence is concerned. First, unlike the Sea Peoples involved in invading Merenptah's Egypt, those identified under Ramesses III were accompanied by women and children and presumably possessions, conveyed in heavy-looking wooden carts drawn by slow- moving zebu-oxen, a piece of pictorial evidence omitted from the accompanying inscriptions (*Medinet Habu* I: pl. 32; but see now also discussion *contra* in Drews 2000). Apparently, the vessels of the Sea Peoples were not suitable for these purposes. Second, while the polities attacked by the Sea Peoples all had shipping, capable to some degree of opposing the seaborne advance of the former, they also had extensive inland territories more effectively overcome or reduced by forces moving by land.

Since the land contingent was organized specifically by peoples all identified as "islanders", a very considerable organizational effort is implied. Indeed, there is archaeological evidence for destructions at numerous sites – both inland and coastal – in the Aegean, Anatolia, Cyprus, and Syria-Palestine, all occurring within a 50-year period from ca. 1225–1175 BC. The question which has been debated for the past century or more is whether the Sea Peoples caused all of these destructions or if, in fact, they are even all related – various alternate theories proposed during the past century have included earthquakes, drought, famine, internal rebellions, and systems-collapse (Drews 1993; Nur and Cline 2000; Stiebing 2001; also Betancourt

2000; Sandars 1985: 83). However, that the Sea Peoples' route to Egypt went via Ugarit in North Syria seems beyond question, if a letter found at that site is any indication:

> Say to the king of Alashiya [Cyprus], my father: Thus says the king of Ugarit, your son: My father, now the ships of the enemy have been coming. They have been setting fire to my cities and have done harm to the land. Doesn't my father know that all of my infantry and [chariotry] are stationed in Khatte, and that all of my ships are stationed in the land of Lukki? They haven't arrived back yet, so the land is thus prostrate. May my father be aware of this matter. Now the seven ships of the enemy which have been coming have done harm to us. Now if other ships of the enemy turn up, send me a report somehow(?) so that I will know.
>
> (RS 20.238 – *Ugaritica* 5.24 (trans. Beckman 1996: 7); Sandars 1985: 142–143; Schaeffer 1968: 87–89)

However, the Egyptian sources also raise some significant geographical issues. First, why are the two lists of Sea Peoples (Merenptah's and Ramesses III's) so different in composition? This raises the possibility that the two sets of peoples were geographically remote from each other, e.g. perhaps along the eastern and western sides of the Aegean respectively, or perhaps in one case west of the Aegean altogether. The two sets have in common only the Shekelesh for certain, though possibly also the Shardana and the Teresh. Possibly, quite different factors were at work, involving political and other relations amongst the various Sea Peoples rather than their geographical disposition. However, given our still very imperfect understanding of the Sea Peoples, any reasonable possibility suggested by the Egyptian sources needs to be kept in play until definitive evidence to the contrary emerges.

In some instances the Egyptian sources display a selectivity that may be significant, but whether in relationship to the Sea Peoples themselves, or to specific compositional needs (written or pictorial) is debatable. For example, two of Merenptah's documents highlight only one of the several Sea Peoples accompanying the Libyans, noting that the Libyan leader mobilized the Shekelesh and "every foreign country involved" (Edel 1961; also Bakry 1973), i.e. the other Sea Peoples mentioned on the other stelae of Merenptah. Presumably, the compression was for reasons of space, but it is not known why the Shekelesh were chosen as the specific representative of the entire group. Only the Shekelesh may have been involved in both of the initiatives against Egypt: perhaps there was something especially distinctive about them.

A similar kind of selectivity is seen in the texts of Ramesses III. The full list of the relevant Sea Peoples is provided only twice, and in different texts (Edgerton and Wilson 1936: 53, 131); all five are (except for perhaps substituting Shardana for Shekelesh) also listed in P. Harris (Breasted [1906] 2001, 4: 201). Elsewhere in the Medinet Habu texts, when limited space or a desired compositional emphasis required that not all the Sea Peoples be listed, it is typically the Tjekru and the Peleset who are named.

For example, in a scene showing prisoners from a fifth year campaign against Libyans and from the 8th year conflict with the Sea Peoples being presented to Amun-Ra, the compositional structure allowed only two registers. One appropriately depicts Libu, but the other (Figure 7:2) only the great fallen ones of Tjekru, as if they are more significant than the other Sea Peoples, or – perhaps the same thing – can stand for all the others (Edgerton and Wilson 1936: 44–46). Moreover, in a text primarily describing the 5th year Libyan campaign, the essentials of conflict with the Sea Peoples are reported laconically, but while the northern countries are specified, only the Tjekru and Peleset are named, as if the two are more significant than the others (Edgerton and Wilson 1936: 30).

The Peleset are singled out in other ways. In an elaborate depiction of arms being issued, for both the 5th year (Libyan) and 8th year (Sea Peoples) campaigns, Tjemehu (an archaic term for Libya) stands for the former, and the Peleset for the latter, as if somehow representative of the entire confederation of Sea Peoples (Edgerton and Wilson 1936: 35). Moreover, in the especially important and large-scale representation of the king presenting Sea Peoples prisoners to Amun-Ra (west wall, first court) the text epitomizes his defeat of the Sea Peoples by referring only to the Peleset, Danuna and Shekelesh, while the three registers of prisoners are labelled, from top to bottom, as leaders of every country (i.e. implicitly, all the Sea Peoples?), the Danuna and the Peleset (Edgerton and Wilson 1936: 47–48). Finally, the Peleset are once described as "hidden in their towns" (Egyptian *dmiw*; Edgerton and Wilson 1936: 35).[1] Towns are not otherwise associated with Sea Peoples in Egyptian sources.

Much of the information concerning the Tjekru and the Peleset may be due to variations in usage, or misused conventional terms. However, given the paucity of

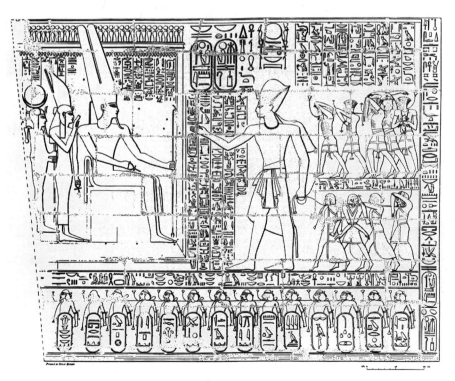

Figure 7:2 The presentation of Tjekru Sea Peoples and Libyan prisoners to the god Amun-Ra; Medinet Habu (Oriental Institute, Chicago).

evidence about Sea Peoples the possibility that more was implied should not be overlooked.

Finally, the historicity of the textual records, both of Merenptah and Ramesses III, is an important issue. First, are the historical records of Ramesses III's reign, as displayed at Medinet Habu, actually those of Merenptah, copied from his nearby, and now largely destroyed, mortuary temple? The case has been made (Lesko 1992), but is not supported by most scholars. In any event, it would simply push the question of the historicity of the texts about the Sea Peoples back into an earlier reign, without changing the essentials.

The second, more important point is the common suggestion that the demands of temple symbolism, royal ideology and, more crudely, propaganda mean that the records of Ramesses III are not to be taken at face value. On the same grounds, the historical narratives describing Merenptah's contacts with Libyans and Sea Peoples should be equally suspect. An extreme example of this scepticism is provided by Cifola (1988), who argued that the Sea Peoples in Ramesses III's time were not a coherent body, or a confederation; and that the process of their migration into the eastern Mediterranean was not unitary, but involved different groups at different times. This resulted in many small-scale clashes between Egyptians and Sea Peoples, which the Egyptians transformed into two great, but nonexistent, battles in the Medinet Habu records.

However, the explicit Egyptian statements must be accepted at face value, at least for now. Under Merenptah, some Sea Peoples joined Libyans in a substantial, if abortive invasion of the western Egyptian Delta. Relatively soon after, another group of Sea Peoples created an effective combined military and migratory force that moved along the southern coast of Anatolia, and then down along the Levantine coast, and coastal lands. The Egyptian sources appear to claim that the kingdoms encountered *en route* were unable to resist; and the process was relatively rapid, even if it involved a few years, rather than a few months. Finally, the Sea Peoples offered a very substantial threat to Egypt and, as the attack on the Nile mouths indicates, intended to penetrate and settle in Egypt. The Egyptians successfully prevented this, but did settle their many Sea Peoples prisoners in royal strongholds in Egypt and perhaps elsewhere (Breasted [1906] 2001: 201), in part as a military resource. In fact, at Medinet Habu, Sea Peoples are shown fighting on the Egyptian side in the battles against the Libyans, Nubians (Figure 7:3) and others, although in theory these events sometimes antedate the eighth year victories.

For example, Sea Peoples with feathered headdresses appear fighting on the Egyptians' side against Nubians (*Medinet Habu* I: pl. 8) and, with horned helmets, in attacks on two cities in the Levant (*Medinet Habu* II: pls. 88, 94). All these events are undated, and may be unhistorical, included in the decorative programme to fill out its cosmographic coverage. However, in the Egyptian campaign against Libyans in the fifth regnal year of Ramesses III (i.e. three years before the conflict with the Sea Peoples), several relevant scenes show Sea Peoples in both feathered headdresses and horned helmets fighting on the side of the Egyptians (*Medinet Habu* I: pls. 17, 18, 19, 24). This could have been anachronism, since the scenes were probably designed and carved after the eighth regnal year; or the Egyptian army might have included Sea Peoples before Ramesses III's conflict with the Sea Peoples. They could have been

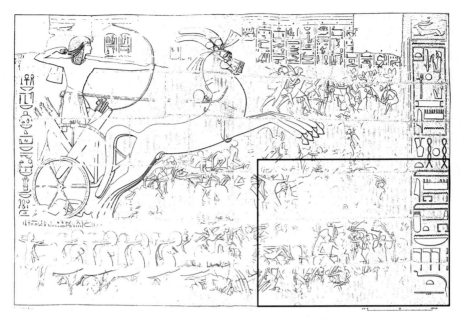

Figure 7:3   Ramesses III slaughtering Nubians; Sea Peoples are included in the Egyptian army.
Lower right detail shown below; Medinet Habu (Oriental Institute, Chicago).

Sea Peoples employed in the Egyptian army.

former prisoners of war of King Merenptah captured only 11 years before. This likelihood is reinforced by the fact that Ramesses III's battles with the Sea Peoples themselves included Sea Peoples (horned helmets only) fighting on the Egyptian side (*Medinet Habu* I: pls. 30, 35, 32)! Finally, in the battle against Libyans in the eleventh regnal year of Ramesses III, Sea Peoples, wearing both feathered headdresses and horned helmets, join the Egyptians in the conflict (*Medinet Habu* II: pl. 71).

In Djahy, however, Egypt – while victorious in battle – was less successful in stemming or controlling Sea Peoples' settlement in the area. No surviving record after Ramesses III refers to the Danuna, Shekelesh or Washosh (this last people in fact is attested only at Medinet Habu) but the case is quite different as regards Tjekru and Peleset. After Ramesses III, Egypt's domination of the area now occupied by Lebanon and Israel seems to have gradually but unceasingly contracted (Weinstein 1981: 22–23) while the demographic and cultural composition of the region changed considerably. Sea Peoples were part of this change. As discussed above, an Egyptian text of ca. 1100 BC, less than a century after Ramesses III's victory, shows that Shardana, Tjekru and Peleset were settled in the coastal regions of Canaan (Redford 1992: 292). The Peleset went on to become the Philistine kingdoms of the Bible (Redford 1992: 298 ff), and a fictional, but historically based description of an Egyptian envoy's adventures in ca. 1082 BC reveals that Dor (on the coast of modern Israel) was a Tjekru town (see above, Tjekru). We have no clear indication as to where the defeated remnants of the Eqwosh, Danuna, Teresh, Washosh, and the Lukki settled, but the Lukki may well have simply made their way back home to south-western Anatolia, while the Danuna may conceivably have settled in the biblical area of Dan – what is now northern Israel.

Pictures worth a thousand words?

So far, this discussion has been based mainly on Egyptian textual sources: but at Medinet Habu these are complemented by a rich pictorial record concerning the Sea Peoples.

The pictorial record (Figure 7:4) comprises several large-scale scenes (complemented by relatively short texts) extending along the external face of the north side of the mortuary temple of Ramesses III. Usually, the scenes are demarcated from each other by vertical dividers of text. The subject matter comprises, from west to east, the equipping of the Egyptian army; its march to or into Djahy; the land battle against the Sea Peoples; a royal lion hunt; the battle against the Sea Peoples' ships in the river mouths; and – in this one instance not divided off from the preceding scene – the

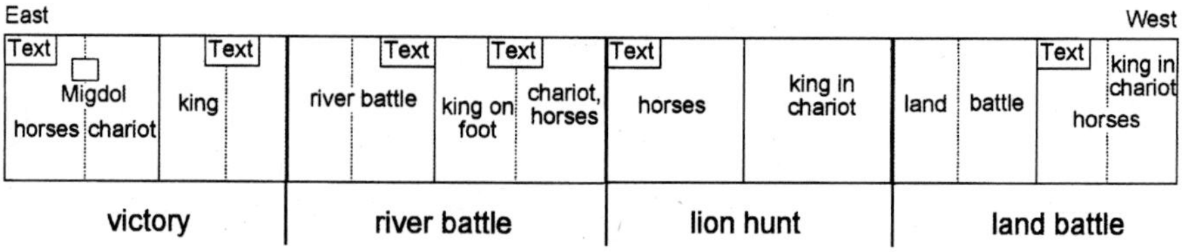

Figure 7:4 Diagrammatic representation of the scenes relevant to the Sea Peoples on the north external wall of the temple of Medinet Habu.

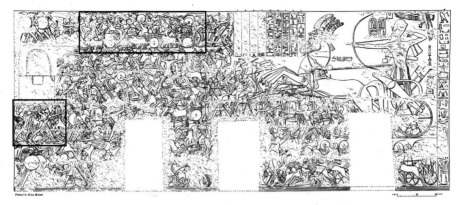

Figure 7:5   The land battle against the Sea Peoples; Medinet Habu. Note the ox-carts in the upper register, and Sea Peoples fighting on the Egyptian side, centre left, detail of both shown below (Oriental Institute, Chicago).

Ox-carts of the Sea Peoples.

Sea Peoples employed in the Egyptian army.

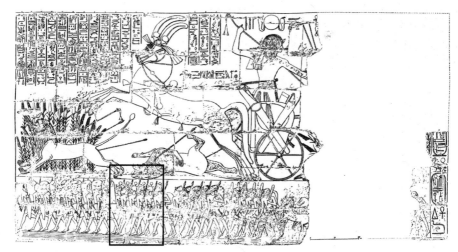

Figure 7:6   The lion hunt of Ramesses III; Medinet Habu. Below: the second contingent of troops from the left are Sea Peoples, detail shown below (Oriental Institute, Chicago).

Sea Peoples employed in the hunt.

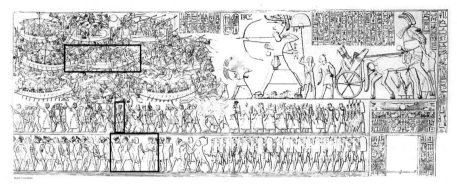

Figure 7:7 The battle of the river mouths against the Sea Peoples; Medinet Habu. Note the distinctive Sea Peoples' ships, with a bird head at either end; and an apparent Sea Peoples 'leader', details shown below (Oriental Institute, Chicago).

Sea Peoples' ship.

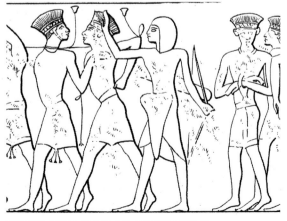

Sea Peoples' leader.

Heraldic group and Sea Peoples' leader (?).

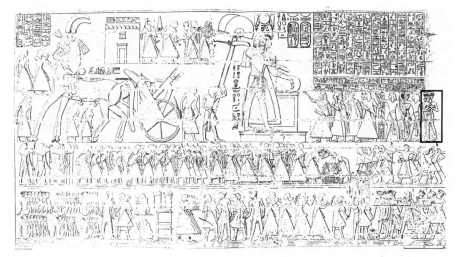

Figure 7:8   The celebration of victory
over the Sea Peoples (Oriental Institute,
Chicago). Right: detail of a single
manacled Sea Peoples individual,
perhaps a/the leader; Medinet Habu.

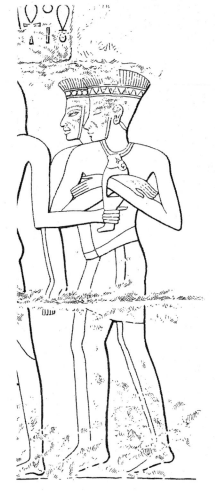

celebration of victory, with emphasis upon the water battle (Figures 7:5–7:8). Finally, a last scene shows the king presenting Sea Peoples prisoners and Libyans to Amun-Ra (for the entire sequence see *Medinet Habu* I: pls. 29–43), the Libyans referring back to scenes depicting the 5th year conflict with Libyans, scenes which precede those dealing with the Sea Peoples and run along the west (north half) and north (western segment) external wall faces.

The other relevant scene occurs on the west wall (south half) of the first court, and depicts Sea Peoples' prisoners presented to Amun-Ra (*Medinet Habu* I: pl. 44). It is balanced on the north half by the long text describing the conflict and its causes (Edgerton and Wilson 1936: 49–58). It should be noted that the temple proper begins at this point, with a pylon and a second court; the first court and its pylon are, functionally, an add-on.

The texts relevant to Sea Peoples at Medinet Habu contain a core of historical actuality (see above) and this should be true of the scenes as well. However, the ways in which actuality is presented in both contexts are powerfully shaped by two factors. First is the cosmography and symbolism of the Egyptian temple in the New Kingdom and later times (Baines 1995; Finnestad 1997). In the New Kingdom temples, scenes of victory over foreign foes were typically rendered, in emblematic or more realistic form, on the entrance pylon and other exterior faces around the temple. One reason for this was that victory was a boon from the deities, hence appropriately depicted on the temples built by the king as thanks offerings for this and more. These scenes also recorded, almost like a symbolically rendered legal document, the transfer of prisoners and booty to the temple's estates.

Moreover, each temple was also a miniaturization of cosmos, depicting in architecture and scene heaven, earth and netherworld. This situation was due in part to cosmos' equation with perfect beauty, a quality thus imparted to the temple as well; but also to the fact that temple rituals and festivals, while varied in content, were patterned after myths describing the creation and continual re-creation of cosmos and hence appropriately played out in an architectural rendering *of* cosmos.

Hence there are cosmographic reasons for the peripheral location of scenes concerning the Egyptian king's defeating and dominating foreign foes. From a terrestrial perspective, the foreign lands fringed and surrounded Egypt, a perfect social order equated with the perfection of the temple. From a pan-cosmic perspective, the scenes had another significance. Cosmos was surrounded by limitless formlessness which had a dynamic negative force, called Isfet (Assmann 1989: 55–88). Isfet was the source of cosmos' actualized life, but of its very nature also ceaselessly but vainly sought to destroy cosmos, and especially the solar cycle whereby the sun god brought life and repeated renewals to cosmos. Thus, by analogy, the triumph of pharaoh on earth equates with the deities' defence of cosmos, and the king's foreign foes are equivalent to the demons and monsters who vainly attack cosmic order. The relationship is quite explicit: Ramesses III for example, in defeating foreign foes is identified with the god Seth who "rages, overthrowing the enemy in front of the sun bark" which carries the sun god around cosmos (Edgerton and Wilson 1936: 38, 42, 47, 57). Such scenes also had the positive power of actually repelling real supernatural danger which attempted to penetrate any temple, destroy its cult and thus contribute to the collapse of the cosmos (Essche-Merchez 1994).

The second factor shaping the treatment of historical actuality at Medinet Habu is the fact that not only the long rhetorical text (west wall, first court) but also the externally located scenes (and their textual complements) each constitute a "King's Novel" (*Königsnovelle*), a genre with its own particular rules and practices. Loprieno has shown that this genre incorporates a great variety of literary forms, and that all are structured around a common theme, the king fulfilling "at the same time all roles of societal representation; he is the *image*, the *trace* and the *symbol* of the country's cohesion" (Loprieno 1996b: 277). As image, the king stands for Egypt as a whole; as trace, his existence is causally tied to Egypt's well-being; and as symbol, "he is theologically equated to entire spheres of the Egyptian conception of the world" (Loprieno 1996b: 277–278), and thus can be identified with some or all deities, or with the powerful forces and beings of nature. Narrative in the King's Novel therefore emphasizes the king's function in the "interface between the divine plan and human condition" (Loprieno 1996b: 281).

These are the conceptual contexts which must be taken into account when we try to understand what the scenes (and texts) at Medinet Habu tell us about the Sea Peoples. The four relevant scenes are those depicting the land battle (Figure 7:5 above); the lion hunt (Figure 7:6 above); the battle of the river mouths (Figure 7:7 above); and the celebration of victory following the latter (Figure 7:8 above). These scenes are represented diagrammatically, in their sequence on the wall, in Figure 7:4 above (see also Essche-Merchez 1992).

That the scenes (and those preceding them, i.e. equipping the army, and the march to Djahy) comprise a largely pictorial King's Novel is evident from the narrative sequence in which the king is visually and verbally (in the accompanying short texts) extremely prominent. In each of the four scenes the king, his chariot and his magnificent horses – all on a superhuman scale, as compared to all the other participants in each scene – occupy much of the visual field; on average, 34 per cent in the two battle scenes, and about 63 per cent in the other two.

The accompanying texts (and, in much expanded form, the long text on the west wall of the first court) make it clear that as image, the king is identified as the embodiment of Egypt; and that as trace, he is the recipient of the powers transferred to him especially by Amun-Ra, but also other deities, thus ensuring Egypt's victories. Finally, as symbol, Ramesses III is identified with a number of deities, which vary appropriately according to context. For example, when a scene is focused more on Egypt and the king's benevolent roles *vis à vis* Egypt, Ramesses is typically identified with Ra, the epitome of rulership (e.g. in the equipping scene, and the celebration of victory), but in the battle scenes the king is equated with the aggressive god Seth, who defends the solar bark against monstrous attackers (compare Edgerton and Wilson 1936: 35, 38–39, 42, 48). Ramesses is also identified with powerful natural forces – the whirlwind, and lions, wild bulls and falcons (Edgerton and Wilson 1936: 36–37, 39, 41, 43). Above all, the king is a flame, or an all-consuming heat, in fact the embodiment of the solar orb itself, and its fiercely protective uraei (Edgerton and Wilson 1936: 37, 39, 40). This point is rendered pictorially as well; when the king is not in battle (in the equipping, march and celebration scenes) the sundisk and its two uraei float over his head. They do not in the battle scenes, because the king there is totally identified with the solar orb and radiates intense and burning power.

At the same time as the scenes form a King's Novel, they also, from the perspective of temple cosmography and symbolism, represent Egypt and the foreign lands around it, which are totally crushed when they attack or resist Egypt; and, at another level, the sun god (embodied in the king) triumphantly traversing the solar path around cosmos while his demonic enemies (here represented by foreign foes) are overthrown.

The imagery of the Sea Peoples is therefore manipulated so as to service these two conflated forms, namely the King's Novel and cosmographic symbolism. In the two battle scenes significant vertical axes – the central and sub-central (one-quarter) ones – of each scene are subtly manipulated so the king and his environs are visually presented as epitomizing order and power, while the defeated enemy represent chaotic, orderless forces reduced to impotence and death by the exercise of that power and order; literally, in these scenes, order (*Maat*) confronts chaos (*Isfet*). Thus, in the land battle scene (Figure 7:5 above; see also Figure 7:4) the royal (western) half comprises a highly symmetrical arrangement of king, chariot and horses around the sub-central axis, while the foreigners (eastern) half is filled with a disorderly mêlée of panic-stricken Sea Peoples fleeing, being slaughtered or surrendering at the onset of pharaoh and his army. In the scene of battle in the river mouths (Figure 7:7 above), the king is allocated a western half (approximately) in which he, on foot, and his horses and chariot, are posed symmetrically around the sub-central axis. The other, eastern (approximate) half shows Sea Peoples' ships attacked by Egyptian ships (Nelson 1943); the former are being grappled, and literally overturned, the lowest placed being completely capsized. As for the Sea Peoples themselves many have tumbled into the water, to be killed as they try to get ashore, while others, taken prisoner, are packed, manacled, into Egyptian vessels. The conceptual contexts described above explain the highly unrealistic nature of these scenes. There is no *real* battle: the enemy collapse immediately before pharaoh, just as demons collapse before the sun god's defenders (Groenewegen-Frankfort 1987: 138–189; on New Kingdom battle scenes in general see Heinz 2001).

As for the Sea Peoples, they also verbally (in the texts) fulfil the roles assigned them by context. More by implication than explicitly, they are bulls killed by a lion (the king), bulls gored by a greater bull (the king) and small birds ripped apart by a falcon (the king). Moreover, if the king is Seth, then the Sea Peoples by implication are demons, and like such demons they are butchered and reduced to ash by solar fire, i.e. the destructive solar heat radiating from the king.

Elsewhere in the scenes, Sea Peoples are emblematic of these themes in other ways. Thus, under the river mouth battle representation (Figure 7:7 above), two registers – one above the other – showing Sea Peoples prisoners being led off both feed into the two registers below the celebration of victory scene (Figure 7:8 above). The upper register in the river mouth battle scene represents Sea Peoples captured at the river mouths battle, and they run on to form part of the celebration of victory scene, in which these prisoners, and a pile of severed hands representing the slaughtered Sea Peoples, are presented to pharaoh. The lower register under the river mouths battle seems to represent Sea Peoples captives in general (i.e. the products of both battles) and runs on below the celebration of victory scene, where the prisoners are shown being branded and then registered for service within Egyptian institutions, temple estates surely (given the context) but also perhaps royal strongholds. Thus, in the celebration of victory scene, Sea Peoples prisoners, now arranged in orderly rows and integrated into Egyptian society (at an appropriately subordinate level), form part of a larger icon celebrating the societal and cosmic order embodied in the king. Again, central and sub-central vertical axes are manipulated so as to create a highly symmetrical image representative of that order. On either side of the central axis are two symmetrically opposed groups: the king (on foot, at a podium) receiving his chief officials and important Sea Peoples prisoners (west) and the royal chariot and horses (east). The notion of order dominating disorder (here, the Sea Peoples) is represented in more subtle ways as well.

On the west sub-central (one-quarter) vertical axis is a vizier or chief minister, the highest ranking officer of government hence representative of order, while below on the same axis order dominates chaos in the form of severed hands counted by an official, or chaos is transmuted into order when, further below, and still on this axis, an official brands a prisoner. Moreover, at the top of the east sub-central vertical axis stands an emblem of royal power, a migdol or fortified tower, while at its bottom Egyptian officials grasp Sea Peoples prisoners who are being registered, a further example of disorder transmuted into order.

The Egyptians seem to have admired, as well as been enraged and frightened by, the invading barbarians. The evidence for this is partly negative: in the Medinet Habu texts the metaphors and imagery applied to Sea Peoples are few, whereas the treatment of Libyan foes is much more explicitly derogatory (Edgerton and Wilson 1936: 7–34, 60–94). More powerful however is the significance of the lion hunt scene (Figure 7:6 above; see also Figure 7:4 above). Whether this event, shown between the land battle and that of the river mouths, actually happened is unknown, but its symbolic significance *vis à vis* the Sea Peoples is substantial (Essche-Merchez 1992: 224–225). Compositionally, the lion hunt scene is presented as part, and even the central part, of the Sea Peoples scenes. It is literally one of them, but also has strongly emphasized centrality. First, it literally occupies the spatial centre of the series of Sea Peoples scenes, from equipping to celebration scene. Second, compositionally the lion hunt emphasizes the king's centrality in a unique way, as compared to the other Sea Peoples scenes. In the latter, the emblematic, highly symmetrical representation of royal power (king, chariot, horses) is always placed to one side of each scene's visual field. In the lion hunt scene, however, the entire visual field is occupied by the royal component, arranged symmetrically around the central, rather than a sub-central, axis. Finally, the lion hunt is rendered in a mannered style, which further contrasts with the other scenes, and again emphasizes the lion hunt's compositional, and implicitly ideological, centrality.

In terms of compositional position and content, the lion hunt scene equates with the defeats of the Sea Peoples on either side, a notion further supported by the associated text, which opens: "The lions are in travail and flee to their land" (Edgerton and Wilson 1936: 39–40), while generally they are described in the same terms as defeated human foes. However, the lion was symbolically of high value to the Egyptians (in the lion hunt text the king himself, as elsewhere, is described as "The lion, lord of victory" – Edgerton and Wilson 1936: 39), indicating that the Sea Peoples were considered worthy opponents. Other hunting scenes at Medinet Habu indicate a hierarchy of foreign foes with Levantines equated with wild bulls, rated lower than lions, and the nomadic Libyans – more risibly – with desert animals such as gazelle, wild asses and even hares (O'Connor 2000: 95).

Elsewhere, more historically specific information about the Sea Peoples is provided, albeit subordinated to the larger aims described above. Especially interesting is the appearance of the Sea Peoples warriors. Although five specific Sea Peoples are identified as comprising the invaders, in the land battle scene (and the representations of Sea Peoples prisoners in various scenes) all the soldiers wear identical costumes, specifically a helmet or headdress resembling feathers and a distinctive type of kilt. Apart from their capacity for uniting into a confederation, this is the principal indication in the Egyptian sources that the Sea Peoples (at least, those represented at Medinet Habu) shared to a significant degree a common culture. If Sea Peoples' costume varied significantly from one people to another the Egyptians were likely to have indicated that fact, a supposition made likely by the unique treatment of Sea Peoples' costumes in the battle in the river mouths scene (Figure 7:7 above).

Here, *two* types of Sea Peoples costume are carefully distinguished (Stadelmann 1984). Some of the Sea Peoples' ships are manned exclusively by men wearing the costume described above, others exclusively by men with a similar kilt but wearing round, smooth profile helmets, each with a pair of projecting horns. In the horizontal register below, Sea Peoples prisoners of both iconographic types are mingled together, but in the actual battle scene they operate quite separately from each other. The implication is clear: one or more of the Sea Peoples was costumed differently from one or more of the remainder, and thus there was a considerable difference in material culture within the Sea Peoples. Moreover, those wearing horned helmets associate solely with sea travel in the Medinet Habu scenes – yet a further example of differentiation.

Unfortunately, comparative evidence is insufficient to equate specific peoples with specific costumes. Many scholars identify the wearing of horned helmets with the Shardana (see Edgerton and Wilson 1936: 36 n. 39a), but at Medinet Habu there is no indication that Shardana were involved in the Sea Peoples invasion. P. Harris does indicate this, but is a less significant source, and omits the Shekelesh, a further indication of unreliability.

The Sea Peoples as a whole are also characterized by a type of ox-drawn cart, unique amongst Egyptian representations (land battle only: Figure 7:5 above) and a distinctive type of ship, with 'bird heads' at the prow and stern (battle of the river mouths; Figure 7:7). These ships were powered only by sail, not by oarsmen, conspicuous on the Egyptian ships in the river mouths battle scene. As an example of how ideological needs can influence historical conclusions, Wachsmann (2000: 105–115) has interpreted the depiction of a capsized Sea Peoples ship as showing that such ships had rowers guards, and hence *were* rowed. However, it seems more likely that the ship is shown breaking up (its sail also has a huge hole torn in it) and the 'rowers shield' is more probably a plank separating from the vessel's body (O'Connor 2000: 99).

The success of the Sea Peoples' invasion before encountering Egyptian forces suggests that they were militarily effective on land and sea, and that they may well have had some form of centralized leadership (*contra* the arguments in Cifola 1988; or the example of the Vikings?). Neither of those characteristics are highlighted in the Medinet Habu scenes, which of their very nature must show the Sea Peoples as totally disorganized and bereft of leadership, and thus fully equivalent to the malevolent yet chaotic force of Isfet, which is continually reduced to impotence by the overwhelming power of cosmic and societal order, as manifest in the triumphant Egyptian king. Moreover, the leaders of Egypt's foreign foes are typically (but not always; see Edgerton and Wilson 1936: 60–68) minimized or overlooked in such scenes in general, because the enemy, if chaotic, should be leaderless; and actual leaders should not be given visual or verbal prominence because as embodiments of leadership their role in opposing pharaoh, the ultimate embodiment of leadership, is considered, by definition, to be so despicable.

This said, it can be observed that in the Medinet Habu scenes clues as to these aspects of the Sea Peoples are provided, within the interstices of the larger, ideologically driven compositions. For example, the land battle scene does provide indications of Sea Peoples' military capacities (Figure 7:5 above). It reveals that the Sea Peoples deployed chariotry as well as infantry (with no indication of the former in the texts) and the Sea Peoples warriors fleeing the carnage in the upper and lower right hand corners do so in good order, perhaps reflective of the military discipline of Sea Peoples warriors as a whole. Visually, the river mouths battle scene does not provide such indications of the Sea Peoples' military effectiveness at sea; here, the described Egyptian preparations are a more significant indication of the Sea Peoples' anticipated strength – the king states: "I caused the Nile mouth to be prepared like a strong wall with warships, galleys and coasters" (Edgerton and Wilson 1936: 54), while a "stockade of lances" surrounded the Sea Peoples along the shore (Edgerton and Wilson 1936: 55).

Finally, even the issue of Sea Peoples' leadership is raised, in a subtle and understated way – making use of the sub-central vertical axes, the compositional roles of which have been discussed above. In the river mouths battle scene (Figure 7:7 above) the western sub-central axis is marked by a unique heraldic arrangement of two Sea Peoples prisoners in the lowest horizontal register: they confront each other in a way not seen elsewhere in the Medinet Habu scenes. Immediately above them, on the same sub-central axis, is a rare representation of a Sea Peoples prisoner, not cruelly bound at the elbows (the usual situation in presentation scenes) but wearing the less agonizing manacles, in the form of a lion emblematic of Egyptian royal power. This same figure recurs to the right or east of the heraldic figures in the register below (which depicts a different, later stage in the experiences of the prisoners) and yet again in the presentation of high ranking prisoners to the king in the celebration of victory scene (Figure 7:8 above). In all three cases the circumstances indicate that the same individual is being represented and subtly indicated as the ultimate leader of the Sea Peoples' invasion (O'Connor 2000: 99). Ideologically, he may be present as a foil to the opposing, and by definition unique, ultimate leader on the Egyptian side: pharaoh himself. In reality Sea Peoples' leadership may have been complex: a possible indication of centrality is provided here, generated but perhaps also distorted by the compositional and ideological needs of the Medinet Habu scenes.

Summary and conclusion

It could very well be argued from the above review of the available evidence that it is the very complexity of the Sea Peoples themselves which constitutes the chief difficulty in reconstructing the details of their culture(s), let alone their origins. Alternatively, some would argue that this is not the case at all, rather that the available textual evidence almost always derives from – and represents – exclusively Egyptian perceptions (in both text and depiction), as well as interests. It is even possible to argue that a unified 'Sea Peoples' never did exist but were merely a useful Egyptian construct which could often act as an 'explanation' for a host of varied incidents: on this view, a varied set of peoples would have been artificially grouped together by the Egyptians under the rubric of 'foreigners from the sea' (Breasted [1906] 2001: 255).

However, even the available textual and representational evidence can appear puzzling in their own right. It is not only that virtually all the available evidence for names of places and rulers are Egyptian, but also that – for instance – texts of King Ramesses III (1187–1156 BC) describe the Sea Peoples invading the eastern Mediterranean and, on the most dramatic reading of the sources, bringing an end to long-standing polities there until meeting defeat at the hands of the Egyptians. Yet, while such Egyptian texts identify five peoples as involved, the accompanying representational scenes seemingly represent only two.

But, in truth, it is likely to be the un-thought-out nature of the methodologies that have been applied to the 'mystery' of the Sea Peoples which lies behind the current exceedingly unsatisfactory nature of our understanding of the relevant events. It has to be admitted that two centuries of research and a spate of recent volumes about the Sea Peoples[2] have left us with much circumstantial evidence and many circular arguments. In all these cases, scholars have used all sorts of evidence coming from all kinds of chronological periods in their attempts to trace the Sea Peoples. It is clear that a rigorous set of methodological principles needs to be formulated to tackle the available, varied, and necessarily partial evidence accessible for study. Such principles are available in the disciplines of archaeology and historical text criticism. For example, standard historiographical practice would require of the historian that the sources are weighted according to context and date. At the simplest level, where there is, for example, a Hittite document discussing the Lukki, which can be considered both contemporary and relevant, it should be assigned a higher priority than, for instance, a later document concerned with the foundation of Salamis on Cyprus, and so on. Above all, the archaeological evidence, the material evidence for peoples in each region, must provide the framework for discussion. Some historians (e.g. Kuhrt 1995: 392) would reject outright almost all of the naming equations that are such a prominent feature of most discussions of the Sea Peoples.

Therefore, at least of equal importance is to decide the relative weight to be given in interpretation and analysis to texts when they are accompanied by archaeological information, *vis à vis* when texts exist in isolation, as the only available evidence. Given the inevitable and long-accepted bias involved in the creation of all written sources, the importance of any archaeological supporting evidence to identify, and thereby access, the possible activities of different Sea Peoples cannot be overstressed (Kuhrt 1995: 386). Indeed, it seems difficult, if not inherently impossible, to critically assess the claims for naming correlations (between Egyptian term and alleged place name) on the basis of linguistics, without supporting archaeological evidence to determine what was actually going on on the ground in terms of changes in population and/or changes in material culture.

Of course, the nature and dependability of any such archaeological evidence will be very variable, and must be assessed and evaluated in its own right; nevertheless, the potential evidence to be derived from pottery and other dateable artefacts – quite apart from human skeletal material – cannot be overestimated. To be plain, it seems unlikely that it will really prove possible to 'make sense' of the Egyptian record of the Sea Peoples before it becomes possible to isolate relevant material culture of the peoples concerned, and to be able to relate it to the archaeological evidence of the activities of the 'Mycenaeans' or other Mediterranean people. Archaeological evidence must be deemed to be the primary source material for an understanding of cultural and population change and movements at the end of the Late Bronze Age (ca. 1250–1000 BC) of the region. Currently, convincing association between archaeological and textual evidence is often impossible.

Also important should be the comparative analysis of the later archaeological evidence for another 'great cultural upheaval' in the Mediterranean, the Greek and Phoenician colonizations from the eighth century BC onwards. It will be instructive to see whether the archaeological distribution on the ground will reveal a different pattern between the two alleged 'invasions' of the area. Currently, the existence and distribution of the 'degraded Mycenaean' pottery is the best evidence of what may have been happening in the earlier of the two periods.

Meanwhile, however, we find ourselves still asking the most basic of questions about the Sea Peoples. They remain a mystery, because the sources for their existence and impact are confined to a large extent to the ancient Egyptian expression of the world in writing and art. Until more archaeological evidence emerges to correct that imbalance, the Sea Peoples seem destined to epitomize a classic disjunction between archaeological and historical accounts of the past. Few other peoples present such a stimulating challenge.

Notes

1   *dmiw* can be just the point where the boat touches the land (*dmiw* = "touch").
2   Other recent publications include Dothan 1982; Dothan and Dothan 1992; Drews 1993; Gitin *et al.* 1998; Leahy 2001; Nibbi 1975; Oren 2000; Sandars 1985; Ward and Joukowsky 1992; Zangger 1994, 1995. On the ships of Medinet Habu, see Artzy 1997; Raban and Stieglitz 1991; Wachsmann 1981, 1982, 1997, 1998, 2000.

Appendix: some translations of relevant inscriptions concerning the Sea Peoples

Merenptah: Year 5

Great Karnak Inscription:

[Beginning of the victory that his majesty achieved in the land of Libya] Eqwosh, Teresh, Lukki, Shardana, Shekelesh, Northerners coming from all lands.

... the third season, saying: The wretched, fallen chief of Libya ... has fallen upon the country of Tehenu with his bowmen – Shardana, Shekelesh, Eqwosh, Lukki, Teresh, taking the best of every warrior and every man of war of his country ...

List of the captives carried off from this land of Libya and the countries which he brought with him ...

Sherden, Shekelesh, Eqwosh of the countries of the sea, who had no foreskins:

Shekelesh 222 men

Making 250 hands

Teresh 742 men

Making 790 hands

Shardana – –

[Making] – –

[Ek]wosh who had no foreskins, slain,

whose hands were carried off, (for) they

had no [foreskins] – –

Shekelesh and Teresh who came as enemies of Libya – –

– – Kehek, and Libyans, carried off as living prisoners 218 men

(after Breasted [1906] 2001, 3: 241, 243, 249)

The Cairo Column: Year 5, second month of the third season (tenth month):

One came to say to his majesty: "The wretched [chief] of Libya has invaded [with] – , being men and women, Shekelesh and every foreign country – – ."

(after Breasted [1906] 2001, 3: 253)

The Heliopolis Text: Year 5, second month of the third season (tenth month):

One came to say to his majesty: "The wretched chief of Libya has invaded and the land of Libya, being men and women, Shekelesh and every foreign country, which is with him, to violate the borders of Egypt."

(after Edel 1961; see Bakry 1973)

The Athribis Stela:

... Eqwosh [of] the countries of the sea, whom had brought the wretched [fallen chief of Libya, whose] hands [were carried off]   2,201 [+x] men

Shekelesh	200 men
Teresh	722 [+x] men
– – Libya, and Shardana, slain	– men

(after Breasted [1906] 2001, 3: 255)

Ramesses III: Year 8

Text inscribed in interior courtyard at Medinet Habu:

Year 8 under the majesty of (Ramesses III) ... The foreign countries made a conspiracy in their islands. All at once the lands were removed and scattered in the fray. No land could stand before their arms, from Khatte, Qode, Carchemish, Arzawa, and Alashiya on, being cut off at [one time]. A camp [was set up] in one place in Amor. They desolated its people, and its land was like that which has never come into being. They were coming forward toward Egypt, while the flame was prepared before them. Their confederation was the Philistines, Tjekru, Shekelesh, Denye(n), and Washosh, lands united. They laid their hands upon the lands as far as the circuit of the earth, their hearts confident and trusting: 'Our plans will succeed!'

Now the heart of this god, the Lord of the Gods, was prepared and ready to ensnare them like birds ... I organized my frontier in Djahy, prepared before them: princes, commanders of garrisons, and maryanuu. I have the river-mouths prepared like a strong wall, with warships, galleys and coasters, (fully) equipped, for they were manned completely from bow to stern with valiant warriors carrying their weapons. The troops consisted of every picked man of Egypt. They were like lions roaring upon the mountain tops. The chariotry consisted of runners, of picked men, of every good and capable chariot-warrior. The horses were quivering in every part of their bodies, prepared to crush the foreign countries under their hoofs. I was the valiant Montu, standing fast at their head, so that they might gaze upon the capturing of my hands.

Those who reached my frontier, their seed is not, their heart and soul are finished forever and ever. Those who came forward together on the sea, the full flame was in front of them at the river-mouths, while a stockade of lances surrounded them on the shore. They were dragged in, enclosed, and prostrated on the beach, killed, and made into heaps from tail to head. Their ships and their goods were as if fallen into the water.

I have made the lands turn back from (even) mentioning Egypt: for when they pronounce my name in their land, then they are burned up. Since I sat upon the throne of Har-akhti and the Great-of-Magic was fixed upon my head like Ra, I have not let foreign countries behold the frontier of Egypt, to boast thereof to the Nine Bows.

(after Edgerton and Wilson 1936: pl. 46, lines 1,16–25;
revised trans., Wilson 1969: 262–263)

Inscription in interior courtyard at Medinet Habu labelled "The Inscription of the Year 5" (but most probably recording events from the Year 8):

The northern countries quivered in their bodies, the Peleset, Tjek[er and ...]. They cut off their (own) land, and were coming, their soul finished. They were teher warriors on land: another (group) was on the sea. Those who came on [land were overthrown and killed ...].

Amon-Ra was after them, destroying them. Those who entered the river-mouths were like birds ensnared in the net ... Their leaders were carried off and slain. They were cast down and pinioned ...'

(after Edgerton and Wilson 1936: pls. 27–28, lines 51–56;
revised translation following Wilson 1969: 263)

Text (*Medinet Habu* I: pl. 14) inscribed at Medinet Habu, accompanying a scene of a naval battle with vessels of both Egyptians and Sea Peoples, and the pharaoh and his infantry fighting from the shore:

Now the northern countries, which were in their isles, were quivering in their bodies. They penetrated the channels of the Nile mouths. Their nostrils have ceased (to function, so that) their desire is <to> breathe the breath. His majesty is gone forth like a whirlwind against them, fighting on the battlefield like a runner. The dread of him and the terror of him have entered into their bodies: (they are) capsized and overwhelmed in their places. Their hearts are taken away; their soul is flown away. Their weapons are scattered in the sea. His arrow pierces him whom he has wished among them, while the fugitive is become one fallen into the water. His majesty is like an enraged lion, attacking his assailant with his paws: plundering on his right hand and powerful on his left hand, like Set destroying the serpent Evil of Character. It is Amun-Ra who has overthrown for him the lands and has crushed for him every land under his feet: King of Upper and Lower Egypt, Lord of the Two Lands: Usermare-Meriamon.

(after Edgerton and Wilson 1936: pls. 37–39, lines 8–23)

Text (*Medinet Habu* I: pl. 15) inscribed at Medinet Habu:

Spoken by his majesty to the royal princes, the officials, the royal chamberlains, and the charioteers: See ye the great strength of my father Amun-Ra! As for the countries who came from their land in the isles in the midst of the sea, as they were (coming) forward toward Egypt, their hearts relying on their hands, a net was prepared for them, to ensnare them. They that entered into the Nile mouths were caught, fallen into the midst of it, pinioned in their places, butchered, and their bodies hacked up. I have caused that you see my strength, which was in that which my arm has done, while I was alone. My arrow hit the mark without fail, while my arms and my hand were steadfast. I was like a falcon in the midst of small fowl, for my talon did not fail upon their heads. Amun-Ra was on my right and on my left, and the awe of him and the terror of him were in my person. Rejoice ye, for that which I commanded is come to pass, and my counsels and my plans are perfected. Amun-Ra repels my foe and gives to me every land in my grasp.

(after Edgerton and Wilson 1936: pl. 42, lines 1–13)

Year 12: A stela at Medinet Habu to the south of the main gateway, on the face of the first pylon, begins with the phrase "Year 12 under the majesty of Horus", and includes the following brief statement:

I overthrew the Tjek[er], the land of Pele[set], the Danuna, the [W]eshesh, and the Shekelesh; I destroyed the breath of the Mesh[wesh], – – , Sebet, – – , devastated in their (own) land. I am fine of plan and excellent of – – – .

(after Edgerton and Wilson 1936: pl. 107, lines 7–9)

P. Harris:

I extended all the boundaries of Egypt. I overthrew those who invaded them from their lands. I slew the Danuna [who are] in their isles, the Tjekru and the Peleset were made ashes. The Shardana and the Washosh of the sea, they were made as those that exist not, taken captive at one time, brought as captives to Egypt, like the sand of the shore. I settled them in strongholds bound in my name. Numerous were their classes like hundred-thousands. I taxed them all, in clothing and grain from the store-houses and granaries each year ... I made the infantry and chariotry to dwell (at home) in my time; the Shardana and Kehek were in their towns, lying the [length] of their backs; they had no fear, (for) there was no enemy from Kush (nor) foe from Syria. Their bows and their weapons reposed in their magazines, while they were satisfied and drunk with joy. Their wives were with them, their children at their side; they looked not behind them, (but) their hearts were confident, (for) I was with them as the defense and protection of their limbs. I sustained alive the whole land, whether foreigners, (common) folk, citizens, or people, male or female.

(after Breasted [1906] 2001, 4: 201; Sandars 1985: 133)

Onomasticon of Amenemope:

(268) *Sherden*; (269) *Tjeter*; (270) *Psset*

(Gardiner 1947: 194–205)

Ugarit Letters: Letter from the king of Alashiya (Cyprus) to Hammurabi, king of Ugarit (RSL 1; *Ugaritica* 5.23):

Thus says the king (of Alashiya): say to Ammurapi, king of Ugarit: May you be well, and may the gods protect you in well-being! Concerning that which you wrote (me): "Enemy ships have been sighted at sea" – if it is true that ships have been sighted, then make yourself very strong. Now where are your infantry and [your] chariotry stationed? Are they not stationed with you? No? Who is sending you after(?) the enemy? Surround your cities with walls. Bring (your) infantry and chariotry into (them). Be on the lookout for the enemy and make yourself very strong.

(after Beckman 1996: 27; Sandars 1985: 142–143; Schaeffer 1968: 85–86)

Letter from Hammurabi, king of Ugarit, to the king of Alashiya (Cyprus) (RS 20.238; *Ugaritica* 5.24):

Say to the king of Alashiya, my father: Thus says the king of Ugarit, your son:

I fall at the feet of my father. May my father be well! May your palaces, your wives, your infantry, and everything which belongs to the king of Alashiya, my father, be very, very well!

My father, now the ships of the enemy have been coming. They have been setting fire to my cities and have done harm to the land. Doesn't my father know that all of my infantry and [chariotry] are stationed in Khatte, and that all of my ships are stationed in the land of Lukki? They have not arrived back yet, so the land is thus prostrate. May my father be aware of this matter. Now the seven ships of the enemy which have been coming have done harm to us. Now if other ships of the enemy turn up, send me a report somehow (?) so that I will know.

(after Beckman 1996: 27; Sandars 1985: 142–143; Schaeffer 1968: 87–89)

CHAPTER 8

"AS FOR THEM WHO KNOW THEM, THEY SHALL FIND THEIR PATHS": SPECULATIONS ON RITUAL LANDSCAPES IN THE 'BOOK OF THE TWO WAYS'

Peter Robinson

Throughout their history the ancient Egyptian elite was buried with elaborate ceremony, though the precise customs varied greatly from one period to another. At first, those buried on the edge of the desert were interred either directly in the ground, or in matting or basketwork. With time, the material protection for the body became more solid and more elaborately decorated, and the body itself received increasingly refined treatment against decay. By the end of the third millennium BC, the wealthier Egyptians were laid to rest in rectangular wooden coffins. These showed a trend towards intricate combinations of depictions and writing, peaking in the magnificent cedar coffins of the twelfth Dynasty (20th–19th centuries BC).

el-Bersheh

Surveyed at various times during the 19th and early 20th centuries, by a number of archaeological teams (e.g. Griffith and Newberry 1894; Newberry 1891; Willems 1988: 68), the site of el-Bersheh (Figure 8:1) was the last resting place of several members of an important family of administrators (Figure 8:2). This family, the descendants of a *wab*-priest of the eleventh Dynasty called Kay, were hereditary rulers of the Hare Nome, the administrative region around the town of Hermopolis, known to the ancient Egyptians as Khemenu or "town of the 8 [gods]". The tombs of el-Bersheh, now badly damaged through quarrying at various times in the past, are nonetheless known for their fine decoration. Most notable amongst these is that of Djehutyhotep, whose tomb contains a famous representation of the transport of a colossal statue. From the tombs and rock inscriptions at the nearby Hatnub quarries there is evidence of some eight generations of the nomarchal family from the reign of Mentuhotep II (ca. 2055–2004 BC) to that of Sesostris II (1880–1874 BC). El-Bersheh and its interred souls are also an important source of distinctive Middle Kingdom coffins. One feature almost unique to these el-Bersheh coffins is the inclusion of a particular set of texts now known as the 'Book of the Two Ways'.

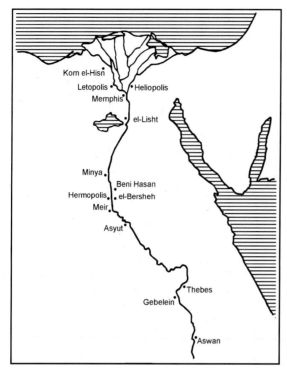

Figure 8:1 Map of selected Middle Kingdom sites.

Coffin texts and the 'Book of the Two Ways'

The 'Tale of Sinuhe', a Middle Kingdom text, indicates one desire of a Middle Kingdom Egyptian for a rich burial:

> ... have in mind the day of burial,
> the passing to blessedness.
> A night vigil will be assigned to you, with holy oils,
> and wrappings from the hands of Tayet.
> A funeral procession shall be made for you on the day of joining the earth,
> with a mummy case of gold,
> a mask of lapis lazuli,
> a heaven over you, and you placed in a hearse ...

(Parkinson 1997: 36)

The 'Tale of Sinuhe' (Loprieno Chapter 3, this volume) was composed some time during the first half of the twelfth Dynasty, shortly after the accession of Sesostris I to the pharaonic throne (Parkinson 1997). As such, it is a text contemporary with the rule of the el-Bersheh nomarchs and gives an idea of the expectation of a goodly burial that they might have had.

Several hundred non-royal coffins are known from the Middle Kingdom, found from sites as far apart as Aswan in the south and the Memphite cemeteries in the north. Unlike the anthropoid coffins from later periods, these Middle Kingdom coffins were usually rectangular in form, with vaulted or flat tops. The finest were made of

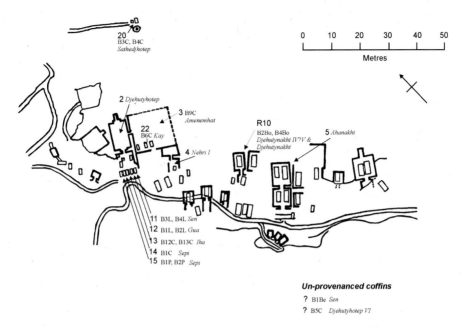

Figure 8:2   The tombs of el-Bersheh showing locations of coffins and tombs with texts including the 'Book of the Two Ways' (after Griffith and Newberry 1894: pl. 2; Willems 1988: 69).

large planks of imported cedar timber, neatly constructed with well-cut mitred joints. In construction, they contrast sharply with the simpler Old Kingdom and First Intermediate Period wooden coffins (Spencer 1982: 168–169). Whilst many have little or no decoration, a number of coffins have images, texts and artistic representations of a variety of ritual objects on their external or internal surfaces.

Although much of the decoration of Middle Kingdom coffins consisted of decorative elements, depictions of objects, painted renditions of 'false doors' and *wedjat* eyes (Willems 1988: 41–44), a significant part of the coffin surface, both inside and out, was taken up with extended selections of larger religious compositions. These so-called 'Coffin Texts' have only been fully accessible to Egyptologists since the transcription and publication of the corpus by de Buck between 1935 and 1961. He identified 1,185 individual spells within the Coffin Texts, some found only in one source and others widespread amongst the 154 source documents which he used. He numbered the individual spells more or less according to the frequency of their appearance. In addition, there are a number of text compositions already attested in the Old Kingdom, in the 'Pyramid Texts', that have found their way into the non-royal contexts of these coffins. De Buck did not count these textual survivals within his transcriptions, however. The three-volume work by Faulkner (1973, 1977, 1978) provides the standard English translation of the Coffin Texts.

The Coffin Texts are often said to represent a 'democratization' of the Pyramid Texts following the breakdown of a central royal control during the First Intermediate Period. It is now being suggested amongst some Egyptologists, however, that this might be an over-simplification or misunderstanding of social changes during the

Middle Kingdom. It may also be indicative of the desires of private individuals to 'tap into' the resurrecting potentials of the Osirian tradition of an afterlife previously apparent only amongst royalty (Bourriau 1991: 4). Nonetheless, many of the Coffin Texts contain extracts of the Pyramid Texts and depictions of the symbols of royalty, such as crowns, staffs of office and other insignia. These royal objects appear in the so-called 'object frieze', a graphical depiction of a variety of items associated with the mummification of the deceased and burial rituals (Willems 1988: 220–221).

A number of the coffins from el-Bersheh not only place a great emphasis on the royal insignia in their object friezes, but are also noted for the inclusion of a set of afterlife texts, rarely attested elsewhere. Whilst much of the decoration is included on the inner and outer sides of the Middle Kingdom coffins from most of Egypt, many el-Bersheh coffins also put the lids and floors of the coffins to good use. Many coffins use their lid as a 'sky', with reference to, if not an image itself of, the sky goddess Nut, spread out over the deceased's mummy (Allen Chapter 2, this volume): sky hieroglyphs are painted along the tops of the side panels of many of the el-Bersheh coffins, symbolizing, no doubt, the height of the ordered cosmos, from the Earth's surface to the upper reaches of the sky. This symbolism well reflects the words of Sinuhe's anticipated coffin design, quoted above. The floors of the el-Bersheh coffins are used for a set of somewhat enigmatic texts known as the 'Book of the Two Ways'. Like many other coffin decoration schemes with floor decoration, the Book of the Two Ways appears to be a counterpart to a sky theme, representing perhaps a descent into and a journey around an underworld. With an emphasis on solar barks and travelling with the sun god Ra, however, the text appears also to have a sky-orientated sub-theme, beginning at the eastern horizon at the moment of sunrise.

The Book of the Two Ways has been described as the first Egyptian cosmography (Hornung 1999: 11). It was investigated early in the 20th century by Schack-Schakenburg (1903) who published the texts from the coffin of Sen. It includes many spells (the 'long version' has 101 separate spells and the 'short version' 54), and instructs the deceased, amongst other themes, on the routes and paths through the lands of Rostau, or the mythical netherworld. Simply put, the 'Two Ways' of its modern title are two pictorial routes that zig-zag past a number of obstacles, demonic and monumental. In addition, however, there are a number of other textual elements as well as demonic habitations, and the two roadways take up only about one-third of the coffin floor area. Elsewhere within the text, we see numerous gateways of darkness and of fire. There are walls of flame to trap the unwary and high walls of flint to exclude others. The text also contains, in some examples, an 'image of a mansion', a walled and compartmented building plan, in some sections inhabited by a variety of monstrous creatures. We can imagine, therefore, that these texts were seen as a kind of map for the deceased. Like the later afterlife texts from royal contexts, such as the Amduat in the royal necropolis of the Valley of the Kings, we can perhaps envisage the Book of the Two Ways as a guide and *aide-mémoire* of the paths through the afterlife. This guide would perhaps enable the deceased to travel safely through the realms of the dead to achieve his or her ultimate goal of a blessed existence in the company of the gods.

Although the text of the Book of the Two Ways might have originated elsewhere within the Nile Valley, this group of afterlife spells is unique as a genre of Coffin Texts.

The spells appear on the scene in the Middle Kingdom, within a small number of surviving coffins from a specific locality. Although absence of evidence is never evidence of absence in archaeological terms, nonetheless, the impact of the Book of the Two Ways in the locality of el-Bersheh and for the perhaps four generations of its incorporation in coffins (Figure 8:3) is considerable. There are no similarly detailed attempts at portraying the landscape of the afterlife in such numbers known elsewhere in Egypt at this time, nor indeed are there any attempts made by the ancient Egyptians to show the landscape of the afterlife in such a form before or since. It may be true that attempts were made to represent some aspects of the afterlife landscapes within royal and high-status tombs from the New Kingdom onwards. These descriptions of landmarks and features were carved or drawn onto coffins or written upon papyrus texts from the eighteenth Dynasty until the end of pharaonic Egypt, but they are generally separate isolated images of what must have been considered but part of the underworld environment. In most cases, these later images are just lists of landmarks or landscape features, to be either avoided or visited, and incorporating 'words of power' or a means of placating the demonic or divine inhabitants passed on the way. The Book of the Two Ways, on the other hand, should be seen as a detailed road-map laid out on the floor of the coffin, for the expressed benefit of guiding the deceased through a journey to his or her destination at the side of the sun god Ra.

Lesko (1972) began a critical analysis of the Book of the Two Ways. Using the various textual elements and the detailed plans of coffins as published by de Buck (1961: pls. 1–15), Lesko was able to identify and sub-divide the Book of the Two Ways into some nine sections. The texts and plans combined follow one of two formats – the

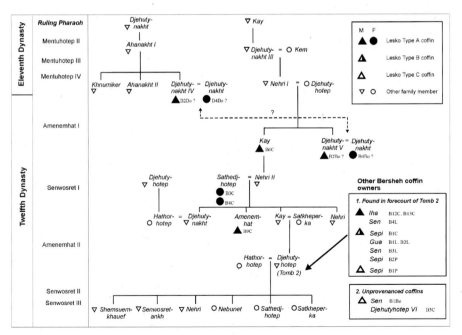

Figure 8:3   The nomarchal genealogy and coffins depicting the 'Book of the Two Ways' (after Willems 1988: 71).

'long version' (Types A and B, see below) and a 'short version' (Type C, see below) that is present in just three of the examples cited by de Buck.

The major themes of the Coffin Texts build upon some of the earlier traditions of Afterlife Texts more commonly found within the Pyramid Texts. We see a number of descriptions of the landscape of the afterlife, of the sort that includes the Book of the Two Ways. The deceased is also identified with both the god of the deceased, Osiris, and the sun god, Ra. In addition, the main corpus of Coffin Texts contains many spells to ensure the integrity of the spirit of the deceased in the afterlife. These texts, for example, enable him or her to be sustained with food throughout the long eternity of a blessed existence, or to be revitalized by the correct rites at the moment of translation from this world to the next. The Book of the Two Ways also includes additional specific information as to the world of the afterlife. This information may be due, however, to the specific contexts and actual regional geography of the coffin owners of el-Bersheh. We therefore need to penetrate deeper into this Middle Egyptian landscape to discover more about the Book of the Two Ways in its setting.

As noted above, de Buck records the Book of the Two Ways from some 15 coffin plans. In addition, Lesko includes a couple of other examples in his analysis. These 17 copies are all found within the 40 coffins discovered from contexts at el-Bersheh that Willems (1988: 20–21) enumerated. A number of further examples have been found by others, mainly in tomb relief contexts. Of these, there is a single example from a non-Bersheh context, that of the western Delta tomb of Khesu the Elder at Kom el-Hisn (Silverman 1996: 132–133). Of those coffins containing texts, some are either outer or inner coffins for individuals, whilst others are single unpaired coffins.

Two major strands emerge from el-Bersheh coffins. The first strand, designated by Lesko as Types A and B (actually slightly different textual versions of the same text), includes most of the coffins. The administrators of the Hare Nome, descendants of Kay referred to above, make use of Type A texts exclusively (representing six of the 17 coffin examples). Three other examples of Type A coffins survive, from individuals outside the hereditary nomarchal line (Figure 8:3 above). These include the inner and outer coffins of a 'great *wab*-priest' by the name of Iha. Willems suggests that this priest lived during the mid-twelfth Dynasty on the palaeographical evidence of his coffin (Willems 1988: 78), corresponding with the reigns of Sesostris II and III. The third example is the outer coffin from the burial of the Chief Physician Sen, who may have been buried in Shaft 11, in the forecourt of Nomarch Djehutynakht's Tomb 2 (Willems 1988: 76). Whilst these Type A coffins date from the reigns of Mentuhotep IV through to Sesostris III (ca. 1992–1855 BC), the remaining coffins all date typologically from the time of Sesostris II and III (ca. 1880–1855 BC) and all belong to private, non-nomarchal individuals. Type B coffins are encountered in the burial Shaft 14, belonging to the general Sepi, Shaft 15, the inner coffin of the steward Sep, the Chief Physician Gua (Shaft 12) and the inner coffin of the Chief Physician Sen whom we have just encountered (Willems 1988: 75–76).

The shorter version of the Book of the Two Ways is said by Lesko (1972a: 134) to be the oldest version, although Lesko's chronology has been questioned (Willems 1988: 235). This version appears in the outer coffin of the steward Sepi (type C), a "scribe of the documents of the king" Djehutihotep and another man called Sen

(Willems 1988: 77–78). These coffins have been designated as Type C coffins by Lesko and comprise the second strand.

Cartographically, the Book of the Two Ways may be an insight into the spatial and temporal geographies of the Middle Kingdom Egyptian. It is always dangerous to transfer upon long-dead societies values from our own cultures and times, especially since we now have our own expectations of religion and belief, mostly built up over two and a half millennia of Greco-Roman philosophy and Judaeo-Christian worship. Indeed, some of our modern-day beliefs are quite alien to the ancient Egyptian notions of the Cosmos and Nature. There are some aspects of these 'landscape texts', however, that share common features with elements of modern cartographic design and usage of today, as well as those that may show what the key elements of Egyptian art might have been. To begin an analysis of the Book of the Two Ways with such an approach, however, we must start by considering what we mean by 'maps' and to what purpose we put them.

A map is more than just a pictorial record of a landscape, or a mirror of reality. It can portray visible (and invisible) features of the world or equally fantasy-lands and products of one's imagination. A map can use symbols to conventionally depict features, whether they are physical, such as mountains, buildings or rivers, or notional concepts, such as sovereignty, accessibility to places, or perceived danger. Maps do not even have to be spatially to scale, or on a hard, printed medium such as paper, to be an effective tool. It is not the purpose of this chapter to discuss the techniques of modern cartography, but we need to think of maps as cultural artefacts that can be understood in one of two ways (Wood 1993: 116). First, they can present a visual representation of spatial relationships, giving us locations and directions of features that we can use to analyze or predict the world around us. In effect, they describe a real (or perceived as real) landscape that we are part of, or hope to visit at some time in the future. Second, maps can be understood as portraying 'mythical' worlds that are subject to the ideas and beliefs of their makers, whether these be political and propagandist or simply constructed within the bounds of the belief systems of their makers.

Like the *mappae mundi* of medieval Europe with their architecturally inspired margins and aspirations of a journey from the here-and-now to an eternal existence (Kline 2001: 73–75), many maps take the form of representations of journeys. Furthermore, such *mappae mundi* as that of Hereford Cathedral reflect and parallel on paper the passage of people through the body of a religious or cultic building. In a church or cathedral, for example, such movement can be seen from the perspective of moving from the main doorway along a central nave to its ultimate goal, the high altar with its image of Christ in majesty. It can also appear in the symbolic movement between ceremonies and rituals, halting at 'stations' associated with various events or activities, for instance baptism, communion, intra-mural burial or similar ritual journeys. In a similar format, the Middle Kingdom artists who composed the Book of the Two Ways no doubt planned the graphic image of the text as a way for the deceased literally to walk through the 'afterlife'. With its paths and structures, rivers and inhabitants, the Book of the Two Ways shows a map of a landscape, with points of entry and gateways and culminating in an eternal destination for the deceased to live within the realm of the gods. These rites of passage initiating the deceased into the afterlife were also marked by a number of points where metaphysical barriers had to be crossed. Furthermore, a map on a coffin floor and a representation of sky on its lid may be more than just a representation of a landscape for a now inanimate dead soul. Modern cartography provides us with a curious parallel as to one possible purpose behind these images. In the Aberdeen Royal Infirmary, maps upon the ceilings of wards and upon the floors of corridors are used to help stimulate and guide the infirm, allowing them to focus upon familiar landscapes, although they might be bed-bound (Addison 1995: 48). It might be just such an intention that the ancients had in mind as they portrayed landscapes upon the floors of their coffins.

It has been suggested that as texts of the Book of the Two Ways survive almost exclusively from el-Bersheh contexts, they represent a regional variety of the Coffin Texts. Hoffmeier (1996: 46–47), however, also points out that the lack of references to the patron god of the el-Bersheh region, Thoth, might indicate that the texts were originally composed elsewhere. One obvious location might be the twelfth Dynasty Residence at Itjtawy. However, lack of papyri buried with the deceased, as well as destruction of the cemeteries over the intervening centuries, results in us having very little evidence to confirm whether the texts were composed around the royal court or at scribal centres in Thoth's cult centre at Khemenu. What we can be sure of, however, is that one or more now long-lost exemplars were available to the makers of high-status coffins in this part of Middle Egypt, and that these exemplars may have arrived from elsewhere within Egypt.

The hidden paths of Rostau and the seven gates

The Book of the Two Ways contains a number of references as to its purpose. Thus, "This is the path to the abodes of those who live on sweet things" (CT1053), and, "The paths by water and by land which belong to Rostau" (CT1074), culminating, in the 'long version' at least, in an indication of the objectives of the text: "I know him and am not ignorant of him, I am one who is equipped, skilled in opening portals" (CT1130).

Clearly the importance of the Book of the Two Ways as a geographical way-book was envisaged by its authors from the beginning. The layout of the Book of the Two Ways can best be described as an image with two main bands (Figure 8:4). The shorter, C version, opens with Lesko's Section II, an image of a ground plan of a palace and shrine with high walls of darkness or flame. These features take up most of the upper band of text. The longer A and B versions commence with a description of the rising sun upon the eastern horizon, indicating, perhaps, the sky-based nature of this section of text. The deceased here is about to board a solar or lotus bark of Ra to commence his or her journey. On both versions, the next texts contain the actual two pathways, one a blue, upper way, and the other a darker lower way, which comprise Sections III and IV respectively. These two pathways are separated by a spell designating a red band, noting the "Lake of Fire of the knife-wielders". The two pathways meander and wind around in their sections. In some cases, we see multiple paths, areas surrounded by paths, and paths crossing the main ways. Textual descriptions of sections of these paths indicate some of the geographical features of this landscape crossed by the deceased. Hence, we read of waterways and basins, fields and shrines. At many of the bends in these pathways, texts record the presence of demons and monsters. In some

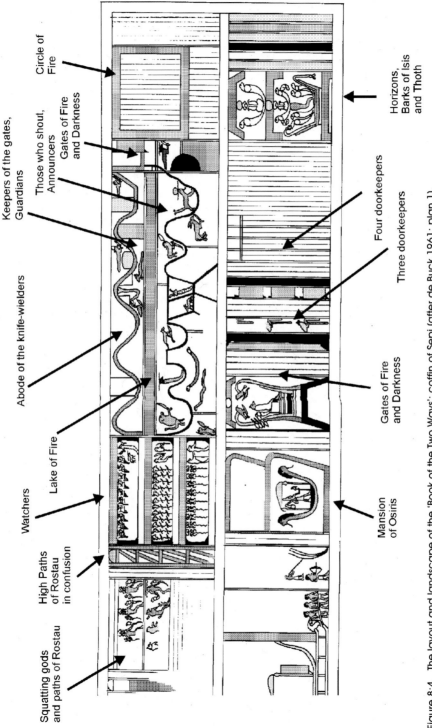

Figure 8:4 The layout and landscape of the 'Book of the Two Ways': coffin of Sepi (after de Buck 1961: plan 1).

coffins, images of these monsters and fantastic beasts, many armed with knives or other weapons, are depicted in the landscape. The deceased traverse this landscape and we can imagine them reading through the spells, learning and repeating the texts and using them as protection against "Large-face who drives off aggressors ... a spell for passing by him which is below the waterway ..." (CT1167) or "He who swallows; he who is alert ..." (CT1044) and others encountered on the way. Finally, the deceased reaches the end of these waterways and pathways and receives special clothing and staffs of authority to show his or her successful initiation through the landscape (CT1069).

Once through the obstacles of Sections III and IV, the deceased leaves the paths and waterways behind to emerge in perhaps a more forbidding landscape in Section V. We are now in Rostau, a place whose name means 'necropolis', but whose etymology is perhaps 'ramp', used for moving a sarcophagus into a tomb (Carter and Gardiner 1917: 137; Faulkner 1991: 146). Crossing across a hall divided into three compartments by flaming walls, the deceased, calling upon the protection of Thoth, passes by groups of "watchers". At either end of the hall, sky symbols form the walls, maybe representing the horizon that the deceased claims to be in (CT1071). Beyond this hall of watchers, the deceased continues to a realm of paths of confusion, shown symbolically in the coffin as a region of many routes crossing over each other. As these routeways are often painted blue upon the coffins, they may have been located within the sky, or might have been waterways. Textually, however, they are said to be "high on the flint walls which are in Rostau, which is both on water and on land" (CT1072). Further gods and demons, scarab-headed and holding snakes and lizards in a number of examples, lie in wait for the deceased as he or she progresses through this land, before arriving in the presence of Osiris, to live eternally as Osiris, breathing and never perishing.

At this point the shorter 'C' version of the text finishes, marking the end of an earlier or simply an abbreviated version of the text. The longer version, however, continues with another four sections before the ultimate goal of an eternal existence is reached. Lesko (1972a: 93) suggests a Hermopolitan tradition for the next section of spells, and we may see here a later addition to the original texts, that originated in el-Bersheh amongst the court of the nomarchs. Evidence of the provinciality of Section VI is to be found in the numerous calls and references to the god of the region, Thoth. The deceased asks to be brought before Thoth (CT1089), greets Thoth (CT1092), travels along Thoth's path (CT1093), meets Thoth in the 'suite of Ra' (CT1094), and finally joins him in his sacred bark (CT1096–1098).

A single, long spell forms the next section, an identification by the deceased with Ra. Unlike the other sections, this section included no vignettes or images of the afterlife. Instead, the deceased gives a justification of his or her actions, denying any false deeds that may be attributed to him or her. Then the deceased takes his or her place in the solar bark of Ra.

Moving into Section VIII, the deceased confronts a number of gates in two regions. The first region consists of four gates. After passing through them, the deceased reaches a second region of three gates of fire behind a wall of darkness. The deceased, therefore, encounters seven gates in this region. Each of these gates has its own guardian. The text here explicitly names the seven guardians in turn, equipping the deceased with the power of the knowledge of their names. In addition, whilst the spells for the first four gates seem to be the words of the deceased in repelling the individual guardians, those spells concerned with the final three guardians are more like the words of guides and protectors of the deceased or words said by the deceased himself to justify his passage through these final gates.

Having succeeded in passing through the seven gates, the deceased now enters Section IX, the final section of the text. Here is the ultimate end of the journey, as the deceased meets with Osiris, the 'god of the Underworld', offers him the 'Eye of Horus', becomes Thoth, son of Osiris, and meets up with the divine beings who exist around the solar bark, before finally spending an eternal existence witnessing a speech by Ra of his mighty deeds. The text concludes by comparing the deceased to Ra at the moment of sunrise and Osiris in the underworld and we realise that the journey 'has come happily to an end' (CT1130).

A potential geography of the afterlife from Two Ways?

We can therefore use the texts of the Book of the Two Ways to begin to understand the environment of the afterlife as seen by the Egyptian of the Middle Kingdom. This landscape can be envisaged both as a sky-borne world of celestial pathways and as a dark and foreboding underworld traversed by paths and canals. There are buildings and structures, and unnamed towns. Fire and darkness occasionally block the way and we must negotiate a number of gateways and portals with their guardians. Care must also be taken in traversing other pathways, since demons and monsters are there to trap the unwary and those who do not know the way. There are waterways, lakes and sources of magical flames. Yet, with our texts in hand, we can find our way through the obstacles to reach the end of our journey.

One striking feature of the journey depicted in the Book of the Two Ways is the number of demons and monsters ("An imaginary animal, either partly brute and partly human, or compounded of elements from two or more animal forms" (OED 1973: 1351)) that lie along the route.

Many of the monsters that appear within the Book of the Two Ways are shown within the bends of the various routeways, within Sections III and IV. In two published coffin plans we are given images of these fabulous beasts (de Buck 1961: plan 1 – coffin of Sepi, plan 14 – coffin of Djehutyhotep). Some are indeed composites with human heads and animal bodies, or mammalian heads and serpentine bodies. In many cases, these creatures are shown brandishing knives. Even when not illustrated in vignettes, we can get some idea of the nature of these demonic forms within the texts. "This is ... a spell for passing by the abodes of the knife-wielders and of those who shout ..." (CT1053) or "His name is Dog-face, whose shape is big ..." (CT1064) and "Those who are in it. Hot of face. Loud of voice. Oppressor. Monster. His name is 'he who is hot'" (CT1152).

Clearly, there are many dangerous creatures to be passed. But the question remains as to whether these beasts are confined to the el-Bersheh coffins, or represent a general understanding of the afterlife. Generations from the New Kingdom and later were to see the afterlife with its portals as teeming with demonic creatures.

Perhaps the creatures of el-Bersheh were just part of a much larger Middle Kingdom menagerie.

Though badly damaged in the years since they were first created, the tombs of el-Bersheh, like many of the nomarchal tombs along the length of Egypt, appear to have been highly decorated. Whilst much of the decorative schema of these tombs included scenes typical of much of tomb decoration from the Old Kingdom until the Late Period, such as agricultural and industrial scenes, images of the deceased in symbolic hunting and fishing expeditions and the deceased with his family, nonetheless there are some curious images within the registers (Figure 8:5). Tomb 5, for instance, belonging to the Great Chief of the Hare Nome, Ahanakht, and dating to the reign of Mentuhotep II or III (ca. 2000–1990 BC), depicts hunting and desert scenes in its outer chamber. Amongst the animals portrayed is one described as *tesh-tesh* or "Tearer in pieces" which takes the form of a composite beast, with a lion's body, a hawk's head, eagle's wings and divine horns and feathers (Griffith and Newberry 1894: 34–5, pl. XVI; Figure 8:5a). In the nearby Tomb 4, belonging to Nehri I and dating to the end of the eleventh Dynasty, the fragmentary remains of the wall plaster depict the head and shoulders of an eared and hawk-headed creature described as a *sagt*, similar (Figure 8:5b) to the *tesh-tesh* referred to above, as well as reference to another creature depicted in Tomb 5 (Griffith and Newberry 1894: 29, pl. XI). However, such creatures are not

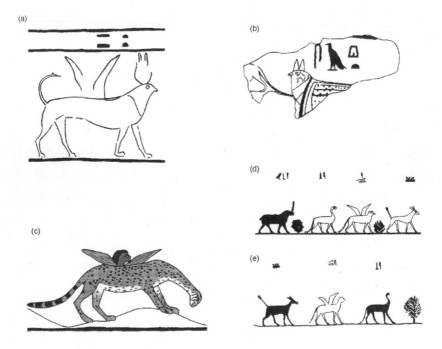

Figure 8:5   Monsters from Middle Kingdom tomb reliefs: (a) *tesh-tesh* from tomb of Ahanakht, el-Bersheh, (b) *sagt* on painted fragment from tomb of Nehri I, el-Bersheh, (c) leopard-spotted *tesh-tesh* from tomb of Khnumhotep II, Beni Hasan (author's own drawing from photograph), (d) desert creatures in tomb of Baket, Beni Hasan, (e) desert creatures in tomb of Khety, Beni Hasan.

confined to el-Bersheh. Beni Hasan, the necropolis of the Oryx-nome administrators and court, also has its creatures upon its walls. There is a *tesh-tesh*-like animal, with a leopard-spotted body, long striped tail, long neck and hawk's wings surrounding a human head sprouting from its back, in the tomb of Khnumhotep II (Tomb 3; Figure 8:5c). The tomb of Baket (Tomb 15) contains images of a standing quadruped Seth-beast, a snake-headed and long-tailed quadruped, a *tesh-tesh*-like animal, and a unicorned quadruped (Griffith and Newberry 1893: pl. IV; Figure 8:5d). The nearby tomb of Khety (Tomb 17) presents a similar sequence, including again a *tesh-tesh*-like animal amongst other fabulous creatures (Newberry 1893: pl. XIII; Figure 8:5e). These griffins and other fantastic beasts are usually found within the hunting scenes in the desert landscapes. Clearly, at the time that these tombs were under construction the Egyptians believed that such demonic beasts were not only a feature of the afterlife, but of another chaotic and dangerous environment: that of the desert, beyond the ordered Nile Valley.

If monsters appear on early Middle Kingdom tomb walls and on coffin floors, so are they widespread in the symbolic imagery of magical and cult objects that are found in later contexts. Many late Middle Kingdom tombs along the Nile Valley contain examples of ivory 'wands'. These curved objects, made from the large tusks of hippopotami, contain images of a variety of creatures and amuletic symbols. Though primarily made for the use of the living, many of these wands were included in the late Middle Kingdom burials at various places along the Nile Valley. It has been suggested that the living used these objects to magically ward off snakes, insects and other dangers. The points of these wands are often worn down, as if they had been used to draw 'enclosing circles of protection' on the floors around someone or something; and because of the texts inscribed upon them, it is generally considered that they might have been used to protect young children whilst asleep (Hayes 1953: 247–248). Although the use of such wands in tomb contexts indicates a shift in funerary ritual away from an earlier depiction of dangerous creatures on tomb walls and coffins to one that uses amuletic magic to ward off demons, the use of such wands may have provided a protective area to help guard the deceased. We may interpret this as a belief that the deceased, reborn into a new afterlife, must also have been seen as vulnerable and requiring the protection of apotropaic magic (Robins 1997: 114–115). We ought also to see this shift in ritual as a move away from the use of objects specifically manufactured for the deceased, to one that used objects of daily life for their intrinsic magical properties.

Many of the magical wands found in tombs bear images reminiscent of the earlier tomb wall reliefs, with their griffins and long-necked quadrupeds (Figure 8:6a), but also a number show bipedal creatures brandishing knives similar to those encountered in the Book of the Two Ways' vignettes from Spell 1069 (Figure 8:6b). It may be significant that ivory wands form part of the *frise d'objets* depicted on early Middle Kingdom coffins and are especially associated with images of beds in these decorative elements (D'Auria *et al.* 1988: 127–128). Altenmüller (1986) and Bourriau (1991) further suggest that these objects, with their associations with a battle between the sun god and his enemies, may have replaced solar spells from coffins of the onset of the Middle Kingdom.

(a)

(b)

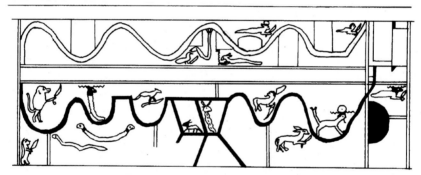

Figure 8:6   Monsters from Middle Kingdom funerary contexts: (a) magic wands (after Petrie 1927: pl. XXXVI; Jeffreys 2003a: Figure 11:1), (b) details of the coffin floor of Sepi, showing creatures from Spell 1069 of the 'Book of the Two Ways' (after de Buck 1961: pl. 1).

Around 1450 BC, when anthropoid coffins were replacing rectangular coffins, and some 400 years after the later sources for the Book of the Two Ways, it became customary to place a scroll of papyrus within the elite burial, which contained another selection of funerary literature, known today as the 'Book of the Dead' and in ancient times as the "formulae for going out by day". There are many passages within the Book of the Dead that are more or less heavily revised versions of the Middle Kingdom Coffin Texts. In fact, it has been suggested (Grapow 1909: 79) that as much as one third of the Book of the Dead may have its origins within the Coffin Texts.

But it is with the geographical and gateway sections of the Book of the Two Ways that we find some interesting comparisons. The Book of the Dead contains a section of

'Glorifications' that describe, amongst other things, seven gates through which the deceased must pass to achieve eternal existence. The gate chapters are often labelled as "Spells for knowing the gates of the house of Osiris in the West and the Gods who are in their twin caverns" (Chapter 147; Allen 1974: 137). In a second version they are introduced as "Knowing the names of them that are at the seven gates and their guardians and the announcers in them" (Chapter 144; Allen 1974: 121). Clearly, the function of these texts is to introduce the deceased to the various creatures that block the way to those not permitted to the afterlife. They can therefore be seen to operate in the same way as various sub-texts within the Book of the Two Ways and we may suspect that they have roots in the Middle Kingdom texts. An analysis of these various inhabitants shows that indeed there is a correlation between the Book of the Two Ways and these specific later Chapters. However, unlike the lists of demons lying in wait along the banks of the various pathways, these Book of the Dead creatures are arranged in groups of three at each of the seven gates.

We can see from the Table (p. 159) that the compilers of the Book of the Dead adapted a number of the various demons from the Book of the Two Ways, using them in the text of the 'Book of Coming Forth by Day' or Book of the Dead (BD in Table). The images of the various demons, however, differ widely between the Coffin Text examples and those in the Book of the Dead. In some of the New Kingdom examples, these gateways are guarded by mummiform spirits (P. Yuya: Davis 1908: pls. XIX–XX); in other examples, they are depicted as standing mammal-, reptilian- or bird-headed, human-bodied creatures (P. Nu: Lapp 1997: pl. 74); and further as seated similar animal-headed divinities (P. Ani: Faulkner 1972: 134–135). In many cases, however, the demons, where depicted, brandish knives or branches. There are, of course, a number of demonic guardians in the Book of the Two Ways who do not appear to have been carried through to the Book of the Dead. Conversely, a number of demons who appear in the Book of the Dead appear to have no antecedents in the Book of the Two Ways or other spells in the Coffin Texts.

A further geographical treatise appears, apparently uniquely, in the Bersheh coffins, in 11 coffins of 10 individuals that contain the Book of the Two Ways (Lesko 1972b: 89) and then re-emerges in the Book of the Dead. This is the text that describes the "Fields of Iaru" or "Fields of Hetep", a mythical place of fields and waterways, temples and towns that is introduced at Bersheh as CT466 and 467 (Parkinson 1991b: 134–136). Here, geographical locations are enumerated and named, in a 'map' reminiscent of an offering table (Willems 1988: 235). The diagram and accompanying captions and formulae continued in use in the New Kingdom, as the Book of the Dead, Chapter 110 (Figure 9:5 below).

The purpose and meaning of an afterlife geography in the Book of the Two Ways

The Coffin Texts in general and the Book of the Two Ways in particular provide illuminating insights into numerous aspects of the Middle Kingdom, its society and its religious development. A number of scholars have suggested that the Egyptian coffin, like the various objects included within the burial, the reliefs on the tomb walls and the tomb itself, acted like a machine to transport the deceased at the moment of interment from this world to the sought-after afterlife (Willems 1988: 238–239). Much of this 'ritual machine' is now lost, namely the words and rites of the funerary liturgy, and the activities at the coffin side before the sealing of the tomb (Bourriau 1991: 4), all of which presumably had a significant role in such a metaphysical transfiguration.

In his study of a Middle Kingdom coffin from Aswan, Willems (1996) has analysed the decoration of the coffin and its religious and ritual significance. This coffin, of a man called Heqata, belongs to a southern tradition, represented by a number of coffins found in the Theban, Gebelein and Aswan cemeteries. As such, it includes some features and schema not found within the el-Bersheh tradition. On the other hand, there are a number of decorative features which, if not the same as those on el-Bersheh coffins, at least appear to share a common design and purpose (Figure 8:7). Like the el-Bersheh coffins, Heqata's coffin had an object frieze painted around its internal walls. It also contained a number of spells from the Coffin Texts, with references to gods, rituals and hopes for the afterlife. Willems (1996: 91) has also shown how these elements within the coffin's decorative schema work together to depict a journey from this life to the next, with a metaphysical landscape as backdrop. An analysis of this schema helps explain and understand the key moments from the decoration within the coffins from el-Bersheh. Heqata's coffin has little decoration on its floor, and certainly nothing like the Book of the Two Ways. It contains a star clock on the inside of the lid, representing a night sky and helping 'orientate' the deceased within geographical space. Within the coffin, the object frieze around the head and the associated texts indicate a representation of the Opening of the Mouth ritual, ensuring the protection of the deceased's head and neck. We are perhaps seeing a virtual ritual being played out for the deceased for all eternity. In addition to this ritual, images of vessels and sacred objects are associated with lists of sacred oils and perfumes within the texts (Spell 934) and allude to the embalming of the deceased within a *wabet* or 'place of embalming', usually a temporary structure close by the tomb. Around the internal walls of Heqata's coffin, numerous references to watchers and snake-charmers within this structure perhaps indicate nightly vigils, which, as they are represented in a metaphysical afterlife, are somewhat demonic and require placating with texts, offerings or words of power, for example in Spell 236.

But the rituals that take place around the deceased's head are just the culmination of a rite of passage from this life to the next. Willems believes that the traditional start for this journey lay in the west, near to present-day Letopolis. Heqata here reaped emmer wheat from the divinities, which he would eventually offer to Osiris in his '*wabet*' at the end of his journey. Much of this journey is recounted in Spells 397 and 398. Prior to his arrival at his '*wabet*', Heqata boarded a divine ferry, having first proved his worthiness to cross into his afterlife. Travelling in this "Bark of Sokar", Heqata sails along the "Winding Waterway", avoiding a group of seven demonic fishermen and other spirits aiming to stop the unworthy. On the way, he approaches the "Fields of Hetep", which might be located, like his ultimate destination, in the environs of Heliopolis. Eventually, Heqata reaches the end of his ferryboat journey, disembarking at Rostau, to enter into his '*wabet*' as Osiris and to be ritually embalmed to become an initiate into his afterlife.

Heqata's coffin offers certain clues to the interpretation of the Book of the Two Ways. Whilst the Coffin Texts have some 1,185 individual spells in their corpus, it is

A. Interpretation of Heqata's Coffin *(based on Willems 1996)*

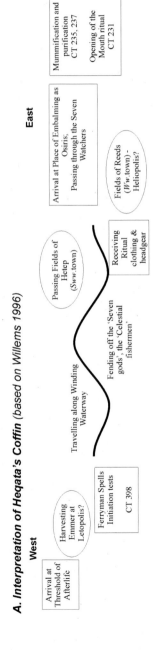

B. Interpretation of el-Bersheh coffins

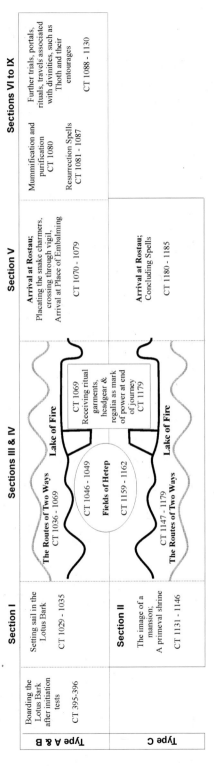

Figure 8:7   Interpreting the ritual landscape of the 'Book of the Two Ways' in comparison with the coffin of Heqata.

important to remember that not all spells occur on all coffins of the Middle Kingdom. The Book of the Two Ways, as already seen, is confined to a limited number of coffins from a specific locality. We can, however, draw the parallels between the el-Bersheh texts and those of Heqata (Figure 8:7). On A and B type coffins, the text begins as the deceased is about to board a "Great Bark of Ra". Prior to this, the deceased's worthiness to travel has been confirmed (Spell 395), where mention of the Lotus Bark and its parts seems to parallel Heqata's interrogation by the divine ferryman, mentioned above. Type C coffins begin at an 'image of a mansion' or a primeval shrine at the moment the doors to the afterlife are flung open to allow the deceased to enter. Once aboard his or her Lotus Bark, the deceased travels down waterway or darkened path, meeting guardians and watchers intent on holding back the unworthy. On the way, the deceased stops at the Field of Hetep (Spells 1048–1052 – versions A and B; Spells 1159–1162 – version C) to prepare a meal or harvest for Osiris. These references to the Fields of Hetep are not as detailed as Spells 466 and 467 noted above. Nonetheless, they form part of the crucial journey from this life to the next, enabling the deceased to collect food on the way to offer to Osiris at the Place of Embalming.

Arriving at the end of his or her voyage, the deceased disembarks at Rostau, only to come across more guardians and paths of confusion (Spells 1070–1079). Significantly, some of these guardians are shown carrying lizards and snakes (Spell 1076: B1C – coffin of Sep; B5C – coffin of Djehutyhotep), protecting Osiris' embalmed corpse in the manner implied in Heqata's coffin (Willems 1996: 127–131). At this point, Spell 1080 indicates the collection of the "efflux of Osiris", the liquids of putrefaction drained from the deceased's corpse as part of the process of mummification and which were believed to hold life-giving properties. The sacred *snw* vases depicted upon Heqata's coffin were perhaps used to collect these liquids, which were associated with the regenerative powers of the corpse of Osiris. Undoubtedly this part of the Book of the Two Ways (the end of Lesko's Section V, Spells 1080–1087) represents the process of mummification of the deceased. Version C of the text ends here. Versions A and B continue as the deceased traverses further realms and re-visits the 'Winding Waterway' and its spirits (perhaps as a duplication or re-stating of Sections III and IV) until he or she reaches an eternity as Osiris in his sarcophagus and as Ra at the moment of sunrise in the east (Spells 1088–1130).

The Middle Kingdom coffin genre carried on the traditions of the Old Kingdom decorated tombs, with their false doors, representations of scenes and objects of both daily life and symbolic ritual, and various architectural features. Some of the demonic aspects of the coffins are related to the tomb reliefs from Beni Hasan and el-Bersheh itself. It may be significant that the tomb paintings of demons cited above occur early on in the Middle Kingdom, whereas the demons of the Book of the Two Ways date from a generation or two later. In addition, the coffin, through its magical texts inside and out, offered a means to meet with the solar god Ra, underworld god Osiris and other divinities for those possessing it. Now, however, these detailed images were painted in bright colours upon the inner and outer surfaces of the deceased's coffin. The use of the Book of the Two Ways within the locality of el-Bersheh may also be a regional representation of the liturgy and imagery of funerary rituals and beliefs. This imagery shows a stage of transition, crossing from the world of the living, via a testing journey to a blessed existence in eternity and the achievement of rebirth. Furthermore, the Book of the Two Ways is perhaps to be interpreted as an elaboration or detailed explanation of the ferryman spells, as depicted on Middle Kingdom coffins such as that of Heqata (Figure 8:7 above).

These Coffin Text spells should perhaps be seen as existing in a variety of exemplars – scraps of significant spells, selected by the intended coffin owner for inclusion on his or her final resting place. With this is mind, the chronological development of the Coffin Texts as envisaged by Willems (1988: 247–248) becomes clear. After the re-unification of Egypt at the start of the Middle Kingdom, there must have been a rapid development and flowering of these afterlife texts whilst some texts may have remained regional specializations. With time, the genre of Coffin Texts became more fully developed, but other social, political and religious forces began to influence their use and distribution.

Certain individual spells or groups of spells might have been perceived as more efficacious at guiding the deceased into his or her afterlife during the Middle Kingdom. El-Bersheh texts emphasized the journey between death and the Place of Embalming with their representation of the Book of the Two Ways. Elsewhere, emphasis was given to other parts of the post mortem ritual. Some of these texts continued to be used after the end of the Middle Kingdom, possibly combined with textual and liturgical elements from other, now lost traditions. The effects of this recombination may perhaps be seen in the re-use of the Book of the Two Ways demons in Chapters 144–147 of the Book of the Dead. These chapters included some of the watchers, announcers and doorkeepers from part of the Coffin Text spells, yet do not include demons from other sections of the text, including instead references to guardians, portals and creatures derived perhaps from other textual sources. This combination of earlier spells in new and novel ways may constitute further evidence for what Hornung (1999: 11) has described as "government-funded research into the hereafter", albeit to enable the priests of the New Kingdom to map out their own ideas of the landscape of the afterlife.

In many cases, the creation of the Books of the Dead out of the remains of the Coffin Texts and Book of the Two Ways is also characterized by a conversion of the format of the spells from the three-dimensional surface of the coffin sides to a two-dimensional papyrus roll. Although this transition is marked by the survival of a number of motifs, such as the guardian gatekeepers, the change highlights a move away from a pictorial and diagrammatic expression of the landscapes of an afterlife and journeys across and through it. The New Kingdom Book of the Dead, for example, presents the gateway information of Spells 144–147 not as a map reminiscent of the el-Bersheh coffin genre but as simple vignettes, with the appropriate descriptive and ritual texts usually arranged below, as in P. Nu (Lapp 1997: 59). Although the use of papyrus to produce an extended religious map re-emerges with the Book of the Fayum (Tait Chapter 10, this volume), during the New Kingdom the afterlife landscape is presented in a more itemized format of a list of locations. The cartographic methods of the coffin makers at Bersheh therefore represent an isolated peak of underworld mapping knowledge in non-royal contexts during the twelfth Dynasty. The true New Kingdom heirs of this envisioning of the afterlife landscape lie not within the realms of the papyrus Books of the Dead produced for the elite across Egypt, but instead amongst the royal tombs of the Valley of the Kings, with their graphical descriptions of the journey of the sun god through the hours of the night.

These texts, the 'Book of what is in the Hereafter' (or Amduat) and 'The Book of Gates', found on the walls of the tombs of kings in the Theban necropolis, enumerate and locate divinities, events and places encountered by the solar entourage as the sun god Ra is magically reborn at the moment of sunrise. The earliest existing source for these texts may date to the reign of Tuthmosis I (Hornung 1999: 27) but their origins are obscure. On the basis of current lack of knowledge of what was held within the royal libraries of the Middle Kingdom, it is not possible to explain the origins of these cartographic interpretations of the metaphysical world, within both the Middle Kingdom contexts of the el-Bersheh coffin text genre and also any royal texts that might have given rise to those geographical interpretations of the afterlife during the New Kingdom. Just how these texts arose and evolved may never be known.

The published examples of Middle Kingdom coffins, funerary offerings and architecture afford an ancient perception of the afterlife at that period, none more so than those coffins with depictions of the post mortem landscape. El-Bersheh coffins especially reveal a world of danger and challenge for the deceased. Undoubtedly the evidence that survives to the present day is dwarfed by the volume of evidence lost during the millennia since the original interments. When many of these tombs were first explored and excavated, the practices of excavators and techniques of recording fell far short of those demanded by present-day archaeology. At Meir, for instance, many fragments of coffins that now would be regarded as valuable and important evidence were destroyed by archaeologists who burnt much of the then apparently insignificant wood fragments for fires during the cold nights of the excavations (Willems 1988: 82).

Finally, in analyzing these spells of el-Bersheh and elsewhere, we must be mindful of the context of each individual text. As Willems (1996: 363) points out, Coffin Text spells work at a number of levels. At individual spell level, we can read certain key elements and see depictions of objects in the object friezes. As we move to broader contexts, we begin to see first the component sections of the coffin, then the coffin itself, until we reach the complex of the tomb, its chamber and superstructure, the burial chamber and coffin and all the objects found within. In today's digital age, many things are now perceived as 'object oriented', with 'classes of objects' being a key to understanding the world around us. The tomb, the coffin, the Coffin Text spells themselves, can now be envisaged as 'containers', holding symbolic, if not actual, objects within. Maps are just one class of container, retaining within defined boundaries, as it were, a landscape with all its appurtenances and symbolic features. The rituals recalled within the Book of the Two Ways, it can be argued, are just another form of symbol class included within the symbolic landscape of the afterlife as developed by the ancient Egyptians. As the depictions on the insides of the coffin suggest, we also see a transfer of some of the functions of the tomb itself to the coffin. Indeed the coffin might be described as a model tomb or even miniature of the universe itself, inheriting some of the forms, functions and ritual space of the higher object class of the tomb complex, its parent object (Willems 1988: 239–242).

Clearly, however, whatever one's orientation, analysis of the ritual space and landscape of the Book of the Two Ways goes some way in helping to interpret and understand the complexities of the ancient Egyptian conceptions of the cosmos, both physical and metaphysical.

Table   *Demons in the Book of Coming Forth by Day (BD) and their Coffin Text (CT) antecedents*

Coffin Text Demon	CT Spell	CT Section	BD name	BD gateway	Function
The sad-voiced one	1038	III	Sad of voice	1	Announcer
Fiery	1039	III	Burner	2	Announcer
He who curses	1039	III	He who curses	3	Announcer
He who swallows (*3sbw*)	1044	III	*3sbw*	5	Guardian
He who is alert	1044	III	Alert of mind	4	Guardian
He who is vigilant	1044	III	Alert of face	3	Guardian
He who is sharp sighted	1044	III	Watchful of face	2	Guardian
He who listens	1044	III	Eavesdropper	1	Guardian
Great face who repels the aggressors	1056	IV	Big of face, repeller of the crocodile	4	Announcer
Hippopotamus face, bellowing of power	1062	IV	Hippopotamus faced, raging of power	5	Announcer
He who stretches the Bow warp, keeper of the outer gate, spy	1100	VIII	Spy	2	Doorkeeper
He who eats the droppings of his hinder parts, keeper of the third gate	1102	VIII	Eater of the excrement of his posterior	3	Doorkeeper
He who glowers, keeper of the fourth gate	1103	VIII	He who defends from the noisy(?)	4	Doorkeeper
He whose face is inverted, the many shaped, keeper of the first gate	1108	VIII	Face downward, numerous of forms	1	Doorkeeper
He who lives on maggots, keeper of the middle gate	1109	VIII	He who lives on rotten meat	5	Doorkeeper

CHAPTER 9

MEASURING THE UNDERWORLD

Stephen Quirke

> I was given a reed like a measuring rod and was told, 'Go measure the temple of God and the altar, and count the worshippers there'.
>
> (Book of Revelation 11: 1)

Exact measurements of other-worldly objects are a recurrent feature of religious literature well within traditions familiar to western scholarship. The citation is from the Revelation of St. John, at the end of the New Testament, the sacred writings of the Christian East and West, dated to the late first century AD. Its directive to measure receives confirmation in the mathematically expressed lengths within the same visionary landscapes, as in the following description of the fate of evil forces:

> They were trampled in the winepress outside the city, and blood flowed out of the press, rising as high as the horses' bridles for a distance of 1,600 stadia.
>
> (Book of Revelation 14: 20)

Several passages from ancient Egyptian funerary literature include linear measurements for features in the underworld. While they are not the dominant strategy in describing an unknown world, they, like the measuring in Revelation, are among the most striking assertions of knowledge in the religious domain. The numerical values provided with the units of measurement offer rich data for an understanding of the symbolism of numbers. However, preceding the specific associations of those numbers, there is the broader question of measurement itself. What lies behind this strategy of combining a unit of measurement with a number, in contexts so remote from the measurable world? For this is far less common than the use of numerals with other nouns in Egyptian religious literature. Some vision has prompted a creative writer to express mathematical precision, when the object is not available in this world to human touch. If a spirit is said to be seven cubits high, or a mountain is 300 leagues long, this information must have its impact both on the person transmitting it, and on the person receiving it. Perhaps that impact determines the use of a measurement, rather than a belief in the truth of the measurement. The decision to assert knowledge of the underworld by means of a measurement could be more important to the ancient writers and readers than the particular numeral and unit given. The measurements may be intrusive, imports into the religious domain from a world of accountancy or a world of literary narrative. This exact description of the world, a mathematical cosmography, is in the end an inevitable projection into the afterlife of the dominant technologies of knowing in an urbanized and socially stratified society – writing and calculating, with in first place the calculation of time. None of these questions can be addressed without some knowledge of how prominent or marginal a place was taken by linear measurement within the full range of Egyptian writing for the afterlife.

Ancient Egyptian funerary literature

Elite burial in Ancient Egypt involved elaborate procedures for preserving the dead body, requiring attention over several months between death and funeral. A sequence of days copied on the back of one papyrus of the late Middle Kingdom (ca. 1800 BC) indicates that, already by that date, embalming required 70 days, as recorded in ancient Greek writings on Egypt (Gardiner 1955). From the mid-third millennium BC, written and pictorial sources refer to rituals performed during these weeks and months. The rites find their way into the surviving record indirectly, because the same or related words of those rites were copied onto select objects in the tomb or inscribed on the walls of the tomb. The exact manner of inscribing the space of the afterlife with this religious literature varied greatly over time, and was entirely absent in several periods. However, the scale of the surviving output is colossal, and this quantitative context is vital for appreciation of the few passages with measurements of the underworld. Taken together, this discontinuous practice of writing for eternity amounts to the greatest body of written, and even of the known oral, funerary literature in human history. So much composing might well encourage variation in expressing the encounter with death and the underworld. Measurement is one minor strand in the armoury of the ancient Egyptian composer of funerary literature.

Egyptologists have divided the constantly evolving stream of writing into three principal groups: Pyramid Texts, Coffin Texts, and Book of the Dead, according to the date of their first appearance and the predominant writing surface of that period. At any one place and time, there would be well over 100 compositions in circulation. 'Composition' here denotes a unit separated from the preceding and following units in a set, principally by the framing devices of title and/or end-note in the original inscriptions and manuscripts. The compositions range in length from pairs of phrases, corresponding to just a line of modern printed text, to more substantial passages which amount to several pages of modern printed text. The proportion of pictorial accompaniment varies over time, and can be absent.

1 **Pyramid Texts:** miscellaneous compositions in the Old Egyptian phase of the Egyptian language, as written in the third millennium BC. These are first found inscribed in hieroglyphs on the walls of chambers inside the pyramid of the king in the late fifth to eighth Dynasties (ca. 2400–2200 BC), with many later found in non-royal contexts down to the early Roman Period, first century AD. There are no images accompanying these compositions.

2 **Coffin Texts:** miscellaneous compositions in the Middle Egyptian phase of the Egyptian language, some derived from Pyramid Texts, mainly known from copies in cursive hieroglyphs on the walls, lids and floors of coffins of the late eleventh

to mid-twelfth Dynasties (ca. 2000–1850 BC). There are few illustrations directly included in this corpus, but, on most coffins, columns of cursive hieroglyphs form large blocks of writing beneath a broad horizontal register containing colourful depictions of objects from a funeral offering ritual (Willems 1988).

3 **Book of the Dead:** a pool of about 200 Middle Egyptian compositions, more than half of which derive from the Coffin Texts, and mainly known from copies in cursive hieroglyphs (later in full hieroglyphs and in the more cursive hieratic script) on papyrus scrolls from non-royal burials from the mid-eighteenth Dynasty to the end of the Ptolemaic Period (ca. 1450–50 BC). Most compositions are now accompanied by illustrations, although the proportion of these to the writing varies greatly, from manuscripts with no illustrations to illustrated manuscripts without any writing.

Despite what at first seems a bewildering mass of material, these groups represent a continuous flow of writing, evolving over time. The compositions echo the words that accompanied the weeks of embalming, the day or days of funeral, and the subsequent rites for the cult of the dead. The Book of the Dead introduces visual imagery on a larger scale.

A fourth group of funerary compositions is in a separate category, both in its content and in the emphatic focus on the images rather than the words – the Underworld Books. These are compositions dominated by visual imagery but with accompanying Middle Egyptian passages written in a cursive hieroglyphic script, first found on the walls of the tombs of kings in the mid-eighteenth to twentieth Dynasties (ca. 1450–1100 BC), later on papyrus scrolls and coffins of the early Third Intermediate Period (ca. 1050–850 BC) and stone sarcophagi from non-royal burials as late as the thirtieth Dynasty (380–343 BC).

A reductive synthesis was the initial response of modern European scholarship to the hundreds of compositions on the hundreds of sources from dozens of such varied types of object. In the decades following their discovery around 1880, the Old Egyptian compositions on pyramid walls were reduced to order, and finally converted by Sethe into a single printed corpus of Pyramid Texts in numerical sequence (Faulkner 1969; Sethe 1908–1922). This had been the strategy of Naville (1888) for the chaotic mass of Book of the Dead manuscripts from the New Kingdom. De Buck adopted the same approach between the two World Wars, as he produced a sequence of 1,185 numbers in seven volumes of Coffin Texts, the compositions on dozens of early Middle Kingdom coffins distributed around the world (de Buck 1935–1961; Faulkner 1973–1978). In these reductive syntheses, the original sources had to take second place to the production of a printed and final 'Text'. This European application of numerical sequences to the originally numbered Egyptian funerary literature reflects both practical necessity for reference in modern academic publications, and, at a different level, a human psychological need for control. It has been argued that, in disciplining its unruly object of study, orientalist philology provided an academic mirror of, or even foundation for, the colonization of Africa and Asia (Said 1991). Archaeology, anthropology, the museum and cartography share this disciplining role in the development of the modern world (Biggs 1999; Preziosi 1996; Thomas 1994). All arguably present efficient techniques for imposing a particular world order, in the interests of colonial domination. They and their numbering systems are unlikely to be as politically innocent or scientifically objective as they appear to claim. The ordering of Egyptian funerary literature needs to be considered in the context of such western approaches.

A synoptic edition of original sources produces a comfortingly invariable Text out of manuscript and inscription, but it is not the only option. In the first Egyptological imposition of order by numbers, for the Book of the Dead, Lepsius (1842) retained the ancient source material in the foreground, by adopting a single manuscript as his anchor. He selected the longest papyrus known to him among those presenting the most common sequence of funerary compositions, the Book of the Dead of a man named Iufankh, from the late Ptolemaic Period (ca. 150–30 BC). He then allotted numbers 1 to 165 for each item as he encountered it in sequence on this papyrus, including some illustrations without words (Chapters 16, 143, 150), and some repeated compositions (e.g. Chapters 100 and 129, the same content at different points in the manuscript of Iufankh). In later phases of the study of funerary literature, some researchers have returned to this focus on the source material, with publication of individual monuments, as in the Piankoff editions of the inscriptions in the pyramid of King Unas and the tomb of Ramesses VI, the Bonn-Cologne Book of the Dead publication project, and the publications of individual coffins by Lapp (1997; Munro 1995; Piankoff 1968). Other researchers, such as Assmann (1990), have redirected the focus from text to context, which is taken to be more illuminating of past practice. The two different approaches – abstract text numbering and object-oriented cultural study – have both advanced modern understanding of the ancient writings and images, and can both be rigorously source-critical. However, for the meaning of measurements in these compositions, the object-oriented approach seems to offer more direct guidance in questions of personal belief. The guiding source in what follows is a now fragmentary papyrus with a selection of Book of the Dead formulae copied for a woman named Satiah.[1]

The Book of the Dead of Satiah

According to the surviving papyrus fragments, Satiah had a second name, Id, and her parents were Herira and the lady of the house Sembu. The style of these names, the handwriting and the selection of compositions included on the papyrus indicate a date soon after the introduction of funerary papyri, ca. 1450 BC. Elite burials of the period 1450–1350 BC clustered at Thebes (modern Luxor and Qurna), where the kings of the day were buried, and most papyri of this date come from the cemeteries there. It seems likely, although it cannot be proven, that the burial of Satiah too lay at Thebes. The female ownership of this funerary manuscript is an extraordinary feature in the context of the time, and deserves further comment. During the period 1450–1350 BC, the rites for the cult of the dead had their home in decorated rock-cut offering chapels, located above the burial chamber cut into the rock (for Thebes see Manniche 1987). Without exception the primary cult in these chapels served the male head of a family unit; the women of the family took second place in the decorative programme. Nearly all surviving Books of the Dead follow this primary male gendering of the afterlife, with men as owners, followed by the women; even stock manuscripts, where spaces were left blank for later insertion of the name of the deceased, show a man, with the wife behind the man in just a few key scenes, and otherwise omitted. As a Book of the Dead without a man, P. Satiah is set against a norm that is statistically overwhelming (Quirke 1999). Only two secure parallels can be cited from among the 70 or more papyri surviving from the period 1450–1350 BC. The first is an exceptional woman, Hatnefer, mother of the influential high official Senenmut, who served an exceptional sovereign, Queen Hatshepsut, ca. 1450 BC. The second is Meryt, wife of the head of royal works Kha, ca. 1375 BC.[2] A possible third female owner of papyrus is known from a fragment only, and it is not certain that the whole scroll was dedicated principally to her, or to her husband. Women own funerary papyri regularly only from the mid-twentieth Dynasty, ca. 1150 BC. The virtual exclusion of women from New Kingdom papyri before that date follows a change in the type of object chosen as writing surface for the literature securing a good afterlife. The papyrus scroll had only become a regular medium for funerary compositions in the joint reign of Hatshepsut with Tuthmosis III, ca. 1450 BC. In the preceding period, 1550–1450 BC, linen shrouds bore the funerary compositions: since a shroud accompanied each individual wrapped body, both men and women were equipped with their own series of compositions for separate survival in the afterlife. A late example of this practice is the shroud of a woman named Resti, also, judging from the style of its illustrations, from ca. 1450 BC. Once papyrus became the normal support for copies of funerary compositions for the afterlife, the practice of copying them on shrouds disappeared, and the male gendering emerged for the single scroll buried with the couple. The Book of the Dead of Satiah is a rare find, then, documenting the possibility of autonomous female gendering of identity in papyri for the afterlife in the period 1450–1150 BC. The scarcity of parallels reinforces the impression that the manuscript dates not long after 1450 BC, when the tradition of a separate manuscript for the woman may still have been a strong memory. Neither Satiah nor her parents are known from other sources. Therefore we do not know whether she, like Hatnefer, was related to some influential official of the day, or was herself an outstanding woman, or, and whether, some exceptional event or status entitled her to her own funerary papyrus.

Since literacy appears central to status in Ancient Egypt, it is reasonable to ask what relation Satiah herself might have had to her Book of the Dead. What part, if any, she or any other member of the Egyptian elite played in the selection of the religious compositions to be copied onto a funerary papyrus is not recorded. The surviving fragments of her Book of the Dead bear compositions found on numerous other manuscripts, giving an impression of social rather than individual selection. Nevertheless, the compositions are each copied explicitly for the named individual; a personal relationship is established at least in theory by the rubric title, which specifies that these words are spoken by the person, on the model 'formula for sailing in the boat of the sun god ... words spoken by Satiah'. These are the surviving compositions that Satiah recites to obtain eternal life, numbered by the 'Chapter' sequence established by Lepsius:

- Book of the Dead Chapter 99, a formula for addressing the ferryman of the underworld;

- Book of the Dead Chapter 125, declarations of purity before Osiris, god of the dead;

- Book of the Dead Chapter 136, a formula for sailing in the boat of the sun god Ra;

- Book of the Dead Chapter 149, address to each of 14 mounds in the underworld.

The end of the papyrus was taken up by the illustration numbered by Lepsius Chapter 150, assembling 15 diagrams of mounds in a different sequence to Chapter 149 (Figures 9:1 and 9.2).

Figure 9:1 Images of the mounds of the Underworld, 'Book of the Dead' Chapter 149 from P. Nu (after Lapp 1997: pl. IV) (British Museum EA 10477).

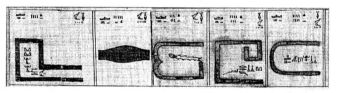

Figure 9:2 The mounds of the underworld, in images, 'Book of the Dead' Chapter 150 is two different versions. Left, fragment from P. Sabtah (author's drawing); right, a complete version from P. Nu (Lapp 1987: pl. IV) (British Museum EA 10477).

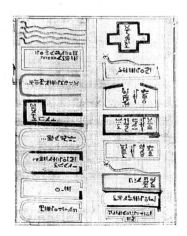

These five Chapters are among the most common on funerary papyri of the period 1450–1350 BC, when Chapters 149 and 150 regularly form the closing section of a manuscript (Lapp 1997:42). The end of Chapter 99 and two of the 14 sections of Chapter 149 are the principal Book of the Dead passages to include linear measurements of features in the underworld. There is no fragment bearing Book of the Dead Chapter 110, which is the only combination of linear measurement in any diagram of a landscape. However, that Chapter is also common in New Kingdom manuscripts, and so it is quite possible that the Satiah Book of the Dead originally contained that Chapter too, giving her every underworld measurement available to a person of her status and time. Even if it had included Chapter 110, the measurements would not have constituted more than a small proportion of the writing for her afterlife. The copies of Chapters 99 and 149 in the Book of the Dead of Satiah are fragmentary, and my translation of the relevant passages is therefore based on two better preserved parallels: P. Yuya, ca. 1375 BC, and P. Nu, ca. 1400 BC.

Chapter 99, instructions written in red at the end of the composition (following P. Yuya, recent republication Munro 1994: pl. 64, lines 681–684):

This formula is to be recited, and he is to go out by day from in the marsh, and is given loaf, beer-jug and cake, joint of meat, barley and emmer wheat 7 cubits high (?); it is the followers of Horus who reap it for him. Then he is to chew this barley and wheat, and then he is to rub his body with it, and then his body will be as these gods. He is to go out from the marsh of reeds in any form in which he wishes to go.

This instruction appears later than, and is therefore probably inspired by, the earliest sources for the next item, Chapter 149, mound 2.

Chapter 149, mound 2 (following P. Nu, published in Lapp 1997: pl. 82, lines 6–19):

I am the lord of wealth in the Field of Reeds.
O Field of Reeds, whose walls are of iron,
whose barley grows 7 cubits tall,
whose grain ears are 2 cubits, its stalk 5 cubits.
Spirits of 7 cubits in their length reap them beside Horakhty.
I know the middle door of the Field of Reeds
through which Ra goes out in the east of the sky.
Its south is in the lake of kharu-geese,
its north is in the wave of the ru-geese,
and the place where Ra sails with the winds and in rowing.
I am the keeper of reports in the boat of the god.
I am the one who rows untiring in the barque of Ra.
I know those two sycamore-trees of turquoise,
through which Ra goes out, which sprouted at the shooting of Shu
at the eastern door, through which Ra goes out.
I know that Field of Reeds of Ra,
whose barley grows 5 cubits tall,
whose grain ears are 2 cubits, its stalk 3 cubits.
Spirits of 9 cubits in their length reap them beside the eastern powers.

Chapter 149, mound 4, first part (following P. Nu, published in Lapp 1997: pl. 83, lines 25–28):

O he who dominates the secret mound,
O this tall and mighty mountain that is in the underworld
on which sky and earth alight,

measuring 300 rods in length and 10 rods in width,
with a serpent on it called Shooter of Two Knives,
measuring 70 cubits in its circuit,
living on cutting down spirits and damned in the underworld.
I stand in your stronghold, so that the sailing may be smooth,
for I have seen the way past you.

Finally, the fifth mound in Book of the Dead Chapter 149 is said to contain fearsome beings "7 cubits in their buttocks", an apt excremental image for these devourers of the shadows of the damned. Although another part of the composition accompanying the fifth mound derives from the Coffin Texts, the measurement is not found there, and seems to belong to the rewriting of the passage as part of Chapter 149, perhaps in the early New Kingdom.

The title phrases 'words spoken by Satiah' raise the question of what these phrases, and most particularly, these measurements signify for her afterlife. It is possible that she never saw or heard the words during her lifetime. However, their inclusion on the papyrus copied for her burial implies at least a social setting where these words carried sufficient value to form part of the strategy for her survival. One important possible meaning can be ruled out: the words do not guide Satiah to or from anywhere – they identify features already reached by the dead woman. Even with as many as 14 mounds, they offer insufficient information to define underworld geographies. The mounds are perhaps the most extended description of afterlife landscape features in the Book of the Dead, with both diagram and pigmentation as well as cast of characters. Yet, despite the image of precision evoked by the outlines in the diagrams illustrating the mounds, the reader receives no more visual information from the series as a whole. With the one exception of the fourth mound, the mountain 300 by 10 rods, the series goes unmeasured. Most important of all, in terms of mapping, although the mounds are numbered from "first" to "fourteenth", not one mound is spatially related to any of the others to form a connected landscape. At most, this is an implicit journey for the deceased through the underworld. The creator of the composition has not found it necessary to make the wider landscape or the journey, if such it is, explicit. Without measurements, the mound illustrations are not even necessarily an accurate guide to appearance, at least for a western reader. With a camera- and television-tuned eye we might assume that each outline is intended to be in proportion, but proportionate relative length and width is not the only possible underlying principle of depiction. Equally powerful principles include the relative importance of features, which could greatly distort any physical correlation. This can be seen consistently in Egyptian formal art with the outsize leading human figures in compositions such as offering to the deceased or the king overpowering animal and human enemies (Robins 1997: 21).

The nature of the 'mounds' are not clear, and they resemble ancient Egyptian plans of buildings as much as images of natural landscape features. Buildings are depicted in funerary literature, among the Coffin Texts, in the Book of the Two Ways (see Robinson Chapter 8, this volume), but none takes any of the forms indicated for the Book of the Dead mounds. Buildings are absent from the one other Middle Kingdom chart of an underworld landscape, the Marsh of Offerings (discussed below). Ancient Egyptian diagrams of buildings in the world of the living are not so common; surviving examples generally include measurements in cubits, and the western reader needs to learn more of the principles of depiction in ancient Egyptian

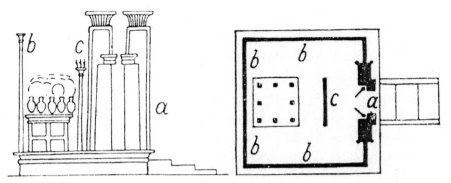

Figure 9:3   Ancient Egyptian (left) and modern (right) plans of the same building (after Schäfer 1930: 131, fig. 84).

formal art, to be equipped to decode each diagram. The difficulties in reading can be appreciated by comparing an ancient Egyptian sketch of a plain rectangular building with a plan of the same construction using conventions of modern western architectural drawing (Figure 9:3). Most of these spatial diagrams survive from later in the New Kingdom, principally from the activities of craftsmen responsible for the cutting and decoration of the king's tomb in the Valley of the Kings 1300–1100 BC. These are later than the earliest sources for the series of mounds in the Book of the Dead. However, there are three previously unpublished examples for rendering space in two-dimensional diagrams that predate the Book of the Dead, and offer possible sources of inspiration for these visual compositions.

Spatial diagrams in a Middle Kingdom town

Flinders Petrie retrieved thousands of papyrus fragments from his two 1889 seasons of clearance at the late Middle Kingdom town site at Lahun. These include just three with coloured schematic illustration (as distinct from figurative illustration, for which there is only one certain fragment):

- UC 32110H (Figure 9:4, left) Papyrus fragment with part of a coloured illustration on one side, and traces of an accounts table in red and black on the other. The closest parallels are renderings of desert space with red dotted pink area, demarcated in black – yellow adjacent area. This fragment is dated by the handwriting of the accounts table on the other side to the late Middle Kingdom (distinct phase in

Figure 9:4   Spatial diagrams on Middle Kingdom papyri fragments from Lahun: left UC 32110-H, centre UC 32316, right UC32327 (part).

material cultural history of Egypt, 1850–1700 BC). If a spatial diagram, it predates the parallels by around six centuries. The radically earlier date is supported by the early Middle Kingdom funerary visual and written composition known in Egyptology as the 'Book of Two Ways' (see Robinson Chapter 8, this volume).

- UC 32316 (Figure 9:4, centre) Papyrus fragment with on one side a red field demarcated at its only preserved edge by a thick black line; on the other side it too bears remnants of accounts.[3]

- UC 32327 (part) (Figure 9:4, right) One fragment in UC 32327, the papyrus fragments from lot XXVI, bears a drawing which appears to indicate a narrow-necked vessel, with black outlines and an internal curving black cross-line below the neck; the open end of the neck is coloured blue, as if for a stopper, and there are blue dots along the space above the internal black line, while the wider area below that line appears to have been painted green; on the other side of the papyrus sheet, there are again parts of an account, this time a name list with one name in each line, and each line ending with the mark 'south' in red. This diagram may provide a more appropriate home for the outlines of mounds in the Book of the Dead, within the general category of diagrams, rather than in their westernized space as proto-maps.

Lost libraries and the origin of maps

These fragments reveal a tradition of illustration otherwise lost to us. Papyrus is as bad at surviving as modern paper, in contrast to the clay used as writing support in the Near East. In quantity, even in Egypt, where the Saharan desert fringe provides a hyperarid nest, it has been estimated that one manuscript out of every 150,000 reaches the modern researcher (Hombert and Preaux 1952: 148). Knowledge of the range of content in ancient Egyptian writing is seriously limited by the ancient destruction of royal libraries in Egypt; fire preserved the clay tablets of the Assyrian kings, but the same force in an Egyptian palace would have obliterated this innermost circle of literacy. In a land as centralized as Egypt, the manuscripts at the royal court would probably have included the most innovative and the finest. The modern reader has only outer circles of papyrus production and use imperfectly reflected in the surviving record. Manuscripts and copies on organic materials such as wood survive principally among funerary goods in rock-cut tombs, and to a lesser degree as waste paper on the few settlement sites overlapping the hyperarid desert edge. The 'Book of the Fayum', a Roman period chart for another region, is described by Tait (Chapter 10, this volume). Apart from this late and emphatically religious composition, there is only one surviving ancient Egyptian diagram of a landscape in the world of the living, the 'Gold Mine Papyrus' (preserved in the Egyptian Museum, Turin: Harrell and Brown 1992). It charts gold mines within the area of stone quarries in the Wadi Hammamat, a valley cutting across the mountainous desert between the Nile and the Red Sea at the level of modern Qena and Qift. The manuscript comes from the principal source for surviving New Kingdom papyri, Deir el-Medina, on the West Bank at modern Luxor, ancient Thebes. Deir el-Medina was the desert settlement, simply called "the village" in ancient Egyptian sources, for the royal craftsmen and their teams cutting and decorating the tomb of the king in the Valley of the Kings, over the hill. There is no immediate reason why a royal craftsman or the accountant of that specialized village should own a guide to gold mines far removed from the horizon of work of the villagers. Possibly a royal project required the presence of a royal craftsman on an expedition, or a levy of some of the workmen from the royal tomb. Possibly, though, the 'Gold Mine Papyrus' reached the village of royal craftsmen as waste paper; this seems to have happened with one other unique document from Deir el-Medina, the 'Turin Canon', which is the only extended king list surviving on papyrus. How many more manuscripts bore plans like that of the gold-mining area remains an open question.

Ancient spatial diagrams are readily labelled 'maps' in contemporary western reception and translation of other cultures. There is a broad range of meanings for 'map', and the ancient illustrations discussed above often feature as early examples of maps in histories of cartography. It would seem strange not to use the word 'map' for the New Kingdom papyrus with the guide to gold mines. However, words are least innocent when common sense is invoked. The predominant contemporary map is not a random sketch of space, but a highly refined spatial diagram resting on histories of development of such techniques as surveying, each with specially adapted tools. When the word 'map' is used in modern English, it refers most often not to spatial diagrams in general, but to a product of a specific technology, which has arguably transformed people's vision of the real world, with dramatic impact on political, economic and social relations (cf. Walsh 1999: 19–20). Like any projection of three-dimensional space in two dimensions, the modern map does not express a view passively, but is an active, indeed a major constitutive, factor in a worldview. In common with other material products of western technologies, such as watches and telephones, its existence as object seduces the western consumer into accepting it as an automatic, even 'natural', adjunct to human society. The social relations that bring the object into existence and use can hide behind that object. By contrast, institutions can be problematized and revealed as forces in a specific historical drama of domination. This vulnerability may affect most strongly institutions with physical incarnations, such as the museum (Walsh 1992: 38). It applies also to more abstract institutions, such as archaeology and anthropology (Hirschkind 1991; Thomas 1994). By contrast, as an object, the modern map 'tells space' apparently innocently, as if inherently objective, much as the wrist watch 'tells time' while keeping its economic ideology in the background. Ironically, not despite but by its physical presence, the object becomes the most invisible of ideological weapons, and therefore among the most effective. The object is most invisible when it is not used to create another object. Such involvement in a productive process with visible and tangible product again leaves the object vulnerable to more penetrating analysis and discussion; perhaps for this reason, the positivism of the camera and the illusory and even deceptive qualities of the photograph have received greater attention than the inert map, a finished product for direct application in a real world. Despite, or thanks to, less intuitive visual coding than the photograph, the map seems to have escaped the same degree of deconstructive enthusiasm. Precisely because the word has not been made a problem, it is dangerous to apply it unproblematically, particularly when discussing other cultures. Once the word, the object and their histories have been made objects of discussion, it becomes safer to use them again in discussion of other human societies. In this instance, I argue that it is not safe to apply the word 'map' to two-dimensional renderings of space in other cultural and artistic traditions, before the transformative power of the map has been fully acknowledged.

The history of cartography involves the intricate elaboration of specific technologies. The emergence of the 'map' from the 15th to the 19th centuries AD runs in parallel to the early modern histories of printing and engraving. The contemporary world order is unthinkable without these three. Archaeology too could not come into existence to join the colonial armoury until these and the related technologies were sufficiently advanced. Accepting early spatial diagrams as paradigmatic equivalents of the modern cartographic map obscures the history not only of the map, but of our knowledge and our deployment of that knowledge to secure power. If we return the spatial diagrams of other cultures to a different cultural space, we have a better chance of understanding both those cultures and their products. 'Their' 'maps' are nothing to do with us; they do not belong to us or to our cartographic vision. The Lahun fragments may be the earliest examples of the type of spatial diagram seen in the chart of gold mines, but this does not make them the first map on paper. Conceptually they are not a forerunner, but a crucial 'other', to our maps.

Landscape in the Book of the Dead

As compared with the earlier Lahun fragments or the later Deir el-Medina material, the outlines of the mounds in the Book of the Dead produce a rather different impact. Although each mound is numbered in a sequence in Chapter 149, there is no information on the broader context, no directions for reaching the 'fourth' from the 'third', and no landscape. It is not excluded that they reflect or even directly represent a series of structures created for the rituals of embalming or burial. However, there seems to be no other evidence for any such structure in the extensive surviving stock of depictions related to elite burial. The forms, like the inhabitants, seem to belong within the underworld. If they have one main function, it may be to assert variation in the underworld. Whereas, in the natural landscape, there are generic repetitions, with similar profiles for mountains and trees, in the series each mound is an identifiably individual form. Perhaps, then, the outlines vary in shape precisely because their purpose is to be different from all the others. Creating difference also seems the main purpose of the diagrams that make up Chapter 150. In P. Satiah, as regularly in manuscripts from the New Kingdom to the Ptolemaic Period, the 14 mounds of Chapter 149 are followed immediately by the slightly different set of Chapter 150, a table summarizing 15 mounds without any accompanying "words to be spoken". From the rigid arrangement in two vertical registers divided by double framing line, this spatial configuration reflects not geographical order, but more a bureaucratic ordering akin to the frequent tabulated offering-lists. They do not create a map in the sense of a guide to the relative position of features in a landscape. Nor do other numerically ordered sets of features in other chapters of the Book of the Dead preserved on other manuscripts – the 21 portals of the Marsh of Reeds in the domain of Osiris (Chapters 145 and 146), or the seven approaches of the domain of Osiris (Chapters 144 and 147). All these gates are presented in images lined up one after the other, most often without distinguishing characteristics. Like the mounds, they confront the deceased as if at any moment in a sequence that is not charted visually;

we are not told what stage of journey the deceased reaches them, or how far it is from one portal to the next, or how to get from one to the other. These are rites of passage that take the deceased past an obstacle from one condition into another. The emphasis seems to be on the act of passing, not on charting the underworld landscape. After 700 BC, in the Late Period sequence of chapters for Books of the Dead, all these chapters are brought closer together, but still without reference to one another. Before 700 BC, they do not form a unified section in the Book of the Dead; it is not known whether Chapters 144–147 were present at all in P. Satiah, and in other manuscripts, such as P. Nu, Chapters 144 and 145 are separated from Chapters 149 and 150 by miscellaneous other compositions in the corpus. The one diagram of landscape is kept separate in the Book of the Dead both in the New Kingdom and in the Late Period sequence, from which Lepsius numbered it Chapter 110. That diagram is taken directly from the Coffin Texts of the Middle Kingdom, and is discussed below.

Measurement in the Coffin Texts

If mapping is not the focus, what do the sporadic measurements of underworld harvest, mountain and dwellers achieve? A different perspective on these passages is offered by other manuscripts, including P. Nu, where the invocations of the second and fourth mounds of Chapter 149 recur as separately titled compositions, without any reference to the rest of the mounds. The invocation with crop measurements, used for mound 2, also occurs as a "formula for knowing the eastern powers", Chapter 109 in the Late Period sequence. The paragraph with mountain and serpent, in mound 4, recurs as a "formula for knowing the western powers", Chapter 108, and in this version the mountain is identified by name as Bakhu. Though brought together in the Late Period, in the New Kingdom – the period of Satiah – these passages can occur at widely disparate parts of the manuscript; they come 34th and 74th respectively in the sequence of compositions on P. Nu (Lapp 1997: 68). Crucially for understanding of their contents and the intention behind their composition, both passages can be shown to have existed earlier as separate units than as parts of the set of 14 mounds, for they also occur with their own titles as single formulae in the early Middle Kingdom funerary literature, the Coffin Texts.

BD Chapter 49	BD separate Chapter	Coffin Text (de Buck numbering)
mound 2	109	160
mound 4	108	159

In contrast to their position in the New Kingdom Book of the Dead, on Middle Kingdom coffins the two compositions generally occur together, with the recurrent sequence Coffin Texts 154–160. Other recurrent sequences of funerary compositions in the sources have been interpreted as funeral liturgies, and this group too may reflect an original liturgy in the embalming or funeral rites (Assmann 1990). The decision to use measurement for the underworld can therefore be dated to the early Middle Kingdom, and it can be identified as a single but binary strategy addressing on one side the powers of the west, on the other those of the east. The other compositions in the sequence Coffin Texts 154–160 do not include measurements; instead, their strategy for overcoming death involves short passages evoking myths of origins, including some of the earliest narrative passages in Egyptian religious literature. Like the measurements, these 'tales of gods' are exceptional in the funerary literature, and they too survived into the Book of the Dead (Chapters 112–116). In both Coffin Texts and Books of the Dead each of these compositions carries the title "formula for knowing the powers" of a particular city in Lower or Middle Egypt. In the Book of the Dead versions these are as follows, giving the ancient Egyptian name of the city before the Greek name (Greek names are more often cited in Egyptological translations and commentaries):

Chapter	City
112	Pe/Buto
113	Nekhen/Hierakonpolis
114/116	Khemenu/Hermopolis
115	Iunu/Heliopolis

Like the mounds of Book of the Dead Chapters 149 and 150, none of these apparently 'geographical' compositions makes explicit the relation between cities; the distance between places and their location within the world is either not important to the composition, or at least does not need to be made explicit. There is no explicit atlas of either world. The power of measuring and the power of place names are two aspects of knowledge of space; they are adjacent, but not fused, in these rituals that were intended to secure eternal life.

In the two compositions with dimensions, there are differences in measurements as compared with the New Kingdom Book of the Dead. In Coffin Text 160 the mountain of the underworld, Bakhu, is said to measure 300 by 120 hundred-cubits, rather than the 300 by 10 given in the Book of the Dead version. The serpent of Bakhu is 30 cubits long, the first 3 cubits in flint. These, at least, are the numerals most often found in extant examples. De Buck recorded 14 copies of Coffin Text 160, on a total of 12 coffins – 10 from el-Bersheh and two from Asyut. The passages with the numerals are preserved in 11 of these; all give the same lengths for mountain and serpent, but the width of the mountain is sometimes recorded as 150 hundred-cubits (on four of the el-Bersheh coffins). This seems not to reflect any discernible difference in time or workshop, as coffins from the same group at el-Bersheh offer both 120 and 150. Perhaps the precise number was less important than the presence of a number. The itemized list of mounds in Book of the Dead Chapter 149 was composed at some point after the coffin production of the early Middle Kingdom, and perhaps as late as the first surviving copy, from the early New Kingdom. Many of the written invocations accompanying the mounds are not known in the earlier sources, and the series of diagrams used as illustrations for the Chapter are also not found before the New Kingdom. In other words, the 14 to 15 mounds represent a prominent part of the massive expansion of visual imagery into the funerary literature, ca. 1450 BC, when papyrus scrolls rather than linen shrouds became the medium of choice for carrying that literature into the tomb. The increase in proportion of illustration to written word may be seen in other defining sections of the new manuscript Book of the Dead tradition: illustrations either occupy all or part of a horizontal register along the top of the manuscript, or take up the full height of the scroll. Full-height vignettes include one diagram showing canals and fields for Chapter 110 taken directly from the Coffin Texts of the Middle Kingdom, but the others are new visual compositions, notably the scenes of offering to Osiris, god of the dead, and the image of the judgment of the deceased before Osiris, for Chapter 125.

The transmission history is important, because it reveals that the measurements do not originate in a setting where visual imagery was the focus. The project of defining three-dimensional geographical space in two-dimensional visual form is exemplified by the diagrams of mounds for Chapters 149 and 150 in the Book of the Dead, but it is not yet present within the Coffin Texts that precede. Instead the measuring belongs to a different, earlier world in which communication is primarily verbal, not visual communication, the context of Coffin Texts 159 and 160. This earlier context helps to explain the absence of measurements for the rest of the mounds of Book of the Dead Chapter 149; the descriptions of the other mounds derive from other sources. Some of the Chapter 149 mound descriptions may have been newly composed in the early New Kingdom, to fill the space for verbal description allotted beneath each diagram. The dominant motif of Book of the Dead Chapter 149 is form and appearance, not the exact measuring of individual and relative space. The numbers must have remained important enough to be retained in the passage in this new series of 14 mounds. However, the Coffin Texts are the earlier setting, and we should look there for any evidence of the way in which the measurements might have been formulated, and the reasons for using measurements to define underworld phenomena. Within the corpus of Coffin Texts, these crop and mountain passages offer almost the only examples of linear measurement (for the Marsh of Reeds, see below). Even the 'Book of the Two Ways' (see Robinson Chapter 8, this volume) does not specify dimensions. However, unlike the Book of the Two Ways, and in contrast to their later life in the Book of the Dead, the two Coffin Texts with measurements are not accompanied by images. They fall entirely within the written domain, within which they appear unique in their emphasis on numbered units of measurement.

As an exception, the impact of the strategy of citing an exact size such as 'seven cubits' must have been all the stronger. Whereas the unit of linear measurement is rare, numbers themselves are not, and the associations of the particular numerical value depend on the frequency and nature of the other passages where the number is cited. This introduces a difference between smaller and larger scale units. The smaller numerals in the measurement passages are bound to carry heavy weighting from the use of lower digits in numbering contexts other than linear measurements. If a spirit or combined stalk and ear of barley is said to be seven cubits, this might establish an intentional association with ideal portions of sustenance in other passages, where the deceased receives, for example, seven loaves – four from heaven, three from earth. Units from one to 10 occur throughout the literature, and are more likely to enrich a passage with numerical symbolism on the strength of that broader pattern of language usage. This is less likely to hold for some of the higher numerals given for measurements in the funerary literature. It is hard to establish a point of reference or meaning for the dimensions given for the mountain of Bakhu, at 300 by 150 or 300 by 120, or even in the Book of the Dead version at 300 by 10. In these larger scale measurements again, an apparently unmeasurable object – a mountain in the underworld – receives precise definition. Both the why and the how of this measuring operation seem 'poetic' questions. The combination of numeral with unit of measurement achieves its effect by the poetic impact of the words and the contrast between operation (measuring) and context (unmeasurable underworld); the transmission of the words creates its own world of religious knowledge. In their transmission, rather than in genesis, the measurements assert control over the uncontrollable: death. This is presumably a key function of funerary literature, and perhaps from this perspective it is less surprising that the measurements exist in these passages, than that the measurement passages are so rare.

Landscape and measurement in the Coffin Texts

Chapter 110 is the one visual rendering of a landscape in the Book of the Dead, in which measurements combine with an illustration connecting different features of the underworld. It occurs already among the Coffin Texts, in the same setting that preserved the Book of the Two Ways, the early Middle Kingdom coffins from el-Bersheh (Robinson Chapter 8, this volume). De Buck gave the combined visual and written composition the number 466 in his Coffin Texts edition, and recorded it from seven coffins; an eighth gives the diagram but without captions. The eight coffins range in time across the two centuries of the early Middle Kingdom (ca. 2050–1850 BC).[4] In each case, the illustrators at the coffin placed the diagram on the side to be faced by the deceased as she or he lay in the coffin. The composition is identified by the words "being the Offerings-god, the Lord of this Marsh", suggesting that this diagram depicts the "Marsh of Offerings" mentioned frequently in both the Coffin Texts and the Book of the Dead, often in parallel to a phrase "Marsh of Reeds". The "Marsh of Reeds" appear in Book of the Dead mound 2, and the "Marsh of Offerings" later in the sequence at mound 11 (Allen Chapter 2, this volume). Research has not settled the question of whether the two terms refer to one or two areas of the underworld (Lesko 1971–72). The various writings indicate that the deceased would be sustained from grain harvested in these underworld marshes. Egyptologists have tended to translate the Egyptian word *sekhet* as "field", but until the first millennium BC the term tends to refer to marsh land. This indicates that the "Marshes" are a miraculous area where, despite the unpromising marshy terrain, crops of supernatural quality are able to grow, to feed the blessed dead.

The diagram occupies a rectangular space dominated by several horizontal registers coloured blue, indicating watery channels (Figure 9:5). These, numbered by de Buck in the sequence of features on the diagram, bear the following labels:

- Section V: "this is a thousand river-lengths in its length and in its breadth; its name is Mistress, Lady of Horns"

- Section X: "the lake of the White Hippopotamus; this is a thousand river-lengths in its length; its breadth is not told; there is no male fish and no female serpent within it"

- Section XI: "its length is the length of the sky; lake of offerings before Upper and Lower Egypt"

- Section XVI: "this is a thousand in its length; its breadth is not told; raiser of storm-clouds is its name"

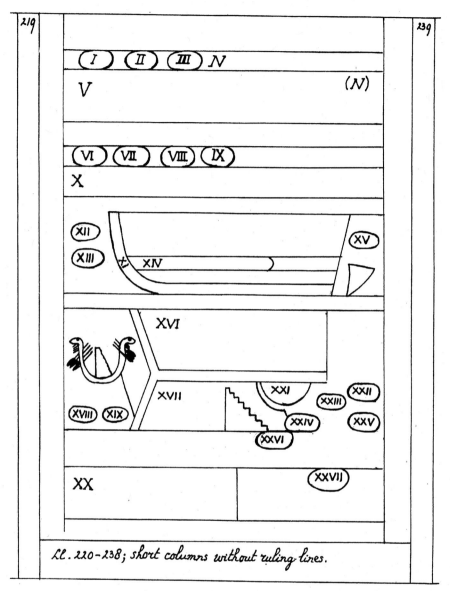

Figure 9:5   The plan of the Marsh of Reeds in the 'Coffin Texts', the ancestor to 'Book of the Dead' Chapter 110.

- Section XX: "this is the Great Green Expanse of the gods; its length and its breadth are told to Osiris" (two coffins, B5C and B9C, give instead the version "its length is not told, its breadth is not told to Osiris").

This composition offers longer lengths that seem to be rounded off or to simply high numerals for effect – a "thousand" or the "length of the sky". The ancient Egyptian "river-length" has been calculated as about 10.5 km, and is the regular unit of measurement for longer distances. With the phrase 'its length is not told', the composition also specifies limits to knowledge, even for the god Osiris, ruler of the underworld. This may add a feeling of authenticity for the measurements that are given, since the writer is not claiming universal knowledge. The phrasing also indicates that the writer has probably not measured the distances himself, but has been told them. The speaker is not revealed; it might be human or divine, and the source might be oral or written. The combination of visual and written information on a landscape is unique to el-Bersheh coffins, but only this diagram survived in the New Kingdom funerary literature. As with the Book of the Two Ways it is not possible to identify the original setting for the composition. el-Bersheh is the necropolis of Khemenu/Hermopolis, city of Thoth. Since Thoth was god of writing and knowledge, it is an intriguing possibility that his city not only preserved but developed the compositions. However, in so strongly centralized a state as Ancient Egypt, the palace of the king seems as likely a home for the creation of both the visual expression and the measurements assigned to the underworld.

Measurements in the Amduat

Measurements of length on a still larger scale are found in the Amduat, the earliest of the Underworld Books in the New Kingdom (Hornung 1999). Amduat is the 19th century Egyptological rendering of the ancient Egyptian phrase "that which is in the underworld", an original abbreviation for the longer title "writings of the hidden chamber which is in the underworld". The "hidden chamber" designated the burial chamber, and the composition occupied all the wall space of the burial chamber in the tombs of the kings, and of one vizier, in the period 1450–1400 BC. The style of these earliest versions evokes an aged papyrus manuscript, with brown background to red and black images and inscriptions arranged in three registers and unfurling around the walls, with some sections even marked by the word "gap" in hieroglyphs, a device to indicate damage to a papyrus scroll in actual manuscripts. The cursive figural depiction of the journey of the sun god Ra through the night sky dominates the accompanying cursive hieroglyphic inscriptions. The fourth to twelfth hours of the night take the boat of the sun god across sandy and rocky underworld terrain, but the first three hours are still on water, and for these waterways the inscriptions specify exact lengths, using the river-length unit employed for longer tracts along the Nile in the world of the living (Figure 9:6). Here, in contrast to the mountain of Bakhu, linear measurements appear within a broader account of time and space – at least a journey, if not a map. The first hour of the night is the passage to a region called Wernes, and the inscription specifies:

> entry of this god in the western approach of the horizon,
> with Seth standing at the shore,
> being 120 river-lengths for reaching this doorway,
> that he may ascend after to (the waters of) Wernes.

In his edition Hornung noted that this number surpassed the length of Egypt as 106 river-lengths from south to north as recorded in inscriptions, the earliest instance being on the White Chapel of Amun in Karnak (East Thebes), dating to ca. 1950 BC (Hornung 1963: 24). The second hour is described as:

Figure 9:6   The journey of the sun god through the first hours of the night (after Hornung 1963).

> resting in Wernes by this god,
> making the rowing of the reeds in the channel of Ra,
> 309 river-lengths being the length of this marsh,
> 120 in its width.

The third hour is labelled:

> resting in the field of the grain-gods by the majesty of this great god,
> making the rowing in the channel of Osiris,
> 309 river-lengths being the length of this marsh.

Hornung drew attention to the far greater distance in each of the second and third hours, 309 river-lengths as compared with 120 for the first (Hornung 1963: 40 with n. 1). The repetition of the number 309 for second and third hours could, though, be interpreted in a different way; possibly the waterway of Ra and the waterway of Osiris are two expressions for the same underworld passage, like a road that changes its name from one stretch to the next. This would give the boat 120 river-lengths to travel in the first hour of the night, and 309 in the following two hours together. This may be less likely than the traditional interpretation of two separate stretches of 309 river-lengths, but the composition itself leaves the options open: the wording might be intended to evoke a journey of great length rather than to pinpoint details. As with the mountain of Bakhu in the Coffin Texts and Book of the Dead, these high numbers are not instantly explicable by the use of the same numerals in other contexts. Possibly the figure of 120 might multiply the hours of the night by 10, following the usual ancient Egyptian decimal system. The other numbers cannot be so easily explained either in themselves or as multiples of other significant numbers. This does not exclude the possibility that some calculation produced these measurements from specific numerical symbols. However, the numbers ending in a digit as opposed to the numbers in multiples of 10 leave the impression that a fixed length has been reached from exact measurement, using the same unit of measurement as that employed for distances along the River Nile. As a rhetorical device the 309 river-lengths produce a specific impact on the receiving mind; the writing seems to assert a literal knowledge of, and therefore power over, the world beyond the visible and tangible world of the living.

Ancient reception is the crucial and open question – would Satiah or her funeral-reciter read Book of the Dead Chapter 149 mound 4 as an imaginary mountain, measurement as a poetic expression, or would the passage carry literal force? In the range of intensity of belief, this is as much a matter of expression as the measurements themselves. In the New Testament account of Pentecost, tongues of flame appear on the heads of the disciples of Jesus. Are the flames real or metaphor? The reader has to decide what such a question of reality means. The Book of Revelation cited at the outset includes one extended description of a city beyond this world:

> The city was laid out like a square, as long as it was wide. He measured the city with the rod and found it to be 12,000 stadia in length, and as wide and high as it is long. He measured its wall and it was 144 cubits thick, by man's measurement, which the angel was using. The wall was made of jasper, and the city of pure gold, as pure as glass. The foundations of the city walls were decorated with every kind of precious stone. The first foundation was jasper, the second sapphire, the third chalcedony, the fourth emerald, the fifth sardonyx, the sixth carnelian, the seventh chrysolite, the eighth beryl, the ninth topaz, the tenth chrysoprase, the eleventh jacinth, and the twelfth amethyst. The twelve gates were twelve pearls, each gate made of a single pearl. The great street of the city was of pure gold, like transparent glass.
>
> (Book of Revelation 21: 16–21)

Believers have responded in different ways to such details over the millennia. In the Christian western traditions, afterlife measurements also emerge in more literary settings, as in the Divine Comedy of Dante:

> From the edge where it borders space,
> to the foot of the other bank as it rises,
> would measure three times a human body
>
> (Purgatory, Canto X: 22–24)

Here, in one of the defining poetic works of European literature, the psychological impact of the measuring can be appreciated without the distraction of the question of whether we should understand the passage literally or as metaphor. The account of this realm of the afterlife gains sharp definition by this introduction of the verb 'to measure' and a number related to the human body. The less 'religious' the literary context, the easier it may be to appreciate the artistic deployment of words. A literary writer may still be asking an audience to believe, but in poetic rather than dogmatic vein. Before presuming a rigid literal reading by ancient Egyptian audiences, it should be noted that, a century or two after Satiah, another New Kingdom manuscript contains a harpist's song with the reminder:

> no-one comes from that side
> to tell of their condition,
> to tell of their needs,
> to calm our hearts
> until we go where they have gone.
>
> (British Museum EA 10060; Lichtheim 1976: 194–197)

Ancient responses to mortality and the unknown clearly varied in form and expression as widely as they do today. The remarkable spatial diagrams and exact measurements in ancient Egyptian funerary literature form one revealing aspect of the range in perception and construction of life after death.

Notes

1   The remains of this manuscript were conserved by Renée Waltham in 2002 with funds from the Friends of the Petrie Museum of Egyptian Archaeology, University College London, where it is now preserved as UC 71001.

2   This papyrus – in which she is cited more often than her husband – was acquired for the French National Library decades before the discovery of the intact tomb of her husband and herself. Curiously, the tomb equipment of Kha included a magnificent papyrus for the husband, with the wife in the usual secondary position; it is not known why the second papyrus for the wife existed, and it remains a mystery how and where it survived outside the intact tomb chamber excavated by Ernesto Schiaparelli (1924).

3   This second fragment retains the original 1890s labelling, identifying it as 'VII.2' or the second item in a 'lot' or single acquisition of papyrus fragments. Unfortunately, there is no information on the precise findspot within the areas of the site cleared by Petrie; the low Latin number suggests a date of discovery within his earlier 1889 season of work, but even this is uncertain, and is not in any case enough to provide a social context – already lots I to VI appear to come from a range of small to palatial houses from the west end to the central part of the ancient town (Gallorini 1998).

4   De Buck (1935–1961) coffin: B6C, Ahanakht (eleventh Dynasty, ca. 2050–2000 BC); Coffin: B9C, Amenemhat (reign of Senusret I, ca. 1950 BC); Coffin: B1C, B5C, B1L, B3L, B2P and the coffin with illustration only, Coffin: B4L, all from the tombs associated with the great rock-cut tomb of Djehutyhotep (reign of Senusret II, ca. 1900 BC).

CHAPTER 10

THE 'BOOK OF THE FAYUM': MYSTERY IN A KNOWN LANDSCAPE

John Tait

The 'Book of the Fayum' is the modern name for a group of Greco-Roman period Egyptian texts providing a 'map' or description of the Fayum district, a name that has become standard since Beinlich's (1991) publication of all the material then known. Since then, he (Beinlich 1996, 1997) has been able to add some further fragments to the corpus.

The Book of the Fayum survives in several versions (Figures 10:1–10:7). The primary form is likely to have been a hieroglyphic text written upon papyrus, with extensive illustrations; several copies survive, some extremely fragmentary. The best preserved (Figures 10:2–10:7) found its way in sections and fragments into at least three modern collections, and thus is termed by Beinlich (1991) 'Boulaq/Hood/ Amherst'. Beinlich (1991, i: 35–39), while seeing the Book of the Fayum as a unity, argues that this chief hieroglyphic manuscript was from the start divided between two papyrus rolls. The Egyptian practice with a very long text was probably to paste together rolls of standard length to provide the necessary space to accommodate the entire text. For example, P. Harris measures over 40 m in length, but, as a celebratory record of royal benefactions, may not have been frequently consulted (Grandet 1994– 1999; i: 32; Leach and Tait 2000: 236). However, the complete text of the Book of the Fayum would probably have occupied less than 10 m, and thus was in no way exceptional among Egyptian papyri. Whatever view is taken on the original state of the Boulaq/Hood/Amherst manuscript, it is occasionally convenient to use Beinlich's terminology of a first and second half of the text.[1]

Another hieroglyphic version of a few sections of the text exists on the walls of the temple of Kom Ombo (Bianchi 1999) in southern Upper Egypt (Beinlich 1991, i: 64–65; Yoyotte 1962: 99–101) (Figure 10:1). There, the text is clearly divided into two halves by a separating border, and is without any accompanying illustrations. One half reproduces a substantial section of text devoted to the Heavenly Cow (see below), while the other copies a series of disparate short passages. There are numerous variations between the two versions, above all in orthography, but the basic intention seems to have been to copy out the same text passages. Kom Ombo was the second most conspicuous centre (Gutbub 1977) of the cult of the crocodile god Sobek after Crocodilopolis (this Greek form of the name will be used here; its Egyptian name was *Shedet* in the Book of the Fayum; it is modern Medinet el-Fayum), the capital city of the

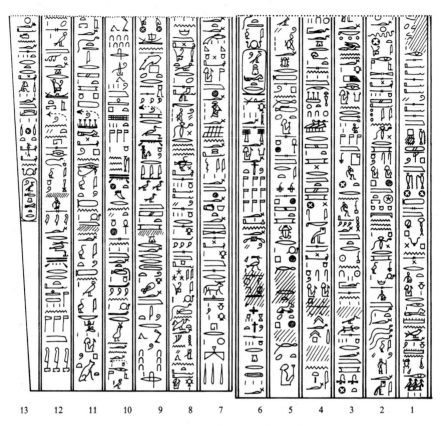

13   12   11   10   9   8   7   6   5   4   3   2   1

Figure 10:1   A version of the 'Book of the Fayum' on the walls of the temple of Kom Ombo (Beinlich 1991, i: fig. 17).

Fayum (Gomaà 1980: 1,254–1,255). The inscribed passages presumably derived from a copy of the hieroglyphic text on papyrus, although there could conceivably have been some intermediate, excerpted source. Their chief interest is that they demonstrate that the Book of the Fayum was known outside the Fayum itself.

A further possible hieroglyphic source is the wood sarcophagus of Ankhrui, discovered by Petrie (1889: 9) at Hawara at the mouth of the Fayum, which bears at least three illustrations which resemble those found in the hieroglyphic papyrus version (Griffith 1889: 21–23, pl. 2 – who did not note the similarities; cf. Beinlich 1991, i: 65–66).

The remaining sources for the Book of the Fayum are found in a number of hieratic transcriptions on papyrus (Botti 1959) which lack illustrations, and which are divided up only by the conventional use of phrases in red ink (rubrics). The majority survive merely as a small fragment or fragments, but one (Botti's version A) is a substantial roll, lacking the beginning but preserving text amounting to about five-sixths of what is known in the hieroglyphic papyri, including the end of the text.

General character of the text and its contents

Like nearly all Egyptian papyrus rolls, the hieroglyphic version of the Book of the Fayum is basically to be held and viewed with its length, as it is unrolled, stretching from side to side horizontally in front of the reader. The overall structure of the text is that of a series, running along the length of the roll, of several hundred representations of deities or their emblems and occasionally of other symbols. Their size and their arrangement vary very greatly from one part of the text to another. However, the whole sequence of the images from start to finish can be read (see below) as a deliberate and meaningful progression. As examples (each discussed further below) of the variety of the layout, at one extreme, the large-scale figure of the sky goddess Mehet-Weret[2] (95) stands seemingly alone. Other figures form obvious groups, in a kind of separate representational 'scene', of which the simplest example is the symmetrical grouping of the eight primeval deities of the Ogdoad (Allen Chapter 2, this volume), almost at the very end of the text (1181–1204). Typically, others are arranged in a series, in horizontal registers, above and below a stylized representation of landscape, while the numerous deities in crocodile-form almost at the beginning of the second half of the text are simply organized in a 'tabular' arrangement in five horizontal rows along the roll.

Almost without exception, each individual representation of a deity, and also each representational scene, is accompanied by text, which acts as a 'label' for it and identifies it. This occasionally may consist merely of a name. Normally additional information is given: there is either a short section of text, or both a naming 'label' and a section of text. A brief example, from within a representational scene, is the god Sobek, seated in a divine boat, simply labelled "This is Sobek, as he travels (by boat) in the Northern Lake (i.e. Northern Fayum)" (152). The whole scene is prefaced by the label "This is the place of the Ogdoad: Ra lives there; Osiris is at rest (satisfied) there; those of the West (i.e. the blessed dead) are (properly) buried there" (148).

The text as a whole is concerned with places, and is not a catalogue of deities. Therefore, in the various horizontal series of depictions of deities, their names lead directly to their cult places. A straightforward example from the early part of the text has a representation of the mummified Hesis-cow (in the Greco-Roman period identified with Isis), whose cult and burials were at Atfih on the east bank of the Nile, not far south of Memphis. She is labelled as 'The Mistress of Atfih', and a short accompanying text (66) reads, "This place, its name is 'The Severing of Heads', the place of offering (cult) things to Sobek of Crocodilopolis, and to his mother, Isis, Mistress of the Knife-nome (i.e. the 22nd administrative district of Upper Egypt, in which Atfih lay)". The word 'place' (*s.t*) is ubiquitous in the text, and often, as here, might be translated 'cult-place', although in the 'place of the Ogdoad' mentioned above, a translation 'domain' or 'proper home' might be considered: the Egyptians no doubt saw no difference in these usages.

It remains surprising to the modern reader that a work concerned with places contains so few depictions of individual localities. The Fayum as a whole is represented in a variety of ways, but the only specific places in any way 'illustrated' (Figure 10:7) are the large 'hieroglyphic' image of the temple of Sobek at Crocodilopolis at the very end of the text, and perhaps the naos of the goddess Neith by her sacred tree (1109).

The organization

Three separate technical questions arise concerning the organization of the text. At which end of the papyrus roll should the reader begin to read the text, if it is meant to be read in a particular direction, or indeed meant to be read consecutively at all (for example, it makes little sense to ask in what order the street names are to be read on a map of London). What is to be made of the order of the individual columns within each subdivision of the text? What is the significance of the fact that most of the hieroglyphs face to the right, but in some portions of text they face to the left?

For the last point, a right to left orientation of the script is normal in Egyptian, and is obligatory for the cursive hieratic script, while it is almost always the rule to read through a text on a papyrus roll from right to left. In hieroglyphic texts, the script may occasionally be written from left to right. There are three main reasons why this may happen. First, there may be a desire to arrange text symmetrically, for example around a doorway or on a piece of furniture (Tait 1996: 2). Second, there are conventions in funerary and temple material, whereby hieroglyphic texts 'face' in the same direction as a divine or human figure who utters them, or to whom they closely relate in some other way (Fischer 1977a, 1986). The figure is normally present, adjacent, for example in a relief scene, but may be implicit rather than explicit. Third, certain kinds of religious texts employ so-called 'retrograde hieroglyphs' (Fischer 1977b: 1,192–1,193): a clear example is the New Kingdom 'Amduat texts' (Piankoff 1957). Such texts are nearly always written entirely in vertical columns (as is the case with most of the material in the hieroglyphic Book of the Fayum). The hieroglyphs of the text face to the right, which would normally imply the need to read from right to left, but the columns should be taken in the reverse order, and it is necessary to begin reading each section of text from the left.

All three practices can be seen in the Book of the Fayum. Retrograde hieroglyphs are consistently used in the text passages accompanying each deity in the various extensive horizontal series, as is immediately obvious from the sense of the text. The first examples (Figure 10:2) are in the section close to the opening of the text (17–90), in which, for example, the seven short columns of text accompanying an image of Khnum-Ra are to be read in order from the left, although the hieroglyphs face to the right (17–19). In the second half of the text, a few self-standing blocks of continuous text adopt the retrograde arrangement. The usage in making the hieroglyphic text face in the same direction as the figure they accompany varies. In the first half of the papyrus, the upper and lower horizontal series of deities consistently face the same way as the hieroglyphs, i.e. to the right. In the series of mummified crocodile images in the second half, the text passages are written in exactly the same retrograde fashion as in the first, but the crocodiles all face to the left (Figure 10:6); thus text and image fail to match in orientation. In the two sections where figures of the Ogdoad appear, arranged facing each other symmetrically, their names are each written with the matching orientation. Elsewhere there is a tendency to lapse into presenting a short labelling piece of text in the right to left format that is standard in Egyptian texts in general, even if a figure faces to the left. There is one clear example of text arranged symmetrically, even when the accompanying representation does not demand this: a section of text arranged symmetrically on either side of the goddess Mehet-weret (Figure 10:3) begins with three horizontal lines to her left, reading from right to left, and continues with three lines to her right, reading from left to right (101–107). There are just a few other examples of text written in horizontal lines, always in order to fit in with the illustrations and layout. The very beginning of what survives of the text (1–13) is written in horizontal lines, both reading from right to left, although half of the text stands upside down: this relates to the way in which the text here represents the two sides of the canal leading into the Fayum (see below).

The arrangement within the various individual subdivisions of the sections of the manuscript with horizontal series of deities, as outlined above, suggests that the text as a whole should be read from left to right, and this is confirmed by a final single column at the right-hand end of the second half of the papyrus (1270): "It has gone accurately from(?) the nome of Meret; none of its substance has been divided in the words of God (i.e. hieroglyphs). It has come (to an end)." Despite the obscurity of the first two statements, this matches the kind of traditional phrases used to mark the end of Egyptian manuscripts (colophons) sufficiently, assuring the reader of the accuracy of the copy – and the last phrase has good contemporary parallels.

There are two indications to suggest that the text was intended to be read through in a particular continuous sequence. First, certain sections at the beginning of the text have been numbered with ordinal numbers in demotic script (Figures 10:3–10:5), in two separate sequences (Beinlich 1991, i: 45–53). Plainly, the numbering provided a guide to the correct order in which to read through the sections of the text (whether or not the numbering was also concerned with a process of transcribing the text). Second, the best preserved example of the continuous hieratic transcriptions of the text gives an unambiguous order to a large proportion of the text. This ordering closely matches the evidence of the demotic numberings in the hieroglyphic version. In fact, in much of the hieroglyphic text, even if the general left to right ordering is assumed, the order in which to take the individual depictions and sections is far from self-evident. Sometimes a simple principle is followed: for example, at the beginning of the text (17–90) the order is middle register, upper register, and finally lower register (Beinlich 1991, i: 49–51). However, in some of the more pictorial sections (see below) no simple rule of thumb will suffice. These two pieces of evidence are consistent and conclusive as to one particular way in which the Egyptians could use the Book of the Fayum. Of course, this does not of itself prove that the papyrus could not also have been viewed in other ways. It is in the nature of a papyrus roll that it has to be worked through sequentially; it is impossible to flick from one passage to another. The indications are that, just as when writing, the reader normally scrolled through the papyrus on the lap, with just a short portion of the text visible at any one moment. This does not necessarily mean that the hieroglyphic version of the Book of the Fayum could not have been used in a different manner. Its visual qualities could hardly have been appreciated unless a broad view could have been taken of the roll.

The large finds of papyri from the Egyptian temple-complexes of the Greco-Roman period can be interpreted as comprising rolls that had been discarded as having been torn beyond repair (Tait forthcoming). The Book of the Fayum, even if taken in two sections, is too long to be completely opened and handled, even by two persons. Of course it could have been fully unrolled on the ground and left displayed. The hieroglyphic version does fall into clearly marked sections, and a possible interpretation is that two among the longest of these (17–90; 590–824) are, deliberately, of about the maximum length that can be displayed in the traditional Egyptian way upon the lap. We do not know if the Egyptians had any other way of displaying large-scale texts and images, except of course upon tomb or temple walls.[3]

It has been suggested that the more than 40 m long P. Harris, cited above, was 'published' by being affixed to the wall at the entrance to the Ramesses III temple at Medinet Habu (Grandet 1994–1999, i: 125–127). There is, however, no direct evidence for such an exhibition of a papyrus scroll, and the coloured illustrations on that particular document seem too well preserved to have been exposed to daylight in antiquity (for the effect of such exposure, compare the colour photographs on the front covers of Grandet 1994–1999: i and ii, with Grandet 1994–1999: iii, front cover, where the original sheet has suffered from exposure to daylight in modern times).

Contents

The beginning of what survives of the hieroglyphic version – only a few preceding sections of which are lost, if we are to believe the demotic numbering inserted into our chief hieroglyphic source – introduces the problematic "Channel of the Great Water-way" (Gardiner and Bell 1943). Beinlich's plausible interpretation is that this refers in some way to the Bahr Yusef as it enters the Fayum. The chief preoccupations of the whole text are alluded to in this passage, however obliquely. The scribe seems to have found some difficulties with the text, which shows many of the features of the ingenious orthography of the Greco-Roman temple inscriptions, and also must be partly corrupt. A possible translation (with many unresolved obscurities) is:

Upper line of text
The Channel of the Great Water-way: it is a great water(-way), and great (i.e. numerous) are its deities, so the body of Sobek of Crocodilopolis may flourish every day. Ra is resident in its Channel. The road of Osiris (is?) with the inundation of the fields of Upper Egypt (blank space - presumably text missing) ... cult-places of Egypt.

Lower line of text
The Channel of Horus, resident in Crocodilopolis: it is divine order upon earth, (and) Mehet-weret;[4] Upper Egypt and Lower Egypt have come from its possessions (riches?), giving it (or life) to its children.
The Mother of all the deities, who lives there every day. She gives breath to her son Horus at her brow/horns, and life is brought into being at her brow/horns because of it.
Deities and humans live in peace/satisfaction. It flows (northwards) from Elephantine,[5] to reach (its proper) place, to bring possessions (riches) from Elephantine, which proceed from the leg of the Child, to inundate the two districts of Osiris, who endures and is strong in body for ever.

Next – in the prescribed order of reading the text (although visually seeming to mark the beginning of the papyrus as preserved) – two large versions of the hieroglyphic signs for desert hill-slopes frame the start of a substantial section in which fish, birds and plants in separate registers (Figure 10:2) flank what must be a body of water. Above and below this representation, and thus presumably to be seen as on either side of the body of water, are representations of deities, with 13 short passages of accompanying text, following the formula, 'This place, it is (such and such a cult-

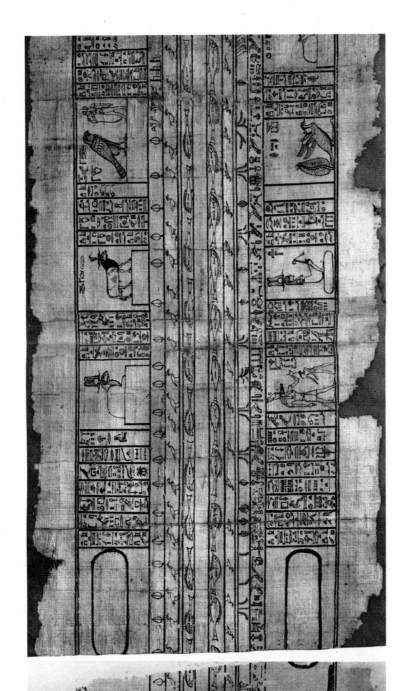

Figure 10:2 The opening of the 'Book of the Fayum': the Bahr Yusef and its cult centres (Beinlich 1991: pl. 44 (part)).

place)'. There are indications that the upper register is to be seen as 'South', and the lower as 'North'.

Here (as throughout the hieroglyphic version) the text passage that is relevant to an illustration can be readily identified by the reader (apart from one or two scribal mistakes), and they can be viewed together in the normal fashion of scrolling through a papyrus.

The next section of text is dominated by a depiction (Figure 10:3) of the goddess Mehet-weret, in completely human form, well preserved in two of the hieroglyphic versions. She is clearly labelled "This is Mehet-weret making her two arms (i.e. stretching them up and apart); she gives cool water to the two lands (i.e. all Egypt), which flows to the south and the north of the Fayum". The division of the waters of the Bahr Yusef into two chief canals is thus shown symbolically by the two outstretched arms of the goddess. In Boulaq/Hood/Amherst there are also two crude depictions of canals: on each side a pair of curved parallel lines have the appearance of springing from the goddess' elbows and of conveying the water onwards at the top and the bottom of the papyrus roll, thus continuing the schematic map-like nature of the text (they are not present in the Copenhagen version of the text). The actual two arms of the goddess, however, are from this point of view pointing backwards, in the wrong direction. Presumably the particular gesture of the goddess was dictated by what was appropriate to a sky/solar goddess; it would have been unthinkable to reverse her stance by 180 degrees. As the text is read from left to right, she would then be standing on her head, which is a fate that, for example, the deceased in the 'Book of the Dead' is anxious to avoid. Elsewhere in the Book of the Fayum the great majority of figures stand the right way up for a reader viewing the roll in the conventional way across their lap. Some others, for reasons of cosmic symmetry, are the other way up, by 180 degrees, for example the image of (Sobek)-Ra as opposed to Sobek (see below). A few others are orientated exactly as the figure of Mehet-weret. The only well preserved figure that is shown with head towards the end of the roll (i.e. at 180 degrees in relation to the figure of Mehet-weret) is the extraordinary representation of Ra (see the next paragraph) who is shown up to his knees in water, in such a way that his feet and calves are invisible (Figure 10:4). This is not a normal Egyptian method of representation: parts of a figure that are 'under water' are usually still visible.

There follows a depiction of the Fayum lake, seen as the lake of creation and perhaps also as the sacred lake of a temple. It is prefaced by the horizontal line of text, written across the height of the roll, already quoted: "This is the place of the Ogdoad: Ra lives there; Osiris is at rest (satisfied) there; those of the West (i.e. the blessed dead) are (properly) buried there" (148). The god Ra is seen partially immersed in a pool or lake: "It is Ra, who goes off to swim" (150 – the hieroglyphic determinative suggests 'swimming', but the meaning may be of a less athletic activity, and the god is shown in a very standard, static pose; yet perhaps there was no way of showing a deity, in proper iconography, swimming).[6] The god Sobek, wearing two forms of the double crown, is shown voyaging in a solar boat: once "it is Sobek, as he rows on the northern lake"; and a second time: "it is Ra, as he rows on the southern lake, chief(?) of the lake." This is an instance where the papyrus would, in theory, have to be turned completely on its head to read the texts relating to Sobek in his form as Ra. After the depiction, there follows a terminating vertical column of text (156): "This Ennead, who gave birth

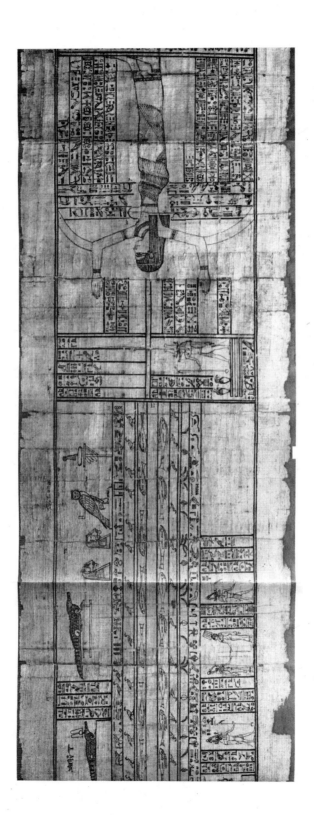

Figure 10:3 The Goddess Mehet-weret: the major canals of the Fayum irrigation system (Beinlich 1991: pl. 44 (part)).

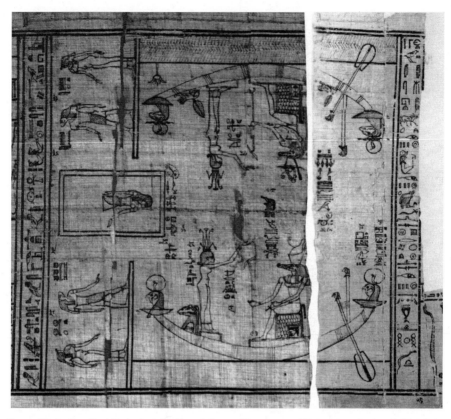

Figure 10:4   The God Ra 'swimming' in a lake and two forms of Sobek in solar boats (Beinlich 1991: pl. 44 (part)).

to the Ihet-cow, the forms of Ra, and the forms of his mother; one has never got to know (i.e. truly comprehended) them; their earthly forms endure for ever and eternity." This apparent reference to the Heliopolitan Ennead probably signifies only the entire corporation of the gods.

The next section (again concentrating upon the chief source illustrated by Beinlich) is a representation of the Fayum as a whole (Figure 10:5). Running along the middle of the papyrus is a long rectangle, presumably showing the Fayum as raised, cultivable land (another source makes more of the aquatic nature of the Fayum). Cult-places are shown above and below. Mentions of the 'Southern Lake' suggest that the previous convention is continued: namely, that the upper register concerns the south, and the lower the north. Within the central long rectangle are various forms of divinities: crocodile and solar, with two forms of heavenly/cosmic cows, Mehet-weret, and the Ihet-cow. Then there follows a substantial catalogue of the forms of Sobek in the various nomes of all Egypt, with figures given for the number of 'offerings' that they each receive in the Fayum (Figure 10:6). An example is: "Sobek: lord of the fish nome (12th Upper Egyptian administrative district); he is Ra; 10,700 offerings are given to him in the Lake." Next are depictions relating to a cult-place (the first to be given such individual prominence) – Ra-sehui – which Beinlich argues must be on (what we see

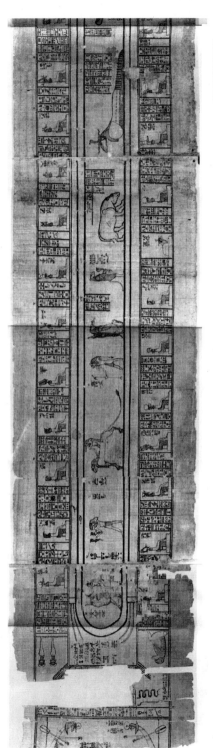
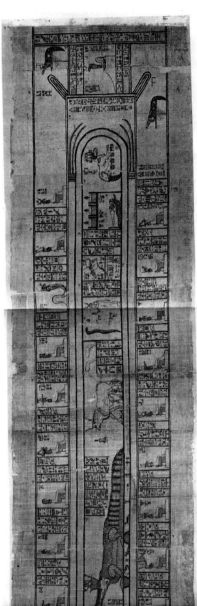

Figure 10:5 The Fayum as a whole (Beinlich 1991: pl. 44).

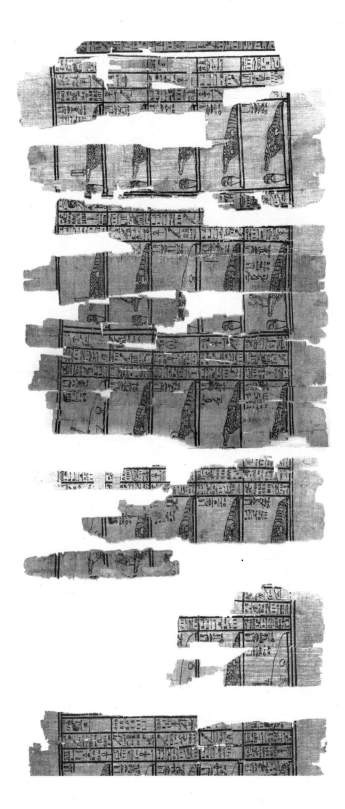

Figure 10:6   The forms of Sobek in the nomes of Upper and Lower Egypt (Beinlich 1991: pl. 45 (part)).

as) the north shore of the Fayum lake. Then there is a figure of the goddess Neith accompanied by Sobek before a shrine (the kind of naos that houses a single cult-statue) and facing the sacred tree of Neith, which is said to be on "a great mound". After this there is a representation of the eight deities of the Ogdoad, who are prominent in the creation myth of Hermopolis, four male with frog-heads, and four female with snake-heads, symmetrically arranged on a rectilinear system of sand banks; again, four stand the right way up for the reader, four are inverted by 180 degrees.

The text closes (hieroglyphic and hieratic versions make it clear that this is the close) with a depiction of the Fayum as a plain rectangle, upon which sit (i) a representation of the temple of Sobek in Crocodilopolis (Medinet Fayum), clearly labelled "The temple of Sobek of Crocodilopolis", (ii) a vertical cartouche, in which stands text which could be translated as "This lake is Ra, Osiris, Horus, pharaoh" (Figure 10:7). The sequence of deities and king makes sense, but whether or not the lake should be identified with them, or rather belongs to them, or whether the cartouche should be included in the reading, 'The name (of) this lake is Ra, Osiris, Horus, pharaoh', is not certain.

There is certainly an element of a map about the Book of the Fayum. Although only a small proportion of cult centres named in the text can be certainly identified today, there was plainly an attempt to relate to what we would think of as geographical reality (Zecchi 2001). A basic structure is assumed for the Fayum: a feeding channel, and two major canals, and a lake, as opposed to cultivable land, and an overriding division of the oasis into north and south, all very clearly reflected in ancient terminology in Egyptian language of the Greco-Roman period. In fact the administrative and hydrological structure of the Fayum was far more complex in many ways (Rathbone 1996), even allowing for changes over time. Yet the Egyptian audience would surely have seen links with the landscape they knew.

The Fayum, as we see it today, is a roughly triangular oasis (Figure 10:8). The irrigation system has been modified again and again, but its basic shape as a broad region of cultivation, even with changing limits and the changing area of the lake itself, has never altered. To the modern visitor, it essentially seems to be a wide, flat area, surrounded by modest hills. Why does the Book of the Fayum reduce it to a narrow strip? (The depicted confined entrance through hills may simply relate to ideas of the sources of the Nile.) The most obvious answer is that this is demanded by the presentation on a papyrus roll. But it is not entirely satisfactory to suggest that the presentation is a one-off distortion for immediate technical reasons. Possibly there may have been a wish to conform to the traditional Egyptian format of the onomastica, which took the form of lists (Gardiner 1947). However, as far as we know, these were never illustrated. The way in which the onomastica and other texts treat the Delta, a region as little linear as the Fayum, is problematic (Gardiner 1947, ii: 131–204), and so is the Egyptian treatment of the states of Syria/Palestine in the New Kingdom.

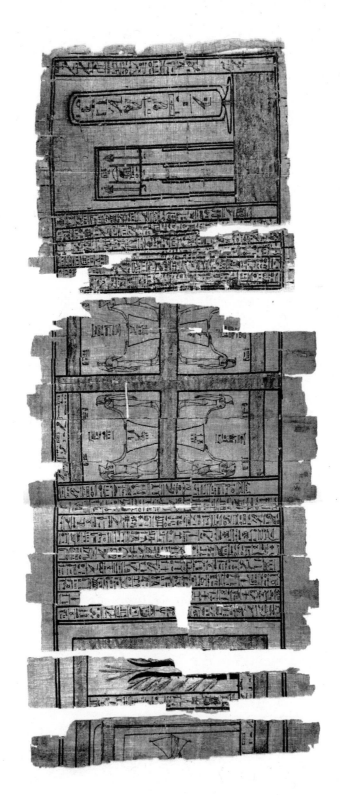

Figure 10:7 The close of the 'Book of the Fayum'; the shrine of the goddess Neith (left), the eight primeval gods of the Ogdoad (centre), and the temple of Sobek at Crocodilopolis (right) (Beinlich 1991: pl. 45 (part)).

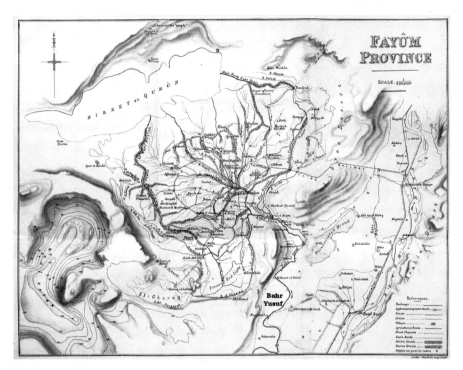

Figure 10:8   Map of the Fayum Province (Brown 1892: map at end of book).

Discussion: reasons for particular fascination with the Book of the Fayum

An interesting consideration is why the text was accorded so much attention in the later 19th century. After all, three publications of hieroglyphic versions appeared between 1871 (Mariette) and 1896, and Brugsch (1879) had already cited many of the geographical names in the text, as Lanzone (1896: 3) and Pleijte (1884: 2) had been at pains to point out. In the mid- to late 19th century, there was a strong optimism that the growing corpus of Egyptian textual material would yield factual information of many kinds. The geography of Egypt was one focus of interest, and the two monumental publications were Brugsch's geographical dictionary and Dumichen's collection of texts. Pleijte's edition of the Book of the Fayum was justified as the first combination of all the major papyrus sources into one text, and Lanzone's (1896: 5) large-format publication made available some fragments that he himself had identified.

One further reason for especial interest was that the text was also thought to provide information on the famous but elusive Egyptian labyrinth, as described by Herodotus and also mentioned by other classical writers (Lloyd 1975–1988, iii: 120–121; Uphill 2000: 82–91). Herodotus drew special attention to the labyrinth, which he claimed to have visited himself. He gave some indication of its location, 'a short way above Lake Moeris, near the place called the City of the Crocodiles',[7] and 'next to'

Lake Moeris, but the visitor in modern times, since the earliest travellers, has never been able to see any remains to match his impressive account. The structures he described seem to combine features of several types of Egyptian monument. The real problem, therefore, is to explain Herodotus' account, contrary to Lepsius (1897–1913, ii: 11–24) and Petrie (1889: 4–8; 1912: 28–35), who interpreted the site of the labyrinth, and its material remains, while also paying attention to the classical accounts. Herodotus' description illustrates why such high hopes were held of the Book of the Fayum in the 19th century. Towards the end of Book II (147), he turned to a fanciful narrative of the rise of the Egyptian Saite Dynasty. This led to an account of the history of the dynasty, and of the first significant contacts of the Greeks with Egypt, which indeed took place in this period. Thus, at the beginning of Book III, Herodotus was ready to return to his wider theme, with Cambyses the Persian's invasion of Egypt under the Saite king Amasis. Herodotus (II.148–149) related that Egypt was amicably divided among 12 kings (one of them the future Saite king Psammetichos I):

> To strengthen their unity, they decided to leave behind a shared monument to their reign, and to this end constructed a labyrinth a short way above Lake Moeris, near the place called the City of the Crocodiles. I have seen this edifice, but it is beyond my abilities to describe it. It must have cost more labour and money than all the forts and public buildings of the Greeks, although no one can deny that the temples at Ephesos and Samos are exceptional buildings. The pyramids also are amazing structures, each of them rivalling many of the most ambitious projects of Greece. However, the labyrinth surpasses them. It has twelve covered courts, six in a row facing the north, and six the south, and the gates of one row are precisely opposite the gates of the other, with a continuous wall around the outside of the whole. Within this, the edifice is in two storeys and comprises three thousand rooms, half of which are subterranean, while the other half are immediately above them. I was taken through the rooms in the upper storey, and so I can speak of them from my own observation, but I can speak of the subterranean ones only from hearsay, because the Egyptians in charge refused to permit me to see them, on the grounds that they contained the burials of the kings who constructed the labyrinth, and also the burials of the sacred crocodiles. The upper rooms, however, I did actually see, and it is difficult to believe that they are the work of mortals. The bewildering and complicated passages from room to room and from court to court were a perpetual wonder to me, as we passed from a courtyard into rooms, from rooms into galleries, from galleries into further rooms, and then into yet more courtyards. The roof of every room, courtyard and gallery is, like the walls, of stone. The walls are covered with figures in relief, and each courtyard is elegantly built of white marble and encircled by a colonnade. Near the corner where the labyrinth ends, there is a pyramid, two hundred and forty cubits high, with large images of animals carved upon it, and it may be entered by an underground passage.

> Although the labyrinth is miraculous, the Lake called Moeris, next to which it stands, is possibly more amazing. Its circumference is 3600 stades, or 60 *skhoinoi* ...

Diodorus (I.61.1–2) has the following account:

> When this king (the Kushite "Aktisames") had died, the Egyptians regained their (independent) power and installed a native king, Mendes, whom some call Marros. He did not accomplish any military feat whatever, but he prepared a tomb for himself, called the Labyrinth, not so much amazing for its size as inimitable in point of its skilful design.

He (I.61.4) then compared the Cretan labyrinth, and continued, "However, the one in Crete has entirely disappeared ..., but the one in Egypt has survived intact in its whole structure down to our own lifetime".

In a later passage, he gave an account of 12 rulers of Egypt (the idea of 11 rulers and Psammetichos, the eventual founder of the Saite Dynasty, is presumably derived entirely from Herodotus):

> When they had ruled for fifteen years according to their oaths and agreements, and had preserved their unity, they embarked upon a project to construct a common tomb for themselves ... (I.66.2).

> For, selecting a location beside the entrance-waterway to the lake of Moeris in Libya (i.e. to the west of the Nile Valley), they constructed the tomb of the finest stones, and they designed it as square in shape, and with each side a *stadion* in length, and they left to those who came after them no scope for them to be surpassed in the carving and other forms of workmanship. For anyone who was entering the enclosure wall encountered a peristyle building, with each side made up of 40 columns, and of this the roof was monolithic, carved into coffers, and decorated with outstanding depictions. It had reminders (*or* emblems?) of the home territory of each of the kings and of the temples (*or* rites?) and sacrifices in each, artistically crafted in the most splendid depictions (I.66.3–5).

Strabo's (XVII.1.3) account is as follows:

> The country was in the first place divided into *nomes*; the Thebaid had ten, the territory in the Delta ten, the territory in between sixteen. As some maintain, the entire total of the nomes was the same as that of the halls of the Labyrinth – but those were less than thirty (*or* than these thirty-six?).

> In addition, the structure of the Labyrinth – and the adjacent tomb of the king who constructed the Labyrinth – is a work quite equal to the pyramids ... with a settlement, and a great palace made up of many palaces, as many as there formerly were nomes. For there are this same number of peristyle courts, adjoining one another, all in one row, and at one wall – as though it were a great wall with the courts situated in front. The routes to them are directly opposite the wall. Large and numerous 'crypts' lie in front of the entrances, which have crooked routes passing from one to another, so that, without a guide, no stranger would be able to negotiate the entrance to each court and the exit. The amazing thing is that the roofs of each of the chambers are monolithic, and the breadth of the crypts are similarly roofed with monoliths, exceptional in size, with no timber incorporated anywhere, or any other kind of material. If one goes up onto the roof – not at a great height, as it is a single storey – one can see a 'plain' of stone, made up of such stones. If one from there descends again into the courts, outside one can observe that they are arranged supported by 27 monolithic pillars, and the walls consist of stones of no less magnitude. At the far end of this building, which extends for more than a *stadion*, there is the tomb: a four-sided pyramid, having each side measuring some 4 *plethra*, and the same height. Imandes is the name of the (king) interred. They say that the courts were made to this number because it was the custom for all the nomes to come together there by rank(?) with the local priests and priestesses, for sacrifices and offerings to the deities, and legislation(??) concerning the most important matters. Each of the nomes was led to the court designated for it (Strabo XVII.1.37).

At XVII.1.42, Strabo simply comments that the Memnonion at Abydos was of the same workmanship as the Labyrinth.

Pliny the Elder is generally agreed to have relied upon existing written sources (Lloyd 1970: 89). He discussed labyrinths in general: "One survives even now in Egypt in the Herakleopolite nome, which – the first – was made 3600 years ago by King Petesuchus or Tithoes, although Herodotus states that the whole work was that of the twelve kings, and of the last of them, Psametichus." (Pliny *Nat. Hist.* XXXVI.84 (19).) He went on to state that the Egyptian Labyrinth was a model for the Cretan, although he appears to have understood the Egyptian Labyrinth to have been a kind of 'maze', in which he may possibly have followed his contemporary Pomponius Mela (*Chorographia*, I.9.56), who had probably tried to interpret the written sources available to him (Lloyd 1970: 86–87, 89). He continues: "An account cannot be given of the lay-out and individual parts of the structure (*opus*), because it is divided between the 21 regions and administrative districts, which they call nomes, having the same number of vast halls attributed to them by their names; and besides it contains temples of all the Egyptian deities, and in addition Nemesis.[8] It included in the 40(?) shrines several pyramids, 40 cubits in height, with a ground area of 6 *arourae*. ... Within are columns of the stone porphyry ('imperial porphyry') and images of the deities, and statues of kings, and monstrous effigies" (Pliny *Nat. Hist.* XXXVI.87–88 (19)).

The possible points of contact with the Book of the Fayum in Herodotus' fifth century account include the various series of cult-places in the papyrus (Herodotus does not say what, if anything, went on in the upper storey of rooms that he himself saw), the series of mummified crocodiles, the 'images of animals' in the central registers, and also the dimensions of the Fayum (cf. 912–913; 939–940). Later descriptions seem either to see the labyrinth as a kind of 'maze', in accordance with the general Greek view of the Cretan labyrinth, or to try to understand it in the light of the Greek experience of Egyptian temples. The common notion that the sub-sections of the labyrinth in some sense represented all the nomes of Egypt can be related to the listings in the Book of the Fayum. Whatever uncertainties remain in the interpretation of the text, there seems no possibility of seeing the papyrus or any part of it as relating to a single complex monument such as Herodotus describes, let alone incorporating a plan of the labyrinth. The text does more than once mention 'pyramid-regions', probably including Hawara (61), now generally favoured as the site of Herodotus' labyrinth, but there is no hint of a reference to a monument of this kind.

Another reason for fascination with this Book must presumably have been the attractive and intriguing nature of the papyri. Even if the orthography of the texts bears some similarity to the difficult and idiosyncratic style of the Greco-Roman temple texts, these had been well studied and understood by the later 19th century. The pioneers in the study of Egyptian had used them, as they had tended to be more accessible and better preserved than earlier texts (Sauneron 1972: 46–50). The Book of the Fayum text, because of its systematic layout, was expected to reveal reliable information about the place names and geography of the Fayum. Lanzone (1896: 2) records that his own interest in the texts arose from his work on mythology. The subject of the geography of the Fayum had been haunted, and remained haunted for many years, by disputes as to what were the Egyptian terms for the Fayum, its lake, and the canal that fed it with water from the Nile (Gardiner and Bell 1943): that is, the canal that transmits the flow of the natural branch of the Nile now known as the Bahr Yusef (see Figure 10:8).

Conclusion

The context in which the Book of the Fayum was copied, and no doubt used, is unproblematic. There is no evidence for the use of any of the Egyptian scripts (hieroglyphic hieratic or demotic) in the Greco-Roman period except by priests in temple communities. Two of the more fragmentary hieroglyphic versions of the text are now housed at Copenhagen, as part of a purchase of papyri stemming from finds at Tebtunis in the southern Fayum. This material was recovered from a cache of discarded papyri in the vicinity of the temple of the local form of Sobek, Soknebtunis. Several hieratic versions came from the same source. Although the text focuses upon Sobek lord of Crocodilopolis, there is other evidence from Tebtunis to suggest that the priests there were content to recognize the supremacy of the cult of Sobek in the capital city of the Fayum. No papyri seem to have come to light at Tebtunis until the very end of the 19th century, so that it is possible to be confident that the chief hieroglyphic source (Boulaq/Hood/Amherst), found much earlier, came from elsewhere, even if it is likely that the various parts of this manuscript came from the Fayum.

What the text was for is less clear. Of course, it would have been of negligible utility as a practical map – and its chief audience seems to have been priests within the Fayum, who would least need such help. It in no way resembles the form of Egyptian liturgical material. Although parts of the text would be appropriate upon temple walls, the text as a whole would not. The various surviving versions show that it was a fixed and well known text, and not an *ad hoc* compilation. It seems to fit best with the general scholastic activities of the Greco-Roman temples, endeavouring to record and so maintain traditional Egyptian culture at a time when in Egypt as a whole this may have seemed under threat from Greek culture. The text was known at Kom Ombo. There are indications that the temples of the Fayum in the Greco-Roman period collected manuscripts from other parts of Egypt, and there is no reason to doubt that manuscripts could have moved in the opposite direction. The priests responsible for the temple texts at Kom Ombo were not short of material, and we should perhaps assume that the Book of the Fayum was simply admired there.

The Book of the Fayum can be seen as a scribal *tour de force*. It shows the rich diversity of ways in which text and image can be combined, and considerable variety in the use of the hieroglyphic script itself. It is conceivable that the text was a work that young scribes copied to prove their skill. Beinlich has shown that more than one illustrator was at work upon the hieroglyphic version Boulaq/Hood/Amherst, but this does not necessarily support either side of the case. The best preserved hieratic version of the text is from Tebtunis, and ends with a colophon:

> This writing has been accomplished by the (... several priestly titles ...), whose name is Pa-Geb. He has written it for the First Prophet of Sobek-Ra, the lord of Bekhen, also (holding the office of) the First Prophet of Sobek, lord of Tebtunis and Geb, the prince of the gods. His name – as he is called – Ra-Sobek, also the wab-priest who carries out the cult in Betenu. It was written in regnal year 20 of Hadrian, the god who protects, first month of Akhet, day 8.

It is not unreasonable to deduce from this, and from the sheer number of hieroglyphic and hieratic copies known from Tebtunis, that at least some of the priests wished to possess their own copies of the text. As far as the evidence goes, it was one of the most successful of Egyptian texts, rivalling in this respect the classics of the Middle Kingdom. We can assume that its mix of scribal and artistic dexterity and the eloquence of its longer textual passages were seen as essential in priestly training.

Notes

1   Beinlich (1991) numbers the lines of text on the pages of his parallel edition of the various sources in a purely conventional series from 1 to 1,289, and these are used here as a conveniently brief form of reference.

2   'Mehet-weret' literally – and appropriately for the Fayum – means 'Great Flood'.

3   The issue of the possible existence of pattern books for Egyptian tomb scenes is notorious. In the case of the Gurob shrine plan (Smith and Stewart 1984), we seem to have evidence for the use of two extraordinarily large sheets of papyrus (each about 80 cm x 54 cm), which could hardly have been handled in the supposed traditional scribal way, but possibly were commonplace in drawing offices.

4   Beinlich (1991, i: 139) suggests that this phrase means that the Channel is truly the earthly incorporation of Mehet-weret.

5   Elephantine was for the Egyptians a 'mythical' source of the Nile, and this is reflected in Herodotus II.28.

6   Beinlich points to the puzzling passage at 198: "The swimming of Ra ... his body is hidden in the meadow(?)."

7   This would most naturally be taken to signify 'Crocodilopolis', the capital of the Fayum, situated in the south-east Fayum.

8   This troublesome passage has often been interpreted along the lines of Lloyd (1970: 86): "... while in addition, Nemesis placed in the building's 40 chapels many pyramids ..."

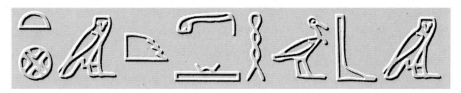

CHAPTER 11

MYSTERIOUS LANDS – THE WIDER CONTEXT

Robert Layton

There were two types of encounter between Egypt and other lands: those that actually occurred – some of which are only known through Egyptian sources – and those with imaginary lands invented by the Egyptians. The two are not absolutely distinct. Real encounters can only be portrayed in the artistic or literary styles within which their recorders work. The imaginary can never be totally novel, only projected as an extension or inversion of the known. Further, Ancient Egypt is itself a somewhat mysterious land for the modern European, posing its own problems of representation and translation in academic discourse (and see Quirke Chapter 9, and Robinson Chapter 8, both this volume).

Encounters through art

Gombrich (1960) commented on the puzzling persistence of what was seen by Europeans as "twisted perspective" in ancient Egyptian art, where the human body is depicted with the torso viewed from the front, while arms and legs are viewed from the side. If they depicted people in that fashion for some 2,000 years, did the Egyptians really see the world like that? If not, why did they persist in so depicting the human body? Gombrich argues against an evolutionist theory of art that construes it as progressing constantly toward greater realism. If that were the case, how did classical Greek artists succeed, in a mere 200 years, in mastering the tricks of foreshortening, of light and shade, to achieve a real *trompe d'œil*? "Surely only a change in the whole *function* of art can explain such a revolution" (Gombrich 1960: 108, my emphasis). Nor is a style merely adapted to its social function. Gombrich concludes that no art style can depict the world in all its detail. "Styles, like languages, differ in the sequence of articulation and in the number of questions they allow the artist to ask" (Gombrich 1960: 78). A correct representation of a building or landscape is one that conveys no false information to those who know how to read the artist's style.

Of course, the absence of classical "perspective" did not prevent the portrayal of complex narrative scenes, nor carving convincing portrait figures of individual pharaohs in bas-relief. A low relief carving (Figure 11:1) displayed in the Bologna Civic Archaeological Museum from the tomb of a high-ranking military official dates from the 14th century BC. The official is shown with his servants, in and around a

Figure 11:1   The late eighteenth Dynasty low relief carving of the estate of Horemheb, a high official (Archaeological Museum of Bologna).

small two-storey building. One servant pours water, another sweeps the threshold. Outside, a third servant seems ruefully to 'rub his shoulder', while his overseer walks away, whip in hand. Whether people see the world the way they depict it remains debatable. Styles are developed to depict what is considered significant or useful, according to the cultural context in which the style is deployed. Art may teach us to see the world in a different way, yet our representations of the world are always restricted by the techniques we have acquired for transforming our perception into material media (see Layton 1991: 156–173). Thus, in the Egyptians' encounter with the mysterious Sea Peoples, victory was a favour given by the gods, who were rewarded by the transfer of prisoners and booty to the temple's estates. It was appropriate to record this reciprocal thanks offering in detail, almost like a symbolically rendered legal document (Cline and O'Connor Chapter 7, this volume). Yet the records of conflict with the Sea Peoples were patterned after myths describing the creation and continual re-creation of cosmic order. It was appropriate to place scenes of the king's victory over foreigners on the entrance and exterior of the temple because foreign lands fringed and surrounded Egypt, whose perfect social order equated with the perfection of the temple. The king was depicted larger than other people, whereas the enemy, if chaotic, should be leaderless and actual leaders should not be given visual or verbal prominence. Like the king of Benin in West Africa, the pharaoh was the defender of order. The Oba of Benin is depicted (Figure 11:2) grasping leopards by the tail, to show his mastery over the king of the untamed bush (Ben-Amos 1976: 248). Pharaoh was similarly "the *image*, the *trace* and the *symbol* of the country's cohesion" (Loprieno 1996b: 277).

The challenge is to learn how to construe Egyptian art in the manner intended, to read through the conventions and, if possible, sift out what *we* would want to find in a historical record. The Medinet Habu land battle scene (Cline and O'Connor Chapter 7, this volume: Figure 7:5) provides indications of the Sea Peoples' military capacities. It reveals that the Sea Peoples used chariots as well as infantry (with no indication of the former in the texts). The apparent recurrent depiction of the Sea Peoples' leader belies the representation of them as chaotic barbarians. Since this aspect of the art goes against the grain of conventional depiction, we feel more confident of seeing through the representation to the event.

Similarly, ancient Egyptian representations of the world were mostly symbolic images of the cosmos intended for sacred purposes, rather than illustrations of routes

Figure 11:2   The Oba of Benin holding leopards by their tails (British Museum 1898, 1–15–30).

of earthly journeys (and see Harvey Chapter 5, this volume), yet this did not preclude the exceptional, particularly detailed geological map of a gold-mining region preserved on papyrus, and there may have been other maps for military or trading purposes. How, then, should the archaeologist interpret Queen Hatshepsut's murals depicting the mysterious land of Punt? Her temple contains the most elaborate of the rare pharaonic period examples of a country outside Egypt depicted with inhabitants and a landscape. What appears strange is that although there are many written accounts of Punt in Egypt, no other contemporary culture mentions it. The question is what information these accounts contain that tell us about Punt, rather than about the Egyptian imagination. For example, the skin colour of Punt's inhabitants is the same as that of Egyptians, whereas African skin colour was shown differently in Egyptian wall paintings. We can ask whether this detail reveals that Punt was located in Arabia rather than sub-Saharan Africa (see Baines 1985 on Egyptian conventions for the use of colour). Hatshepsut's murals show stilted, thatched-roofed houses, precious trees and exotic animals, while the queen of Punt is depicted as enormously fat. But the question remains whether the unconventional nature of this image is evidence for its veracity. The Egyptians were not solely interested in Punt as a source of economically valuable resources (live incense trees, ebony logs, gold, incense, electrum, ivory, baboons, panthers, and ostrich eggs). Punt had a parallel existence as a literary landscape, at the border between the human world and the world of the gods (and see Meeks Chapter 4, this volume). Perhaps the queen's girth was an expression of a concept of foreign royalty, in the same way that the pharaoh's relative size designates social status. The goddess Hathor was frequently termed the 'Lady of Punt'. The Punt expedition evokes the theme of departure to the God's Land and return to Egypt, accompanied by the divine scents and qualities of distant places.

In certain compositions we can see the effort of reducing what Gombrich (1960: 182) called the incalculably large quantity of information reaching us from the physical world to a restricted and granular artistic medium. In the 'Book of the Fayum' the god Ra is shown partially immersed in a pool or lake. According to the explanatory text, 'It is Ra, who goes off to swim' but the god is shown in a very standard, static pose; perhaps there was no way of showing a deity, in proper iconography, swimming. More challengingly, the division of a watercourse into two major canals is shown symbolically by the two outstretched arms of the goddess Mehet-weret. The two arms of the goddess are however pointing backwards, in the wrong direction. Tait (Chapter 10, this volume) concludes that the particular gesture of the goddess was dictated by what was appropriate to a sky/solar goddess; it would have been unthinkable to reverse her stance by 180 degrees: as the text is read from left to right, she would then be standing inappropriately on her head.

Another example can be seen when an artist grapples with the problem of representing three-dimensional space on a two-dimensional surface, in one of the earliest maps showing the world to be round. The sundisk at the top of the outer circle and the images inside the inner ring belong in the same dimension as the deities of earth, air and sky, while the rest of the circle is to be understood as rotated through 90 degrees from these. Despite their size, the images inside the inner ring should be seen as covering the full extent of the outer circle: they represent the visible world, at the top, and the Duat beneath the earth at the bottom (and see Allen Chapter 2, this volume).

Translating categories of representation

The question of whether or not the Book of the Fayum is a map raises the issue of appropriate categories in translation. The issue is familiar in anthropology: is it opportune to speak about 'land ownership' among hunter-gatherers, or is 'custodianship' a more satisfactory term (cf. Malinowski 1922: 116–117 on 'ownership' in the Trobriand Islands)? When the Azande say *boro mangu* are people who harm others by wishing them ill, is it appropriate to say that they believe in witchcraft, or is that term tainted by the history of European witch hunts (Ahern 1982; Evans Pritchard 1937)? The Book of the Fayum (Tait Chapter 10, this volume) contains a series of several hundred representations of deities and their emblems. The text is concerned with places. The papyrus roll therefore clearly has elements of a map but its users would not have needed a map. The association of deities with places recalls Australian totemism, where each clan is associated with a semi-human, semi-animal ancestor whose travels and stopping places bestow rights to land on the ancestors' human descendants. Each clan is responsible for looking after sites where the ancestors camped, sang or fought in their country. The well known Central Australian tradition of 'dot' painting originated, as a commercial enterprise, in the community of Papunya (Bardon 1979). It derives from traditional ground paintings and rock art that portray the ancestors' travels. Paintings often depict sacred sites in the landscape, linked by the tracks of ancestors. Yet they are not maps in the contemporary western sense, because sacred sites are not positioned relative to one another in a strictly topographic fashion. Sites are often (re)arranged to provide a symmetrical composition. Aboriginal people are of course expert in navigation through the desert landscape and, in fact, rely on the topographic relations between sacred sites to find their way (Lewis 1976). Designs (even commercial ones) validate their users' ancestral rights. If they are maps, they map the social position of the artist in his or her regional community.

Ancient ritual landscapes depicted or described on Egyptian coffins share some common features with elements of modern cartographic design. Yet, the danger is that in postulating the notion of Egyptian 'proto-maps' this becomes an act of intellectual colonialism, annexing *their* independent cultural tradition to assert our superior power of representation. There are many gradations between landscape painting, which presents the view from a single point, and maps plotted as if the eye were always directly over any position in the landscape. A 16th century view of Carrickfergus, illustrated in Harvey 1993, depicts the town from an imaginary, highly elevated viewpoint. The streets are laid out in plan below the viewer, yet the side walls of buildings facing the viewer stand between the eye and what lies beyond. Ogilby's route maps, drawn a century later, adopt the convention of an eye that moves along above the route taken, occasionally glancing to left or right as it passes a settlement (Delano-Smith and Kain 1999). Landscape painting is itself a geographically and historically specific artistic tradition, associated at one time with the celebration of the landed gentry's success during the enclosures (Daniels and Cosgrove 1988; Green 1995; Olwig 1993). Other cultures are not 'at fault' for failing to develop landscape art!

Describing real encounters in words

Gombrich's discussion of style and representation in art parallels Foucault's account of discourse in literature (see Layton 1997a). "Knowledge is that of which one can speak in a discursive practice" (Foucault 1972: 182). Foucault observed that medical statements cannot come from anyone, only someone who is authorized as a doctor. Medical discourse is shaped by the social context within which it is practised. The doctor's social standing was greatly modified at the end of the 18th century when the health of the population became one of the economic norms required by industrial societies (Foucault 1972: 51). The rules of a discourse specify what can usefully be said about a subject and what is irrelevant. Functionalist theory, in anthropology, established that it was irrelevant to write about the history of a society, but essential to describe evidence gained through participant observation. Plato's *Republic* starts with a detailed description of the circumstances in which Socrates debates the nature of justice.

> I went down to the Piraeus yesterday with Glaucon, the son of Ariston. ... Polemarchus saw us from a distance as we were setting off for home and he told his slave to run and bid us wait for him ...
>
> (Grube 1974: 2)

Weber (1947: 87) writes within different discursive parameters. He begins:

> An introductory discussion of concepts can hardly be dispensed with, in spite of the fact that it is unavoidably abstract and hence gives the impression of remoteness from reality ... It attempts only to formulate what all empirical sociology really means when it deals with the same problems, in what is hoped is a more convenient and somewhat more exact terminology.

If artistic categories such as maps and landscape are culturally specific, the same is true of literary categories such as myth, novel and travelogue. Michaels (1994: 31), who studied the beginnings of Aboriginal television in central Australia, discovered that the Walpiri deny fiction, both in their oral tradition and in film-making. In oral transmission, "the narrative imagination and memory are consumed by the requirement of preserving knowledge over time by encoding it as true stories collectively authored". Walpiri therefore do not 'make things up' for the camera; they are careful to perform everything in a true and proper manner, after consulting their kin. To characterize the foundational narratives of the ancestors' journeys as myth is highly misleading. Since translation depends on finding the nearest equivalent term in the language into which a discourse is converted, the translator has a certain amount of power, particularly when the original authors cannot pass comment (Derrida 1976: 113).

Thus, there are real difficulties of drawing on *our own* culture and time to elucidate ancient ritual landscapes depicted on Egyptian coffins, since we have our own expectations of religion and belief, mostly built up over two and a half millennia of Greco-Roman philosophy and Judaeo-Christian worship. We also find certain correspondences between the traits that we regard as crucial in defining our own literary discourse and similar traits in ancient Egyptian sources. Loprieno (Chapter 3, this volume) argues that the 'Tale of Sinuhe' has features which might today be termed a 'fictional' autobiography, with an intentionally literary character. The argument that ethnography (descriptive anthropological writing) is a form of 'fiction' (Geertz 1988) caused considerable debate in anthropology (see Layton 1997b: 200–211 for a summary). 'Fabricated' is more apt than 'fictional' since 'fiction', in this sense, means conventionally fashioned rather than invented. Clifford (1986) challenged Shostak's (1981) claim to have produced the biography of Nisa, a Kalahari gatherer-hunter woman, in her own words. Shostak rearranged Nisa's recollections into a coherent life-story. The narrative she constructed transcends Nisa's individual life by revealing an allegory of womanhood that makes the story compelling to a cross-cultural audience. The narrative is also constructed according to the specific concordances between what Nisa says and Shostak's own experience, as a feminist North American academic. While no one supposes that Malinowski or Evans-Pritchard invented their accounts of the Trobriand Islanders or the Nuer (as Geertz appeared to suggest in 1988), it is now clear that they, like all anthropologists, worked within a stylistic tradition shaped to their particular theoretical interests.

Maybe this helps to explain why although most Egyptian kings of the first millennium BC were of western (Libyan) descent and had un-Egyptian names, there is little prior evidence, textual or archaeological, for Libyan society. The Nubian conquest of Egypt in the eighth century BC only lasted 50 years, but was better recorded than the more enduring Libyan presence. Earlier, the Nubians were more interesting economically to ancient Egyptians, and were perceived as more of a threat. Perhaps the nomadic, clan-based society of ancient Libya was harder for Egyptians to conceptualize and represent than the centralized Nubian state.

Herodotus has been accused of fabricating Egyptian and Scythian society through a series of inversions upon the Greek society he was familiar with. Gould (1989) assesses this claim, while Harrison (2003) notes that Herodotus avoids the common, overt prejudices of classical Greek writers on Egypt. His accounts of the deeds of pharaohs explore and theorize the nature of monarchy. But, writes Harrison, Herodotus was working within a long tradition. His treatment of Egypt as the geographical and cultural inversion of Greece, while not necessarily pejorative, inevitably restricted the number of features of Egyptian society that could be described.

The new can only be described in terms of the familiar. The first Australian Aboriginal depictions of horses or cattle show them as a variant on the motif for kangaroo, with shorter front than back legs, but with a hairy tail and hoofed feet (Layton 1992: 122; Rosenfeld 1982: 208–209). The colonists, meanwhile, were searching for Aboriginal 'kings' through whom they could practice indirect rule, plucking innocent men from among their peers and presenting them with brass plaques inscribed 'King Billy' or 'King Tommy'. Howard (1981: 59) quotes the 'installation' of such a 'king' in south-west Australia, during the 1870s:

> After admonishing the blacks to give up fighting and stealing ... Governor Weld proceeded to select the most suitable man amongst them to be the King of the tribe in the district. This exalted position fell to a native locally known as Left-handed Billy.

When King Billy tried to act according to the authority bestowed on him, his supposed subjects rebelled. Many years later, the anthropologist Daisy Bates encountered him again:

In the streets of Geraldton I met a solitary old Bibbulmun with a brass plate dangling from his neck – 'King Billy of Geraldton' inscribed thereon ... We talked for a little while of the rites and true relationships and then I touched the plate and asked,

> 'What is this brother?'
> 'That is a lie,' said Dongaluk, 'but the jugga give me bacca and money for it when they laugh at me.'

(quoted in Howard 1981: 59–60)

During the 17th and 18th centuries, newly discovered societies were used to validate competing philosophies concerning the original human condition. Hobbes depicted native Americans as living in the state of war which he imagined would precede a social contract, "For the savage people in many places in America ... have no government at all; and live at this day in that brutish manner" (Hobbes [1651] 1970: 65). Rousseau, borrowing from the more sympathetic account of du Tertre, countered that the unfettered desires Hobbes attributed to the original human condition were in fact created by the invention of property. The native Caribbean was peaceable because he did not covet belongings (Rousseau [1755] 1963: 163; du Tertre [1667] 1992: 133; see also Whitehead 1995). We have not escaped the tendency to exoticize other cultures. Fabian (1983) argued that anthropology consistently projects contemporary small-scale societies into the past. The 'Tale of Sinuhe' is one of the earliest examples of narrative in Egyptian texts. Loprieno (Chapter 3, this volume) relates how the hero's journey from Egypt to Asia is dramatized as entry into a strange land. The wealth of topographical and psychological details included in the account of the hero's transition from Egypt to Asia makes it clear that the protagonist is entering a new phase in his life, an increased level of awareness. The land of Retjenu, where he is going to spend a sizeable portion of his adult life, is portrayed in Utopian terms, motivated by the hero's psychological state rather than by the objective observation of Palestinian landscapes. Van Gennep ([1905] 1960) identified journeys as a widely distributed inspiration for 'rites of passage' celebrating a change of status such as birth, adulthood or marriage. The shipwrecked sailor appears to be journeying through his own rite of passage.

The notion of 'Possible Worlds' has been elevated to a scientific concept by Basalla (1988). It is possible to imagine a world in which the steam car triumphed over the internal combustion engine, or China underwent a Capitalist revolution, and then ask which particular historical variables prevented such outcomes. Basalla finds that the once popular Stanley Steamer was still being constructed by craftsmen, while Henry Ford was already using a production line to mass-produce his petrol-engine cars (Basalla 1988: 189). If printing, gunpowder and the magnetic compass revolutionized Western culture, why did they not have the same effect in China, where they were invented? The Chinese were enthusiastic about the uses of all three. Basalla (1988: 170–175) considers several possible explanations. The bureaucratic feudal administration of China, for example, may have inhibited the rise of a merchant class. Social stability led to slow and continuous scientific and technological change, rather than a series of revolutions. Cheap transport, rather than technical innovation, was used to solve economic problems in 18th century China.

Projecting the imaginary

In the history of European fiction, the complexity of an organized geography tends to replace the magic topography of the traditional tale rooted in oral tradition. This trend is reversed in Egypt. Middle Kingdom literature reveals the emergence of a different stylistic genre, from 'narrative' to 'moral' discourse. The protagonist in 'The Eloquent Peasant' begins as a simple hunter-gatherer taking his goods to trade in Egypt, but on the way his travel becomes a moral journey. A description of exotic products gives way to an analysis of the deep problems facing Egyptian society.

Academics have taken different approaches to the variety of Coffin Texts describing the journey of the soul. Some have provided synoptic editions while others take one good example as a reference point. A similar dilemma has been encountered in anthropological analyses of myth. Lévi-Strauss, who was interested in revealing the universal cognitive structures underlying a diversity of myths, tended to take one telling as representative; '*the* Bororo myth of the parrot catchers', etc. (Lévi-Strauss 1970, 1973). Bourdieu (1977) criticized this approach, arguing that the 'unwritten score' that Structuralists searched for was an artefact created by the analyst. In reality, he argued, each member of a community performs tradition in a slightly different way. Each has internalized a 'habitus' learned by listening to the performances of the previous generation. British 'Functional' anthropologists, who were interested in the political functions of myth, seized upon variations in the way myths were told as indicative of the social position of the narrator (Kaberry 1957; Leach 1954: ch. 9), whereas Bourdieu (1977) was equally interested in the social processes that caused individual 'habituses' to converge.

The form of Egyptian narratives changed as Egyptian political organization changed. Loprieno (Chapter 3, this volume) argues that it is possible to understand the organization of space in Middle Kingdom literature as following the same lines and serving the same interests as those of the bourgeois novel in Europe, that is, the interests of an elite who displayed an emerging national identity. Later confrontation with foreigners caused a new attitude to the fantastic. The Egyptian historical novel in Ramesside times revisits, in a fictive way, past historical periods or figures, offering many parallels with what is called the 'historical novel' of modern European literatures.

If the new can only be described in terms of the familiar, it is equally true that the imagined can only be conceived by extending or reversing the known. O'Connor and Quirke (Chapter 1, this volume) point out that even events that really happened can be treated imaginatively for literary purposes. Rather than an absolute contrast between factual reporting and fiction, there is a continuum between attempts to imagine the completely novel and attempts to describe the unfamiliar absolutely factually. The Ancient Egyptians were not the only community to experience this dilemma. The two meanings of the word 'alien' in American English are revealing: an alien is a foreigner from abroad, or an intelligent being from another part of the universe. The distinctively western genre of science fiction contains endless tales of alien worlds peopled by insect-like beings, of feudal or totalitarian societies, with crazed leaders bent on ruling the universe while a brain-washed proletariat labours in prison camps until democracy comes to the rescue. Details of non-western culture are borrowed to realize the exotic: Princess Leia of Star Wars dresses her hair in the style of Hopi girls (see Connelly 1979: 546), the subjugated community of Stargate lives in a Saharan mud-walled oasis city. Terry Pratchett's Disc World is wittily built upon the theory that the world is a disc supported by four elephants standing on the backs of turtles, a theory that Geertz (1973: 28–9) tentatively locates in India. The best science fiction constructs an alternative world and follows its inverted logic remorselessly, as in Philip K. Dick's (1962) *The Man in the High Castle*, where Japan and Germany have defeated the US and divided it into two occupied zones.

In Middle Kingdom belief, walls of flame and walls of flint confronted the travelling soul, as did a walled building with compartments, some inhabited by a variety of monstrous creatures. (I cannot resist visualizing this as a 20th century computer game.) Measurements supplied for features in the underworld are among the most striking assertions of knowledge in the religious domain. The ancient Egyptian projection of the known into the unknown, further reaches of the (universe), has parallels in other cultural traditions. In dynastic Egypt the earth was male and the sky female; they were held apart by air. In the West African cosmology of the Yoruba, the world is made up of a primeval sky and earth, between which lies *ile aiye*, the subsequently created habitable world. *Ile aiye* denotes both the civilized, ordered world, organized into states governed by kings, and the pattern or idea of life properly lived. It does not include distant, uncultivated bush or forest. Among Oyo Yoruba the Sky is the domain of the Supreme God, while the Earth (beneath the inhabited world) is the domain of the Earth Goddess. South-western Yoruba represent the Sky and Earth as two halves of a closed calabash (Morton-Williams 1964).

The Hopi of south-western North America conceive of a dual division of time and space between the worlds of the living and the dead. The sun has two entrances, described as houses or *kivas* (ceremonial centres). In the morning, the sun emerges from its eastern house and in the evening it descends into its western house. During the night the sun must travel underground from west to east, hence day and night are reversed in the worlds of the living and dead (Titiev 1944, quoted in Hieb 1979: 577). The winter solstice in the upper world coincides with the summer solstice in the lower world. The Hopi altar is a representation of the three-dimensional cosmology (Geertz 1987: 19–24).

While Yoruba and Egyptian culture may perhaps be historically connected (Folorunso 2003), similarities with native North American culture must be the result of parallel conjectures. What lay over the Egyptian horizon could only be surmised through a projection of what was known. Thus, Egyptians were aware of the curvature of the earth's surface, this explaining the afterglow when the sun has set (Allen Chapter 2, this volume). The annual solar cycle showed the world to be round. The Hopi underworld, lived in reverse, parallels the Egyptian *Duat*, both beneath the earth and through which the sun travelled at night.

Like most cultures, Egyptians put their land at the centre of the universe. South was up, north down, a method of orientation shared, for example, with the Alawa of northern Australia, whose country lies on either side of monsoon-fed rivers that flow northward into the Gulf of Carpentaria (Layton 1997a). The 40 nomes (states) into which Ancient Egypt was divided, some of their animal emblems apparently depicted on the protodynastic Narmer Palette (O'Connor 2003: Figure 9:3), recall the totemic clans of Aboriginal Australia. Mithen (1998) has followed early psychologists (e.g. Luquet) in arguing that the representation of animal-headed human figures in the early Upper Palaeolithic of Europe is symptomatic of the emergence of modern human cognition, distinctive in its ability to draw parallels between different realms of experience. The carved lion-man of Hohlenstein-Stadel (Hahn 1993) and the painted bison-man of Chauvet (Chauvet *et al.* 1996) both date to around 30,000 BP. They reveal the ability for imaginative and creative thinking, a fundamental prerequisite for handling encounters with the mysterious. Current approaches to analyses of the 'mysterious lands' of other cultures demonstrate the depth and complexity of human ingenuity. Not so long ago, it was common practice for academics to assume and assert that humans would always posit 'opposites' for 'heaven' and 'hell' (i.e. hot 'hells' for cold 'Eskimos' away from cold (afterworld) 'heavens'). Today, any such assumptions would rightly appear both superficial and simplistic. The wider context of 'mysterious lands' reveals the workings of unmistakable curiosity in the human spirit.

References

Note: references to chapters and books in the *Encounters with Ancient Egypt* series are denoted in bold type.

Adams, W. Y. 1977, *Nubia Corridor to Africa*. London: Allen Lane

Addison, D. 1995, Maps to Sleep and Dream to. *The Cartographic Journal* 32, 48–49

Ahern, E. M. 1982, Rules in Oracles and Games. *Man* 17, 302–312

Allen, J. P. 1988, *Genesis in Egypt: The Philosophy of Ancient Egyptian Creation Accounts*. New Haven: Yale UP

Allen, J. P. 1989, The Cosmology of the Pyramid Texts, in W. K. Simpson (ed.), *Religion and Philosophy in Ancient Egypt*, 1–28. New Haven: Yale UP

Allen, J. P. 2000, *Middle Egyptian. An Introduction to the Language and Culture of Hieroglyphs*. Cambridge: CUP

Allen, T. G. 1974, *The Book of the Dead or Going Forth by Day*. Chicago: University of Chicago Press

Alliot, M. 1951, Pount-Pwane, l'Opôné du géographe Ptolémée. *Révue d'Égyptologie* 8, 1–7

Altenmüller, H. 1986, Ein Zaubermesser des Mittleren Reiches. *Studien zur Altägyptischen Kultur* 13, 1–27

Amigues, S. 1996, L'expedition d'Anaxicrate en Arabie Occidentale. *Topoi* 6, 674–675

Andrews, C. 1972, Introduction, in R. O. Faulkner, *The Book of the Dead*, 11–16. London: British Museum Press

Artzy, M. 1997, Nomads of the Sea, in S. Swiny, R. L. Hohlfelder and H. W. Swiny (eds), *Res Maritimae: Cyprus and the Eastern Mediterranean from Prehistory to Late Antiquity*, 1–16. Atlanta,. Georgia: Scholars Press

Assmann, J. 1969, *Liturgische Lieder an den Sonnengott: Untersuchungen zur altägyptischen Hymnik*. Berlin: B

Assmann, J. 1970, *Der König als Sonnenpriester: ein kosmographischer Begleittext zur kultischen Sonnenhymnik in thebanischen Tempeln und Gräbern*. Glückstadt: Augustin

Assmann, J. 1983, Schrift, Tod und Identität: das Grab als Vorschule der Literatur im Alten Ägypten, in A. Assmann, J. Assman and C. Hardmeier (eds). *Schrift und Gedächtnis*, 64–93. Munich: Wilhelm Fink

Assmann, J. 1989, State and Religion in the New Kingdom, in W. K. Simpson (ed.), *Religion and Philosophy in Ancient Egypt*, 55–88. New Haven: Yale UP

Assmann, J. 1990, Egyptian mortuary liturgies, in S. Israelit-Groll (ed.), *Studies in Egyptology presented to Miriam Lichtheim*, 1–20. Jerusalem: Magnes

Assmann, J. 1991, *Stein und Zeit. Mensch und Gesellschaft im Alten Ägypten*. Munich: Wilhelm Fink

Assmann, J. 1995, *Ma'at: Gerechtheit und Unsterblichkeit in alten Ägypten*. Munich: C. H. Beck

Assmann, J. 1996, Kulturelle und literarische Texte, in A. Loprieno (ed.), *Ancient Egyptian Literature: History and Forms*, 59–82. Leiden: Brill

Assmann, J. 2001, *The Search for God in Ancient Egypt*. Ithaca and London: Cornell UP

Baines, J. 1985, Colour Terminology and Colour Classification: Ancient Egyptian Colour Terminology and Polychromy. *American Anthropologist* 87, 282–297

Baines, J. 1990, Interpreting the Story of the Shipwrecked Sailor. *Journal of Egyptian Archaeology* 76, 55–72

Baines, J. 1995, Palaces and Temples of Ancient Egypt, in J. Sasson (ed.), *Civilizations of the Ancient Near East*, 303–317. New York: Simon and Schuster

Baines, J. 1996, Classicism and Modernism in the Literature of the New Kingdom, in A. Loprieno (ed.), *Ancient Egyptian Literature: History and Forms*, 157–174. Leiden: Brill

Baines, J. 1999, On Wenamun as a Literary Text, in J. Assmann and E. Blumenthal (eds), *Literatur und Politik im pharaonischen und ptolemäischen Ägypten*, 209–233. Cairo: Institut Français d'Archéologie Orientale

Bakry, H. 1973, The Discovery of a Temple of Merenptah at On. *Aegyptus* 53, 3–21

Bardon, G. 1979, *Aboriginal Art of the Western Desert*. Adelaide: Rigby

Barker, G., D. Gilbertson, B. Jones and D. Mattingly 1996, *Farming the Desert: The UNESCO Libyan Valley Archaeological Survey 1: Synthesis*. Paris, Tripoli and London: Unesco Publishing

Basalla, G. 1988, *The Evolution of Technology*. Cambridge: CUP

Bates, O. 1914, *The Eastern Libyans: An Essay*. London: Macmillan

Bates, O. 1927, Excavations at Marsa Matruh. *Harvard African Studies* 8, 125–197

Baum, N. 1994, Sntr: une révision. *Revue d'Egyptologie* 45, 17–39

Baum, N. 1999, *Encyclopédie religieuse de l'univers végétal*. Montpellier: Université Paul Valéry-Montpellier III.

Beaux, N. 1990, *Le Cabinet de Curiosités de Thoutmosis III: Plantes et Aimaux du 'Jardin botanique' de Karnak*. Leuven: Peeters

Beckman, G. 1996, Texts: Akkadian/Ugarit, in A. B. Knapp (ed.), *Sources for the History of Cyprus. Volume II: Near Eastern and Aegean Texts from the Third to the First Millennia BC*, 26–28. Altamont, NY: Greece and Cyprus Research Center

Beinlich, H. 1991, *Das Buch vom Fayum: zum religiösen Eigenverständnis einer ägyptischen Landschaft*. Wiesbaden: Harrassowitz

Beinlich, H. 1996, Ein Fragment des Buches vom Fajjum (W/P) in Berlin. *Zeitschrift für Ägyptische Sprache* 123, 10–18

Beinlich, H. 1997, Hieratische Fragmente des 'Buches vom Fajjum' und ein Nachtrag zu BF Carlsberg. *Zeitschrift für Ägyptische Sprache* 124, 1–22

Ben-Amos, P. 1976, Men and Animals in Benin Art. *Man* 11, 243–252

Bernal, M. 1987, *Black Athena: The Afroasiatic Roots of Classical Civilization, 1, The Fabrication of Ancient Greece 1785–1985*. London: Free Association Press

Bernal, M. 1991, *Black Athena: The Afroasiatic Roots of Classical Civilization, 2, The Documentary and Archaeological Evidence*. London: Free Association Press

Bernal, M. 2001, *Black Athena Writes Back: Martin Bernal Responds to his Critics*. Durham: Duke UP

Bernal, M. 2003, Afrocentrism and Historical Models for the Foundation of Ancient Greece, in D. O'Connor and A. Reid (eds), *Ancient Egypt in Africa*, 23–30. London: UCL Press

Betancourt, P. P. 2000, The Aegean and the Origin of the Sea Peoples, in E. D. Oren (ed.), *The Sea Peoples and Their World: A Reassessment*, 297–303. Philadelphia: University Museum Publications

Betro, M. 1994, Il Domestico, la Lessicografica Botanica e gli Incensi. *Egitto e Vicino Oriente* 17, 39–48

Betro, M. 1996, Punt, la XXVI Dinastia e il Frammento di Statua del Museo Pushkin I.1,B 1025. *Egitto e Vicino Oriente* 19, 41–49

Bianchi, R. S. 1999, Kom Ombo, in K. A. Bard (ed.), *Encyclopedia of the Archaeology of Ancient Egypt*, 418–421. London and New York: Routledge

Bickel, S. 1994, *La Cosmogonie Égyptienne avant le Nouvel Empire*. Fribourg and Göttingen: Editions Universitaires, Vandenhoeck and Ruprecht

Bietak, M. 1966, *Ausgrabungen in Sayala-Nubien 1961–1965: Denkmäler der C-Gruppe und der Pan-Gräber-Kultur*. Vienna: H. Böhlaus Nachf

Biggs, M. 1999, Putting the state on the map: cartography, territory, and European state formation. *Comparative Studies in Society and History* 41, 374–405

Blackman, A. M. 1932, *Middle Egyptian Stories*. Brussels: Fondation Egyptologique Reine Elisabeth

Bonneau, D. 1964, *La Crue du Nil divinité Égyptienne*. Paris: C. Klincksieck

Bonnet, C. 1990, *Kerma, Royaume de Nubie*. Geneva: Museé d'Art et d'Histoire

Borghouts, J. F. 1970, *The Magical Texts of Papyrus Leiden I 348*. Leiden: Rijksmuseum van Oudheden

Botti, G. 1959, La Glorificazione di Sobek e del Fayyum in uno Papiro Hieratico da Tebtynis. *Analecta Aegyptiaca* 8, Copenhagen: Munksgaard

Bourdieu, P. 1977, *Outline of a Theory of Practice* (trans. R. Nice). Cambridge: CUP

Bourriau, J. 1991, Patterns of Change in Burial Customs, in S. Quirke (ed.), *Middle Kingdom Studies*, 3–20. New Malden: SIA

Bowen, C. 1975–1976, The Historical Inventory of the Dindshenchas. *Studia Celtica* 10–11, 115

Bowersock, G. W. 1996, Exploration in North-West Arabia after Jansesen-Savignac. *Topoi Orient-occident* 6, 553–563

Bradbury, L. 1988, Reflections on Travelling to 'God's Land' and Punt in the Middle Kingdom. *Journal of the American Research Center in Egypt* 25, 127–156

Bradbury, L. 1996, *Kpn*-boats, Punt Trade, and a Lost Emporium. *Journal of the American Research Center in Egypt* 33, 37–60

Breasted, J. H. 1906, *Ancient Records of Egypt, Volume 2, The Eighteenth Dynasty*. New York: Russell and Russell

Breasted, J. H. 2001 (reprint of 1906 edition), *Ancient Records of Egypt, Volumes 3 and 4*. Urbana: University of Illinois Press

Brown, R. H. 1892, *The Fayum and Lake Moeris*. London: Edward Stanford

Broze, M. 1989, *La Princesse de Bakhtan*. Brussels: Fondation Egyptologique Reine Elisabeth

Broze, M. 1996, *Les Aventures d'Horus et Seth dans le Papyrus Chester Beatty* I. Leuven: Peeters

Brug, J. 1985, *A Literary and Archaeological Study of the Philistines*. Oxford: British Archaeological Reports

Brugsch, H. 1857, *Die Geographie des Alten Ägyptens* I. Leipzig 48–49; II (Leipzig, 1858), 15–16; III (Leipzig, 1860), 63–64

Brugsch, H. 1879, *Dictionnaire Géographique de l'Ancienne Égypte: contenant par ordre alphabétique la nomenclature comparée des noms propres géographiques qui se rencontrent sur les monuments et dans les papyrus*. Leipzig: Hinrichs

Brunner, H. 1964, *Die Geburt des Gottkönigs. Studien zur Überlieferung eines altägyptischen Mythos*. Wiesbaden: Harrassowitz

Bryce, T. R. 1979, The Role of the Lukki People in Late Bronze Age Anatolia. *Antichthon* 13, 1–11

Bryce, T. R. 1986, *The Lycians: A Study of Lycian History and Civilisation to the Conquest of Alexander the Great. Vol. 1: The Lycians in Literary and Epigraphic Sources*. Copenhagen: Museum Tusculanum Press

Bryce, T. R. 1992, Lukki Revisited. *Journal of Near Eastern Studies* 51, 121–130

Butzer, K. 1977, Geographie, in W. Helck and E. Otto (eds). *Lexikon der Ägyptologie* II, 525–530, Wiesbaden: Harrassowitz

Caminos, R. 1956, *Literary Fragments in the Hieratic Script*. Oxford: OUP

Caminos, R. 1958, *The Chronicle of Prince Osorkon*. Rome: Pontificum Institutum Biblicum

Caminos, R. 1968, *The Shrines and Rock Inscriptions of Ibrim*. London: Egypt Exploration Society

Caminos, R. 1977, *A Tale of Woe. Papyrus Pushkin 127*. Oxford: OUP

Carter, H. and A. H. Gardiner 1917, The Tomb of Ramesses IV and the Turin Plan of a Royal Tomb. *Journal of Egyptian Archaeology* 4, 130–158

Carter, T. H. 1963, Reconnaissance in Cyrenaica. *Expedition* 5/4, 18–27

Casson, L. 1989, *The Periplus Maris Erythraei*. Princeton: Princeton UP

Cauville, S. 2000, *Le Temple de Dendara XI*. Cairo: Institut Français d'Archéologie Orientale

Cauville, S. and D. Devauchelle 1984, Le Temple d'Edfou: Étapes de la Construction. Nouvelles Domes Historiques. *Revue d'Egyptologie* 35, 31–55

Chassinat, E. 1934a, *Dendara I*. Cairo: Institut Français d'Archéologie Orientale

Chassinat, E. 1934b, *Dendara II*. Cairo: Institut Français d'Archéologie Orientale

Chassinat, E. 1935a, *Dendara III*. Cairo: Institut Français d'Archéologie Orientale

Chassinat, E. 1935b, *Dendara IV*. Cairo: Institut Français d'Archéologie Orientale

Chassinat, E. 1965, *Dendara VI*. Cairo: Institut Français d'Archéologie Orientale

Chassinat, E. and F. Daumas 1978, *Dendara VIII*. Cairo: Institut Français d'Archéologie Orientale

Chassinat, E. and M. Rochemonteix 1918, *Le Temple d'Edfou II*. Cairo: Institut Français d'Archéologie Orientale

Chassinat, E. and M. Rochemonteix 1928, *Le Temple d'Edfou III*. Cairo: Institut Français d'Archéologie Orientale

Chassinat, E. and M. Rochemonteix 1929, *Le Temple d'Edfou IV*. Cairo: Institut Français d'Archéologie Orientale

Chassinat, E. and M. Rochemonteix 1930, *Le Temple d'Edfou V*. Cairo: Institut Français d'Archéologie Orientale

Chassinat, E. and M. Rochemonteix 1931, *Le Temple d'Edfou VI*. Cairo: Institut Français d'Archéologie Orientale

Chassinat, E. and M. Rochemonteix 1932, *Le Temple d'Edfou VII*. Cairo: Institut Français d'Archéologie Orientale

Chassinat, E. and M. Rochemonteix 1933, *Le Temple d'Edfou VIII*. Cairo: Institut Français d'Archéologie Orientale

Chauvet, J-M., E. B. Deschamps and C. Hillaire 1996, *Chauvet Cave: The Discovery of the World's Oldest Paintings* (trans. P. Bahn). London: Thames and Hudson

Chermette, M. and J-C. Goyon 1996, Le Catalogue Raisonné des Producteurs de Styrax et d'Oliban d'Edfou et d'Athribis de Haute Égypte. *Studien zur Altägyptischen Kultur* 23, 47–82

Cifola, B. 1988, Ramses III and the Sea Peoples: A Structural Analysis of the Medinet Habu Inscriptions. *Orientalia* 57/3, 275–306

Clifford, J. 1986, On Ethnographic Allegory, in J. Clifford and G. Marcus (eds), *Writing Culture*, 98–121. Berkeley: University of California Press

Cline, E. H. 1994, *Sailing the Wine-Dark Sea: International Trade and the Late Bronze Age Aegean*. Oxford: Tempus Reparatum

Cohen, R. and R. Westbrook (eds) 2000, *Amarna Diplomacy the Beginnings of International Relations*. Baltimore: Johns Hopkins UP

Collombert, J. and L. Coulon 2000, Les Dieux contre la mer. Le début du 'Papyrus d'Astarté' (pBN 202). *Bulletin de l'Institut Français d'Archéologie Orientale du Caire* 100, 193–242

Colls, D., C. Descamps, M. Faure and C. Guerin 1985, The Bronze Black Rhinoceros from Port Vendres III. *Antiquity* 59, 108–110

Connelly, J. C. 1979, Hopi Social Organisation, in A. Ortiz (ed.), *Handbook of North American Indians, vol. 9: Southwest*, 539–553. Washington: Smithsonian

Couyat, J. and P. Montet 1912, *Les Inscriptions hiéroglyphiques et hiératiques du Ouadi Hammamat*. Cairo: Institut Français d'Archéologie Orientale

D'Auria, S., P. Lacovara and C. H. Roehrig 1988, *Mummies and Magic*. Boston: Museum of Fine Arts

Danelius, E. and H. Steinitz 1967, The Fishes and Other Aquatic Animals on the Punt-Reliefs at Deir el-Bahri. *Journal of the American Research Center in Egypt* 53, 15–24

Daniels, S. and D. Cosgrove 1988, Introduction: Iconography and Landscape, in S. Daniels and D. Cosgrove (eds), *The Iconography of Landscape*, 1–10. Cambridge: CUP

Dasen, V. 1993, *Dwarfs in Ancient Egypt and Greece*. Oxford: Clarendon

Davies, N. de G. 1905, *The Rock Tombs of El Amarna. Part II. The Tombs of Panehesy and Meryra II*. London: Egypt Exploration Fund

Davies, N. de G. 1922, *The Tomb of Puyemre at Thebes*. New York: Metropolitan Museum of Art

Davies, N. de G. 1930, *The Tomb of Ken-Amun at Thebes*. New York: Metropolitan Museum of Art

Davies, N. de G. 1943, *The Tomb of Rekh-mi-re' at Thebes*. New York: Metropolitan Museum of Art

Davies, N. M. 1961, A Fragment of a Punt Scene. *Journal of Egyptian Archaeology* 47, 19–23

Davies, N. M. and N. de G. Davies 1941, The Tomb of Amenmose at Thebes. *Journal of Egyptian Archaeology* 26, 131–136

Davis, T. M. 1908, *The Funeral Papyrus of Iouiya*. London: Constable

de Buck, A. 1935–1961, *The Egyptian Coffin Texts*. Chicago: University of Chicago Press

de Buck, A. 1947, *The Egyptian Coffin Texts III*. Chicago: University of Chicago Press

de Buck, A. 1951, *The Egyptian Coffin Texts IV. Texts of Spells 268–354*. Chicago: University of Chicago Press

de Buck, A. 1961, *The Egyptian Coffin Texts VII*. Chicago: University of Chicago Press

de Morgan, J. 1895 *Catalogue des monuments et inscriptions de l'Egypte antique, II. Kom Ombo*. Vienna: Adolphe Holzhausen

Degas, J. 1995, Dom Juan de Castro sur l'itineraire de Pount (1541). *Revue d'Egyptologie* 46, 215–237

Delano-Smith, C. and R. J. P. Kain 1999, *English Maps: A History*. London: British Museum Publications

Derrida, J. 1976, *Of Grammatology* (trans. G. C. Spivak). Baltimore: Johns Hopkins UP

Desanges, J. 1978, *Recherches sur l'activité des Méditerranéens aux confins de l'Afrique*. Rome: École Française de Rome

Desroches-Noblecourt, C. 1989, *Tutankhamun, Life and Death of a Pharaoh*. London: Penguin

Dixon, D. M. 1969, The Transplantation of Punt Incense Trees in Egypt. *Journal of Egyptian Archaeology* 55, 55–65

Dothan, T. 1982, *The Philistines and Their Material Culture*. Jerusalem: Israel Exploration Society

Dothan, T. 1995, The Sea Peoples and the Philistines of Ancient Palestine, in J. M. Sasson, J. Baines, G. Beckman and K. S. Rubinson (eds), *Civilizations of the Ancient Near East*, 1,267–1,279. Peabody: Hendrickson

Dothan, T. 1998, Initial Philistine Settlement: From Migration to Coexistence, in S. Gitin, A. Mazar and E. Stern, *Mediterranean Peoples in Transition: Thirteenth to Early Tenth Centuries BC*, 148–161. Jerusalem: Israel Exploration Society

Dothan, T. 2000, Reflections on the Initial Phase of Philistine Settlement, in E. D. Oren (ed.), *The Sea Peoples and Their World: A Reassessment*, 145–158. Philadelphia: University Museum Publications

Dothan, T. and M. Dothan 1992, *People of the Sea: The Search for the Philistines*. New York: Macmillan

Drews, R. 1992, Herodotus I.94, the Drought ca. 1200 BC and the Origin of the Etruscans. *Historia* 41, 14–39

Drews, R. 1993, *The End of the Bronze Age*. Princeton: Princeton UP

Drews, R. 1998, Canaanites and Philistines. *Journal for the Study of the Old Testament* 81, 39–61

Drews, R. 2000, Medinet Habu: Oxcarts, Ships, and Migration Theories. *Journal of Near Eastern Studies* 59/3, 161–190

Drioton, E. and J. Vandier 1962, *L'Egypte*. Paris: Presses Universitaires de France

Edel, E. 1961, Ein kairener Fragment mit einem Bericht über den Libyerkrieg Merenptahs. *Zeitschrift für Ägyptische Sprache und Altertumskunde* 86, 101–103

Edel, E. 1966, *Die Ortsnamenlisten aus dem Totentempel Amenophis III*. Bonn: Hanstein

Edel, E. 1975, Neue Identifikationen Topographischer Namen in den Konventionellen Namenszusammenstellungen des Neuen Reiches. *Studien zur Altägyptischen Kultur* 3, 49–73

Edel, E. 1976, Die Afrikanischen Namen in der Völkerliste Ramses II. *Studien zur Altägyptischen Kultur*, 75–101

Edel, E. 1983, Beiträge zu den ägyptischen Sinaiinschriften. *Nachrichten der Akademie der Wissenschaften in Göttingen, I. Philologisch-historische Klasse*, 157–185

Edel, E. 1984, Die Sikeloi in den Ägyptischen Seevölkertexten. *Biblische Notizen* 23, 7–8

Edel, E. and S. Wenig 1974, *Die Jahreszeitenreliefs aus dem Sonnenheiligtum des Königs Ne-User-Re*, Vol. 1. Berlin: Akademie

Edgerton, W. F. and J. A. Wilson 1936, *Historical Records of Ramses III: The Texts in Medinet Habu Volumes I and II*. Chicago: University of Chicago Press

Egberts, A. 1987, A Note on the Building History of the Temple of Edfu. *Revue d'Egyptologie* 38, 55–61

Egberts, A. 1998, Hard Times: The Chronology of the 'Report of Wenamun' Revisited. *Zeitschrift für Ägyptische Sprache und Altertumskunde* 125, 93–108

el-Hadidi, M. N., M. abd el-Ghani, I. Springuel and M. A. Hoffmann 1986, *Wild Barley. Egypt. Biological Conservation* 37/4, 1–10

Epigraphic Survey 1986, *The Battle Reliefs of King Sety I*. Chicago: Oriental Institute, University of Chicago

Erman, A. 1894, *Life in Ancient Egypt* (trans. H. M. Tirard). London: Macmillan

Essche-Marchez, E. 1992, La Syntaxe formelle des reliefs et de la grande inscription de l'an 8 de Ramses III Medinet Habou. *Chronique d Egypte* 67, 211–239

Essche-Marchez, E. 1994, Pour une Lecture stratigraphique des Parois du temple de Ramses III à Medinet Habou. *Revue d Egyptologie* 45, 87–115

Evans-Pritchard, E. E. 1937, *Witchcraft, Oracles and Magic among the Azande*. Oxford: Clarendon

Eyre, C. J. 1999, Irony in the Story of Wenamun: the Politics of Religion in the 21st Dynasty, in J. Assmann and E. Blumenthal (eds), *Literatur und Politik im pharaonischen und ptolemäischen Ägypten*, 235–252. Cairo: Institut Français d'Archéologie Orientale

Fabian, J. 1983, *Time and the Other: How Anthropology Makes its Object*. New York: Columbia UP

Fahd, T. (ed.) 1989, *L'Arabie Preislamique et son Environnement Historique et Culturel*. Actes du colloque de Strasbourg 24–27 juin 1987, Leiden: Brill

Fakhry, A. 1937, Blocs décorés provenant du Temple de Louxor. *Annales du Service des Antiquités de l'Egypte* 37, 51–56

Fakhry, A. 1940, Wâdi-el-Natrûn. *Annales du Service des Antiquités de l'Egypte* 40, 837–848

Fakhry, A. 1986, The Battle Reliefs of King Sety I. *The Epigraphic Survey* 59, Chicago

Farout, D. 1994, La Carriére du *whmw* Ameny et l'Organisation des Expéditions au Ouadi Hammamat au Moyen Empire. *Bulletin de l'Institut Français d'Archéologie Orientale du Caire* 94, 143–172

Fattovich, R. 1991, The Problem of Punt in the Light of Recent Field Work in the Eastern Sudan, in S. Schoske (ed.), *Akten des vierten internationalen Ägyptologen Kongresses München 1985, Vol 4*, 257–272. Hamburg: Helmut Buske

Fattovich, R. 1993, Punt: The Archaeological Perspective. *Sesto Congresso Internazionale di Egittologia, Atti, Vol. II*, 399–405, Turin

Faulkner, R. O. (ed.) 1972, *The Book of the Dead: A Collection of Spells*. New York: Limited Editions Club

Faulkner, R. O. 1953, Egyptian Military Organisation. *Journal of Egyptian Archaeology* 39, 32–47

Faulkner, R. O. 1969, *The Ancient Egyptian Pyramid Texts*. Oxford: Clarendon

Faulkner, R. O. 1973, *The Ancient Egyptian Coffin Texts I: Spells 1–354*. Warminster: Aris and Phillips

Faulkner, R. O. 1977, *The Ancient Egyptian Coffin Texts II: Spells 355–787*. Warminster: Aris and Phillips

Faulkner, R. O. 1978, *The Ancient Egyptian Coffin Texts III: Spells 788–1185*. Warminster: Aris and Phillips

Faulkner, R. O. 1991, *A Concise Dictionary of Middle Egyptian*. Oxford: Griffith Institute

Faulkner, R. O. 1999, *A Concise Dictionary of Middle Egyptian*. Oxford: OUP

Favard-Meeks, C. 1991, *Le temple de Behbeit el-Hagara*. Hamburg: H. Buske

Finkelstein, I. 2000, The Philistine Settlements: When, Where and How Many?, in E. D. Oren (ed.), *The Sea Peoples and Their World: A Reassessment*, 159–180. Philadelphia: University Museum Publications

Finnestad, R. 1997, Temples of the Ptolemaic and Roman Periods; Ancient Traditions in New Contexts, in B. Shafer (ed.), *Temples of Ancient Egypt*, 185–238. Ithaca: Cornell UP

Fischer, H. G. 1977a, *Egyptian Studies: The Orientation of Hieroglyphs*. New York: Metropolitan Museum of Art

Fischer, H. G. 1977b, Hieroglyphen. *Lexikon der Ägyptologie* ii, 1,189–1,199

Fischer, H. G. 1986, *L'Écriture et l'art de l'Égypte ancienne*. Paris: Presses Universitaires de France

Fischer, H. G. 1987, The Ancient Egyptian Attitude Towards the Monstrous, in A. E. Farkas, P. O. Harper and E. B. Harrison (eds), *Monsters and Demons in the Ancient and Medieval Worlds*, 13–26. Mainz: Philipp von Zabern

Fischer-Elfert, H-W. 2003, Representations of the Past in New Kingdom Literature, in J. Tait (ed.), *'Never had the like occurred': Egypt's view of its past*, 119–138. London: UCL Press

Flinder, A. 1977, The Island of Jezirat Fara'un. *International Journal of Nautical Archaeology and Underwater Exploration* 6, 127–139

Folorunso, C. A. 2003, Views of Ancient Egypt from a West African Perspective, in D. O'Connor and A. Reid (eds), *Ancient Egypt in Africa*, 77–92. London: UCL Press

Forman, W. and S. Quirke 1996, *Hieroglyphs and the Afterlife*. London: British Museum Press

Foster, J. L. 1974, *Love Songs of the New Kingdom*. Austin: University of Texas Press

Foster, J. L. 1995, *Hymns, Prayers and Songs: An Anthology of Ancient Egyptian Love Poetry*. Atlanta: Scholar's Press

Foucault, M. 1972, *The Archaeology of Knowledge* (trans. A. M. Sheridan Smith). London: Tavistock

Franke, D. 1991, The Career of Khnumhotep III of Beni Hasan and the So-Called 'Decline of the Nomarchs', in S. Quirke (ed.), *Middle Kingdom Studies*, 51–67. New Malden: SIA Publications

Frankfort, H. 1933, *The Cenotaph of Seti I at Abydos*. London: Egypt Exploration Society

Friedman, R. 2001, Excavating in the Nubian Cemeteries. *Nekhen News* 13, 22–27

Frost, H. 1996, Ports, Cairns and Anchors: a Pharonic Outlet on the Red Sea. *Topoi Orient-occident* 6, 869–902

Gaballa, G. A. 1976, *Narrative in Egyptian Art*. Mainz: von Zabern

Gallorini, C. 1998, A Reconstruction of Petrie's Excavation at the Middle Kingdom Settlement of Kahun, in S. Quirke (ed.), *Lahun Studies*, 42–59. Reigate: SIA Publishing

Gardiner, A. H. 1918, The Supposed Egyptian Equivalent for the name of Goshen. *Journal of Egyptian Archaeology* 5, 218–223

Gardiner, A. H. 1932, *Late Egyptian Stories*. Brussels: Fondation Egyptologique Reine Elisabeth

Gardiner, A. H. 1937, *Late Egyptian Miscellanies*. Brussels: Fondation Egyptologique Reine Elisabeth

Gardiner, A. H. 1947, *Ancient Egyptian Onomastica*. Oxford: OUP

Gardiner, A. H. 1955, *The Ramesseum Papyri*. Oxford: OUP

Gardiner, A. H. 1957, *Egyptian Grammar: Being an Introduction to the Study of Hieroglyphs*. Oxford: Griffith Institute

Gardiner, A. H. 1961, *Egypt of the Pharaohs: An Introduction*. Oxford: Clarendon

Gardiner, A. H. and H. I. Bell 1943, The Name of Lake Moeris. *Journal of Egyptian Archaeology* 29, 37–50

Gardiner, A. H., J. Cerny and T. Peet 1952, *Inscriptions of Sinai* II. London: Egypt Exploration Society

Gatier, P-L. 1996 Des Girafes pour l'Empereur. *Topoi* 6, 903–941

Geertz, A. 1987, *Hopi Indian Altar Iconography*. Leiden: Brill

Geertz, C. 1973, Thick Description: Toward an Interpretive Theory of Culture, in C. Geertz (ed.), *The Interpretation of Cultures*, 3–30. London: Hutchinson

Geertz, C. 1988, *Works and Lives: The Anthropologist as Author*. Stanford: Stanford UP

Gennep, A. van 1960, *The Rites of Passage* (trans. M. B. Vizedom and G. L. Caffee). London: Routledge

Germer, R. 1979, *Untersuchung uber Arzneimittelpflanzen im Alten Ägypten*. Dissertation, Hamburg

Gitin, S., A. Mazar and E. Stern (eds) 1998, *Mediterranean Peoples in Transition: Thirteenth to Early Tenth Centuries BC*. Jerusalem: Israel Exploration Society

Giveon, R. 1969–1970, The Shosu of the Late 20th Dynasty. *Journal of the American Research Center in Egypt* 8, 51–53

Giveon, R. 1971, *Les Bédouins Shosou des Documents Égyptiens*. Leiden: Brill

Gnirs, A. M. (ed.) 2000, Reading the Eloquent Peasant. *Proceedings of the International Conference on The Tale of the Eloquent Peasant at the University of California, Los Angeles, March 27–30, 1997*. Göttingen: Seminar für Ägyptologie und Koptologie

Gnirs, A. M. 1996, Die Ägyptische Autobiographie, in A. Loprieno (ed.), *Ancient Egyptian Literature: History and Forms*, 191–241. Leiden: Brill

Gnirs, A. M. 1998, Die Levantische Herkunft des Schlangengottes, in H. Guksch and D. Polz (eds), *Stationen. Beiträge zur Kulturgeschichte Ägyptens Rainer Stadelmann gewidmet*, 197–209. Mainz: Philipp von Zabern

Goedicke, H. 1957, The Route of Sinuhe's Flight. *Journal of Egyptian Archaeology* 43, 77–85

Goedicke, H. 1968, The Capture of Joppa. *Chronique d'Egypte* 43, 219–233

Goedicke, H. 1986, *The Quarrel of Apophis and Seqenenre*. San Antonio: Van Siclen

Goldwasser, O. 1995, *From Icon to Metaphor*. Fribourg and Göttingen: Vandenhoeck and Ruprecht

Gomaà, F. 1980, Medinet el-Fajjum. *Lexikon der Ägyptologie* iii, 1,254–1,255. Wiesbaden: Harrassowitz

Gombrich, E. H. 1960, *Art and Illusion*. London: Phaidon

Gorak, J. (ed.) 2001, *Canon versus Culture. Reflexions on the Contemporary Debate*. New York: Garland

Gould, J. 1989, *Herodotus*. London: Weidenfeld and Nicholson

Goyon, J-C., P. Archier, S. Coen and C. Vieillecazes 1999, Contribution de la chimie analytique à l'étude de vestiges de la XIIe ou XIIIe Dynastie Égyptienne. *Studien zur Altägyptischen Kultur* 27, 107–121

Grandet, P. 1994–1999, *Le Papyrus Harris I* (BM 9999). Cairo: Institut Français d'Archéologie Orientale

Grapow, H. 1909, Zweiwegebuch und Totenbuch. *Zeitschrift fur Ägyptische Sprache und Altertumskunde* 46, 77–81

Green, M. 1983, The Syrian and Lebanese Topographical Data in the Story of Sinuhe. *Chronique d'Egypte* 58, 38–59

Green, N. 1995, Looking at the Landscape: Class Formation and the Visual, in *The Anthropology of Landscape: Perspectives on Place and Space*, 31–42. Oxford: Clarendon

Greenstein, E. L. 1995, Autobiographies in Ancient Western Asia, in J. M. Sasson (ed.), *Civilizations of the Ancient Near East*, 2,421–2,432. New York: Charles Scribner's Sons

Griffith F. L. 1889, The Hieroglyphic Inscriptions, in W. M. F. Petrie, *Hawara, Biahmu, and Arsinoe*, 21–23. London: The Leadenhall Press

Griffith, F. L. 1888, Qantara, in W. M. F. Petrie, *Tanis II. Nebesheh (An) and Defenneh (Tahpanhes)*, 96–108. London: Egypt Exploration Fund

Griffith, F. L. 1900, *Stories of the High Priests of Memphis*. Oxford: Clarendon

Griffith, F. L. and P. E. Newberry 1894, *El Bersheh II*. London: Egyptian Exploration Fund

Griffith, R. D. 1997, Homeric ΔΙΙΠΕΤΕΟΣ ΠΟΤΑΜΟΙΟ and the Celestial Nile. *American Journal of Philology* 118, 353–362

Groenewegen-Frankfort, H. [1951] 1987, *Arrest and Movement: Space and Time in the Art of the Ancient Near East*. Cambridge, Mass: Belknap

Groenewegen-Frankfort, H. 1970, 'Narratives' in Ancient Egypt, in T. B. Hess and J. Ashbery (eds), *Narrative Art*, 36, 112–121. New York: Macmillan

Grube, G. M. A. 1974, *Plato's Republic*. Indianapolis: Hackett

Guglielmi, W. 1983, Eine 'Lehre' für einen Reiselustigen Sohn. *Die Welt des Orients* 14, 147–166

Guksch, H. 1994, 'Sehnsucht nach der Heimatstadt': ein Ramessidisches Thema? *Mitteilungen des Deutschen Archäologischen Instituts. Abteilung Kairo* 50, 101–106

Gumbrecht, H-U. 1996, Does Egyptology Need a 'Theory of Literature'?, in A. Loprieno (ed.), *Ancient Egyptian Literature: History and Forms*, 3–18. Leiden: Brill

Gutbub, A. 1952, Les inscription Dédicatoires du Trésor dans la Temple d'Edfou. *Bulletin de l'Institut Français d'Archéologie Orientale du Caire* 50, 33–38

Gutbub, A. 1977, Kom Ombo. *Lexikon der Ägyptologie* iii, 87–93. Wiesbaden: Harrassowitz

Gutbub, A. 1995, *Kom Ombo I*. Cairo: Institut Français d'Archéologie Orientale

Habachi, L. 1980, The Military Posts of Ramesses II on the Coastal Road and theWestern Part of the Delta. *Bulletin de l'Institut Français d'Archéologie Orientale du Caire* 80, 13–30

Hachid, M. 2000, *Les Premiers Berbères: Entre Méditerranée, Tassili et Nil*. Aix-en-Provence: Édisud; Alger: Ina-Yas

Haeny, G. 1997, New Kingdom 'Mortuary Temples and Mansions of Millions of Years', in D. Arnold, L. Bell, R. Bjerre Finnestad, G. Haeny and B. E. Shafer (eds), *Temples of Ancient Egypt*, 86–126. New York: Cornell UP

Hahn, J. 1993, Aurignacian Art in Central Europe, in H. Knecht, A. Pike-Tay and R. White (eds), *Before Lascaux: The Complex Record of the Early Upper Palaeolithic*, 229–241. Boca Raton: CRC Press

Harrell, J. A. and V. Brown 1992, The Oldest Surviving Topographical Map from Ancient Egypt (Turin 1879, 1899, 1969). *Journal of the American Research Center in Egypt* 29, 81–105

Harris, J. R. 1961, *Lexicographical Studies in Ancient Egyptian Minerals*. Berlin: Akademie

Harrison, T. 2003, Upside Down and Back to Front: Herodotus and the Greek Encounter with Egypt, in R. Matthews and C. Roemer (eds), *Ancient Perspectives on Egypt*, 145–156. London: UCL Press

Harvey, P. 1993, *Maps in Tudor England*. London: Public Records Office and British Library

Hayes, W. C. 1949, Career of the Great Steward Heneny Nebhepetre Mentuhotpe. *Journal of Egyptian Archaeology* 35, 43–49

Hayes, W. C. 1951, Inscriptions from the Palace of Amenhotep III. *Journal of Near Eastern Studies* 10, 35–56, 82–111

Hayes, W. C. 1953, *The Scepter of Egypt I*. New York: Metropolitan Museum of Art

Heinz, S. 2001, *Die Feldzugdarstellungen des Neun Reiches: Eine Bildanalyse*. Vienna: Österreichischen Akademie der Wissenschaften

Heinz, S. 2001, *Die Feldzugsdarstellungen des Neuen Reiches*. Vienna: Österreichischen Akademie der Wissenschaften

Helck, W. 1954, Die Sinai-Inschrift des Amenmose. *Mitteilungen des Instituts für Orientforschung* 2, 189–207

Helck, W. 1967, Eine Briefsammlung aus der Verwaltung des Amuntempels. *Journal of the American Research Center in Egypt* 6, 135–151

Helck, W. 1970, *Die Lehre des ḏꜢA- ꜣjj. Kleine Ägyptische Texte*. Wiesbaden: Harrassowitz

Helck, W. 1971, *Die Beziehungen Ägyptens zu Vorderasien im 3, und 2, Jahrtausend v. Chr*. Wiesbaden: Harrassowitz

Helck, W. 1987, Die Erzählung vom Verwunschenen Prinzen, in J. Osing and G. Dreyer (eds), *Form und Mass. Beiträge zur Literatur, Sprache und Kunst des Alten Ägypten. Festschrift für Gerhard Fecht zum 65, Geburtstag am 6, Februar 1987*, 218–222. Wiesbaden: Harrassowitz

Hepper, N. 1969, Arabian and African Frankincense Trees. *Journal of Egyptian Archaeology* 55, 66–72

Hermann, G. 1968, Lapis Lazoli: The Early Phases of its Trade. *Iraq* 30, 21–57

Herzog, R. 1968, *Punt*. Glückstadt: Augustin

Hieb, L. 1979, Hopi World View, in A. Ortiz (ed.), *Handbook of North American Indians, vol 9: Southwest*, 577–580. Washington, DC: Smithsonian Institution

Hintze, F. 1959, *Studien Zur meroitischen Chronologie unt zur dein Opfertafeln ous den Pyramiden von Meroe*. Berlin: Akademie

Hintze, F. and W. Reineke 1989, *Felsinschriften aus dem sudanischen Nubien, Publikation des Nubien-Expedition 1961–1963*, Band I. Berlin: Akademie

Hirschkind, C. 1991, Egypt at the Exhibition: Reflections on the Optics of Colonialism. *Critique of Anthropology* 11, 279–298

Hobbes, T. 1970, *Leviathan, or the Matter, Form and Power of a Commonwealth, Ecclesiastical and Civil*. London: Dent

Hodjash, S. and O. Berlev 1982, *The Egyptian Reliefs and Stelae in the Pushkin Museum of Fine Arts, Moscow*. Leningrad: Aurora

Hoffmann, F. 1995, *Ägypten und Amazonen*. Vienna: Brüder Hollinek

Hoffmann, F. 1996, *Der Kampf um den Panzer des Inaros*. Vienna: Brüder Hollinek

Hoffmeier, J. K. 1996, Are there Regionally-based Theological Differences in the Coffin Texts?, in H. Willems (ed.), *The World of the Coffin Texts*, 45–54. Leiden: Nederlands Instituut von het Nabije Oosten

Hollis, S. T. 1990, *The Ancient Egyptian 'Tale of the Two Brothers'. The Oldest Fairy Tale in the World*. Norman: University of Oklahoma Press

Hölscher, W. 1937, *Libyer und Ägypter*. Glückstadt: Augustin

Hombert, M. and C. Preaux 1952, *Recherches sur le recensement dans l'Egypte Romaine: P. Bruxelles Inv.E.7616*, Papyrologica Lugduno-Batava 5. Leiden: Brill

Hornung, E. 1963, *Das Amdaut. Die Schrift des verborgenen Raumes* I. Wiesbaden: Harrassowitz

Hornung, E. 1982a, *Conceptions of God in Ancient Egypt* (trans. J. Baines). Ithaca: Cornell UP

Hornung, E. 1982b, *The Valley of the Kings. Horizon of Eternity* (trans. D. Warburton). New York: Timken

Hornung, E. 1999, *The Ancient Egyptian Books of the Afterlife*. Ithaca: Cornell UP

Hounsell, D. 2001, The Occupation of Marmarica in the Late Bronze Age, unpublished PhD thesis, University of Liverpool

Howard, M. 1981, *Aboriginal Politics in Southwest Australia*. Nedlands, WA: University of Western Australia Press

Hulin, L. 1999, 'Marmaric' Wares: Some Preliminary Remarks. *Journal of Libyan Studies* 30, 11–16

Hulin, L. 2001, Marmaric Wares: New Kingdom and Later Examples, unpublished manuscript

Inconnu-Bocquillon, D. 2001, *Le mythe de la Déesse Lointaine à Philae*. Cairo: Institut Français d'Archéologie Orientale

Iser, W. 1991, *Das Fiktive und das Imaginäre. Perspektiven literarischer Anthropologie*. Frankfurt: Suhrkamp

Iskander, S. 2002, The Reign of Merenptah, unpublished PhD thesis, New York University

James, T. G. H. 1962, *The Hekanakhte Papers and Other Early Middle Kingdom Documents*. New York: Metropolitan Museum of Art

Jeffreys, D. 2003a, All in the Family? Heirlooms in Ancient Egypt, in J. Tait (ed.), 'Never had the like occurred': Egypt's view of its past, 197–212. London: UCL Press

Jeffreys, D. 2003b, Introduction – Two Hundred Years of Ancient Egypt: Modern History and Ancient Archaeology, in D. Jeffreys (ed.), *Views of Ancient Egypt since Napoleon Bonaparte: imperialism, colonialsim and modern appropriations*, 1–18. London: UCL Press

Johnson, D. 1973, *Jabal al-Akhdar, Cyrenaica: An Historical Geography of Settlement and Livelihood*. Chicago: University of Chicago Press

Jones, D. 1988, *A Glossary of Ancient Egyptian Nautical Titles and Terms*. London: Kegan Paul

Junge, F. 2000, Die Rahmenerzählung des Beredten Bauern: Innenansichten einer Gesellschaft, in A. M. Gnirs (ed.), *Reading the Eloquent Peasant*, 157–181. Göttingen: Seminar für Ägyptologie und Koptologie

Junker, H. 1958, *Der grossen Pylon des Temples der Isis in Philä*. Vienna: R. M. Rohrer

Kaberry, P. 1957, Myth and Ritual: Some Recent Theories. *Bulletin of the Institute of Classical Studies, University of London* 4, 42–54

Kampp, F. 1996, *Die thebanische Nekropole. Theben 13*. Mainz: Philipp von Zabern

Kees, H. 1933, *Kulture Geschichte des alten Orients I. Ägypten*. Munich: C. H. Beck

Kemp, B. J. 1983, Old Kingdom, Middle Kingdom and Second Intermediate Period ca. 2686–1552 BC, in B. J. Kemp, A. Lloyd, D. O'Connor and B. Trigger (eds), *Ancient Egypt: A Social History*, 71–182. Cambridge: CUP

Kendall, T. 1997, *Kerma and the Kingdom of Kush 2500–1500 BC. The Archaeological Discovery of an Ancient Nubian Empire*. Washington, DC: Smithsonian Institution

Killebrew, A. E. 1998, Mycenaean and Aegean-Style Pottery in Canaan During the 14th–12th Centuries BC, in E. H. Cline and D. Harris-Cline (eds), *The Aegean and the Orient in the Second Millennium: Proceedings of the 50th Anniversary Symposium, Cincinnati, 18–20 April 1997*, 159–169. Liège: Université de Liège

Killebrew, A. E. 2000, Aegean-Style Early Philistine Pottery in Canaan During the Iron I Age: A Stylistic Analysis of Mycenaean IIIC:1b Pottery and its Associated Wares, in E. D. Oren (ed.), *The Sea Peoples and Their World: A Reassessment*, 233–253. Philadelphia: University Museum Publications

Kisnawi, A., P. S. de Jesus and B. Rihani 1983, Preliminary Report on the Mining Survey, Northwest Hijaz, 1982. *Atlal 7*, 76–83

Kitchen, K. A. 1971, Punt and How to Get There. *Orientalia 40*, 184–207

Kitchen, K. A. 1973, *The Third Intermediate Period in Egypt.* Warminster: Aris and Phillips

Kitchen, K. A. 1975, *Ramesside Inscriptions I.* Oxford: Blackwell

Kitchen, K. A. 1979, *Ramesside Inscriptions II.* Oxford: Blackwell

Kitchen, K. A. 1980, *Ramesside Inscriptions III.* Oxford: Blackwell

Kitchen, K. A. 1982a, Punt, in W. Helck and W. Westendorf (eds), *Lexikon der Ägyptologie, vol. IV*, 1,198–1,201, Wiesbaden: Harrassowitz

Kitchen, K. A. 1982b, *Ramesside Inscriptions: Historical and Biographical IV.* Oxford: Blackwell

Kitchen, K. A. 1983a, *Ramesside Inscriptions Historical and Biographical V.* Oxford: Blackwell

Kitchen, K. A. 1983b, *Ramesside Inscriptions Historical and Biographical VI.* Oxford: Blackwell

Kitchen, K. A. 1990, The Arrival of the Libyans in Late New Kingdom Egypt, in A. Leahy (ed.), *Libya and Egypt*, 15–27. London: Society for Libyan Studies

Kitchen, K. A. 1993a, The Land of Punt, in T. Shaw, P. J. J. Sinclair, B. Andah and A. Okpoko (eds), *The Archaeology of Africa: Food, Metals and Towns*, 587–608. London: Routledge

Kitchen, K. A. 1993b, *Ramesside Inscriptions. Translated and Annotated: Notes and Comments I: Ramesses I, Sethos I and Contemporaries (RITANC).* Oxford: Blackwell

Kitchen, K. A. 1999, Further Thoughts on Punt and its Neighbours, in A. Leahy and J. Tait (eds), *Studies on Ancient Egypt in honour of H. S. Smith*, 173–178. London: Egypt Exploration Society

Kline, N. R. 2001, *Maps of Medieval Thought.* Woodbridge: Boydell

Kling, B. B. 2000, Mycenaean IIIC:1b and Related Pottery in Cyprus: Comments on the Current State of Research, in E. D. Oren (ed.), *The Sea Peoples and Their World: A Reassessment*, 281–295. Philadelphia: University Museum Publications

Knapp, A. B. 1992, Bronze Age Mediterranean Island Cultures and the Ancient Near East, Part 2. *Biblical Archaeologist 55/3*, 112–128

Koch, R. 1990, *Die Erzählung des Sinuhe.* Brussels: Fondation Egyptologique Reine Elisabeth

Krauss, R. 1997, *Astronomische Konzepte und Jenseitsvorstellungen in den Pyramidentexten.* Wiesbaden: Harrassowitz

Kuentz, Ch. 1920, Autour d'une Conception Egyptienne Méconnue: L'Akhit ou soi-disant Horizon. *Bulletin de l'Institut Français d'Archéologie Orientale du Caire 17*, 121–190

Kuhrt, A. 1995, *The Ancient Near East c. 3000–330 BC.* London: Routledge

Kuper, A. 1988, *The Invention of Primitive Society: Transformations of an Illusion.* London: Routledge

Kurth, D. 1987, Zur Interpretation der Geschichte des Schiffbrüchigen. *Studien zur Altägyptischen Kultur 14*, 167–179

Lanzone, R. V. 1896, *Les Papyrus du Lac Moeris, Réunis et Reproduits en Fac-simile et Accompagnés d'un Texte Explicatif.* Turin: Bocca Frères

Lapp, G. 1997, *The Papyrus of Nu.* London: British Museum Press

Layton, R. 1991, *The Anthropology of Art.* Cambridge: CUP

Layton, R. 1992, *Australian Rock Art, A New Synthesis.* Melbourne, Vic: CUP

Layton, R. 1997a, Representing and Translating People's Place in the Landscape of Northern Australia, in A. James, J. Hockey and A. Dawson (eds), *After Writing Culture: Epistemology and Praxis in Contemporary Anthropology*, 122–143. London: Routledge

Layton, R. 1997b, *An Introduction to Theory in Anthropology.* Cambridge: CUP

Layton, R. and P. Ucko 1999, Introduction: Gazing on the Landscape and Encountering the Environment, in P. Ucko and R. Layton (eds), *The Archaeology of Landscape*, 1–20. London: Routledge

Leach, B. and J. Tait 2000, Papyrus, in P. T. Nicholson and I. Shaw (eds), *Ancient Egyptian Materials and Technology*, 227–253. Cambridge: CUP

Leach, E. R. 1954, *Political Systems of Highland Burma*. London: Athlone

Leahy, A. 2001, Sea Peoples, in D. B. Redford (ed.), *The Oxford Encyclopedia of Ancient Egypt*, 257–260. Oxford: OUP

Leclant, J. 1964, *Göttinger Vorträge vom ägyptologischen Kolloquium der Akademie*. Fribourg and Göttingen: Vandenhoeck and Ruprecht

Leclant, J. 1978, L'exploration des côtes de la Mer Rouge. A la quête de Pount et des secrets de la Mer Erythrée. *Annales d'Ethiopie* 11, 69–73

Leclant, J. 1978, Voir les remarques de Abdel-Aziz Saleh. *Annales d'Ethiope* 11, 258–261

Leclant, J. 1984, T. P. Pepi Ier, VII: Une Nouvelle métier des FNHW dans les texts des Pyramides. *Studien zur Altägyptischen Kultur* 11, 455–460

Lefkowitz, M. and G. M. Rogers (eds) 1996, *Black Athena Revisited*. Chapel Hill: University of North Carolina Press

Lepsius, K. R. 1842, *Das Totenbuch der Ägypter nach dem hieroglyphischen Papyrus in Turin*. Leipzig: G. Wigand

Lepsius, K. R. 1897–1913, *Denkmäler aus Aegypten und Aethiopen: Texte*. Leipzig: Hinrichs

Lesko, L. 1991, Ancient Egyptian Cosmogonies and Cosmologies, in B. E. Shafer (ed.), *Religion in Ancient Egypt: Gods, Myths and Personal Practice*, 88–122. Ithaca, NY: Cornell UP

Lesko, L. 1992, Egypt in the 12th Century BC, in W. Ward and M. Joukowsky (eds), *The Crisis Years: The 12th Century BC from beyond the Danube to the Tigris*, 151–156, Dubuque, IA: Kendall/Hunt

Lesko, L. and B. Lesko (eds) 1982, *A Dictionary of Late Egyptian volume I*. Berkeley: University of California Press

Lesko, L. H. 1972a, *The Ancient Egyptian Book of Two Ways*. Berkeley: University of California Press

Lesko, L. H. 1972b, The Field of Hetep in Egyptian Coffin Texts. *Journal of the American Research Center in Egypt* 9, 89–101

Lesko, R. 1971–1972, The Field of Hetep in the Egyptian Coffin Texts. *Journal of the American Research Center in Egypt* 9, 89–101

Lévi-Strauss, C. 1970, *The Raw and the Cooked: Introduction to a Science of Mythology* (trans. J. and D. Weightman). London: Jonathan Cape

Lévi-Strauss, C. 1973, *From Honey to Ashes* (trans. J. and D. Weightman). London: Jonathan Cape

Lewis, D. 1976, Observations on Route-Finding and Spatial Orientation in Central Australia. *Oceania* 46, 249–282

Lichtheim, M. 1973, *Ancient Egyptian Literature I: The Old and Middle Kingdoms*. Berkeley: University of California Press

Lichtheim, M. 1976, *Ancient Egyptian Literature II: The New Kingdom*. Berkeley: University of California Press

Lichtheim, M. 1980, *Ancient Egyptian Literature III: The Late Period*. Berkeley: University of California Press.

Lichtheim, M. 1983, *Late Egyptian Wisdom Literature in the International Context*. Fribourg and Göttingen: Vandenhoeck and Ruprecht

Lion, V. B. 1992, La Circulation des animaux au proche-orient antique, in D. Charpin and F. Joannes (eds), *La Circulation des biens, des personnes et des idées dans le proche-orient ancien. Actes de la XXXVIIIe Rencontre Assyriologique*, 357–365. Paris

Lipke, P. 1985, Retrospective on the Royal Ship of Cheops, in S. McGrail and E. Kentley, *Sewn Plank Boats: Archaeological and Ethnographic Papers Based on Those Presented to a Conference at Greenwich in November 1984*, 19–34

Lloyd, A. B. 1970, The Egyptian Labyrinth. *Journal of Egyptian Archaeology* 56, 81–100

Lloyd, A. B. 1975–1989, *Herodotus Book II*. Leiden: Brill

Loprieno, A. 1991, The Sign of Literature in the Shipwrecked Sailor, in E. Graefe and U. Verhoeven (eds), *Religion und Philosophie im Alten Ägypten. Festgabe für Philippe Derchain zu seinem 65, Geburtstag am 24,Juli 1991*, 209–218. Leuven: Peeters

Loprieno, A. 1996a, Defining Egyptian Literature: Ancient Texts and Modern Literary Theory, in J. S. Cooper and G. M. Schwartz (eds), *The Study of the Ancient Near East in the Twenty-First Century. The William Foxwell Albright Centennial Conference*, 209–232. Winona Lake: Eisenbrauns

Loprieno, A. 1996b, The 'King's Novel', in A. Loprieno (ed.), *Ancient Egyptian Literature: History and Forms*, 277–295. Leiden: Brill

Loprieno, A. 1998, Le Pharaon reconstruit. La figure du roi dans la littérature Égyptienne au Ier millénaire avant J-C. *Bulletin de la Société Française d'Egyptologie* 142, 4–24

Loprieno, A. 2001, *La Pensée et l'écriture. Pour une analyse sémiotique de la culture Égyptienne*. Paris: Cybèle

Lüddeckens, E. 1988, Ein Demotischer Papyrus aus Mittelägypten. *Zeitschrift fur Ägyptische Spracher* 115, 52–61

Machinist, P. 2000, Biblical Traditions: The Philistines and Israelite History, in E. D. Oren (ed.), *The Sea Peoples and Their World: A Reassessment*, 53–83. Philadelphia: University Museum Publications

Malinowski, B. 1922, *Argonauts of the Western Pacific: An Account of Native Enterprise and Adventure in the Archipelagoes of Melanesian New Guinea*. London: Routledge

Manniche, L. 1987, *City of the Dead: Thebes in Egypt*. London: British Museum Publications

Mariette, A. [1878] 1999, *Voyage dans la Haute-Égypte: compris entre le Caire et la première Cataracte*. Paris: Editions Errance

Mariette, A. 1875a, *Karnak: Etude topographique et archéologique*. Leipzig: Hinrichs

Mariette, A. 1875b, *Les Listes géographiques des pylones de Karnak comprenant la Palestine, l'Ethiopie, le pays de Somal*. Leipzig: Hinrichs

Mariette-Bey, A. 1871, *Les Papyrus Égyptiens du Musée de Boulaq*. Paris: Libraire A. Franck

Matthews, R. and C. Roemer (eds) 2003a, *Ancient Perspectives on Egypt*. London: UCL Press

Matthews, R. and C. Roemer 2003b, Introduction – The Worlds of Ancient Egypt: Aspects, Sources, Interactions, in R. Matthews and C. Roemer (eds), *Ancient Perspectives on Egypt*, 1–20. London: UCL Press

Mayerson, P. 1995, Aelius Gallus at Cleopatris (Suez) and on the Red Sea. *Greek, Roman, and Byzantine Studies*, 17–24

Mayerson, P. 1996, The Port of Clysma (Suez) in Transition from Roman to Arab Rule. *Journal of Near Eastern Studies* 55, 119–126

Mazar, A. 2000, The Temples and Cult of the Philistines, in E. D. Oren (ed.), *The Sea Peoples and Their World: A Reassessment*, 213–232. Philadelphia: University Museum Publications

McBurney, C. B. M. 1967, *The Haua Fteah (Cyrenaica) and the Stone Age of the South-East Mediterranean*. Cambridge: CUP

Medinet Habu I = *The Epigraphic Survey. 1930, Earlier Historical Records of Ramesses III*. Chicago: University of Chicago Press

Medinet Habu II = *The Epigraphic Survey. 1932, Later Historical Records of Ramesses III*. Chicago: University of Chicago Press

Meeks, D. 1972, *Le Grand Texte des Donations au Temple d'Edfou*. Cairo: Institut Français d'Archéologie Orientale

Meeks, D. 2002, Coptos e le Chemins de Pount. *Topoi*, supplement 3, 267–335

Meyer, E. 1928, *Geschichte des Altertums, II pt. 1*, Stuttgart: J. G. Cotta

Michaels, E. 1994, *Bad Aboriginal Art: Tradition, Media and Technological Horizons*. Minneapolis: University of Minnesota Press

Mithen, S. 1998, A Creative Explosion? Theory of Mind, Language and the Disembodied Mind of the Upper Palaeolithic, in S. Mithen (ed.), *Creativity in Human Evolution and Prehistory*, 165–191. London: Routledge

Moers, G. 1999, Travel as Narrative in Egyptian Literature, in G. Moers (ed.), *Definitely: Egyptian Literature*, 43–61, Göttingen: Seminar für Ägyptologie und Koptologie

Moers, G. 2000, 'Bei mir wird es Dir gut ergehen, denn Du wirst die Sprache Ägyptens hören!' Verschieden und doch gleich: Sprache als identitätsrelevanter Faktor im pharaonischen Ägypten, in F. Paul and U. Sander (eds), *Muster und Funktionen kultureller Selbst- und Fremdwahrnehmung. Beiträge zur internationalen Geschichte der sprachlichen und literarischen Emanzipation*, 45–99. Göttingen: Wallstein

Moers, G. 2001, *Fingierte Welten in der ägyptischen Literatur des 2, Jahrtausends v. Chr.* Leiden: Brill

Moran, W. L. 1992, *The Amarna Letters*. Baltimore: Johns Hopkins UP

Morenz, L. 1996, *Beiträge zur ägyptischen Schriftlichkeitskultur des Mittleren reiches und der Zweiten Zwischenzeit*. Wiesbaden: Harrassowitz

Morenz, L. D. 2003, Literature as a Construction of the Past in the Middle Kingdom, in J. Tait (ed.), 'Never had the like occurred': Egypt's view of its past, 101–118. London: UCL Press

Moretti, F. 1997, *Atlante del Romanzo Europeo 1800–1900*. Turin: Einaudi

Morton-Williams, P. 1964, The Cosmology and Cult Organisation of the Oyo Yoruba. *Africa* 34, 243–261

Moussa, A. M. and H. Altenmüller 1977, Das Grab des Nianchchnum und Chnumhotep. *Archäologische Veröffentlichungen* 21, Mainz: von Zabern

Munro, I. 1994, *Die Totenbuch-Handschriften der 18, Dynastie im Ägyptischen Museum Cairo*. Wiesbaden: Harrassowitz

Munro, I. 1995, *Das Totenbuch des Ian-mes (pLouvre E.11085) aus der frühen 18, Dynastie*. Handschriften des Altägyptischen Totenbuches 1, Wiesbaden: Harrassowitz

Naville, E. 1898, *The Temple of Deir el Bahari*. London: Egypt Exploration Society

Nelson, H. 1943, The Naval Battle Pictured at Medinet Habu. *Journal of Near Eastern Studies* 2, 40–45

Neugebauer, O. and R. A. Parker 1960, *Egyptian Astronomical Texts I. The Early Decans*. Providence: Brown UP

Newberry, P. E. 1891, *El Bersheh I: The Tomb of Tehuti-hetep*. London: Egyptian Exploration Fund

Newberry, P. E. 1893, *Beni Hasan II*. London: Egyptian Exploration Fund

Newberry, P. E. 1942, Notes on Seagoing Ships. *Journal of Egyptian Archaeology* 28, 64–66

Ni Dhomnaill, N. 1996, Dinnsheanchas – the Naming of High or Holy Places, in P. Yaeger (ed.), *The Geography of Identity*, 408–432, Michigan: Michigan UP

Nibbi, A. 1975, *The Sea Peoples and Egypt*. Park Ridge, NJ: Noyes Press

Nibbi, A. 1981, *Ancient Egypt and Some Eastern Neighbours*. Park Ridge, NJ: Noyes Press

Niemeier, W-D. 1998, The Mycenaeans in Western Anatolia and the Problem of the Origins of the Sea Peoples, in S. Gitin, A. Mazar and E. Stern, *Mediterranean Peoples in Transition: Thirteenth to Early Tenth Centuries BCE*, 17–65. Jerusalem: Israel Exploration Society

Nur, A. and E. H. Cline 2000, Poseidon's Horses: Plate Tectonics and Earthquake Storms in the Late Bronze Age Aegean and Eastern Mediterranean. *Journal of Archaeological Science* 27, 43–63

O'Connor, D. 1982, Egypt, 1552–664 BC, in J. D. Clark (ed.), *The Cambridge History of Africa I: From the Earliest Times to c. 500 BC*, Appendix, 925–940. Cambridge: CUP

O'Connor, D. 1983, New Kingdom and Third Intermediate Period, 1552–664 BC, in B. G. Trigger, B. J. Kemp, D. O'Connor and A. B. Lloyd, *Ancient Egypt: A Social History*, 183–278. Cambridge: CUP

O'Connor, D. 1986, The Locations of Yam and Kush and their Historical Implications. *Journal of the American Research Center in Egypt* 23, 26–50

O'Connor, D. 1987, The Location of Irem. *Journal of Egyptian Archaeology* 73, 99–136

O'Connor, D. 1989, City and Palace in New Kingdom Egypt. *Cahiers de Recherches de l'Institut de Papyrologie et Égyptologie de Lille* 11, 73–87

O'Connor, D. 1990, The Nature of Tjemhu (Libyan) Society in Later New Kingdom Egypt, in A. Leahy (ed.), *Libya and Egypt c. 1300–750 BC*, 29–114. London: Society for Libyan Studies

O'Connor, D. 1993, *Ancient Nubia. Egypt's Rival in Africa*. Philadelphia: University of Pennyslvania Press

O'Connor, D. 1997, Egyptian Architecture, in D. Silverman (ed.), *Searching for Ancient Egypt*, 155–161. Dallas and Philadelphia: Dallas Museum of Art and University of Pennsylvania Museum

O'Connor, D. 2000, The Sea Peoples and the Egyptian Sources, in E. D. Oren (ed.), *The Sea Peoples and Their World: A Reassessment*, 85–102. Philadelphia: University Museum Publications

O'Connor, D. 2003, Egypt's Views of 'Others', in J. Tait (ed.), *'Never had the like occurred': Egypt's view of its past*, 155–186. London: UCL Press

OED 1973, *The Shorter Oxford English Dictionary*. Oxford: OUP

Ohshiro, M. 2000, A Study of Lapis Lazuli in the Formative Period of Egyptian Culture. *Orient* 35, 60–74

Olwig, K. 1993, Sexual Cosmology: Nation and Landscape at the Conceptual Interstices of Nature and Culture: Or, What Does Landscape Really Mean?, in B. Bender (ed.), *Landscape: Politics and Perspectives*, 307–343. Oxford: Berg

Oren, E. D. (ed.) 2000, *The Sea Peoples and Their World: A Reassessment*. Philadelphia: University Museum Publications

Oren, E. D. 1987, The 'Ways of Horus in North Sinai', in A. F. Rainey (ed.), *Egypt, Israel, Sinai*, 69–119. Tell Aviv: Tell Aviv University

Osing, J. 1977, Gottesland, in W. Helck and E. Otto (eds), *Lexikon der Ägyptologie, Vol. II*, 815–816. Wiesbaden: Harrassowitz

Osing, J. 1980, Libyen, Libyer. *Lexikon der Ägyptologie* III, 1,015–1,033

Osing, J. 1998, *Hieratische Papyri aus Tebtunis I*. Copenhagen: Museum Tusculanum

Osing, J. and G. Rosati 1998, *Papiri geroglifici e ieratici da Tebtynis*. Firenze: Istituto papirologico 'G. Vitelli'

Paice, P. 1993, The Punt Relief, the Pithom Stele, and the Periplus of the Erythraean Sea, in A. Harrak (ed.), *Contacts Between Cultures. West Asia and North Africa I*, 227–235

Painkoff, A. 1968, *The Pyramid of Unas*. Princeton: Princeton UP

Papanikolaou, A. D. 1973, *Xenophontis Ephesii Ephesiacorum Libri V de Amoribus Anthiae et Abrocomae*. Leipzig: Teubner

Parkinson, R. B. 1991a, *The Tale of the Eloquent Peasant*. Oxford: Griffith Institute

Parkinson, R. B. 1991b, *Voices from Ancient Egypt*. London: British Museum Press

Parkinson, R. B. 1997, *The Tale of Sinuhe and Other Ancient Egyptian Poems, 1940–1640 BC*. Oxford: Clarendon

Parkinson, R. B. 2002, *Poetry and Culture in Middle Kingdom Egypt. A Dark Side to Perfection*. London: Athlone

Parkinson, R. B. and L. Schofield 1993, Akhenaten's Army. *Egyptian Archaeology* 3, 34–35

Pestman, P. W. 1993, *The Archive of the Theban Choachytes*. Louvain: Peeters

Petrie W. M. F. 1889, *Hawara, Biahmu, and Arsinoe*. London: The Leadenhall Press

Petrie, W. M. F. 1906, *Hyksos and Israelite Cities*. London: British School of Archaeology in Egypt

Petrie, W. M. F. 1912, *The Labyrinth, Gerzeh and Mazghaneh*. London: British School of Archaeology in Egypt

Petrie, W. M. F. 1927, *Objects of Daily Use*. London: British School of Archaeology in Egypt

Phillips, J. 1997, Punt and Aksum: Egypt and the Horn of Africa. *Journal of African History* 38, 423–457

Piankoff, A. 1957, *Mythological Papyri* 2. New York: Pantheon

Piankoff, A. 1968, *The Pyramid of Unas*. Princeton: Princeton UP

Pleijte, W. 1884, *Over Drie Handschiften op Papyrus bekend onder der titels van Papyrus du Lac Moeris du Fayoum et du Labyrinthe*. Amsterdam: Müller

Porter, B. and R. Moss 1927–1999, *Topographical Bibliography of Ancient Egyptian Hieroglyphic Texts, Reliefs and Paintings*, 1–8. Oxford: Griffith Institute

Posener, G. 1936, *La Première Domination Perse en Egypte*. France: Imprimerie de l'Institut Français

Posener, G. 1960, *De la Divinité du Pharaon*. Paris: Imprimerie Nationale

Posener, G. 1969, Achoris. *Revue d'Égyptologie* 21, 148–150

Posener, G. 1973, Le Pays de Pount. *Annuaire du College de France* 73, 369–374

Posener, G. 1977, L'Or de Pount, in E. Endesfelder and F. Hintze (eds), *Ägypten und Kusch, Schriften zur Geschichte und Kultur des Alten Orients* 13, 337–342. Berlin: Akademie

Posener, G. 1985, *Le Papyrus Vandier*. Cairo: Institut Français d'Archéologie Orientale

Preziosi, D. 1996, Brain of the Earth's Body, in P. Duro (ed.), *The Rhetoric of the Frame. Essays on the Boundaries of the Artwork*, 96–110. Cambridge: CUP

Pritchard, J. B. (ed.) 1969, *Ancient Near Eastern Texts Relating to the Old Testament*. Princeton: Princeton UP

Propp, V. 1969, *Morfologija Slazki*. Moscow: Academy of Sciences

Quack, J. 1996, *Kftȝw und iȝsy. Ägypten und Levante: Zeitschrift für ägyptische Archäologie und deren Nachbargebiete* 6, 75–81

Quack, J. 2001, Ein neuer Versuch zum Moskauer literarischen Brief. *Zeitschrift für Ägyptische Sprache und Altertumskunde* 128, 167–181

Quibell, J. E. 1900, *Hierakonpolis I*. London: B. Quaritch

Quirke, S. (ed.) 1991, *Middle Kingdom Studies*. New Malden: SIA Publishing

Quirke, S. 1996a, Narrative Literature, in A. Loprieno (ed.), *Ancient Egyptian Literature: History and Forms*, 263–276. Leiden: Brill

Quirke, S. 1996b, Archive, in A. Loprieno (ed.), *Ancient Egyptian Literature: History and Forms*, 379–401. Leiden: Brill

Quirke, S. 1999, Women in Ancient Egypt: Temple Titles and Funerary Papyri, in A. Leahy and J. Tait (eds), *Studies on Ancient Egypt in Honour of H. S. Smith*, 227–235. London: Egypt Exploration Society

Quirke, S. 2001, *The Cult of Ra Sun Worship in Ancient Egypt*. London: Thames and Hudson

Raban, A. and R. R. Stieglitz 1991, The Sea Peoples and Their Contributions to Civilization. *Biblical Archaeology Review* 17/6, 34–42, 92–93

Ranke, H. 1935, *Die Ägyptischen Personennamen I*. Glückstadt: J. J. Augustin

Ransom, C. L. R. 1914, A Late Egyptian Sarcophagus. *Metropolitan Museum of Art Bulletin* 9, 112–120

Rathbone, D. 1996, Towards a Historical Topography of the Fayum, in D. M. Bailey (ed.), *Archaeological Research in Roman Egypt, Journal of Roman Archaeology* supplement, 50–56

Ray, J. D. 1986, Psammuthis and Hakoris. *Journal of Egyptian Archaeology* 72, 149–158

Redford, D. B. 1986, *Pharaonic King-Lists, Annals and Day-Books.* Mississauga: Benben

Redford, D. B. 1992, *Egypt, Canaan, and Israel in Ancient Times.* Princeton: Princeton UP

Redford, D. B. 2000, Egypt and Western Asia in the Late New Kingdom: An Overview, in E. D. Oren (ed.), *The Sea Peoples and Their World: A Reassessment*, 1–20. Philadelphia: University Museum Publications

Redmount, C. A. 1995, The Wadi Tumilat and the Canal of the Pharoahs. *Journal of Near Eastern Studies* 54, 127–135

Richardson, S. 1999, Libya Domestica: Libyan Trade and Society on the Eve of the Invasions of Egypt. *Journal of the American Research Center in Egypt* 36, 149–164

Ritner, R. 1993, *The Mechanics of Ancient Egyptian Magical Practice.* Chicago: Oriental Institute, University of Chicago

Robin, C. 1991, L'Arabie antique de Karib' il a Mahomet: nouvelles donnees sur l'histoire des Arabes grace aux inscriptions. *Revue du Monde Musulman et de la Mediterranée* 61, 72–73

Robins, G. 1997, *The Art of Ancient Egypt.* London: British Museum Press

Roccati, A. 1970, *Papiro ieratico n. 54003, Estratti magici e rituali del Primo Medio Regno.* Turin: Edizioni d'arte F.lli Pozzo

Rochemonteix, M. 1897, *Le Temple d'Edfou I.* Cairo: Institut Français d'Archéologie Orientale

Rosenfeld, A. 1982, Style and Meaning in Laura Art: A Case Study in the Formal Analysis of Style in Prehistoric Art. *Mankind* 13, 199–217

Rousseau, J. J. 1963, *The Social Contract and Discourses.* London: Dent

Rowe, A. 1948, *A History of Ancient Cyrenaica.* Cairo: Service des Antiquités Egyptiennes

Rowe, A. 1954, A Contribution to the Archaeology of the Western Desert II. *Bulletin of the John Rylands Library, Manchester* 36, 484–500

Said, E. 1991, *Orientalism.* 2nd edition, Harmondsworth: Penguin

Saleh, A-A. 1972, The *Gnbtyw* of Thutmosis III's Annals and the South Arabian *Geb(b)anitae* of the Classical Writers. *Bulletin de l'Institut Français d'Archéologie Orientale du Caire* 72, 245–262

Saleh, A-A. 1981, Notes on the Ancient Egyptian *t3-ntr* 'God's Land'. *Bulletin du Centenaire, Supplément au Bulletin d'Institute Français d'Archéologie Orientale*, 107–117

Saleh, M. and H. Sourouzian 1987, *Official Catalogue of the Cairo Museum.* Cairo: Organization of Egyptian Antiquities

Salles, J. F. 1988, *L'Arabie et Ses Mers Bordieres, I, itineraires et voisinages.* Lyon: GS Maison de l'Orient

Salles, J. F. 1989, Les Échanges commerciaux dans le golfe Arabo-Persique ai Ier millénaire avant J-C, in T. Fahd (ed.), *L'Arabie Preislamique et son environnement, historique et culturel*, 67–96. Leiden: Brill

Salles, J. F. 1998, *Le Sinai durant l'Antiquité et le Moyen Age. 4000 ans d'histoire pour un desert.* Paris: Errance

Samuel, A. E. 1965, Year 27=30 and 88 BC. *Chronique d'Egypte* 40, 376–400

Sandars, N. 1985, *The Sea Peoples.* London: Thames and Hudson

Sandman, M. 1938, *Texts from the Time of Akhenaten.* Bruxelles: Fondation Égyptologique Reine Elisabeth

Sanlaville, P. 1988, Des Mers au milieu du desert: Mer Rouge et goye Arabo-Persique, in J. F. Salles, *L'Arabie et ses mers bordières, I, itineraires et voisinages*, 9–26. Lyon: GS Maison de l'Orient

Sauneron, S. 1952, Un Theme littéraure de l'antiquité classique: Le Nil et la pluie. *Bulletin de l'Institut Français d'Archéologie Orientale du Caire* 51, 41–48

Sauneron, S. 1963, *Le Temple d'Esna*. Cairo: Institut Français d'Archéologie Orientale

Sauneron, S. 1972, L'Écriture Ptolémaïque. *Textes et langages de l'Egypte pharaonique I*, 45–56. Cairo: Institut Français d'Archéologie Orientale

Sauneron, S. and J. Yoyotte 1952, La Campagne Nubiene de Psammetique II et sa signification Historique. *Bulletin de l'Institut Français d'Archéologie Orientale du Caire* 50, 157–207

Säve-Söderbergh, T. 1946, *The Navy of the Eighteenth Egyptian Dynasty*. Uppsala: Lundequist

Sayed, A. M. A. H. 1977, Discovery of the Site of the 12th Dynasty Port at Wadi Gawasis on the Red Sea Shore. *Révue d'Égyptologie* 29, 140–178

Sayed, A. M. A. H. 1978, The Recently Discovered Port on the Red Sea Shore. *Journal of Egyptian Archaeology* 64, 69–71

Sayed, A. M. A. H. 1980, Observations on Recent Discoveries at Wadi Gawasis. *Journal of Egyptian Archaeology* 66, 154–157

Sayed, A. M. A. H. 1983, New Light on the Recently Discovered Port on the Red Sea Shore. *Chronique d'Egypte* 58, 31

Scamuzzi, E. 1965, *Egyptian Art in the Egyptian Museum of Turin*. New York: Harry N. Abrams

Schack-Schakenburg, H. 1903, *Das Buch von den zwei Wegen des seligen Toten*. Leipzig: Hinrichs

Schaeffer, C. F. A. 1968, *Ugaritica 5*. Paris: Geuthner

Schenkel, W. 1965, *Memphis, Herakleopolis, Theben*. Wiesbaden: Harrosowitz

Schenkel, W. 1975, Dolmetcher, in W. Helck and E. Otto (eds), *Lexikon der Ägyptologie, Vol. I*, 1,116. Wiesbaden: Harrassowitz

Schiaparelli, E. 1924, *Missione Archaeolgica Italiana in Egitto: Relazione sui Lavori della Missione Archaeologica Italiana in Egitto, Anni 1903–1920*. Turin: R. Museo di Antichita

Schofield, L. and R. B. Parkinson 1994, Of Helmets and Heretics: A Possible Egyptian Representation of Mycenaean Warriors on a Papyrus from el-Amarna. *Annual of the British School at Athens* 89, 157–170

Scholz, P. 1984, Fürstin Iti – 'Schönheit' aus Punt. *Studien zur Altägyptischen Kultur* 11, 529–556

Schulman, A. 1964, *Military Rank, Title and Organisation in the Egyptian New Kingdom*. Berlin: Münchner Ägyptologische Studien

Serpico, M. 1997, Organic Materials: Resins, Amber and Bitumen, in P. Nicholson and I. Shaw (eds), *Ancient Egyptian Materials and Technology*, 430–474. Cambridge: CUP

Serpico, M. and R. White 2000, The Botanical Identity and Transport of Incense during the Egyptian New Kingdom. *Antiquity* 74, 884–897

Servin, A. 1948, Constructions navales Égyptiennes: les barques de papyrus. *Annals du Service des Antiquités de l'Egypte* 48, 55–88

Sethe, K (ed.) 1903, *Urkunden des Alten Reichs (Urkunden I)*. Leipzig: Hinrichs

Sethe, K. (ed.) 1904, *Historisch-biographische Urkunden aus den Zeiten der makedonischen Könige und der beiden ersten Ptolemäer (Urkunden II)*. Leipzig: Hinrichs

Sethe, K. 1906–1957, *Urkunden der 18, Dynastie (Urkunden IV)*. Leipzig: Hinrichs and Berlin: Akademie

Sethe, K. 1908–1922, *Die altaegyptischen Pyramidentexte nach den Papierabdrücken und Photographien des Berliner Museums*. Leipzig: Hinrichs

Sethe, K. 1933, *Urkunden des Alten Reiches*. Leipzig: Hinrichs

Shostack, M. 1981, *Nisa: The Life and Words of a Kung Woman*. Cambridge, Mass: Harvard UP

Sidebotham, S. E. 1986, Aelius Gallus and Arabia. *Latomus* 45, 590–602

Silverman, D. P. (ed.) 1997, *Ancient Egypt*. London: Duncan Baird

Silverman, D. P. 1996, Coffin Texts from Bersheh, Kom el Hisn, and Mendes, in H. Willems, *The Coffin of Heqata*, 129–141. Leuven: Peeters

Simons, J. 1937, *Handbook for the Study of Egyptian Topographical Lists Relating to Western Asia.* Leiden: Brill

Simpson, W. K. 1960, Papyrus Lythgoe: A Fragment of a Literary Text of the Middle Kingdom from el-Lisht. *Journal of Egyptian Archaeology* 46, 65–70

Smith, H. 1992, The Making of Egypt: A Review of the Influence of Susa and Sumer on Upper Egypt and Lower Nubia in the 4th Millenium BC, in R. Friedman and B. Adams (eds), *The Followers of Horus. Studies dedicated to Michael Allen Hoffman*, 235–246. Oxford: Oxbow

Smith, H. S. and H. M. Stewart 1984, The Garob Shrine Papyrus. *Journal of Egyptian Archaeology* 70, 56–64

Smith, W. S. 1962, The Land of Punt. *Journal of the American Research Center in Egypt* 1, 59–60

Snape, S. 1998, Walls, Wells and Wandering Merchants: Egyptian Control of Marmarica in the Late Bronze Age, in C. J. Eyre (ed.), *Proceedings of the Seventh International Congress of Egyptologists*, 1,081–1,084. Leuven: Peeters

Snape, S. 2000, Imported Pottery at Zawiyet Umm el-Rakham: Preliminary Report. *Bulletin de Liaison du Groupe International d'Etude de la Céramique Egyptienne* 21, 17–22

Spalinger, A. 1979, Some Notes on the Libyans of the Old Kingdom and Later Historical Reflexes. *Journal of the Society for the Study of Egyptian Antiquities* 9, 125–160

Spalinger, A. 1996, Sovereignty and Theology in New Kingdom Egypt: Some Cases of Tradition. *Saeculum* 47, 217–238

Spencer, A. J. 1982, *Death in Ancient Egypt.* Harmondsworth: Penguin

Stadelmann, R. 1984, Seevölker, in W. Helck and W. Westendorf (eds), *Lexikon der Ägyptologie V*, 814–822. Wiesbaden: Harrassowitz

Stern, E. 1994, *Dor, Ruler of the Seas: Twelve Years of Excavations at the Israelite-Phoenician Harbor Town on the Carmel Coast.* Jerusalem: Israel Exploration Society

Stern, E. 2000, The Settlement of Sea Peoples in Northern Israel, in E. D. Oren (ed.), *The Sea Peoples and Their World: A Reassessment*, 197–212. Philadelphia: University Museum Publications

Stiebing, W. H. Jr. 2001, When Civilization Collapsed: Death of the Bronze Age. *Archaeology Odyssey* 4/5, 16–26, 62

Störk, L. 1977, *Die Nashörner.* Hamburg: Borg

Störk, L. 1992, Grabakarabis Pillularis-Orientalisches in Johann Fischarts 'Geschichtsklietterung'; II Selims Rhinoceros; III Notizen zum Fischotter in Ägypten; IV Der Skarabäus als Lichtheld, in I. Gamer-Wallert and W. Helk (eds), *Gegengabe. Festschrift für Emma Brunner-Traut*, 319–339. Tübingen: Attempto

Stricker, B. H. 1956, *De Overstroming van de Nijl.* Leiden: Brill

Tait, W. J. (ed.) 2003, 'Never had the like occurred': Egypt's view of its past. London: UCL Press

Tait, W. J. 1976, The Mountain of Lapis Lazuli. *Göffinger Miszellen* 20, 49–54

Tait, W. J. 1996, Egypt, Ancient: XI. Writing and Books, in J. Turner (ed.), *The Dictionary of Art X*, 1–7. London: Macmillan

Tait, W. J. forthcoming, Findspot, Place of Use, and Place of Writing: Some Practical Issues in the Provenance of Demotic Texts. *Acts of the Wurzburg Demotic Conference*

Tertre, J. B. 1992, Jean Baptiste du Tertre and the Noble Savages, in P. Hulme and N. Whitehead (eds), *Wild Majesty*, 128–137. Oxford: Clarendon

Thomas, N. 1994, *Colonialism's Culture: Anthropology, Travel and Government.* Cambridge: Polity

Thomas, S. 2000a, Aspects of Technology and Trade in Egypt and the Eastern Mediterranean during the Late Bronze Age, unpublished PhD thesis, University of Liverpool

Thomas, S. 2000b, Tell Abqa'in: a Fortified Settlement in the Western Delta. *Mitteilungen des Deutschen Archäologisches Instituts Abteilung Kairo* 56, 371–377

Thomson, J. O. 1965, *History of Ancient Geography.* New York: Biblio and Tannen.

Titiev, M. 1944, *Old Oraibi: A Study of the Hopi Indians of Third Mesa.* Cambridge, Mass: Peabody Museum

Trigger, B. G. 1976, *Nubia Under the Pharaohs.* London: Thames and Hudson

Uphill, E. 2000, *Pharaoh's Gateway to Eternity: The Hawara Labyrinth of King Amenemhat III.* London: Kegan Paul

Vagnetti, L. 2000, Western Mediterranean Overview: Peninsular Italy, Sicily and Sardinia at the Time of the Sea Peoples, in E. D. Oren (ed.), *The Sea Peoples and Their World: A Reassessment*, 305–326. Philadelphia: University Museum Publications

Van't Dack, E. 1983, Le retour de Ptolémée IX Sotèr II en Égypte et la fin du règle de Ptolémée X Alexandre I, in E. Van't Dack, P. van Dessel and W. van Gucht (eds), *Egypt and the Hellenistic World: Proceedings of the International Colloquium, Leuven, 24–26 May 1982*, 136–150. Leuven: Lovanii

Vandersleyen, C. 1971, *Les guerres d'Amosis.* Brussels: Fondation Égyptologique Reine Elisabeth

Vandersleyen, C. 1989, Les Inscriptions 114 et 1 du Ouadi Hammamat (11e Dynastie). *Chronique d'Egypte* 127, 148–158

Vandersleyen, C. 1994, L'Asie des Egyptiens et les Iles de la Mediteranée Orientale sous le Nouvel Empire. *Orientalia Lovaniensia Periodica* 25, 37–47

Vandersleyen, C. 1996, Les Monuments de l'Ouadi Gaouasis et la possibilité d'aller au pays de Pount par la Mer Rouge. *Révue d'Égyptologie* 47, 107–115

Vandersleyen, C. 1999, *Ouadj-our. w3d wr. Un autre aspect de la vallée du Nil.* Brussels: Connaissance de l'Egypte Ancienne

Vercoutter, J. 1956, New Egyptian Texts from the Sudan. *Kush* 4, 66–82

Verhoeven, U. 1996, Ein historischer 'Sitz im Leben' für die Erzählung von Horus und Seth des Papyrus Chester Beatty I, in M. Schade-Busch (ed.), *Wege öffnen. Festschrift für Rolf Gundlach zum 65, Geburtstag*, 247–63. Wiesbaden: Harrassowitz

Vinson, S. 1996, Paktun and Paktosis as Ship-Construction Terminology in Herodotus, Pollux and Documentary Papyri. *Zeitschrift fur Papyrologie und Epigraphik* 113, 197–204

Wachsmann, S. 1981, The Ships of the Sea Peoples. *International Journal of Nautical Archaeology* 10, 187–220

Wachsmann, S. 1982, The Ships of the Sea Peoples: Additional Notes. *International Journal of Nautical Archaeology* 11, 297–304

Wachsmann, S. 1997, Were the Sea Peoples Mycenaeans? The Evidence of Ship Iconography, in S. Swiny, R. L. Hohlfelder and H. W. Swiny (eds), *Res Maritimae: Cyprus and the Eastern Mediterranean from Prehistory to Late Antiquity I*, 339–356. Atlanta, Georgia: Scholars Press

Wachsmann, S. 1998, *Seagoing Ships and Seamanship in the Bronze Age Levant.* College Station, Texas: A & M UP

Wachsmann, S. 2000, To the Sea of the Philistines, in E. D. Oren (ed.), *The Sea Peoples and Their World: A Reassessment*, 103–143. Philadelphia: University Museum Publications

Walsh, K. 1992, *The Representation of the Past. Museums and Heritage in the Post-Modern World.* London: Routledge

Walsh, P. 1999, From the Mountains of the Moon to the Neon Paintbrush, in D. Bearman and J. Trant (eds), *Museums and the Web*, 15–24. Philadelphia: Archives and Museum Informatics

Warburton, D. 2003, Love and War in the Late Bronze Age: Egypt and Hatti, in R. Matthews and C. Roemer (eds), *Ancient Perspectives on Egypt*, 75–100. London: UCL Press

Warburton, D. and R. Matthews 2003, Egypt and Mesopotamia in the Late Bronze and Iron Ages, in R. Matthews and C. Roemer (eds), *Ancient Perspectives on Egypt*, 101–114. London: UCL Press

Ward, W. A. and M. S. Joukowsky (eds) 1992, *The Crisis Years: The 12th Century BC*. Dubuque, IA: Kendall/Hunt

Weber, M. 1947, *The Theory of Social and Economic Organisation* (trans. A. M. Henderson and T. Parsons). Glencoe, Ill: Free Press

Weinstein, J. M. 1981, The Egyptian Empire in Palestine: A Reassessment. *Bulletin of the American Schools of Oriental Research* 241, 1–28

Welsby, D. A. 1996, *The Kingdom of Kush: The Napatan and Meroitic Empires*. London: British Museum Press

White, D. 1990, Provisional Evidence for the Seasonal Occupation of the Marsa Matruh Area by Late Bronze Age Libyans, in A. Leahy (ed.), *Libya and Egypt: c 1300–750 BC*. London: SOAS, Centre for Near and Middle Eastern Studies and the Society for Libyan Studies, 1–14

White, D. 1994, Before the Greeks Came: A Survey of the Current Archaeological Evidence for the Pre-Greek Libyans. *Libyan Studies* 25, 31–39

Whitehead, N. 1995, The Historical Anthropology of Text: The Interpretation of Raleigh's Discoveries of Guiana. *Current Anthropology* 36, 53–74

Wilhelm, G. 1995, The Kingdom of Mitanni in Second-Millennium Upper Mesopotamia, in J. M. Sasson (ed.), *Civilizations of the Ancient Near East*, 1,243–1,254. New York: Charles Scribner's Sons

Willems, H. (ed.) 1996, *The World of the Coffin Texts*. Leiden: Nederlands Instituut voor het Nabije Oosten

Willems, H. 1988, *Chests of Life: A Study of the Typology and Development of Middle Kingdom Standard Class Coffins*. Leiden: Ex Oriente Lux

Wilson, J. A. 1964, *Signs and Wonders upon Pharaoh: A History of American Egyptology*. Chicago: University of Chicago Press

Wilson, J. A. 1969, Egyptian Historical Texts, in J. B. Pritchard (ed.), *Ancient Near Eastern Texts Relating to the Old Testament*. 3rd edition with Supplement, 227–263, Princeton: Princeton UP

Winnicki, J. K. 1991, *Ancient Society* 22, 161 n. 40

Wood, D. 1993, *The Power of Maps*. London: Routledge

Yadin, Y. 1968, And Dan, Why Did He Remain in Ships? *Australian Journal of Biblical Archaeology* I, 9–23

Yoyotte J. 1972, Une Statue de Darius Decouverte à Suse. *Journal Asiatique*

Yoyotte, J. 1952, Quelques Toponymes Egyptiens mentionnés dans les 'Annales d'Assourbanipal'. *Revue d'Egyptologie* 46, 101–105

Yoyotte, J. 1962, Processions géographiques mentionant le Fayoum et ses localités. *Bulletin de l'Institut Français d'Archéologie Orientale du Caire* 61, 79–138

Yoyotte, J. and P. Chuvin 1986, Documents Relatifs au Culte Pelusien de Zeus Casios. *Revue Archéologique* 51, 41–63

Yoyotte, J., P. Chaveret and S. Gompertz 1997, *Le voyage en Egypte: un regard romain /Strabon*. Paris

Zangger, E. 1994, *Ein neuer Kampf um Troja: Archäologie in der Krise*. Munich: Droemer Knaur

Zangger, E. 1995, Who Were the Sea Peoples? *Aramco World* 46, 21–31

Zauzich, K-Th. 1987, Das Topographische Onomastikon im P. Kairo 31169. *Göttinger Miszellen* 99, 83–91

Zecchi, M. 2001, *Geographia Religiosa del Fayyum. Dalle origini al IV secolo a.c.* Imola: La Mandragera

Zertal, A. 2001, The Corridor-builders of Central Israel: Evidence for the Settlement of the Northern Sea Peoples?, in V. Karageorghis and C. E. Morris (eds), *Defensive Settlements of the Aegean and the Eastern Mediterranean after c. 1200 BC: proceedings of an international workshop held at Trinity College Dublin, 7–9 May 1999*, 215–232. Nicosia: Anastasios G. Leventis Foundation

Zibelius, K. 1972, *Afrikanische Orts- und Völkernamen in Hieroglyphischen und Hieratische Texten.* Wiesbaden: Ludwig Reichert

Zyhlarz, E. 1958, The Countries of the Ethiopian Empire of Kash (Kush) and Egyptian Old Ethiopia in the New Kingdom. *Kush* 6, 7–38

Index